Genesis
FROM CREATION TO COVENANT

MAGGID

Zvi Grumet

GENESIS
FROM CREATION TO COVENANT

Maggid Books

Genesis
From Creation to Covenant

First Edition, 2017

Maggid Books
An imprint of Koren Publishers Jerusalem Ltd.

POB 8531, New Milford, CT 06776-8531, USA
& POB 4044, Jerusalem 9104001, Israel
www.maggidbooks.com

ISBN 978-1-59264-477-3, *hardcover*

A CIP catalogue record for this title is
available from the British Library

Printed and bound in the United States

Contents

PART III

COVENANTAL FAMILY

Acknowledgments

I am fortunate to have been surrounded by outstanding students, colleagues, and learning groups for many years. It was with these students and peers that I initially floated many of the ideas presented here, and I am grateful for both their challenging of my ideas and their support. Their questions forced me to clarify and refine many times over, and their support encouraged me to continue. There are too many of you to name individually, but you will recognize yourselves in the various groups I will mention.

The nine years I taught at the Torah Academy of Bergen County provided an extraordinary opportunity for me to explore Torah with my many students there. My special thanks to Rabbi Yosef Adler, who gave me the latitude to teach and create in that remarkable institution. I was also privileged to have a group of parents learn with me. The group started so that the parents of students in my classes could discuss with their children what they were learning in my class, but it grew and over time drew other parents as well. The ideas and discussions that came up in those Monday night sessions taught me immeasurably, and I am profoundly grateful.

During those same years, I taught a class to a group at the Riverdale Jewish Center. Those loyal learners came week after week, adopted me into their homes, brought insights from a diverse range of backgrounds, and encouraged me to write. Were it not for them, I doubt that this book would have ever come to light, and I thank them deeply.

Soon after moving to Israel, I was invited by two visionary leaders, Rabbis Dovid Ebner and Yehuda Susman, to found the Tanakh department at Yeshivat Eretz HaTzvi. For the past twelve years, I have been privileged to work side by side with outstanding colleagues and have been surrounded by hundreds of thoughtful, eager, and inquisitive young men who challenged me with questions I had never considered, with novel ideas, and with never accepting a thought if it did not completely satisfy them. They were not just my students but my learning partners as we struggled through difficult passages together. They, too, pushed me to write more times than I can count, and I am afraid that this work will be insufficient for them as it contains some of the product but so little of the process we shared. My gratitude to them is beyond words.

I would be remiss if I did not mention Rabbi Joseph B. Soloveitchik, the Rav, *zekher tzaddik livrakha*, with whom I studied only in his old age. I know that I learned from him only the tiniest drop of what his genius had to offer. More than anything else, I learned an absolute intellectual integrity and educational methodology: to say "I don't know," to make his students his partners in exploration, and to completely revise in the face of a good question. His extraordinary teaching continues to inspire me.

I am indebted to Gila Fine, editor in chief at Maggid Books. She embraced this book long before it was ready and encouraged me to rewrite and refine to continually improve the content and presentation. I appreciate her wisdom, guidance, and patience. Thanks are also due to her editorial staff: Deena Nataf, Tali Simon, and Tomi Mager.

My wife, Naomi, is a constant source of support, both in my teaching and specifically in this work. She never misses an opportunity to encourage me. Her love fills these pages. I am blessed with three wonderful children – Ruti, Yair, and Haviva – whose eyes light up whenever we study Torah together. You have helped me understand so much more because of who you are and the questions you ask. I pray that your love for Torah continues to grow even as you learn to question, challenge, and explore deeply.

Finally, I truly believe that somehow, God has guided my path throughout the years. Teaching Torah was not my initial career, and the myriad experiences in my life have shaped my thinking and continue to do so. I pray that what I have written reveals new layers of truth in Your Torah, brings Your people to a deeper understanding and appreciation of Torah, and brings them closer to Torah. It has certainly done that for me.

Zvi Grumet
Jerusalem
Shevat 5776

Introduction

I recall being asked years ago to teach a class on the Book of Genesis at a local synagogue. "Of course," the rabbi continued, "you will begin with *Lekh Lekha*" (the beginning of the Abrahamic saga). I demurred. As much as the uniqueness of the Jewish people is a central thrust throughout the biblical narrative, omitting the context and purpose for which they were chosen misses the Torah's central thesis.

The essence of the Torah is God's search for a meaningful relationship with humanity.[1] The idea itself is not new. It is the centerpiece of the prayer commonly known as *Aleinu* and is prominent throughout the liturgy, especially that of Rosh HaShana – the Jewish New Year and traditionally the day of judgment: "Therefore we place our hope in You, Lord our God, that we may soon see the glory of Your power... when all humanity will call on Your name."[2]

The idea simultaneously supports both the universality of God's concern – He loves all humans, as they are created in His image – and the particularity of His special relationship with the Jewish people.

1. This idea was explicated by Martin Buber, *Darko Shel Mikra* [Hebrew] (Jerusalem: Mossad Bialik, 1978), 65–81.
2. Jonathan Sacks, trans., *The Koren Siddur* (Jerusalem: Koren Publishers, 2009), 180.

God wants to have a direct relationship with all of humanity, but His initial attempts are unsuccessful. After trying twice, with modifications made to the second attempt, to achieve that direct relationship with all of humanity, He tries a third time – first choosing an individual who would start a family, then a clan, and eventually a nation. It is through this select group, cultivated over the course of multiple generations, that God hopes to eventually build a relationship with all people. Abraham and his descendants are chosen to be the conduits for His message.

The Book of Genesis is concerned with how God's covenantal partners rise to that status, and there is a dynamic between His selection of the partner and the partner's readiness. In Genesis, God's covenantal partners are accorded patriarchal status. The identification of God as the God of Abraham, Isaac, and Jacob resonates throughout the book, and, in fact, through the rest of the Bible and subsequent Jewish literature. At what point, however, does each of the Patriarchs achieve that status and through what process?

The Patriarchs aren't born as Patriarchs; they must grow themselves into that status. Abraham starts out as Abram and isn't transformed into Abraham until decades after we are first introduced to him, halfway through the Abrahamic narratives, just as the focus shifts to Sarah. Jacob doesn't become Israel until he returns home after more than twenty years away, just before the focus of the story shifts to his children.

The development of the Patriarchs continues through the narratives in which they are the focus, so it can be argued that Abraham doesn't really become patriarchal until he accepts Sarah as his covenantal partner; Isaac doesn't achieve that status until he learns to accept his father and embrace his own identity; Jacob becomes patriarchal only when the covenantal family emerges.

The search for covenantal partners turns out to be a stepping stone toward cultivating the covenantal family, and that search is fraught with difficulty. Families in the Book of Genesis are, for the most part, failures.[3] Cain and Abel's parents are absent from the conflict

---

3. This might be why Genesis does not hold back critique of its heroes while still extolling them as such.

between the brothers; Noah is violated by his son Ham; Isaac and Rebecca barely speak; Jacob struggles with his wives, his rebellious sons, and the repeated near-fragmentation of his family. Genesis cannot rest until Jacob's family is reunited with a common purpose aligned with the ancestral covenant, and once the covenantal family is in place, the institution of patriarchy can be retired. There is no longer a need for the figurehead when the family, and later the nation, will take on God's partnership.

THE *TOLEDOT* STRUCTURE OF GENESIS

The word *toledot* appears thirteen times in the entire Hebrew Bible, eleven of which are in Genesis. As such it serves as an important structural element of Genesis and could even be said to represent one of its central themes. There is considerable debate about its precise meaning. Some understand it to mean "descendants" or "generations,"[4] while others would translate it as "story," so that the former would read the phrase "*toledot Noaḥ*" as "the descendants of Noah," while the latter would understand it to mean "Noah's story."[5]

I believe that both suggestions are lacking, as is evident from the very first appearance of the word in the Torah: "These are the *toledot* of the heavens and the earth" (2:4). The heavens and the earth neither have children nor do they have a story. Instead, I prefer the word *legacy*.[6] This is the legacy of the creation of the heavens and the earth. It is what eventually emerges from that individual or event.[7]

Genesis is essentially eleven books of *toledot*, each ending just prior to the beginning of the next. Each book of *toledot* concludes with the ultimate legacy of the period, or the identified individual, so that the

---

4. See Nahmanides, 5:1; Rashbam, 6:9. Throughout this book, biblical references to Genesis are identified by chapter and verse only.
5. Ibn Ezra, 6:9.
6. Saadia Gaon, 2:4, defines it as "development." Robert Sacks defines *toledot* as "the story of what came to be." See Sacks, *A Commentary on the Book of Genesis* (Lewiston, NY: The Edwin Mellen Press, 1990), 48.
7. This translation is based on Prov. 27:1: "Who knows what the day will bring forth" (in Hebrew, Y-L-D, literally, "what the day will give birth to"). Ibn Ezra 6:9 references this verse as well.

entire story contained within yields some result or outcome. There is a legacy of the Creation, a legacy of Adam, a legacy of Noah, etc.[8]

These eleven books trace the development of an idea mirroring the central theme of Genesis. For example, the Creation story in Genesis 1 begins with the broadest legacy of all, Creation, and narrows the focus to the legacy of Adam. Of Adam's three children, only one, Seth, has a *toledot*, while the other two are left in the dustbins of biblical history. The legacy narrows even further with the identification of Noah, the only one of Seth's descendants over the course of the next nine generations who warrants his own *toledot*.

Noah represents God's second attempt to establish a relationship with all of humanity as He essentially restarts the entire Creation, this time focusing on the family rather than the individual. Once again, however, the attempt to foster a relationship with all humanity flounders and the focus is narrowed to one family, that of Terah, father of Abraham. It is through this family that God will attempt to have His blessing reach all of humanity. Yet even that family needs refining, and subsequent books of *toledot* continue narrowing the focus to Isaac and ultimately to Jacob.

The *toledot* structure echoes the central thesis of Genesis that God is looking for a partner relationship with humanity. After the two main failed attempts, that of Man and his descendants and that of Noah's family, universal God decides to work with one family in order to reach all of humanity.[9] As God tells Abram, "Through you shall come blessing to all the families of the earth" (12:3).

---

8. One of the features of each book of *toledot* is that it opens by reviewing a critical piece of information from the prior *toledot*. Thus, *toledot* Noah begins with the birth of his three sons, which the Torah had already shared with us; *toledot* Terah begins with the birth of his three sons, which we heard about in the previous verse, the close of the previous *toledot*; *toledot* Isaac begins with his marriage to Rebecca, which the Torah had described in the previous chapter; etc.

9. If Genesis is the book of *toledot*, leading to God's choice of the covenantal family, it is worth noticing the other two *toledot* in the Bible. The first is in Numbers 3:1, which delineates the *toledot* of the priesthood, and the second is at the end of Ruth (4:18), which lists the *toledot* of the Davidic dynasty. Each represents a further narrowing of the focus to the central leadership positions within the chosen nation.

HISTORY, PRE-HISTORY, PROTO-HISTORY

One essential assumption this book makes about biblical chronology is that it need not be consistent with external chronologies, but it does need to be internally consistent so that the narrative makes sense in its own context. The Torah is not concerned with history, just as it is not concerned with biology or chemistry. The Torah *is* interested in God and God's relationship with people. What this means is that we should not try to correlate the stories of the Tower of Babel or the Flood with other events in world history, nor should we expend any energy trying to understand the physics of Creation or figure out whether the world is six thousand or fifteen billion years old. The physics and timing of Creation are for scientists to explore; the religious significance of the Torah's Creation saga or the Tower of Babel is for religious thinkers and students of the Torah to probe.[10]

The same is true with biblical history; it is not meant as a scientific record of what happened but serves as a religious guide to understand the events that are recorded. As such, the internal consistency of the Torah is what yields meaning, not its accordance with external historical annals or archaeological findings.

A corollary to the challenge of chronology in Genesis is the logical implausibility of some of what it describes in its narrative. Let me be clear – I am *not* discussing here things that the Torah describes as miraculous. Miracles are an essential component of the Torah's message that God, as Creator, reserves the right to intervene when it is deemed necessary for reasons that only He determines. Sarah's giving birth to Isaac at the age of ninety is identified by the Torah as God's intervention in the natural order, as are the Ten Plagues, the Splitting of the Sea, the manna in the desert, the Revelation at Sinai, and much more. Those are miracles, and it is perfectly reasonable for God to decide when and how to perform them.

What does seem odd, however, are twenty generations of apparently average people with life spans four to twenty times what might be considered normal – and for the Torah to present that as unexceptional, not as resulting from divine intervention. Similarly, the speaking serpent

---

10. Ibn Ezra, in the introduction to his commentary on the Torah, argues forcefully that the study of Torah is not designed to yield any scientific insights.

in the Garden of Eden is presented as if it were normal for snakes to speak.[11] These extra-ordinary events which are not presented as miraculous demand our attention.

What this suggests is that there is an early period described in the Torah which is unlike our own, in which miraculous events were so much the norm that they are not even described as such. Whether such a period actually existed or is used as a metaphor is less important than the fact that the description of that period is designed to lead us to conclude that it is an otherworldly time, what I would call a *pre-historic* period in which regular rules do not apply. Attempts to rationalize its irrational elements only distort it and distract from its core messages.

This pre-historic era – in which people live nearly a thousand years and there are talking snakes, cataclysmic floods, and the mysterious appearance of languages – is an important transitional stage from before there was time at all. It is particularly pointless in this pre-historic period to imagine correlating biblical events with those of the world outside the Bible. It perhaps should not be surprising that it is in the pre-historic section of Genesis that God is unsuccessful at establishing a meaningful relationship with humanity. The first section of this book corresponds to the pre-historic phase of Genesis.

As Genesis eases us out of the pre-historic era (beginning with Noah's children), life spans are halved, then halved again, bringing the average life span to just under two hundred years. The shortening of life spans signals the transition into the second era, the patriarchal period, or what I might call the era of *proto-history* – including Abraham, Isaac, and Jacob. This era is marked by individuals about whom we know quite a bit and whose development we can trace over the course of many chapters. Although their life spans are double the norm, their lives look remarkably similar to our own, with rare exceptions of divine communication and intervention.

But these figures are not just regular people; they are prototypes for a nation. Nahmanides identifies their uniqueness by describing them as archetypes who blazed the patterns of behavior which their descendants would follow and imprinted patterns of history which

---

11. As distinct from Balaam's donkey, which is described as an act of God.

would be repeated for generations.[12] Those individuals are the forefathers of the nation – real people whose lives have cosmic significance.
It is because they are more than individuals that the Torah ascribes to
them lives which are double the norm. Those life spans are a literary
device used by the Torah to indicate that they are archetypes who lay
the foundations for and character of those who would follow them.
The second section of this book corresponds roughly to this proto-
historic phase of Genesis, one in which God finds individuals with
whom to have a relationship but who have not successfully cultivated
the covenantal family.

Finally, we have the *historical* era, in which people live normal
life spans and are just people, not prototypes or archetypes. God does
not speak directly with these people, nor are there overt divine miracles.
These "regular" people are introduced to us toward the end of Genesis,
namely, Joseph and his brothers, who live slightly longer than the average
but nowhere close to beyond the range of reason. They mark the transition from the proto-history of the Patriarchs to the historical period of
the Bible beginning in Exodus. This era corresponds to the third section
of this book, in which the covenantal family finally emerges. It is only
with the emergence of the covenantal family that Genesis can close and
the Torah can continue with the ongoing interaction between God and
His chosen people.

TORAH AS INSTRUCTION

Ever since the Torah was written, it has been studied as a source of
guidance. With the Enlightenment, in many circles the study shifted from
seeking moral or religious direction to academic study. That academic
examination challenged some of the most fundamental assumptions
and sensitivities of the religiously oriented, and for much of the past two
hundred years there has been an antagonistic relationship between those
who study the Bible from an academic perspective and those who see it
as a sanctified, core religious document. In recent decades, however, a
new approach has begun to emerge, one which is aware of and enlight-
ened by the contributions of two centuries of academic exploration while

---

12. See Nahmanides, 12:10.

remaining committed to preserving the Torah as a book of instruction – which is what its Hebrew name means.

On these pages I aim to participate in this emerging trend. I am fortunate to have been exposed to extraordinary thinkers and a growing body of literature written by people with deep reverence for the text and astonishing insights, including those derived from history, philosophy, philology, archaeology, and most important, an exquisitely refined literary sensitivity. The marriage of traditional reverence for the text with an array of new tools for exploring it has the potential to reveal magnificent insights into the text coupled with deep religious inspiration which otherwise would have remained hidden. I write these pages in an attempt to share with others my own religious experience emanating from this multilayered exploration of the Torah.

TERMINOLOGY AND CONVENTIONS

The word "Torah" literally means teaching, or a guiding manual. In this volume I use "Torah" to refer specifically to the Five Books, and the term Bible to refer to the rest of the biblical canon (what Christians call the Old Testament).

Genesis is filled with multiple names for God. Academic works insist on distinguishing between them, and indeed most translations make those distinctions. With rare exception I do not make those distinctions, as they are mostly irrelevant to what I am exploring. While God is neither masculine nor feminine, convention refers to God using masculine terminology (with the exception of the *Shekhina*, the Divine Presence, which is distinctly feminine). This book adheres to that convention.

When referring to humankind, I try to remain gender-neutral, using terms such as "humanity." There are times when that terminology becomes awkward and I use the capitalized Man. Except when describing Man in distinction to Woman (particularly in the story of the Garden of Eden), the terms Man or mankind refer equally to both genders.

Rendering the biblical text in translation is difficult and robs it of the power of nuance and wordplay embedded in the Hebrew text. Translations in this book are my own and adapted to probe what I believe is the underlying meaning of many of the words in the original Hebrew text, although I regularly consulted Robert Alter's sensitive translation in his *The Five Books of Moses: Translation and Commentary* (New York: Norton, 2004) and the new JPS translation, *Tanakh: The Holy Scriptures* (Philadelphia: Jewish Publication Society, 1988).

Unless otherwise specified, all biblical references are in Genesis. Cited commentaries that are linked to a verse being discussed are generally listed without referencing the verse.

The ideas presented here emerged from a careful reading of the biblical text and they are, by and large, very much grounded in that text. Those readings fall into what Rashbam may have called "the deep *peshat*" (text-based reading), what is nowadays sometimes referred to as an emerging school of theologically driven *peshat,* but what others may call *derash* (homiletic readings). Even though it is important to distinguish between what the text means and the meaning which is imposed on that text, *peshat* and *derash* live on a spectrum of interpretation and there is no clear consensus on the dividing line between them. It should be noted that many midrashim were born out of deep readings of the text, but the rabbis used homiletic rather than exegetical language to express those ideas. As such, it should not be surprising that many of the insights coming from contemporary literary readings of the Bible can actually be found in midrashim. I try to highlight some of those as they relate to my reading of the text.

There is a dance between theology and textual reading. Every reader brings his or her own theological biases to the reading. Were we to leave it at that, there would be few revelations about biblical text other than the creative ways of demonstrating that the text supports our predetermined ideas. To truly uncover the theology of the text requires shedding theological preconceptions. That is both difficult, if not impossible, and rather frightening to those for whom theology is important. And yet it is important to be able to do so, to some extent, if we are to begin to uncover the Bible's theology (as distinct from theology developed over many subsequent centuries). As a result, some of what I wrote here may be jarring to some readers in its boldness, while other readers will be disappointed that I did not go far enough. I hope that, at the very least, my words cause people to consider what their own theological lines are and open up the possibility of expanding those boundaries when they listen to the voice of the text.

I do have some basic assumptions that guided me in this work. First, the biblical text is a unified work, and any attempt to disassemble it into its disparate components does violence to the text (unless accompanied by an equal attempt to reassemble it into a meaningful and coherent whole). Second, the meaningfulness of the Bible emerges organically from a close reading of it and should not be superimposed on it from external sources. This close reading can be enhanced greatly by literary tools such as wordplays, theme words, pacing, patterns, developing themes, and literary structures embedded within the text. And while the enterprise of Midrash is meaningful as its own discipline, it should not be confused with the meaning that emanates from analysis of the text itself.[13]

Third, I assume that the reader has at least a minimum familiarity with the biblical story. The more knowledge the reader has, the better he or she will be able to appreciate the nuances which support and develop the arguments I present, and those with access to the original Hebrew text will benefit even more. That being said, I aim to have the content of this volume accessible to those who do not already possess comprehensive knowledge of the text, though they should be prepared to open the Bible and read along.

Fourth, I believe that as we broaden the scope of our reading of the Torah, our insight deepens. Drawing conclusions from individual passages taken out of context risks missing or distorting the Torah's fundamental message. A direct corollary to this assumption relates to the Torah's presentation of its central characters or heroes. Those characters develop, and not necessarily in a linear progression. Their growth cannot be observed in a single snapshot, and the attempt to draw conclusions

---

13. See Rashbam's comment to Genesis 1:1. Included in this is the presumption that unless there is a compelling reason to suggest otherwise, the Torah is very much chronological and sequential. This accords with the position of Nahmanides (see his comments on Gen. 11:32; 35:28; Ex. 24:1; Lev. 16:1; Num. 16:1), who fundamentally disagrees with the notion popularized by Rashi that the Torah is not written chronologically (see Rashi's comments on Gen. 35:29; Ex. 18:9; 19:11; 21:1, 12; 31:18; Lev. 8:2).

about them from any particular incident is premature and misleading. It is the process they undergo which brings them to their moments of greatness. Thus, Abram does not become Abraham until we have followed him for more than a quarter-century of his life, and Jacob does not emerge as Israel until he is well advanced in years. It is the struggles and the growth of these heroes which make them fitting models as they demonstrate the human capacity.

This opens the way to a humanistic reading of the great biblical characters. The greater insight we gain about them and their challenges, their strengths and weaknesses, their struggles and successes, the more we can see ourselves in them. That humanistic approach guides my understanding of the Bible, and it is my hope that I will help many to find inspiration in their biblical exploration.

Part I

Creation and Re-Creation

Genesis 1:1–25

Conceptualizing Creation

The story of Creation challenges our sensibilities. It is so far removed from our lives that we have no context into which we can place it, no framework from which we can attempt to understand it. Creation asks us to imagine what existed before there was existence. It confronts us with the task of imagining the time before there was time. We are forced to grapple with questions such as defining life itself, why we exist, what it means to be human, and why any of that should matter. In just one chapter, which is completely dominated and directed by God, we move swiftly from the initial amorphous mass to humans, the pinnacle of Creation. We understand nothing, and wonder why we are told any of this at all.

These, of course, are precisely the questions the Torah invites us to grapple with by presenting the narrative. The rabbis of the Talmud were concerned about people delving into these questions, not to mention teaching them publicly or writing about them.[1] Much of what the text says defies our ability to comprehend rationally and meaningfully, yet that is precisely what we will attempt to do in these opening chapters.

---

1. Mishna Ḥagiga 2:1.

TOWARD A CONCEPTUAL MODEL OF CREATION

Ever since the Enlightenment, there has been tension over the biblical account of Creation, which emerging scientific understanding challenged. Most of the attempts to deal with the conflict fell into one of three approaches: (a) rejection of the biblical account, (b) rejection of the scientific approach, or (c) harmonization (either by interpreting science to fit the Bible or by interpreting the Bible to fit science).[2] This is not the place to fully plumb those approaches with their advantages and disadvantages, as we will be operating under a completely different assumption which I believe allows for both intellectual and spiritual integrity.

As I mentioned in the Introduction, the Torah is not and never was meant to be a textbook of science, history, anthropology, cosmogony, or any other discipline. Rather, it deals with matters of faith, religion, ethics, morality, and theology. The Torah is concerned with God, with the nature of humans, and with the relationship between them. Just as scientific inquiry can shed no light on the nature of God, religious inquiry yields no meaningful information about the mechanics of the universe.[3] The conflict between science and religion is artificial, imaginary, perhaps even manufactured.

This fundamental assumption allows us to explore a conceptual model of the Creation story. This model will suggest that the Creation story lays the foundations for my fundamental thesis about the Torah – God creates the human and desires to have a relationship with it. But

---

2. Some recent works grappling with these issues are Nathan Aviezer, *In the Beginning* (Hoboken, NJ: Ktav Publishing House, 1990); Daniel C. Matt, *God and the Big Bang* (Woodstock, VT: Jewish Lights, 1996); Robert Pollack, *The Faith of Biology & The Biology of Faith* (New York: Columbia University Press, 2000); Gerald Schroeder, *Genesis and the Big Bang* (New York: Bantam Books, 1990); and Miryam Z. Wahrman, *Brave New Judaism* (Lebanon, NH: Brandeis University Press, 2002).

3. In Mishna Avot 5:22, Ben Bag Bag states, "Turn it [Torah] over again and again, for everything is in it." Some commentaries suggest that Ben Bag Bag's intention is that all knowledge is included in Torah. I understand him to mean that Torah is limited to all divinely revealed knowledge. Knowledge that humans can derive through their intellect does not need to be divinely revealed. Leon Kass, *Genesis: The Beginning of Wisdom* (New York: The Free Press, 2003), 46, writes, "Genesis is not the sort of book that can be refuted – or affirmed – on the basis of scientific or historical evidence."

what is God? Who is God? If the human is created in the "image" of God, what is that image? This, I believe, is one of the central topics in the opening chapter of Genesis.

Genesis 1 contains the key Creation narrative in the Bible. As it introduces the entire Bible, it focuses not on what God *is* but on what God *does*. A careful investigation of what God does helps paint for us an initial image of God, one which yields insights valuable for this story itself and for the rest of the biblical account as a whole. For example, the simple observation that in Genesis 1, God creates, allows us to describe Him as a Creator. When we delve deeper into this simple statement and break it down based on a thoughtful reading of the biblical text, we will be able to further refine and expand upon the simple "God is a Creator," yielding a richer conception of the "image" of God in the Bible.

THE STRUCTURE OF CREATION

Pervasive throughout Genesis 1 is a profound sense of order. One example is the five-step format which structures each "day"[4] of Creation:

- God said …
- God made/did/created/formed …
- God saw that it was "good"…
- (God named …)
- It was *erev* and it was *boker*, a (number) "day"

The regularity of the structure leaves us with a profound sense that the process has been carefully planned in advance and is methodical. Every stage is introduced by divine thought or speech, and speech is the vehicle through which things are created. At the conclusion of each creative stage, God is reflective about His creations, saying that they are "good."[5] The structure is so reliable that any deviation from it commands

---

4. The word "day" is in quotations because it does not refer to a day as we know it. This will be demonstrated later.

5. See Rashi, 1:7. The phrase *ki tov* indicates completion, which is why it is missing after day two, on which the separation of the raw matter into its different forms – solid, liquid, and gas – had only begun and was not yet complete.

our attention and demands explanation. Thus, for example, when *ki tov* ("it was 'good'") is missing on the second "day" but appears twice on the third, or when the first "day" concludes with a cardinal rather than an ordinal number (that is, *one* day rather than a *first* day), or the sixth "day" concludes with the definite article (that is, *the* sixth rather than *a* sixth), a flurry of commentary rushes to explain the anomaly.

The systematic nature of Creation expresses itself in yet another remarkable way. The six days of Creation are organized so that there are actually two cycles of three days each, with the second cycle paralleling the first; each day in the first cycle has its companion in the second. The first and the fourth discuss creations revolving around *or* (we will discuss the meaning of this term later); the second and the fifth focus on the separation of the "upper waters" from the "lower waters" (on the fifth day, those two domains – the upper waters and the lower waters – are populated by the water creatures and the flying things); the third and the sixth focus on the emergence of land and vegetation, and the beings which inhabit that land and consume that vegetation. The chart below illustrates this succinctly:

First cycle of Creation	*Second cycle of Creation*
Day 1 *Or*	**Day 4** *Meorot* (from the same Hebrew root as *or*)
Day 2 Separation of "lower" from "upper" waters	**Day 5** Sea animals to inhabit lower waters Flying creatures to inhabit upper waters
Day 3 Emergence of land Vegetation	**Day 6** Land animals and humans Consumers of vegetation

What emerges is a picture of a Creation that is not only orderly and sequential, it is carefully planned and organized. It is not six sequential days of Creation but two parallel cycles of three days each, in which the first round lays foundations that are developed or populated in the second.

This sense of structure, pattern, order, and planning is intentional, and stands in stark contrast to many ancient Mesopotamian creation stories in which the world emerges as a result of a clash between gods, is the violent or accidental product of some heavenly conflagration, or came to be to provide the gods with their daily needs.[6] In the Torah there is but a single Creator who plans, decides, controls, and creates everything. Even the strange reference (v. 21) to the *taninim*, the mythical and mighty sea creatures, may be an expression of this same idea.

In some ancient cultures, the terrifying and mighty sea monsters were themselves considered gods, and the emergence of the world was the result of a terrible battle between them, or between them and God.[7] The Torah's version explicitly rejects any such notions. Those *taninim* are not gods, but beings which were created by the one and only Creator, and emerged only when the Creator decided that the waters needed to be populated.

If we return to our discussion of the image of God, it is now reasonable to argue that God is not only a Creator, He is intelligent, thoughtful, organized, and powerful, among other adjectives which we can add based on the above observations. These are all part of our emerging "image" of God. It is no wonder that the Hebrew name for God used in this creation story is *E-lohim*, which translated accurately would yield "the All-Powerful," or "Almighty." God as Almighty is an essential thrust of Genesis 1.

THE CHALLENGE OF LANGUAGE

God creates through speech.[8] Moreover, in Genesis 1 He creates language itself, presenting us with a significant challenge. Language is the primary

6. See Umberto Cassuto, *A Commentary on the Book of Genesis* [Hebrew] (Jerusalem: Magnes Press, 1969), 1–8.
7. See Cassuto. See also Yehezkel Kaufmann, *The Religion of Israel*, trans. Moshe Greenberg (New York: Schocken Books, 1972), 20–70.
8. This has been noted as significant in Psalms (33:6) and in Mishna Avot (5:1), and is featured in the daily prayer *Barukh SheAmar* as well as the first blessing prior to the evening *Shema*.

tool we have in studying text, yet in the Creation story familiar words are used in unfamiliar ways. Five words particularly stand out, demanding attention, including some of the words we take most for granted: *or, ḥoshekh, yom, erev,* and *boker,* usually translated, respectively, as "light," "darkness," "day," "evening," and "morning." All these words appear in the opening passage of Genesis, yet it is only after they are used that they are defined, indicating that they initially mean something other than what we intuitively assume.

Some examples will be helpful in highlighting the difficulty. The words usually translated as "day" (*yom*), "morning" (*boker*), and "evening" (*erev*) are all used on the first "day" of Creation, prior to the creation of the sun (which does not appear until the fourth day). If in conventional terms, a day is defined by one rotation of the earth, what can "day" mean when the earth does not yet exist (as in the first two "days" of Creation)? Similarly, morning and evening are functions of the rotation of the earth and its position vis-à-vis the sun. It is obvious that prior to the creation of the sun they refer to something completely different.[9]

Similarly, in the opening verse we are perplexed by the usage of the terms *shamayim* and *aretz,*[10] usually translated as "heaven" and "land" (or earth), respectively. It is only on the second day that God names something[11] *shamayim* and on the third day that dry land appears, which God then names *aretz.* It seems apparent that these words, prior to their definition and prior to the creations with which they are associated, refer to something other than their conventional interpretation.

The confusion generated by these words begs our attention and generates an opportunity to reexamine the text along with some of our basic assumptions.

CREATING TIME

The Torah describes God as separating *or* from *ḥoshekh,* usually translated as "light" and "darkness," yet if darkness as we know it is the absence

---

9. Maimonides, *Guide for the Perplexed* 2:30, discusses many of these issues.
10. Ibn Ezra, 1:1, s.v. *hashamayim,* struggles with this issue.
11. That "something" is identified in Hebrew as *rakia,* usually translated as "firmament." This translation is based on ancient notions of the existence of a physical barrier separating the various heavenly spheres.

of light, it makes no sense conceptually to "separate" between the existence of something and its absence. Even more problematic is that God afterward gives new names to *or* and *ḥoshekh* – *yom* (daytime) and *laila* (nighttime): "God named *or* daytime and *ḥoshekh* He called nighttime." Accordingly, at least in the opening of Genesis, *or* and *ḥoshekh* are not about light and dark at all, but rather are expressions of time, the lit hours being the productive ones and the dark hours less so.[12] The movement between those two kinds of time helps to mark it, frame it, and measure its passage.

This identification of *or* and *ḥoshekh* as functions of time rather than light and dark is sharpened when we recall that Creation occurs in two parallel cycles. The creation of *or* on the first day is mirrored in the creation of the *meorot* on day four. *Meorot*, based on the root *or*, is usually translated as something like "luminaries," things whose primary function is to provide light. Yet a careful reading of the Torah's account of that fourth day indicates that their primary function has nothing to do with light but with time: "God said, let there be *meorot* in the firmament of the heavens to distinguish between daytime and nighttime; and they should serve as signs, time markers, and for days and years" (1:14). The primary function of these *meorot* is not as sources of light at all, but as timekeepers. Their function as sources of light is secondary, mentioned only after their primary function.

It should not surprise us that the first creative utterance focuses on the creation of time. For an infinite God, time is irrelevant. The creation of time allows for the existence of finite beings. In fact, time is so essential for Creation that its very creation may be alluded to in the opening verse of Genesis. That verse presents a substantive challenge for the attentive reader, since the opening word of the Torah, *bereshit*, means "In the beginning of…." The problem is that the Torah does not fill in that ellipsis, leaving us with a verse which, in its simplest translation, reads: "In the beginning of…, God created the heavens and the earth."

---

12. Using the word "dark" to denote uselessness is both ancient and contemporary, and is true in English as well as in Hebrew.

This difficulty invites the reader to fill in the gap creatively. One of those possibilities is that the Torah leaves it open since an infinite and eternal God needs to first create the possibility, or the beginnings, of everything – including space and time – to allow for the existence of anything besides Himself.[13] If so, the creation of time in Genesis can be viewed as occurring in three stages. In the first stage, time itself is created: "God created the Beginning."[14] In the second stage, time can oscillate between two expressions, and those two phases of time can be used to mark its passage: "God distinguished between time associated with light and time associated with darkness." Both of these stages are created on the first day of Creation, and relate to time as linear. Linear time has a beginning, and any given moment in time exists only once – in either the past, the fleeting present, or the future. These two acts of Creation, even with the oscillation between daytime and nighttime, basically represent time as linear.

Linear time is meaningful because it is limited. Like any resource, endless access to it renders it meaningless. Limited access means that we have to make choices regarding how to use that resource, and the choices we make both say something meaningful about us and are meaningful in and of themselves.

But God does not stop with the creation of linear time. There is a third stage in the creation of time, just as revolutionary as the first two stages – the creation of cyclical time. Cyclical time helps make time manageable and meaningful for humans. In cyclical time we can make statements such as, "I'll meet you tomorrow at the same time," or "Next year in Jerusalem," or "on the first of each month." Viewed cyclically, time becomes an anchor for organizing and evaluating our

---

13. A variation on this would yield, "God created the Beginning with the *shamayim* and the *aretz*." This possibility emerges because the Hebrew *et* can be translated as "with."
14. One implication of this is that anything prior to Creation is beyond human comprehension. R. Yona, cited in Y. Ḥagiga 2:2, suggests that the Torah begins with the letter *bet* because it is closed on three sides, indicating that what came before Creation is closed and unknowable. Interestingly, this corresponds with the concept of singularity in physics, i.e., that which preceded the "Big Bang" is not only unknown but unknowable. See, for example, Stephen Hawking, *A Brief History of Time* (New York: Bantam Books, 1996).

internal and external selves. This is the creation of the fourth day, as the *meorot* distinguish daytime from nighttime, one day from the next, and year from year.

Prior to the Creation there is no time, as there is no need for time – for an eternal God, time has no meaning. The creation of time, both linear and cyclical, allows for the very existence of finite beings like us. More important, it allows for us to make time meaningful in multiple ways. The creation of time is perhaps God's first step in making room for people.

THE PROCESSES OF CREATION

The model of an initial Creation followed by refinement is deeply embedded in the text. We earlier saw that the terms *shamayim* and *aretz*, usually translated as heaven and earth, cannot mean "heaven" and "earth" in the opening verse of Genesis, as those do not appear until the second and third days of Creation. Following the lead of Nahmanides,[15] I'd like to suggest that the terms refer to an initial creation *ex nihilo* of the raw materials from which the rest of the universe ultimately emerges, whose initial state is described as *tohu* and *bohu* – *tohu* meaning perplexing (as in, "What is it?")[16] and *bohu* suggesting that it has the potential in it for everything (*bohu* being a contraction of *bo* and *hu* – literally, "it is in it").[17] While that initial state is chaotic and useless, God will bring its potential to fruition via the processes of separation, formation, and combination.

The theme of separation dominates the first three days of Creation: daytime from nighttime, "upper" waters from "lower" waters,[18]

---

15. 1:1.
16. The adjective *tohu*, meaning amazement or wonderment, describes the initial state of the *aretz*. The initial raw materials were all mixed together, so that they were unlike anything in the human experience. This is akin to the name the Israelites give to the manna, which would roughly translate as "What is it?"
17. Nahmanides, 1:1.
18. The separation on the second day between the "upper waters" and the "lower waters" may refer to the distinction between liquids (lower waters) and gases (upper waters). The Torah text speaks of a *rakia* as something infinitesimally thin, perhaps even merely a conceptual distinction between two states of matter. The "firmament" found in most translations is based on primitive conceptions of the universe.

water from land, etc., and is meaningful in that it takes the raw materials which are initially unidentifiable and unusable, and distinguishes them to make them usable. Following an intensive series of separations, God brings them together in constructive ways – a different form of creation. Water, recently separated from solids, is carefully remixed with those very solids, as it irrigates the dry land to enable the growth of vegetation.

In this light, I'd like to suggest the following as a reading of the opening two verses of Genesis: God created – *ex nihilo*[19] – the Beginning, alongside the raw material of which everything else will be made.[20] Initially, that raw material was in a state in which it was indistinguishable and unrecognizable yet brimming with potential, but since that potential was not actualized, the raw material was effectively useless.[21]

The fundamental process is clear – generate the raw material out of nothingness, separate and refine it into its components so that they become usable, and then make something from them. This process is actually reflected in two of the puzzling words we mentioned earlier, *erev* and *boker*. Etymologically, the Hebrew word *erev*, conventionally understood as evening, comes from the word meaning mixture. Evening became known as *erev* because that is when two days melt into one another, when the light from the sun and the moon mix in ways that render neither of them fully functional, when the world around us grows increasingly murky and unclear.

By contrast, the root of the word *boker*, usually translated as morning, means "to be able to distinguish." The morning time (*boker*) is when we begin to distinguish those things which have been unclear since the previous *erev*, when the new light enables us to see and distinguish that which had been unclear. In fact, Mishna

19. The creation of something where there was nothing before is marked in this story through the verb *bara*. See Nahmanides, 1:1. In the next chapter we will discuss the significance of the fact that this particular verb is used in only three contexts in the Genesis 1 Creation narrative.
20. While the *aretz* is subjected to multiple stages of refinement, what happens to the initial *shamayim* remains something of a mystery.
21. In verse 2 this is indicated by the darkness in which the *tohu*, or *tehom*, is shrouded.

Berakhot 1:2 clearly understands that the defining element of morning hinges on the ability to distinguish a friend's face or the colors on the strings of tzitzit. The movement from *erev* to *boker* refers not to times of day (which cannot exist until the fourth day of Creation) but to the movement from chaos to greater clarity. That movement is one of the landmark features of the Creation narrative, and defines each phase of Creation known as a *yom*, or "day."[22] Thus, a "day" of Creation does not mark time but a meaningful transition out of chaos into functional order.

This reading of the initial verses of Genesis yields a bizarre twist. The word *or* does not refer to light but is a function of time. *Erev* and *boker* have nothing to do with time, but reflect God's overall interest in His world being carefully organized and structured. So too, the word *yom* is not about time but refers to God's achieving a meaningful phase of Creation marked by the movement from disorder to order: "It was *erev* and then it was *boker*; a meaningful stage in the creative process." The creation of time makes room for Man; the move to orderliness within Creation models for Man the creative process.

ORDER AND HIERARCHY

The move from chaos to order almost defines the Creation story: concepts are followed by actions, raw materials are refined and then used. In physics, the law of entropy states that without the input of energy things will naturally tend toward disorder. The Creation story presents a picture of reverse entropy, in which God invests creative energy into the world to move it progressively from chaos to order.

The orderliness in Creation is apparent in numerous other expressions throughout the story. One fine example can be found in the creation of vegetation, where the language is unmistakable:

> "Let the ground carpet itself – grasses which produce seeds, fruit trees bearing fruits of their own species containing their own

---

22. Leon Kass, *Genesis*, 46, writes: "Creation, according to Genesis 1, is the bringing of order out of primordial chaos, largely through a process of progressive separation, division, distinction, differentiation."

seeds on the ground" – and it was so. The ground brought forth its carpet: grasses producing seeds of their species and fruit-bearing trees containing the seeds of their own species. (1:11–12)

Three times in these two verses the Torah emphasizes that vegetation needs to be self-propagating and self-perpetuating – each according to its species. Orange trees need to produce oranges which will contain the seeds necessary for growing new orange trees. The preservation of the species line could not have been made any clearer.

The same emphasis emerges in the description of the imperative for animals to be fruitful. Twice in 1:21, another time in 1:24, and three times in 1:25, we hear variations on the word *lemino*, "according to its own species." God is intent on preserving the distinction between the species, whether in the plant or animal kingdom.

This intensified focus on the self-perpetuation of the species serves as a backdrop for some of the most inexplicable laws spelled out later in the Torah. There are prohibitions on crossbreeding animals and even on hybridization of crops.[23] Those attempts to tamper with the natural order of the world threaten the careful orderliness of Creation itself.[24]

And it is not only the species which must be maintained, the domains of those creatures must be maintained as well. Beings of the water are meant to be in the water, flying creatures dominate the skies, and land animals belong on land. (The land animals even belong to a different day of Creation.) It is fascinating that there is not a single kosher animal that crosses those boundaries (as opposed to turtles, frogs, penguins, water mammals, etc., which are all non-kosher animals). It is almost as if the Torah has boycotted animals that have violated the boundaries of their domains.

The meticulous order of Creation also suggests hierarchy. The Torah begins with inert matter, which contains the building blocks of everything. By the third day we find organic matter, vegetation,

---

23. See Leviticus 19:19, and especially the comments of Rashbam and Nahmanides.
24. A tension will later emerge in the text between this imperative and God's instruction that people "conquer" the earth (1:28).

emerging from the lifeless ground. When we reach the fifth day we are introduced to animate beings, first the creatures of the sea and then the flying creatures. The sixth day brings us land animals, and finally humans.

This hierarchy of life-forms actually finds expression in the Jewish codes of law. Inert matter and vegetation need no special preparation to be rendered kosher – theoretically, you can put your mouth under a waterfall to drink or take a bite out of an apple while it is still attached to a tree. While impolite, it is certainly not forbidden. In the animal kingdom, even kosher animals need some kind of preparation to render them halakhically permissible to eat, and those preparatory acts – which are all related to the need to sever the body of the animal from its life source – have a hierarchy parallel to the hierarchy within Creation. In practical terms, for a kosher fish to be rendered fit for consumption, it must be caught and killed (unlike the apple); for a bird to be rendered kosher, it needs to be slaughtered, with either the trachea or the esophagus being slit; for a land animal to be made kosher, it needs to have both the trachea and the esophagus slit.

The higher the being is on the hierarchy of Creation – that is, the closer it is to the human – the greater the demonstration necessary to make the animal permissible to eat.

IMAGE OF GOD

The biblical Creation story weaves a complex tapestry illuminated by intelligent planning, thought, sequence, order, and hierarchy – all done in a staged, spiral process. Both the content and the structure of the description serve as foundations for understanding some of the more obtuse laws and narrative passages spelled out later in the Torah, and we will later see further examples of this.

Perhaps even more important than what the Creation story teaches us conceptually about Creation is what it teaches us about God. As we discussed above, the description in Genesis 1 presents God as All-Powerful (E-lohim), Independent, Intelligent, Thoughtful, Orderly, Purposeful (even though we do not as yet know what the purpose is), and Creative, along with a host of additional adjectives which emerge upon subsequent careful readings.

This "image" of God is significant not only for our understanding of God but for our understanding of Man. Man will be created in the "image" of God, and the opening chapter of Genesis provides insight as to what that might mean. The description of the Creation paints for us an image of the Creator, and that image will help us understand what makes the creation of Man, the pinnacle of Creation, so extraordinarily unique.

Genesis 1:26–31

Challenge of Humanity

C reation is orderly, planned, systematic, and hierarchical. Everything has its place and the boundaries are set. It involves bursts of creation *ex nihilo* followed by movement from chaos to clarity and purpose. There is even a template for each stage, or "day," of the creative process: God said…God made/did/created/formed…God saw that it was "good"…God named…it was *erev* and it was *boker*, a (number) "day." When it comes to the creation of humans, however, the formulaic pattern is subtly, but significantly, interrupted:

> God said, "Let us make human in our *tzelem* and our *demut*,[1] so that they may dominate the fish of the sea, the birds of the sky, the land animals, the entire land, and all the swarming creatures which swarm on the land." (1:26)

---

1. These words are often translated as "image" and "form." In classical Jewish thought, God has neither an image nor a form. The use of both terms here opens up a complex puzzle, as God proclaims His intention to create humanity with both His *tzelem* and His *demut* yet in the following verse, Man is created only in God's *tzelem*. The puzzle is complicated by 5:1, which describes Man as created in God's *demut* but not His *tzelem*, and even further by 9:1, which describes Man as created in God's *tzelem* but not His *demut*.

Nowhere else in the entire Creation narrative do we find the deliberative voice of "Let us make…." Instead, we find God's word as the vehicle through which He creates: "Let there be…." The deliberative voice prior to the creation of humans suggests a moment's hesitation prior to following through on the idea, as if there were some kind of heavenly debate which is resolved by God's declaration, "Let us make human." What is it about humans that could generate this divine hesitation?

There are a host of fascinating midrashim that provide some insight into the heavenly ambivalence. Here is one:

> R. Shimon said: When The Holy One, blessed be He, came to create the first man, the heavenly angels organized into groups. Some said, "He should be created," while others proclaimed, "He should not be created." Kindness said, "He should be created, for he will do kindness." Truth declared, "He should not be created, for he is full of lies." Justice said, "Let him be created, for he does righteousness." Peace averred, "He should not be created, for he is full of discord."[2]

The different angels in this midrash represent different aspects of God's interaction with humanity, so that what we have is not so much a debate between heavenly beings but God's internal debate about creating humans. The midrash focuses that ambivalence: The human is capable of great things but also has the capacity to destroy. The greatness of the human potential is counterbalanced by the ability to use that potential improperly.

MOVING TOWARD INDEPENDENCE

We've established that Creation is orderly and systematic and follows a clear progression in terms of the sophistication of beings. Yet there is another progression – from static to dynamic. The world of the first three days is essentially fixed. In the first three days, God creates the building blocks of the universe: gasses, liquids, solids, time. Although God is active, there is no movement within the creations themselves. Even

---

2. Genesis Rabba 8. For other midrashim with similar themes see the full discussion there. See also Sanhedrin 38b.

vegetation, created on day three, is relatively static; it is rooted, both literally and figuratively, in its place. With the advent of the fourth day we are introduced to movement. The sun, moon, and stars move across the sky and their positions are always changing.[3]

The movement of the heavenly bodies, however, is fixed, programmed, predictable. It is not until the fifth day, when we hear about the creation of animate life, that we are introduced to independent movement. Not only does the Torah introduce it, the locomotion of the creatures is precisely their most prominent feature.[4] Most English translations render the opening of the fifth day as some variation on "Let the waters swarm with living beings, and birds will fly over the land." The word "swarm" itself suggests movement, but the Hebrew is even more explicit. The Torah uses the word *sheretz*. That word, with the minor modification of a single vowel, yields *sheratz*, which literally means, "that moves."[5] The principal identifying factor of this creation is that it moves. The same is true for the other primary creation of the fifth day, the birds. In Hebrew, the noun for bird is essentially the same as the verb that describes its movement: *of yeofef*, "the flying things will fly."

The significance of the creation of independently moving beings is further highlighted by the choice to describe this creation using the word *bara* – creation *ex nihilo* – a word which has not been used since the opening creative act in which God created the raw materials for the universe. Independent movement is revolutionary in the Creation narrative. It is not a continuation of something that preceded it, but, like time, something completely new.[6]

---

3. Even though, from an astronomical perspective, the sun doesn't move, from the human perspective we speak of sunrise and sunset. Our experience of the heavenly bodies is that they do move.

4. See Leon Kass, "Why the Dietary Laws," *Commentary* 97 (1994): 46.

5. In the Torah scroll, there are no vowels. Grammatically, the vowels which make the "eh" sound and the "ah" sound are often interchanged, especially when there are two sequential "eh" vowels (although in those cases it is the first of those which is transformed into the "ah" vowel).

6. If, indeed, the word *bara* is reserved for creation *ex nihilo* (as claims Nahmanides), then the Torah is making a profound statement that animate life as we know it would not have materialized on its own. The emergence of the first life-forms where there were previously none requires an act of God.

Observers of humanity recognize the importance of locomotion in achieving independence. From the time a child learns to crawl, take her first steps, ride a bicycle, or drive, every stage of increased mobility is accompanied by a profound sense of independence. Just watch the child who crawls away from his parents and turns a corner to be out of sight, or the teen asking for the car keys; each advance is a step on the path to independence.

INDEPENDENCE OF HUMANS

The independence of humans, however, extends far beyond locomotion. Human behavior is directed by willful decisions, not merely by instinct. Humans are, by and large, in control of their decisions, and they are free to change them. Perhaps even more significant, human decisions can have a moral or ethical component, and can make a difference in the lives of others. In other words, human decisions are meaningful and can profoundly impact on the world around them.

This is the gist of the midrash we cited earlier. God created a world; humans can make it a better place or destroy it. The midrash did not invent the idea – it is already implied in the Torah text, as when God plans to make humans He also identifies their function – domination over the rest of the creations on earth (1:26).[7]

This is actually a radical statement with profound theological implications. If humans are to dominate the earthly beings, then God must cede some of His control to them. If human decisions can really make a difference, to the extent that they can impact on the world in both positive and negative ways (per the midrash), then by implication God has empowered them and disempowered Himself at the same time.

The empowerment of humans is closely associated with the fact that they are created in the *tzelem/demut* of God. In the previous chapter we painted the image of God, as it emerges from the Genesis account, as Powerful, Independent, Intelligent, Thoughtful, Orderly, Purposeful, and Creative, to name just a few of the attributes which emerge from a

---

7. *Pirkei DeRabbi Eliezer* 11 presents Man as the singular dominant force on earth, paralleling God, who is the singular dominant force in the heavens.

close reading of the first chapter. Imagine each of those but without the capital letters, and we have the beginnings of a portrait of what it means to be a human created in God's "image."[8]

It is perhaps for this reason that the Torah again uses the reserved term *bara* to describe humans. They – we – are unlike any being created previously, and the difference is qualitative, not quantitative. Humans are not simply one step more advanced than the other creatures; we are endowed with Godlike qualities, created in the image of God. Just as the raw materials for the universe need a divine fiat to come into existence, and just as life cannot emerge without God breathing life into an inanimate world, humans cannot come into existence without a divine spark distinguishing us from the rest of the beasts.[9]

There is an ancient riddle which presents a paradoxical question: Can God create a rock that He can't lift? I believe that there is a simple answer: He already has. The paradox is built on the assumption that God cannot be limited – if there is something He cannot create then He is limited, and if He cannot lift the rock then He is limited. What the riddle does not consider is whether God can choose to limit Himself. A cursory look through the Torah indicates that He does, and He does so repeatedly. When God enters into a covenant with Noah, promising to never again return the world to its primordial state, that becomes binding upon God, and in doing so He limits Himself. When God later enters into a covenant with Abraham or the Israelite nation, He chooses to limit His behavior. He is bound by that covenant, as are the people with whom He establishes it.

What we are suggesting is that the creation of humans requires God to self-limit. God surrenders some of His control, what in kabbalistic

---

8. Leon Kass, *Genesis*, 38, writes:
   Our reading of this text, addressable and intelligible only to us human beings, and our responses to it, possible only for us human beings, provide all the proof we need to confirm the text's assertion of our special being.... Man may be, of all the creatures, the most intelligent, resourceful, conscious, and free – and in these respects the most godlike.
9. This is not to say that human bodies did not evolve from more primitive beings, but that humanity as we know it involves a quantum leap beyond what existed previously. That quantum leap was provided from Above.

literature might be called *tzimtzum*,[10] in order to make room for humans to exercise their power to decide, implement, create, and destroy. Humans are the pinnacle of the progression toward independence – not of independence merely to move, but to exercise their God-given gift to become meaningful beings through the choices they make.

It is this independence of humans, and the necessary sacrifice of control by God, which gives Him cause for hesitation. Is He really prepared to relinquish control of that which He created? Is He prepared to truly empower humans in a way which necessitates that He give up the right to regularly intervene and correct?

EXPLORING SELF-LIMITATION

On some fundamental level, the notion of God limiting Himself makes perfect sense. The perspective of a basic model of human interaction, parenting, can be instructive. Parents are constantly torn between trying to protect their children and raising them to be healthy adults. Overprotective parents deny their children the opportunity to cope and become competent adults. Parents who are *laissez-faire* run the risk of their child making serious mistakes and suffering terrible consequences prior to adulthood.

Take the simple example of learning to cross the street. A parent who is too fearful to ever let their child cross alone cripples the child, but a parent who lets their child cross unaided from too early an age runs the risk of irreversible tragedy. Most people fall somewhere in the range between those two extremes, slowly teaching their child how to be careful and eventually trusting that child to cross alone. That moment of letting go requires a leap of faith – ceding control as the child is empowered. Parents may be afraid to relinquish control, but know that ultimately they must do so in order for their child to become a functioning adult.

For God to create humans in His "image," He too, like the parent, needs to voluntarily limit Himself so that people can fully realize their humanity. That self-limitation and the accompanying empowerment of people is risky, and so God hesitates, even though He knows that

---

10. See Gershom Scholem, *Major Trends in Jewish Mysticism* (New York: Schocken Books, 1954), 260–262.

without empowering His new creation, it will never have the opportunity to fully achieve its potential.

This formulation leads to two significant ideas. First, assuming that God wants people to be able to make meaningful choices, He needs to be prepared for the eventuality that they will sometimes make choices of which He does not approve. Put differently, sin is to be expected as part of the process of exploring what it means to be human. And if God needs to expect that people will sin, then people can expect that God will be tolerant – up to a point – of those mistakes.

The parent-child model once again offers a useful model in which the stakes are not life-and-death issues, but a homework assignment the child was given from school. The parent could do it for the child, and the child will have the homework completed properly but will not have learned anything from it. Alternatively, the parent can let the child make mistakes in doing it, encounter some frustration, and then need to redo it and learn from his mistake. Allowing the child to make the mistake enables the child to learn and is part of a process of empowerment. The child's learning is directly related to his ability to err. Similarly, the actualization of human potential is directly related to our ability to make mistakes, that is, to sin, and to learn from those errors.[11] That model implies divine tolerance of our errors, albeit not without consequences, to enable our ultimate emergence as developed people.

Second, if God can self-limit His *control* over Man's decisions, is it possible that He can also self-limit His *knowledge* of Man's decisions? Thus, the limits on God's knowledge emanate not from His inability to know but from His choice not to know. If this is indeed possible, then God can truly be surprised by Man's decisions, angry at Man for disappointing Him,[12] regret decisions He makes regarding Man,[13] saddened by Man's actions,[14] and can adjust based on what He learns about Man.[15]

---

11. The Hebrew word for sin is *ḥet*, which means "to miss the mark."
12. For example, Ex. 4:14. This theme is central throughout the Bible.
13. Gen. 6:6; Ex. 32:14.
14. 6:7.
15. For example, Num. 14:11–24. For more on this see Yochanan Muffs, *The Personhood of God* (Woodstock, VT: Jewish Lights, 2005).

God's deliberation and hesitation prior to creating humans is now entirely comprehensible. To create humans, by definition, demands that God recede from direct control – and perhaps even foreknowledge – of the daily affairs of the world.

THE NECESSITY OF HUMANITY

Given the immense challenges arising from the creation of people, one must wonder why God would choose to create them. Would it not have made the world a simpler, more pristine place had people not been introduced? Would it not have been easier for God to avoid the necessary self-limitation and remain the Almighty God with no restrictions, albeit self-imposed?

The answer, it seems, is quite obvious. Without the creation of the "unknown" of humanity, the existence of a pristine world has no purpose; it is meaningless. To put this differently, imagine a computer programmer who programmed his screen to regularly flash the words, "You are wonderful!" That praise is absolutely meaningless; it is nothing but an exercise in narcissism. Imagine, however, a programmer so clever that he programmed a computer which would consciously decide whether or not to flash, "You are wonderful!" The programmer's sense of satisfaction will be achieved only when it is clear that the outcome is not fixed or predetermined or known in advance, and that the computer ultimately (perhaps after numerous errors), justifiably decides to declare the programmer as being awesome.

For people to choose – using their divine spark – to encounter God, acknowledge Him, establish a relationship with Him, and fashion themselves in God's "image" is an extraordinary achievement. And that seems to be the essential goal of Creation: for humans to become truly Godlike and exercise their divine quality to achieve that intimate encounter with their Creator.

This, I believe, is the answer to a different question which has vexed readers of the Bible for millennia. When God deliberates the creation of people the Torah introduces that hesitation with the words, "Let us make human." To whom is God referring when He says "us?"[16]

---

16. See Genesis Rabba 8; Sanhedrin 38b. Y. Berakhot 9:1 records R. Simlai's comment that this verse exposes the Torah to heretical challenges, as if there were more than

Many answers have been suggested throughout the ages; I propose that the "us" refers to God and the people themselves; people are empowered to create themselves in God's "image" and thus, paradoxically, become partners with God in their own self-creation.

As people make choices about their actions and attitudes they design their own character. It is for this reason that we are ultimately responsible for our own actions,[17] because God entrusted us with the ability to decide what kind of people we want to become.

THE GLORY OF HUMANITY

It is this uniqueness of humanity that the Torah celebrates as it describes our creation (1:27):

> God created (*bara*) the Man in His *tzelem*,
> in the *tzelem* of God He created (*bara*) him,
> male and female He created (*bara*) them.

We've already seen that the term *bara* used to describe Creation is reserved for creation *ex nihilo*; prior to this verse it had been used only twice in the entire Creation narrative. Yet in this single verse describing the creation of people it is used three times. Moreover, the verse appears to be filled with repetition. It could even be argued that the entire middle phrase is unnecessary. Yet it is precisely this repetition which, I believe, highlights just how extraordinarily different and astonishing this creative act is.

It is almost inconceivable that a human could be created in God's *tzelem*; the Torah needs to say it yet again, almost verbatim. In fact, the first phrase could easily be translated as: God created (*bara*) the Man in his *tzelem*, that is, that the Man is created in his own, but not God's, *tzelem*.[18] The thoughtful reader might have been tempted to read this

---

a single Creator. R. Simlai notes the next verse in response, in which God alone is recoded as the Creator.

17. This principle is deeply enshrined in the halakhic rubric in that a person is always considered responsible for his actions – even for accidents and even when asleep! (See Mishna Bava Kamma 2:6.)
18. Indeed, Rashi and Rashbam read it as such.

opening phrase as such precisely because it is preposterous to suggest that Man is created in God's *tzelem*. It is for that very reason the Torah repeats the phrase almost verbatim, eliminating the possibility of ambiguity – Man is created in God's *tzelem*.

The third phrase catches our attention as well. Weren't animals also created as male and female? Why does the Torah highlight this element regarding humans?

It would seem that the human male and female reflect not only biological diversity but a difference in essence as well. The masculine and feminine voices are different and they reflect different ways of thinking, experiencing, and relating – one which would be identified as more masculine and a second which would be identified as more typically feminine.

Rereading that third phrase, it is even possible that the identification of male and female may, in fact, be an explication of God's *tzelem*. In kabbalistic literature, God is described as relating to the world through multiple modes, including a distant, masculine mode in which God is described as The Holy One, blessed be He, and an intimate, feminine mode in which God is described as *Shekhina*, the One who dwells among humans.[19]

This kabbalistic, male-female dichotomy reflects one aspect of God's complexity, one in which justice and compassion, war and peace, truth and kindness, all coexist. The Torah's description of humans as being created in God's *tzelem* suggests that humans are complex as well. It is that complexity that allows for the sophistication of humanity and the capacity for thoughtfulness, reflectiveness, and change, and it is that complexity which makes us more Godlike and glorious than anything else ever created.

The creation of people is marked by nothing less than a textual celebration of the crowning glory of the entire narrative. What makes this so highly extraordinary is that the very existence of the beings that

---

19. See, for example, Hava Tirosh-Samuelson, "Gender in Jewish Mysticism," in *Jewish Mysticism and Kabbalah: Insights and Scholarship*, ed. Frederick E. Greenspahn (New York: New York University Press, 2011), 191–230. Hasidic liturgy has embraced this imagery; prior to the performance of many mitzvot or prayers, there is a recitation: "For the sake of uniting The Holy One, blessed be He, with His *Shekhina*."

God creates in His *tzelem* will inherently challenge God, and their actions may threaten God's sovereignty in this world; yet God celebrates their creation like nothing else in Creation.

MUTUAL EMPOWERMENT

The story of Creation is the ultimate story of the empowerment of humanity. Not only because God must self-limit – certainly in control and perhaps even in knowledge – but because God empowers those created in His image to decide for themselves how they want to self-create. To contrast the creation of humans with the creation of vegetation, vegetation is designed to be self-propagating and has no choice in the matter. Apple trees produce fruit with seeds to produce more apple trees. Humans, on the other hand, give birth to humans who decide what kind of people they want to be. Each individual is self-creating; no two are identical because each chooses its own identity.

The great irony with people is that those who ultimately tap into the embedded divine spark use it to better themselves and the world around them and to connect meaningfully with their Creator. As they do so, like their own Creator, they voluntarily cede some of their self-authority to submit to God's. Their self-limiting mirrors God's, and their self-empowerment leads to a re-empowering of God in their lives.

Prior to the Creation, God is unquestionably the king of everything, but because nothing as yet exists that sovereignty seems pointless. It is only when He created the world that the creations could crown Him properly. This idea is not new, and is expressed elegantly in the opening lines of the *Adon Olam* prayer:

> Master of the universe, who reigned
> prior to the Creation of anything.
> When ultimately He willed all things into existence,
> it was only *then* that He was proclaimed "King!"

Genesis 2:1–3

The Seventh Day

The division of the Torah into verses is part of an ancient Jewish tradition; in the Talmud there is discussion with regard to the precise number of verses in the Torah.[1] Also part of an ancient Jewish tradition (alternatively called the *mesora*, or the Masoretic tradition) is the division of the Torah into sections with paragraph breaks. Two kinds of breaks appear in a traditional Torah scroll. One, called a *petuḥa*, or open break, leaves a space which is open until the end of the line. The other, called a *setuma*, or closed break, leaves a space the width of nine letters in the middle of a line, with the text continuing afterward on the same line.

Quite different, however, is the division of the Torah into chapters. This organizational system did not emerge until the early thirteenth century, and is usually attributed to Stephen Langton, the archbishop of Canterbury. While these divisions are often logical, they are also a form of exegesis; organizing the beginning and end of a chapter helps define its theme. It is only when we become aware of this that we can

---

1. Kiddushin 30a. The Talmud records that already in its day there were discrepancies between the accepted number of verses in the Torah and the texts available at the time.

detect the exegetical ideas being expressed. Moreover, there are times when a minor discrepancy between the Masoretic paragraph breaks and the chapter division can have dramatic exegetical and even theological implications.[2]

PLACEMENT OF THE SEVENTH DAY

Our first encounter with discrepancy in division comes in the very brief passage in Genesis 2:1–3, which describes the seventh day. Archbishop Langton separated this from the first six days of Creation by making it the beginning of chapter 2. A cursory literary analysis reveals that he had good reason to do so:

> The *shamayim* and the *aretz* and their entire arrays[3] were completed. God completed on/through[4] the seventh day the creative work which He had done, and He desisted on the seventh day from all the creative work which He had done. God blessed the seventh day and sanctified it, for on it He desisted from all the creative work, which He created to do.

---

2. For example, Exodus 31:18 reads: "He [God] gave to Moses, when He finished speaking with him, the two Tablets of Testimony; tablets of stone with God's writing." The Christian chapter division designates this as the concluding verse of the long section describing the Tabernacle. According to their reading, that section begins with preparations to build the Ark of the Covenant and closes with God's delivering the Tablets of the Covenant, which are to be housed in that Ark. God's work is completed and is contrasted with the sinful work of the Israelites building the Golden Calf.

   In contradistinction to that reading, the Masoretic text has the above verse as the opening of the story of the Golden Calf. The Tablets are God's symbol of His attempt to communicate with the Israelites (as per Ex. 25:22), while the Golden Calf was the Israelites' attempt to communicate with God. Moses, understanding that the relationship between God and the Israelites was endangered, shatters both symbols in an effort to demonstrate the fragility of the bond.

3. This is usually translated as "hosts." Below I will justify translating it as "arrays," based on the fine translation of Robert Alter, *The Five Books of Moses* (New York: Norton, 2004).

4. Later in this chapter I will discuss the ambiguity represented here.

We've noted that the Creation narrative follows a template. The pattern repeats six times, albeit with minor variations. On the seventh day every element of that cycle is missing. There is no speech from God, no creative action by God, no indication that anything was "good," no naming, and no *erev* and *boker*. The absence of the creation formula alone is enough to convince the reader that this passage does not belong to the first chapter of Genesis, the Creation narrative, but is the beginning of a new narrative.

Despite the structural evidence just presented, Jewish tradition reads this passage differently, placing it as the coda of the previous chapter rather than as the start of a new one. That placement is also reasonable, as further analysis of the text reveals there is ample literary evidence supporting it. First, it is well known that the name of God used throughout the opening Creation narrative is E-lohim, while the name of God used throughout chapters 2 and 3 is A-donai E-lohim. The name used on the seventh day is E-lohim, linking it to Genesis 1. That alone may be enough to justify identifying the seventh day as the conclusion of the opening Creation narrative, but there is additional support for the Masoretic reading.

The passage above references the seventh day three times. It is meaningless to speak of a seventh without the context of the first six. This point is sharpened when we consider that in all of Genesis 2–3, there is no sense of time or order or days, whereas the opening Creation narrative is filled with order, organization, sequence, time, and "days." Moreover, the opening line of the passage, "The *shamayim* and the *aretz* and their entire arrays were completed," refers explicitly back to the opening line of the complete Creation narrative, "In the beginning God created the *shamayim* and the *aretz*," defining it as a closed literary unit.[5] The unit which begins with the creation of the *shamayim* and the *aretz* closes with the same language.

In fact, there is a strange word introduced on the seventh day, *tzevaam*. In most of the rest of the Bible, as well as in modern Hebrew,

5. This form is sometimes referred to as an *inclusio*, or a literary envelope, in which words, phrases, or themes introduced in the beginning of a section are echoed in the close of that section, in effect "framing" the section as a literary unit.

the word *tzava* typically refers to an army. One significant distinguishing feature of an army is that it is a well-organized collection of individuals called to the service of a commander. While Genesis 1:1 speaks of *shamayim* and *aretz*, the rest of the chapter deals with the things that emerge from and inhabit those domains. They are what the Torah eventually identifies as a *tzava*; they are well organized and follow the instructions of their Commander. Hence the sun, moon, and stars are included in the *tzava* of the *shamayim*,[6] while the vegetation and animals make up the *tzava* of the *aretz*.[7] This sharpens the literary envelope we mentioned earlier. Genesis 1:1 opens with the *shamayim* and *aretz*, continues with a detailed account of the emergence of the *tzava* of each, and closes with the statement that the *shamayim* and *aretz* and the *tzava* of each were finished. The seventh day opens with the declaration that the Creation process which began in Genesis 1:1 is now complete.

THE NATURE OF THE SEVENTH DAY

The somewhat technical discussion of where to locate the seventh day leaves us with a puzzle. In terms of content the passage clearly belongs with the previous chapter, but it is missing the structural elements which define that chapter.

The resolution of that puzzle is actually quite simple. While the passage is the coda to the Creation narrative, this day is distinctly different from the prior six. On the other six, God creates, on this day He refrains from creating, and it is precisely because there is no creative

---

6. It is worth noting that the Hebrew word for the sun is *shemesh*. In the unvocalized Torah, *shemesh* is a play on *shamash*, that is, a servant. Even the mighty sun is part of the *tzava* of the *shamayim*, following the directives of the Almighty Commander. This is a powerful expression of the Torah's negation of sun-worship; the sun is not to be worshiped as a god, as the sun itself is nothing more than God's servant. Poignantly, Robert Sacks, *Commentary on the Book of Genesis*, 41, writes: "This de-emphasis of the heavenly bodies seems also to be implied by the fact that they are merely called the two great lights, rather than being given their proper names."
7. It is for this reason that I chose to translate *tzevaam* as "their arrays," as it indeed refers to the arrays that fill the respective domains of the *shamayim* and the *aretz*.

work on this day that all those elements in the Creation formula are missing. There is no "God said" because God's speech is the creative force and does not belong where there is no creative act. Likewise, there is no "God made," there is nothing for Him to reflect upon that it "was good," and there is no *erev* or *boker* because there is no movement from chaos to clarity. All the structural elements meticulously developed in the Creation narrative are there in the first six days of Creation because they help define the creative process; their absence in the description of the seventh day reinforces the distinction between it and the others, even as the Torah makes it clear that this day is an integral part of the Creation narrative.

Resolving these "technical" questions opens up some thought-provoking ones. Why is there a need for a day of Creation in which nothing is created? What was missing from the world which necessitated a seventh day?

It appears that while the creation of the physical universe – the *shamayim* and the *aretz* – is complete, there is a dimension which is absent. This is how the seventh day is actually introduced: "The *shamayim* and the *aretz* and their entire arrays were completed." But while the physical universe is complete, God's work is not, as there is still something missing. The very creation of the seventh day completes God's work. Perhaps the most significant feature of the seventh day is that it even exists.

This is apparently the intent of the second verse of the passage. It is not *on* the seventh day that God completed His Creation, but *through* the fact that He created the seventh day – in which there would be no creative work – that the Creation is complete.[8]

---

8. The Hebrew, *bayom hashevi'i*, is usually translated as "on the seventh day," but can also mean "through the seventh day." This is apparently the intent of a midrash (Genesis Rabba 10:19). Faced with an internal contradiction in 2:2 – on the one hand it says, "God completed on the seventh 'day' the creative work which He had done," while it continues with, "He desisted on the seventh 'day' from all the creative work which He had done" – the midrash answers that the world was missing rest, and God's resting on the seventh day paradoxically completes the Creation. Thus it is through the very existence of the seventh day that the Creation is complete.

The seventh day is not a day of rest,[9] but a day of desisting from making, forming, clarifying, separating, combining, building, or any of the other processes which mark the previous six. It is the cessation of these activities which allows for investment in a different dimension, and it is that dimension which is introduced in the final verse of our passage.

BLESSING AND SANCTIFICATION

The final verse of our passage reads: "God blessed the seventh 'day' and sanctified it." As opposed to desisting and refraining, which indicate passivity, blessing and sanctification are active, and point to what the day is as distinct from what the day is not. To get a better understanding of the seventh day we need to explore what these two words, "blessed" and "sanctified," mean.

Throughout the Torah, *kedusha*, which is from the same root as the word "sanctified" in our passage, has less to do with notions of sacredness than it does with distinguishing something as being set apart from the mundane. If the six days of Creation are defined by creative acts in the physical sphere, the seventh is set apart from the others by the absence of that work.

Defining "blessed" is somewhat more complicated. There are many types of blessing – people blessing people, people blessing God, and blessing which emanates from God. We will limit ourselves, for now, to defining this last one. In the Creation narrative there are actually numerous blessings which God bestows. The sea and flying animals are blessed on day five, and humans are blessed on day six.

What does it mean when God blesses something? It would seem to mean that God endows that something with potential. When sea animals are blessed to be fruitful and multiply, God is endowing them with special potential in this realm. Similarly, when God blesses humans on the sixth day to be fruitful, to fill up the land and conquer it, He endows them with a special ability to dominate and tame the natural world, but

---

9. The Hebrew verb SH-B-T does not mean to rest, but to refrain or desist. See Ibn Ezra's comment on 2:2. In modern Hebrew, the word for a workers' strike derives from the same root.

that does not necessarily mean they will actualize the blessing. For this to happen, the one who is blessed must act upon that with which God has endowed them.

Applying this to the seventh day, however, is somewhat more perplexing. What could it mean for a "day" – whether a unit of time or a cycle of creation – to be endowed with potential?

THE SEVENTH DAY BECOMES SHABBAT

The verbs "to bless" and "to sanctify" appear together only twice in the entire Torah. Our text in Genesis is the first; the second is in the Decalogue in the Book of Exodus, at the conclusion of the commandment of Shabbat. Let us look at that text:

> Remember the Shabbat in order to sanctify it. For six days you shall labor and do all of your creative work, but the seventh day is the Shabbat, dedicated to A-donai, your God. You shall do no creative work – you, your son, your daughter, your male and female servants, your animal, and the stranger in your gates. Because in six days God created the *shamayim*, the *aretz*, the seas, and all that is in them, and He desisted on the seventh day. It is for that reason that God blessed the Shabbat and sanctified it. (Ex. 20:8–11)

It is in the closing line that we hear our two verbs, "to bless" and "to sanctify," and it is not surprising that the entire presentation of Shabbat paints it in the context of Creation; the description of the commandment of Shabbat in Exodus presents it as a mirror of the Creation text in Genesis.[10] In both, there are six days of Creation during which God creates the *shamayim*, the *aretz*, and all that is in them; in both, God desists from creative work on the seventh day; in both, God blesses *and* sanctifies the seventh day. It is clear that the Exodus text is intentionally built on the Genesis text.

---

10. The text of the Shabbat commandment in the Decalogue in Deuteronomy is markedly different; it makes no reference at all to Creation, focusing instead on the experience of the Israelites as liberated slaves.

There are apparently two things that the Decalogue text adds to our text in Genesis. First, the seventh day is called Shabbat and is dedicated to God. Second, God's refraining from creative work is apparently the model for the legislation which forbids the Israelites to engage in creative work on Shabbat.

Yet there is a puzzling phrase in the Exodus text, and it is precisely in the verse referencing blessing and sanctification: "It is for that reason that God blessed the Shabbat and sanctified it." What is meant by the phrase, "It is for that reason"? Of which reason, precisely, is the Torah speaking?

A careful reading of the text yields a startling conclusion: God blessed and sanctified the seventh day so that we should remember and sanctify it. That is, it is not that we refrain from plastic creativity on Shabbat because God did, but that God desisted from creative work on the seventh day so that we should! This is quite remarkable, as it reverses conventional thinking about the commandment of Shabbat with an interesting implication.

God created the seventh day and endowed it with potential, but God's sanctification and blessing of the seventh day found no concrete expression for thousands of years. It is not until the giving of the Torah to the Israelites that the seventh day becomes identified as Shabbat, and not until their observance of Shabbat that the potential with which God endows Shabbat can be actualized. Shabbat becomes meaningful when people observe it, and God created the seventh day so that people should be able to observe it and mine its potential.

That potential is inherently tied into the prohibitions associated with the day. It is a day designed to free us from any thought of engaging in the creative activities of the other days; it is *kadosh*, set aside for a different kind of activity. That other activity may be in the realm of seeking the spiritual, of personal reflection, of developing relationships, or of a host of other possibilities. What they all have in common is what they are not: they are not creative work in the physical realm. God refrained so that we could, and thereby explore other dimensions of our lives. By desisting on the seventh day, God sets the model for those created in His image.

ISRAEL AND SHABBAT

Shabbat is an integral component of Creation, despite – or perhaps because of – the dramatic difference between it and the first six days. There is a fascinating midrash[11] which describes a dialogue between Shabbat and God: "Each day of the week has a partner," complains Shabbat, "but I am left all by myself." God responds, "Israel will be your partner." Each of the first three days of Creation, which we referred to as the first cycle of Creation, is endowed with a potential which is then developed by its partner in the second cycle of three days. Time, created on the first day, becomes cyclical time with timekeepers on the fourth; the domains of the upper and lower waters created on the second day become populated with their respective denizens on the fifth; the dry land with its vegetation created on the third day is populated on the sixth with creatures that will eat that vegetation. Shabbat, however, is endowed with a potential that does not achieve expression. God's response is that with the giving of the Torah, the potential of Shabbat will find its fulfillment.

In this, Shabbat is truly distinct, or *kadosh*, as its "gratification" is delayed – but that delay brings with it the unique feature that Shabbat is now symbiotically bound to Israel. Shabbat achieves its fulfillment through Israel, and Israel fulfills Shabbat's endowed potential through observing it. That same symbiotic relationship, also a relationship of sanctification, or *kedusha*, finds particular expression later in the Book of Exodus. As God finishes instructing Moses with regard to the construction of the Tabernacle, He introduces Shabbat into the discussion:[12]

> The Israelites shall observe the Shabbat, to make the Shabbat, for all their generations, an eternal sign. It will be an eternal sign between Me and the Israelites, because for six days God created

---

11. Genesis Rabba 11:8. This midrash pairs day 1 with day 2, 3 with 4, and 5 with 6.
12. There are numerous linguistic and conceptual parallels between Shabbat and the Tabernacle. See Joshua Berman, *The Temple* (Northvale, NJ: Jason Aronson, 1995), 13–20.

the *shamayim* and the *aretz* but on the seventh day He desisted, and inspired.[13] (Ex. 31:17)

As Israel observes Shabbat, passively refraining from work and actively seeking to fulfill its potential, God's Creation becomes complete.[14] It is hard to imagine a greater expression of Man expressing his "divine image."

---

13. The Hebrew word is *vayinafash*, from the root *nefesh*. This particular form of the word is unique in the Bible, leading to significant discussion regarding its meaning. In the Creation story the word *nefesh* refers to living beings, or beings that became alive through God's breath (2:7). Onkelos and many of the medieval commentaries suggest that *vayinafash* means "to rest." Alter reverts back to the word's meaning in Genesis and suggests the anthropomorphic "caught His breath," and Everett Fox similarly suggests "paused-for-breath." Everett Fox, trans., *The Five Books of Moses* (New York: Schocken Books, 1983), 436.

   Nahum Sarna, in *The JPS Torah Commentary: Exodus* (Philadelphia: JPS, 1991), 202, translates this as "was refreshed," explaining that it "conveys the notion of a fresh infusion of spiritual and physical vigor, the reinvigoration of the totality of one's being." I chose "inspired" to reflect both the aspect of breath as well as the specifically non-physical association with inspiration, related to the central focus of this chapter: the non-physical quality of Shabbat. It is perhaps from here that the Talmud suggests that on Shabbat the individual is endowed with an additional soul, a *neshama yetera*.

14. Shabbat 88a records a statement suggesting that at Mount Sinai God held the mountain over the heads of the Israelites, threatening that if they did not accept the Torah they would be buried under it. Much ink has been spilled explaining this bizarre comment, which seems to contradict the plain meaning of the text. In light of this chapter, however, its meaning becomes abundantly clear. Should Israel fail to accept the Torah, the potential endowed in the Creation will go unfulfilled, rendering the entire enterprise meaningless. It is not just the Israelites who will be buried under the mountain, but all of Creation itself.

Genesis 2:4–3:24

In and Out of the Garden

The second chapter of Genesis presents a significant challenge to the biblical reader. A cursory read of the chapter tells us that it too is a story of Creation, but dramatically different from the one presented in Genesis 1. In this version humans are created first (in Genesis 1 they are created last), the Man is created before the Woman (in Genesis 1 they are created as one), and there is no sense of time or order (Genesis 1 accentuates time and order). Whereas the first version of Creation is punctuated by "it was good," this second version has only "it was not good" (2:18), and opens with a description of what has not happened: "No shrub of the field was yet on the earth and no grass of the field yet sprouted" (2:5).

In fact, as distinct from the first Creation story which is marked by an exquisite sense of order, planning, and forethought, the second version of Creation sounds haphazard and improvised. Nothing is growing, so God creates Man. In need of a place to put Man, He plants a garden. God realizes that it is not good for Man to be alone, so He creates animals. Those animals, however, are not what Man needs, so He puts Man to sleep and creates Woman from him. The two stories are so different that we are not surprised to find that they each have their own name for God: E-lohim in the first, A-donai E-lohim in the second.

TWO STORIES, MANY APPROACHES

In the mid-eighteenth century, a French physician, Jean Astruc, was so taken by the problem described above that he hypothesized that the two chapters must be the work of two different authors. The idea caught on, and by the nineteenth century it was expanded into what became known as the Documentary Hypothesis, which theorized that the entire Bible was the product of multiple authors living at different times, and edited – or redacted – at some later time. Since then the theory has gone through countless revisions and modifications, but is still considered standard in academic circles.

The traditional world was aware of the problems much earlier. Various midrashim, written some fifteen to seventeen centuries before Astruc, refer to the discrepancies between the two accounts,[1] and the traditional approach generally attempted to harmonize the two stories.[2] For traditional Jews this avenue of interpretation held sway until the twentieth century.

In the latter part of twentieth century, a variety of alternatives began to emerge among the Jewish traditionalists. Rabbi Joseph B. Soloveitchik, in *The Lonely Man of Faith*,[3] suggested that the two versions represented two different typologies of Man, while Rabbi Mordechai Breuer developed a broader approach which theorized that the Torah is actually presenting two different aspects of God's interaction with the world.[4] I would like to add two additional thoughts to this discussion.

First, we've already pointed out that the initial Creation story is magnificently constructed, with symmetry, development, forethought, progression, and more. It seems suited for an omniscient, omnipotent God. It is a world in which all the pieces work together harmoniously and flawlessly. It is a world of *ki tov* (it was good) culminating with *tov me'od* (very good).[5] It is perfect and operates with absolute mechanical precision.

---

1. See, for example, Genesis Rabba 12:15.
2. See Rashi, 1:1, s.v. *bara E-lohim*; 1:27, s.v. *zakhar unekeva*.
3. Joseph B. Soloveitchik, *The Lonely Man of Faith* (Jerusalem: Maggid Books, 2012).
4. Mordechai Breuer, *Pirkei Bereshit* [Hebrew] (Alon Shevut, Israel: Tevunot, 1999), 55–72.
5. 1:31.

The problem is that it may be too perfect. The world in which we live is not perfect, it is messy. It is messy because we inhabit it, and we are not perfect. A mechanical world in which the buttons must be pressed in precisely the right order and which leaves no room for human error is not suitable for human habitation.[6] We make mistakes, sometimes not by accident, and interfere with the perfection of the world. The natural world is also filled with glitches: inexplicable storms, tsunamis, earthquakes, volcanos, genetic mutations, disease, and more. Our world is one of *lo tov*, or not (yet) good.

The first Creation story reflects an ideal, what the world would look like if everything worked the way it should, if there were no competition between people and no enmity, if God's plan were implemented and there was no one to ruin it. It is a model of the world we should strive to emulate. By contrast, the second Creation story depicts the world as it is, as it develops. It is a world which is unfolding, a work in progress, in which even God seems to be trying to figure out what the next step should be. It is a world in which God reflects that things are *lo tov* rather than the *ki tov* of Genesis 1.[7]

My second suggestion is that while the first story is indeed a Creation narrative, the second is less interested in Creation than it is in the emergence of Man.[8] It does not seek to answer the question of the origins of the universe but of the nature of Man. How does Man come to be the kind of being that he is? If Genesis 1 is preoccupied with painting the "image" of God, Genesis 2–3 is interested in exploring the question, "Who is Man?"

---

6. See Genesis Rabba 12:15. God wanted to create a world with the attribute of strict justice, but saw that the world would not survive as such. So He joined justice with mercy and created the world. The attribute of justice is a veiled reference to Genesis 1, where the divine name used exclusively is E-lohim, the Almighty God of justice. Contrast this with the Genesis 2–3, in which the divine name is A-donai E-lohim, justice blended with mercy.

7. For a more developed exploration of this, see Zvi Grumet, "Ideal and Real," *Tradition* 34 (2000): 3.

8. The Torah identifies him as "the Man" and the woman as "the Woman." As such, they are not individuals but they are all men and all women. They do not take on individual identities until their expulsion from the Garden.

PARALLEL UNFOLDING STORIES

The narrative opens with a presentation of the problem: nothing is growing. At the same time, it suggests that there are two causes for the problem; on the one hand God did not bring rain, and on the other hand there is no one to work the land. Immediately afterward, the Torah describes in two successive verses two solutions to the problem: God brought a mist to irrigate the ground, and God formed the Man from the dust of that ground.

The problem seems to be resolved, but this opens up an interesting question. Why are both necessary; would not one have been sufficient? Are there not places on earth which can flourish without human intervention, and are there not places where there is no rain but humans have made the desert bloom?

It appears that these questions point to the underlying question of this story: Will it be God, or the human, who makes the world flourish? Both options are equally viable – one of a perfect world with God at the helm and running flawlessly like a fine Swiss watch, the other of an imperfect world in which Man plays a significant role laboring to improve it. This question serves as the backdrop to our story.

MEANINGFULNESS VS. IMMORTALITY

To explore this further, it is valuable to place it in a conceptual framework. The "image" of God which the Torah introduced in Genesis 1 has two basic components, God's immortality and what I will call God's "meaningfulness." By meaningfulness I mean all those things which we earlier identified in the first Creation story: independence of thought, creativity, purposefulness, etc. By definition, for humans to lead a meaningful existence it must necessarily be limited. It is precisely because of humans' limited resources that their decisions and choices can be meaningful. We can readily imagine the inverse of the human model: beings who live forever but who lack the capacity to make meaningful decisions. Some of us may recognize these beings throughout a broad range of Jewish literature; they are called angels. The Hebrew word for angel, *malakh*, actually means a messenger.[9] Angels are generally

---

9. See Genesis Rabba 50:2.

understood as incapable of making independent decisions; they are sent by God to fulfill a task.

In this binary model we thus have two possible options for human existence, a meaningless immortality or a meaningful mortality.[10] Only God can exist in a meaningful immortality.

TWO TREES, TWO PATHS

This story presents a problem with two options: either God makes the world flourish or Man does. Immediately afterward it presents a Garden with two distinctive trees, the Tree of Life at its center and the Tree of Knowledge of Good and Evil.[11] It now seems clear that these two trees are the symbols of those two possibilities. The Tree of Life is the symbol for the path of meaningless immortality, in which Man's existence will be essentially the same as that of the angel. By contrast, the Tree of Knowledge of Good and Evil represents the alternative path, the one in which life is filled with the possibility for meaning (as in the choice between good and evil) but is temporally limited.

Upon more careful reflection, it appears that the Tree of Life is actually the symbol of life in the Garden itself; hence, it is the only tree described as being at the center of the Garden.[12] In the Garden, there is no mortality, and because there is no mortality there is no need for procreation, and thus Man is created alone. That absence of mortality, however, comes with a price – Man's existence is effectively meaningless. There is little for Man to

---

10. This idea, that of the impossibility of leading a meaningful, immortal life, has been pursued and explored extensively in literature, philosophy, and popular culture. See Bernard Williams, "The Makropulos Case: Reflections on the Tedium of Immortality," in *Problems of the Self*, ed. Bernard Williams (Cambridge: Cambridge University press, 1973). See also A. W. Moore, "Williams, Nietzsche, and the Meaninglessness of Immortality," *Mind* 115 (2006). In popular culture the topic has been explored by L. Janáček (1925) in his opera, *The Makropulos Case*, and more recently in the figure of the character "Q" in the *Star Trek: The Next Generation* television series.
11. This second tree is presented in a grammatically puzzling verse, in which it is an extra limb dangling off the edge of the sentence: "God caused to sprout from the soil every tree lovely to view and good for eating, and the Tree of Life in the midst of the garden and the Tree of Knowledge of Good and Evil" (2:9).
12. The Woman describes the Tree of Knowledge of Good and Evil as being at the center (3:3), precisely because her attention has been drawn to it. For her, it is at the center.

do there other than "work and guard" the Garden (which the Torah leaves mysteriously undefined); there are no meaningful or significant decisions to be made. Man's existence is essentially indistinguishable from that of the heavenly angels. They serve their Master faithfully, but that service is fixed, much like the rotation of the earth or the orbits of the planets around the sun – or the computer program which sings the praises of its creator.

The Tree of Knowledge of Good and Evil, by contrast, represents an existence dramatically different from the meaningless immortality of the Garden. In this existence, the human recognizes – and chooses between – good and evil, and it is that capacity which renders each decision significant. That meaningfulness is bundled with mortality, and therefore Man is warned that that on the day he eats from the Tree of Knowledge of Good and Evil, he will become mortal.[13] It is also why after he eventually does eat from that tree he must be expelled from the Garden. He is a different being from what he was previously, so immortality would be inappropriate.

The impossibility of anyone other than God being able to "eat" from both trees – that is, to both be immortal and lead a meaningful existence – is highlighted by God's words at the end of the story: "Behold, the Man has become like one of us, as one who knows good and evil. Now, lest he extend his hand and eat also from the Tree of Life and live forever…" (3:22). Prior to becoming a "knower of good and evil," there is no barrier to the Tree of Life because Man's existence is that meaningless immortality, but once he has chosen a meaningful existence, his life span must be limited and the Tree of Life placed out of bounds.

This dichotomous model, in which there are two paths for humanity represented by the two key trees, presents us with a paradox. If Man is created without the knowledge of good and evil, how can he freely and meaningfully choose the alternate path? In the context of the story, how could Man – absent the ability to make meaningful choices – make the choice that is considered evil?[14]

---

13. Without context, the text is easily readable as meaning that Man will die on the day he eats from the tree. The continuation of the story makes it clear that this is not God's intention.

14. This question has troubled thinkers throughout the ages. Maimonides, *Guide* 1:2, grapples with it and Abrabanel asserts that this paradox led R. Nissim to avoid commenting on this passage altogether.

GOD'S CHALLENGE

If we take a step back, it seems as if not just the readers of the Torah are troubled by this paradox, but the Author of the Torah is bothered by it as well.

Consider the following: Is it possible that God wanted Man to lead a meaningful existence, albeit tinged with mortality? To put this into the language of the story itself, is it possible that God wanted Man to eat from the Tree of Knowledge of Good and Evil?

Let us reframe this into the context of the two paths we laid out earlier. Were Man to remain an eternal, angelic (or robotic) creature following God's instructions to care for the Garden, he would essentially be redundant. After all, God had already brought the mist to water the earth, and that would have been sufficient. For there to truly be two viable paths, one as an alternative to the other, Man would have to eat from the forbidden tree and become a different kind of being.

The challenge faced by God is that despite the temptation, an eternal, meaningless Man will not eat from the tree. Imagine placing a child in a room filled with toys and telling him that he may play with every toy except for one; it is natural for the child to gravitate to the forbidden toy. As humans, we are all subject to temptation, experimentation, and exploration – even, or especially, when forbidden. But eternal, meaningless Man will never make the leap from curiosity to disobeying a direct command; once commanded he will obey and will not fall for the temptation of God highlighting the forbidden tree. In this, immortal Man is not fully human.

The Man who will not eat from the forbidden tree, who will not succumb to temptation, presents God with a problem. God's solution to the puzzle is to introduce a helping character for the Man: "It is not good for Man to be alone. I will make for him a helpmate," says God. The job of that helpmate is to bring Man to become the kind of person who is subject to temptation, and thereby transformed into someone for whom choices are meaningful.[15]

---

15. From God's perspective in this story, Woman is not the temptress seducing Man into sin but the one who empowers Man to begin to achieve. In this light, Man's ultimate response to God's interrogation after eating from the fruit is fascinating:

The problem, of course, is that the nature of Woman is identical to that of Man: "This time," exclaims Man, "bone of my bone and flesh of my flesh. This one shall be called *isha* (Woman), for this one was taken from *ish* (Man)" (2:23). If Woman's nature is the same as Man's and she too is commanded to keep away from the tree, she, like he, will avoid eating the forbidden fruit. She, like he, will live an eternal, meaningless existence. Woman is too much like Man to help him become different. Creating Woman did not seem to solve the problem at hand.

There is, however, one essential distinction between Woman and Man. Man hears the prohibition to eat from the tree directly from God, while Woman hears it from Man – and this opens the door to new possibilities.[16]

TORN BETWEEN TWO TRUTHS

Man will not eat from the tree on his own, and even with the help of Woman, he will apparently not approach it. It is then that God introduces a third character, the serpent: "The serpent was more cunning than all the beasts of the field" (3:1), and cunning implies both intelligence and slyness.[17]

"The Woman whom You gave [to be] with me, she gave me from the tree, and I ate" (3:12). Many read this response as a feeble attempt to shift the blame (Sarna, *The JPS Torah Commentary*). A careful reading, however, yields a simpler, more innocent, truth. It was God's idea to present Man with Woman as a helpmate. Man had every reason to believe that everything she did was authorized by God; that was the *raison d'être* for her creation. Hence his response to God would be read as: "You gave her to me to be a helpmate, and she gave me from the fruit to eat. Was that not Your intention?" (Nahmanides, 3:12.) By extension, Woman's response is equally compelling, as she has no reason to believe the Man any more than she believes the serpent. Both present convincing arguments.

16. Interestingly, when God later admonishes Man and Woman, He introduces His rebuke of Man saying, "Because you listened to your wife and you ate from the tree which I commanded you," but when rebuking Woman there is no such prologue. Woman never heard the command directly from God and cannot be held directly accountable for its betrayal. This accords with the rabbinic tradition that sees Woman as being created after Man (e.g., Genesis Rabba 17:4). According to the traditions that seek to harmonize the two Creation narratives, Woman was part of Man in the initial Creation (Genesis Rabba 8:1). As such, she would have heard the directive directly from God.

17. Later folk literature, such as Aesop's Fables, ascribes these characteristics to the fox.

From the end of this incident it becomes clear that prior to this story and its consequences, the serpent had legs. One midrash even asserts that the serpent walked upright.[18] Furthermore, the Hebrew word for cunning, *arom*, is clearly a play on the description of Man and Woman being naked, *arumim*, just one verse before the serpent is introduced. What is the significance of all this?

Let us put ourselves in the place of Woman. She hears from Man, an intelligent being whom she trusts, that eating from the forbidden tree will bring about death. She hears from the serpent, also an intelligent being (with amazingly human qualities of being *arom*, walking upright, and speaking) whom she has no reason to distrust, that eating from the tree will not bring about death. In fact, says the serpent, the prohibition against eating is motivated by God's fear that she and Man will become Godlike knowers of good and evil.

Ironically, the second half of the serpent's claim is true[19] – she will, indeed, become a knower of good and evil, and will become Godlike in that way. This is actually explicit in the epilogue to the story: "Behold, Man has become like one of us in that he is a knower of good and evil" (3:22). Moreover, the serpent presents a compelling argument. Implicit in his words is that he himself ate from that tree. How else did he become an intelligent being capable of speech, unlike all the other animals?[20]

Torn between two equally compelling truths, Woman needs to make a decision. In a world of eternity she can decide to listen to Man an almost infinite number of times. All it takes is but a single

---

18. *Pesikta Zutreta*, Gen. 3:1.
19. As far as the serpent is concerned, it is of no real concern to the biblical narrative. After Man and Woman eat and are challenged by God, the serpent is neither asked a question (as were Man and Woman) nor provided an opportunity to respond. In the language of filmmaking, the serpent is an "extra" in the story, a necessary catalyst to allow for the events to unfold, but discarded as soon as its function is served.
20. The strength of the serpent's argument is attested to by Woman herself. Challenged by God as to why she did what she did, she replies simply, "The serpent convinced me." Her reply is not merely an attempt to "pass the buck" but a truthful indication of her appraisal of the events.

time of accepting the serpent's compelling argument to change everything.[21]

BECOMING HUMAN

Before continuing with the repercussions and implications of eating the forbidden fruit, let us pause to consider a simple question. If God wants Man to be a knower of good and evil, why not simply create him as such? Why go through the complex subterfuge?

To answer this, it is necessary to reopen the story of the creation of Woman. After God decides that Man needs a helpmate, He creates all the beasts of the field and brings them to Man, who proceeds to give each of them names. Only afterward does God create Woman. Why is this interruption in the presentation of Man's helpmate necessary?

Apparently, while God declares that it is not good for Man to be alone, Man does not understand that there is a problem. In order for Man to be able to appreciate Woman he first needs to become aware that he is, indeed, lacking something significant. Giving meaningful names to the animals requires him to first understand what they are, and as he meets each one he becomes increasingly aware of how different he is from them. Man's discovery of Woman is preceded by a discovery of self, and it is only after understanding who he is that he becomes open to engaging meaningfully with Woman. One major commentary expresses this quite graphically: Man tried mating with each of the animals (i.e., getting to know them intimately before naming them) but repeatedly found it unsatisfying.[22] Only after exhausting all the possibilities do we hear, "As for Man, he found no helpmate for himself" (2:20). It is only after realizing his own uniqueness that Man is able to appreciate the uniqueness of Woman: "This time, bone of my bone and flesh of my flesh" (2:23).

It is perhaps for this reason that God puts Man to sleep prior to creating Woman. Were Man to know that Woman is created from him,

---

21. According to the sequence of the text, it would seem that this time it was Woman who, after partaking of the fruit, realized it was not good to be alone in her new status, and that it was she who effectively created Man in her image, virtually reversing the roles of their creation.

22. Rashi, 2:23, s.v. *zot hapaam*.

his relationship to her would be quite different; he would view her as an extension of himself rather than as an individual living parallel to him. It is his self-discovery that brings him to recognize that he needs a partner, and the process which brings him to understand himself enables him to identify that Woman is appropriate for him.[23]

Man's experience in self-discovery prior to meeting his mate is an essential component of his becoming more human. That experience is subtly but significantly expanded after meeting her, when he names the Woman *isha*, deriving from *ish* (Man). The careful reader will note that prior to this, Man is never called *ish*; he is consistently called *haadam* (the man). In the self-discovery emerging from the process of finding his own partner, Man creates for himself a new identity, distinguishing himself from the other animals. *Haadam* derives from *adama*, or soil – the stuff of which Man is made (2:7) and the same stuff of which animals are made (2:19). Naming himself *ish* expresses his understanding of just how different he is from the other animals.[24]

The self-discovery is repeated again, albeit with differences, with the forbidden fruit. The very fact that Woman and Man are centrally involved in the decision to eat the fruit, regardless of whether it is intended as an act of rebellion against God, has a profound impact on their own sense of selfhood. It is their decision to eat it,[25] and their decision to try to become knowers of good and evil. Woman and Man

---

23. In the conclusion of that scene the Torah writes, "Therefore, Man will leave his mother and father and cleave unto his wife." The process of leaving the mother and father is an expression of the discovery of self and of creating an independent identity, significant stages prior to forging a meaningful, committed relationship with another. Man in the Garden is the paradigm for all people.

24. By extension, naming the Woman *isha* emphasizes his understanding that she, like him, is distinct from the other animals.

25. The text is ambiguous as to whether the Woman gives the fruit to the Man to eat only *after* she eats it or if they eat it simultaneously. The sequence of the text suggests the former, yet the phraseology ("she gave to her man with her" [3:6]) and the simultaneous consequence ("their eyes were both opened" [3:7]) suggests that they leap together into their new reality. If she does eat first, then her giving of the fruit to her man is an expression of the same loneliness he experiences prior to her creation.

become truly human (as we know it) through their own doing; they created themselves, figuratively, in God's image.[26]

We first explored this idea to explain why God uses the plural in describing the plan to create Man: "Let *us* make man." Humans became God's partners in creating themselves. This also explains the next time God refers to Himself in the plural: "Behold, Man has become like one of us in that he is a knower of good and evil" (3:22). The "us" refers to the Godlike humans. The psalmist (8:5) expresses this beautifully, citing the complaint of the heavenly creations: "What is Man that You should note him and the human that You pay him heed, that You made him almost like God and You crown him with glory and grandeur?"

The story of the Garden is not a second Creation epic at all. Rather, it is a story of how humans became the glorious creations we are. It is a description of the choices we make, and how those choices are transformative in the process of how we become who we are.

REFORMULATING GOD'S CHALLENGE

Thus far we explored God's challenge to get naïve Man to eat from the tree from which he is forbidden to eat. Formulated as such, the story of the Garden describes the various steps God takes to bring Man to becoming fully human. Yet what if the challenge were reformulated as an experiment?

We earlier suggested that God self-limited His control, and perhaps even His foreknowledge, to allow for true human independence and meaningfulness. Those limitations open up the possibility of a genuine experiment in which the result is unknown. That experiment takes place in the controlled environment of the Garden, in Hebrew a *gan*, or a protected area.

In the first phase of the experiment, God places Man in the *gan* and forbids him to eat from a particular tree, in an attempt to determine

---

26. Erich Fromm, in *Escape from Freedom* (New York: Farrar & Rinehart, 1941), 28, writes:

> From the standpoint of man, however, this is the beginning of human freedom. Acting against God's orders means freeing himself from coercion, emerging from the unconscious existence of prehuman life to the level of man. Acting against the command of authority, committing a sin, is in its positive human aspect the first act of freedom, that is, the first human act.

whether the instruction will prevent Man from eating from the tree or impel him to do so. When it becomes clear that naïve Man will not violate the rules, God retries the experiment under the same controlled conditions, but this time after introducing Woman. In doing so, not only is there an additional player in the story, but Man himself changes as a result of his discovery of her. Still, even with the new dynamic, the result of the experiment does not change. Man remains naïve, living a meaningless existence. It is not until God introduces a third element, the serpent, under the same controlled conditions of the *gan*, that Man is brought to cross the line. In doing so, God discovers naïve Man's limits.

The experiment continues with the new, transformed Man, but under less-controlled conditions. The ten generations until Noah, the story of the Dispersion, the ups and downs of the Patriarchs, and the rest of the biblical narrative are part of the unfolding experiment. Man must continually learn from his mistakes, while God repeatedly monitors and adjusts His expectations. As with any experiment, for it to be genuine it must have the potential for failure. And as with any experiment, failure is an essential component of the learning process, which ultimately leads to success.

In our story, the success of God's experiment has less to do with discovering the limits of naïve Man than with the transformation of naïve Man into meaningful, but mortal Man. It is that Man who has acquired for himself his own "image" of God.

IMPLICATIONS AND REPERCUSSIONS

There are at least two sets of implications of the choice made by Woman and Man, and not surprisingly, the first relates directly to their new mortality while the second results from their status as meaningful beings (knowers of good and evil).

The drive to reproduce emerges from the realization that as individuals our lives are terminal, and from the deep instinct that we want something of ourselves to continue beyond our passing. That is why, as humans, we understand the death of children as a profound tragedy, as it threatens our very permanence. Prior to Woman and Man's eating from the forbidden fruit, when humans could have lived eternally, there was no need for procreation. Hence, the Torah describes them as being naked but not ashamed; the sexual drive is absent. It is not until after they eat that they sense their own mortality, and it is only then that they intuit a sexual drive and run to cover themselves. Their new-found sexuality is not the product of sin but the result of recognizing their own mortality.

The second set of repercussions emerges from their new status as meaningful beings. In fact, a careful look at God's responses to the Man and the Woman reveals that they are parallel, each consisting of three central elements – the ability to be productive, the pain involved in doing so, and subservience to one's origin. Here are God's words to them:

Woman (2:16)	*Man (2:17–19)*
I will greatly increase your pain (*etzev*) and pregnancy; with pain (*etzev*) shall you bear children. Your craving will be to your husband, and he will dominate you.	Cursed be the ground on your behalf; with pain (*etzev*) shall you eat from it all the days of your life. It will grow for you thorns and thistles and you will eat the grasses of the field. By the sweat of your brow you will eat bread until you return to the ground-dust, for as you are dust you were taken from it, and to dust shall you be returned.

The chart below highlights the three central elements in God's responses:

	Woman	*Man*
Fruitfulness	Pregnancy, childbearing	Bread
Pain	*Etzev* – pain in bearing children	*Etzev* – pain in bringing forth produce
Subservience to source	Subservience to Man, from whom Woman is created	Subservience to the ground-dust, from which Man is created

While the tone of God's words suggests that His response is punishment for some sin, a careful consideration of the substance of those words reveals a dramatically different idea.[27] In the Garden, Man is a caretaker and Woman a helpmate. In their new reality, outside the Garden, both Man and Woman become producers – Woman producing human fruit from her womb[28] and Man producing fruit from the ground. Both of those acts involve extraordinary, Godlike empowerment: Woman can become a partner in the creation of other humans (as opposed to her and Man's own self-creation) and Man can take the grains of nature and from them manufacture bread, the staple of life.

In the halakhic mindset, bread and wine are the symbols of ultimate human empowerment. Generally, when plant products lose their original form, the blessing recited for them is demoted from a more specialized one to a more generic one. Bread and wine, symbolizing human improvement on the natural world, represent movement in the opposite direction, and the blessings for those are the most highly specialized of all foods. What is more, the blessing for bread covers all the food consumed in that meal, while the blessing for wine covers all the drinks. The expulsion from the Garden brings with it human empowerment. It is this empowerment, combined with the pain and sacrifice necessary to capitalize on it, which is the essence of the new reality for humans – a meaningful mortality.

I've long understood how early humans could have accidentally discovered cooking (a forest fire which "cooked" the animals that did not escape), but I have always been fascinated by the discovery of baking. How could humans have accidentally decided to take a grain, dry it to the point that it is inedible, grind it to a powder, mix it with water,

---

27. As opposed to the serpent, neither Woman nor Man is cursed. The closest we find to a curse is God's cursing the land in its production for Man. Moreover, as opposed to the stories of the Flood or Sodom, nowhere in this story do we find any explicit expression of God's anger, frustration, or disappointment. (In a fascinating midrash, Genesis Rabba 20 finds blessing even within the serpent's curse.) In general, the Torah uses language of punishment even when God's response is designed for our betterment. This is implied in Maimonides' *Guide* (3:32) as he addresses the inevitability of the Israelites' forty-year wandering in the desert.
28. The power of this experience will become abundantly clear in the beginning of Genesis 4, which we will address in the next chapter.

and then bake it? This same sense of wonderment must have impelled the Midrash to suggest that as God banished Man from the Garden, He taught him to bake bread.[29] Put differently, God acknowledges Man's new creative self and teaches him how to begin to act upon it, so that the empowerment of Man is not an accidental byproduct of the expulsion but an essential feature of it.

Together with the empowerment of Man and Woman, however, comes a sobering message. Since eating from the fruit is not an act of betrayal but one of seeking Godliness, both Man and Woman need to have that craving moderated by a dose of humility.[30] They need to be cautioned that as lofty and empowered and creative – even self-creative – as they may be, they are nonetheless beings that derive from a source. They are created, and may never supplant the Creator. They need the ever-present reminder that places their new reality and status in perspective. There is still a Master, a Creator, who created them from their source. Hence both Man and Woman need to become subservient to their respective origins.

PREPARING FOR A NEW REALITY

There is yet another implication of the transformation of Man and Woman into creative, meaningful, mortal beings. The Garden is no longer an appropriate place for them. A life of meaningfulness is marked by challenges and adversity; the Garden, like a womb, is a place in which all a person's needs are taken care of. In the Garden there is fruit ready to eat and no need for shelter; outside the Garden people need to toil to produce food and find shelter for themselves.

It is for this reason that even though Man and Woman fashion primitive clothes of fig leaves for themselves while in the Garden, God makes leather clothing for them as He sends them out of the Garden. In the Garden the only function of their clothing is to cover their newly

---

29. This idea is implicit in *Yalkut Shimoni* I:32. For years I have searched, but not yet found, the explicit midrash which I first saw in my youth.

30. I did not address the serpent, as he is a character introduced solely for the purpose of enabling the Godliness of humans. Nonetheless, God's response to the serpent parallels the subservience of both Man and Woman, as God ensures that the distinction between human and beast is never again to be blurred. Hence, missing from God's response to the serpent is the elevation and empowerment witnessed for the humans.

realized nakedness, but outside the Garden they need to learn to protect themselves from the elements. As God sends them from the Garden, He prepares them for their new reality.

There is an additional aspect of this new reality. Since the Garden is a place where time stands still and death holds no power, there is no need for procreation.[31] Hence there is just a single immortal Man and a single immortal Woman – archetypical humans without names as individuals. As they prepare for life outside the Garden, a life of mortality, they become individuals for the first time. Man gives Woman a name, calling her Ḥava (Eve), the mother of all living beings. She, with her reproductive abilities, is the key to the immortality of humanity. But she also, for the first time, has an identity as an individual, a name.[32] Within the Torah, it is only humans who have names as individuals; all the other creatures carry only the name of their species.

Neither the serpent nor any other beast is a knower of good and evil. Moreover, no other beast wears garments; clothes are the mark of humans. As God prepares the humans for life outside the Garden He makes for them garments reflecting the dignity of their Godlike status as humans. It is not surprising, then, that the word chosen to describe their garments is "*kutonet.*" There are many other terms the text could have chosen, but throughout the Torah the word *kutonet* always has the implication of a special garment, one worn by important figures of a particular stature.[33] As Man and Woman leave the Garden, prepared for their new world, God affirms their unique status among all the creations. What is more, in the final line of this story God not only prepares the clothing for them but dresses them in their new clothes as well.

The combination of God preparing for Man and Woman clothing of animal skins (highlighting the distinction between them and the beasts) and Himself dressing them affirms our central theme in this

---

31. See *Pirkei DeRabbi Eliezer* 11, in which Man (in the Garden) – like God – is described as having no need for procreation.
32. Man will get his own individual name at the end of the following chapter.
33. The word is used primarily in two contexts: the special garment Jacob made for Joseph (seven times in Genesis 37) and with regard to the priestly clothing (ten times throughout the narratives of the consecration of the priests in Exodus and Leviticus).

story. The story of the Garden is not one of sin and punishment and it is not about the fall of Man. Rather, this is the story of the emergence of Man as a meaningful being, capable of Godlike creativity and choice. As God inaugurates humanity into its new role, He clothes us with vestments appropriate for our status and stature.

INNOCENCE LOST

The story of the Garden is not another version of Creation; it is the story of how humans become truly human. The Man and the Woman of the Garden are every man and every woman as we all exit our mother's womb and enter into a world of exploration, discovery, and creativity. It is a passage fraught with pain and terror and is the first, and perhaps most traumatic, experience of life as a human – and it is irreversible. The loss of innocence can never be regained. A wonderful talmudic legend describes life in the womb as a virtual Garden of Eden – in all our innocence we are taught the entire Torah by a heavenly angel, only to be made to forget it as we prepare to enter the world.[34] The moment of birth changes everything forever; from then on we must toil and strive to achieve.

The moment of childbirth is terrifying and exhilarating for the newborn, but it is equally so for the parents. They are gifted with the opportunity to care for and teach that young child; they will delight in his successes and help him to recover from his failures, and will stand by with mixed emotions of loss and pride as he moves toward greater independence. They will admonish that child when he crosses boundaries but stand firm with their endless love to help ensure that he becomes a mature adult like themselves.

As God's children, we, as humans, expect the same from Him as we do from our own parents. This is where our story, the path we choose, really begins.

---

34. Nidda 30b.

Genesis 4:1–26

Grappling with Mortality

E merging from the womb of the Garden as creative beings, Man and Eve are keenly aware of their mortality, and are driven to perpetuate themselves: "The Man was intimate with his wife, Eve." We are also not surprised that the ensuing birth, the first human birth, is accompanied by extraordinary exhilaration: "She conceived and gave birth to Cain (*Kayin*), saying, 'I have created (*kaniti*) a human together with God'" (4:1). The sense of power surging through Eve at that moment is indescribable. She created a person, an accomplishment she believes is reserved for God: "I am God's partner in creation," she effectively declares.

Aside from being a donor to the cause, the Man is notably absent from the discussion of the birth. In the background, however, he apparently does have some influence. Cain becomes a farmer, working the ground, just like his father. This is, after all, the destiny of humans outside of the Garden.

Our initial picture of Cain is that he is the apple of his mother's eye, the product of her divine-like quality to create life; even his name reflects her excitement. While Cain's mother basks in her creation, his father, proverbially, takes him into the family business, as he is inducted into the most quintessential of human tasks – farming. In addition to the image generated by his parents, we also have the image which he himself generates. Cain, without prodding or precedent, brings an offering[1] to God from the very produce which he toiled with "the sweat of his brow" to produce. Cain is the first to offer thanks to God.

THE BROTHER

The description of Abel is profoundly different. Missing from the narrative is intimacy or conception. Also missing is an explanation of his name or a justification for his profession as a shepherd (consumption of meat is not yet permitted). Instead, the first thing we hear about Abel is: "Additionally, she gave birth to his brother, Abel." In stark contrast to Cain, there is no recorded excitement surrounding the birth of Abel. He is merely the additional child, the brother. Even his name has dark overtones. In Hebrew, the word *hevel* (which is his Hebrew name) means worthless, vanity, hot air.[2] And even Abel's profession seems pointless – what is the value-added produce of a shepherd when meat is prohibited?[3]

If we pause to reflect upon the life of the shepherd, we discover that there is an inherent tension between farmers and shepherds. Farmers labor by tilling the soil to grow produce; sheep consume and destroy that produce. Farmers and shepherds cannot coexist on the same land. When Joseph's brothers join him in Egypt he instructs them to inform Pharaoh that they are shepherds, and must therefore live far from mainstream Egypt, the great grain-producing empire. While the farmer needs to live near his crops and is rooted in his home, the shepherd wanders

---

1. In Hebrew it is called a *minḥa*, or offering. The text is mum on how the offering was presented; there is no mention of an altar or a fire. While Rashi, Nahmanides, and many others assume that this refers to a sacrifice, the Torah text avoids describing it as such. It is worth noting that there are only three sacrifices mentioned in all of Genesis: one by Noah upon exiting the ark (8:20); one by Abraham, who offers the ram instead of Isaac (22:13); and one by Jacob as he leaves his Promised Land for Egypt (46:1).
2. The word *hevel* features prominently in Ecclesiastes, describing the futility of man's endeavors.
3. Kass, *Genesis*, 129, suggests that Abel's chosen profession harkens back to God's charge to Man in Genesis 1 to have dominion over the animals. If so, then Abel is an expression of Genesis 1 while Cain, tiller of the soil, embodies Genesis 2–3.

with the flocks to wherever there is grazing. In fact, one description in the Torah for the shepherd is that he dwells in tents.[4]

The picture that emerges of Abel is quite disturbing. In addition to the lack of excitement surrounding his birth, he is the "extra" one, the brother; he works in a profession which has limited value; and his name suggests that he is regarded as being worthless. He is relegated to spending much of his time living away from the family home as he tends his sheep, while the beloved Cain is very much connected to the family plot and destiny.

With the disparity between the brothers, it is no surprise that Abel tries to surpass his brother and bring an offering that is superior to Cain's. How else can Abel possibly compete for attention if not by outdoing his elder sibling? "Abel also brought, from the choicest and fattest of his sheep" (4:4). Abel is still an "also," and he must do better than Cain in his attempt to be counted.

GOD'S ROLE

The internal dynamics of the family are disrupted when God enters the picture: "God paid heed to Abel and his offering, but to Cain and his offering He paid no heed" (4:4–5).[5] Note that the primary focus of this verse is on the person, not on the offering. God pays heed to Abel (and his offering), but not to Cain (and his offering). Contrary to the popular notion,[6] this is not a statement of the quality of one offering versus the other, but a statement of giving attention to the person, to Abel.[7]

The attention God gives to Abel is an attempt to redress a fundamental injustice done to "the brother." No one else seems to regard Abel as worthwhile, and God wants to let Abel (and perhaps the rest of the family) know that Abel does matter. In fact, this message is so significant that in order to drive the point home God must pay no heed to

---

4. See Genesis 4:20, where this is explicit. This is also the apparent plain meaning of the Torah's description of Jacob as a tent-dweller (25:27).
5. The precise meaning of the Hebrew *vayisha*, describing God's actions toward both Abel and Cain, is unclear. I suspect that it comes from the root SH-A-H, meaning time, which would yield a literal translation of "God gave time to Abel and his offering."
6. Popularized by Rashi, 4:3. See note 8.
7. Saadia Gaon reflects this nuance in his commentary.

Cain (and his offering). This is not a rejection of Cain or an implication that Cain did anything improper, but a necessary step to try to restore some balance. Cain *always* receives attention, while Abel *never* does; to give Abel a sense of importance or specialness it is vital that he receive something which Cain does not.

For Cain, this new turn of events is intolerable. First, it is inconceivable to him that Abel has any value. Abel is the other, the brother, the rejected one forced to wander from the family estate. Second, since Cain has never had to share the limelight with anyone, he takes the attention given to Abel as a rejection of himself. For Abel to receive *any* attention completely disrupts Cain's world; for Abel to receive *exclusive* attention is utterly devastating. Hence, "Cain was extremely distressed, and his face fell."

Cain's experience is the quintessential experience of the firstborn. Every firstborn is, at some point, an only child, the recipient of the exclusive devotion of his parents. The introduction of a sibling, a rival for his parents' attention, can easily bring about feelings of jealousy and rejection.

GOD'S MYSTERIOUS MESSAGE

God does not ignore Cain's dejection, but the message He delivers is shrouded in mysterious poetry:

> If you do good, there will be uplift
> And if you do not do good ... the sin crouches at the entrance.
> His craving is toward you
> And you will dominate him. (4:7)

While there are many interpretations of this vexing poem,[8] we will look to the textual clues to help unravel its message. Our first clue comes in the last two lines, which are essentially identical to God's earlier message to the Woman: "Your craving will be to your husband, and he

---

8. For example, Rashi understands this as a rebuke to Cain for bringing an inferior offering and a call for him to repent. Nahmanides, on the other hand, reads this as God's call to Cain to rein in his jealousy of Abel.

will dominate you." Once again, God is establishing or identifying some sort of hierarchy. No matter how much consideration Abel receives, by virtue of the fact that he is the younger sibling he will always be looking up to his elder brother. Abel's need to supersede Cain's offering is the result of Abel's desire to emulate Cain, and the only way for him to equal his older brother is to best him. God's closing message to Cain is to accept that Abel's need to compete is ultimately an act of admiration and esteem, and that Cain should learn to embrace (and be honored by) it rather than fight it.

If Cain focuses only on doing the right thing ("If you do good"), regardless of what his brother does or receives, then, given his status as the elder brother, he will always have the upper hand ("there will be uplift"). Interestingly, Ibn Ezra points out that the Hebrew word for "uplift," *se'et*, appears in a similar context at the end of Genesis in the context of Jacob's blessing to his eldest, Reuben: "Reuben, you are my firstborn, with extra *se'et*" (49:3). The word, then, refers to the special status accorded the firstborn by his younger siblings,[9] and God's message is essentially that Cain need not look over his shoulder since his brother will always be there.

If, however, Cain cannot accept the notion that someone else can potentially equal, or almost equal, himself, then his situation will be unbearable. If Abel's inevitable and perpetual competitiveness are too much, if Cain would prefer a simple life in which there is no competition and no jockeying for position, then the only recourse would be a return to the Garden. That option, however, does not exist. The entrance to the Garden is blocked by the two cherubs with the revolving swords. In other words, there is no going back. This is God's message in the second line of the poem. If you are not prepared to focus just on doing the right thing without looking over your shoulder at Abel, then…the entrance to the Garden is blocked as a result of the sin.

---

9. Of course, in Reuben's case, his additional *se'et* did not help him, as he lost his premiere status due to his impetuous behavior. This is reflected in the continuation of Jacob's blessing: "You were impetuous and unstable as water; you will have nothing extra" (49:4).

IN THE FIELD

It initially appears that Cain understands God's message, and he shares it with Abel: "Cain said to his brother, Abel" (4:8). The text does not specify what Cain said, but it seems obvious that he shared the message he just heard, or at least the parts he thought would be valuable for Abel to hear.[10]

It is at this point that something unexpected happens. The brothers meet in the field. The field is Cain's domain; Abel had been banished to grazing grounds. What is Abel doing in the field?

Various midrashim consider the venue for the confrontation significant, seeing a turf war between Cain and Abel.[11] Indeed, it appears that after God's acknowledgment of Abel and his offering, or perhaps *because* of God's emboldening of Abel, he returns from his wandering to reestablish himself close to home, perhaps even allowing his sheep to overrun Cain's crops. Cain will tolerate none of this and repeats the message *he* heard from God, that Abel is to be subservient. Each comes with his own divine communication, and their mutual misunderstandings of those communications leads to conflict.

To be sure, none of this is explicit in the Torah text. The text hides the conflict, as it seems less important than the outcome of that clash. Abel is dead, and his death comes at his brother's hand.

And here we are faced with a significant question. Does Cain intend to kill Abel or merely to subjugate him? Even more, does Cain know that it is possible to kill someone? These questions are important far beyond what they tell us about Cain the individual. They reveal much about God and His reaction to Abel's violent death.

PREMEDITATED MURDER OR UNINTENTIONAL KILLING?

The opening lines of the conversation between God and Cain afterward are quite striking:

---

10. This is how Ibn Ezra reads the verse.
11. See, for example, Genesis Rabba 22:7. The opinions there include struggles over land, religion, and a woman.

God: Where is your brother Abel?
Cain: I do not know. Am I my brother's keeper?

God opens with a rhetorical question, one to which He certainly knows the answer. Questions of this sort appear throughout Genesis,[12] and wherever we find a divine being (God or an angelic figure) asking a rhetorical question – usually using some variation on the word "where" – it is always a rebuke.[13] After Man eats from tree God asks, "Where are you?" After Hagar flees from Sarai an angel asks, "From where are you coming?" Here too, God asks, "Where is your brother Abel?" God is clearly displeased with Cain's actions.

Cain's response, however, is fascinating. Standing over his brother's corpse his first response is, "I don't know." There are two ways to read this – either he is an arrogant and brazen liar,[14] or he really does not know. He sees the body but does not know what happened to Abel. His attempts to subjugate his brother seem to be working, but Abel is completely unresponsive. Does Cain even know what death is?

One mishnaic comment, which sees Cain as an evil, premeditated murderer, suggests that Cain knows about death but does not know how to bring it about.[15] As a result, Cain wounds his brother multiple times in an attempt to kill him. The comment is sparked by an anomaly in God's response to Cain: "The bloods of your brother are screaming to Me from the ground." Noticing that the text says "bloods" (plural) and not "blood" (singular), the Mishna envisions Abel spurting blood from multiple wounds. Yet that textual observation can easily be read in the reverse. Cain has no concept that he can kill. The multiple wounds, part of his attempt to put Abel in his place, result in Abel's death, but that is certainly not Cain's intention.

God's final message to Cain is that he will be a wanderer, exiled from his land. In the books of Exodus, Numbers, and Deuteronomy

---

12. See 3:9, 11; 16:8; 18:9; 21:17. Outside of Genesis, see God's question to Balaam in Numbers 22:9.
13. A variation on this is God's question to Elijah upon his arrival at Horeb: "What are you doing here, Elijah?" (I Kings 19:9).
14. This is Rashi's approach.
15. Sanhedrin 37a.

the Torah spells out the punishments for the intentional and accidental killers. There is no mercy for the intentional murderer; he is to be put to death. The one who kills by accident must be exiled. Is not Cain the prototype for that, as he, too, is exiled?

GOD'S MEASURED RESPONSE

Cain thinks that being the elder accords him rights, but no responsibilities. "Am I my brother's keeper?" he asks. God's response is carefully constructed:

> And now, you are cursed from the land which opened its mouth to take your brother's blood from your hands. When you work the land it will no longer give its strength to you. You shall be a wanderer and a nomad in the land. (4:11–12)

Cain, the son who worked the land, will no longer be able to produce from the land. He is not only banished from his father's occupation, he must become dependent on others. Cain's wandering is not his punishment, it is the consequence of his being unable to produce. He has been reduced to a meaning*less* mortality, accorded none of the benefits of the choice his parents made in the Garden. He has become Abel: worthless, a wanderer with no place to call home.

God's response brings Cain to a growing awareness of the gravity of his deed. "My sin is too great to bear!" he exclaims.[16] Cain is moved not only by the severity of the repercussion, but by the awareness of the fragility of life itself: "Anyone who finds me will kill me." If one man can bring about the death of another, what prevents any human from taking the life of any other? And especially now, as Cain begins to consider his life as Abel, the worthlessness of his own existence is terrifying.

If the source of Cain's misdeed is his self-centeredness and inability to make room for his brother, Cain begins to see life through that brother's eyes. Banished from the family home, forced to wander

---

16. An alternate reading has this punctuated as a question: "Is my sin too great to bear?" The formulation as a question is an integral part of Cain's discovery of the severity of his act. This view is challenged by Rashi, who sees Cain, like many other biblical characters, as a paradigm of pure evil. See his comments on 4:3, 8-9, 10, and 13, where he misses no opportunity to interpret the text as a condemnation of Cain.

and dependent upon others, regarded by all as worthless, Cain lives the life of Abel. God ensures that he will never repeat his mistake.

CAIN'S RECOVERY

Cain's immediate response provides our first indication that he is beginning to understand. He is shamed before God, needing to hide himself from God's presence. And he begins to understand the tenuousness of Abel's life. The story, however, does not end yet. Cain travels to a familiar place – the land of wandering, east of Eden – where he hopes to find the entrance to the Garden.[17] If the land will not produce, if his work is meaningless, then he prefers a life of meaninglessness in the Garden. The problem, of course, is that as God told him earlier, the entrance is blocked. He cannot return; there is no going back. So Cain marries, bears a child, and builds a city. In the context of the story, how are we to understand his actions?

Simply put, Cain's reaction to his destiny of living a meaningless mortality is to seek to redress both. Just like his parents, who upon being confronted with mortality feel impelled to reproduce, Cain seeks an alternative form of immortalizing himself;[18] and just as Abel had tried living a life that was meaningful to him even if no one else considered it valuable, Cain attempts to live a life of meaning by building a city – the significance of which cannot be overstated.

Urban life differs from agrarian life in multiple ways. For one, the farmer can essentially live a life of self-sufficiency; he grows what he needs and can live isolated from others. This is essentially Cain's life before the killing. Cain the farmer needs no one else. His self-sufficiency dovetails nicely with his self-centeredness. Urban life, by contrast, demands interaction with others. It is marked by division of labor and specialization. In a city, others can produce the food while Cain can be a carpenter or tailor. He can trade his services for that which he needs, enabling himself to both survive and be productive. Through interaction with others, Cain finds a way to redeem his existence as Abel, and learns that part of being human includes making room for others.

---

17. See 3:24.
18. The language used in both Adam's and Cain's attempts to immortalize themselves is nearly identical, involving intimacy, conception, and birth.

THE MYSTERY OF LEMEKH

Cain is on the path to rehabilitation, and his story should end – but it does not. In rapid succession the Torah describes six generations of Cain: Cain, Ḥanokh, Irad, Meḥuyyael, Metushael, and Lemekh – only to slow down the description with an extended discussion of Lemekh's family.

Lemekh has two wives, Ada and Tzila; three sons, Yaval, Yuval, and Tuval-Cain; and a daughter, Naama. Not only does the Torah describe the family, it even discusses the occupations of Lemekh's sons.[19] Yaval is the father of tent-dwelling shepherds, Yuval is the father of musicians, and Tuval-Cain is the father of copper- and iron-forging. Moreover, Lemekh composes a cryptic poem for his wives:

> Ada and Tzila, listen to my voice,
> Wives of Lemekh, hear my speech.
> Have I killed a man with my wounds,
> Or a boy through my bruises?
> If Cain is granted a seven-generation reprieve,
> Then Lemekh seventy-seven. (4:23–24)[20]

What is the Torah's fascination with Lemekh and his family?

This is not the first cryptic message in this chapter. Earlier, following Cain's fears that he could also become a target for killing, God gives him a sign, and says, "Therefore, anyone who kills Cain ... for seven generations shall Cain stand."[21]

---

19. The daughter, Naama, is curious, as she is mentioned explicitly but never referred to again in the text.

20. All translation involves a substantive layer of interpretation. This translation is my own and reflects my understanding of Lemekh's comments. As with God's mysterious message to Cain, there are numerous interpretations of Lemekh's poem, including a fantastical one involving a blind hunter (Rashi). Likewise, contemporary translations of the text are based on the translators' and commentators' interpretations of the text and will obviously differ from each other dramatically.

21. See the previous note about translations. There is a medieval interpretation of this story in the penitential prayer (*seliḥa*) composed by Benjamin ben Zerah for the Fast of Gedalia:

Two of the Hebrew words used in God's statement to Cain and later in Lemekh's poem to his wives, *shivatayim* and *yukam*, are obtuse and hence the subject of intense debate. I translated the former as referring to seven generations[22] and the latter as "will stand," as in "will be allowed to live" or "granted a reprieve."[23]

It is entirely possible that not only does the contemporary reader struggle with the ambiguity, but the biblical characters themselves were unsure of God's intent. This means that God's message to Cain leaves him and his descendants with an impending fear: is God issuing a writ of protection for Cain that would last seven generations, or is God promising to take vengeance for Cain's deed at some later time? The text is obtuse – so much so that we may never know. And perhaps the biblical characters themselves may not have known either. The enigmatic message leaves them anxiously wondering what would happen in the seventh generation.

This discomfort can easily generate hesitation in Lemekh's wives to bear children, the seventh generation. Why should they bring children into the world who will bear the brunt of the curse of Cain? It is this concern which Lemekh addresses in his poem. If Cain, who does kill a man, is granted a seven-generation reprieve, shouldn't innocent Lemekh be granted a reprieve of seventy-seven generations? Whatever the anticipated punishment is, argues Lemekh, it will not come upon the seventh generation.

LEMEKH'S INNOVATION

But Lemekh does not stop with his reasoned morality. He takes two additional steps. First, the names of Lemekh's sons – Yaval, Yuval, and Tuval-Cain – echo Abel's Hebrew name, Hevel. Lemekh effectively

---

[Adam]'s son erred in spilling his brother's blood
You afflicted him with wandering, walking to and fro
He returned to You and abandoned the evil of his path
You granted him a seven-generation reprieve that he not be struck by others.

22. Rashi and Ibn Ezra understand this word similarly. Seforno renders it as "seven times over," while Saadia Gaon and Radak read it as an idiom for "many times over."

23. Most of the classical commentaries read this word as related to vengeance. See Rashi, Ibn Ezra, Seforno, Radak.

names his sons after Abel. Abel's name lives, and through his redemption, perhaps the decree resulting from his death can be reversed.

Second, the professions of Lemekh's children are significant. Yaval is the father of shepherding, taking up Abel's profession. Reviving Abel's profession renders Abel's life meaningful. He is no longer the worthless one. His innovation is recognized, hence he lives on. Yuval, the second son, introduces musical instruments. Music is often associated with shepherding, and Yuval is credited with leaving behind a cultural legacy which can also be associated with Abel. Finally, we have Tuval-Cain, which is actually a play on the names of both Abel and Cain, who is the father of metalsmithing.[24]

Each of Lemekh's sons bears a variant of Abel's name to immortalize him and takes on some innovation associated with Abel but which will be his own legacy nevertheless. The concept of legacy is yet another version of the quest for immortality – some piece of the person lives on beyond his own lifetime. Lemekh apparently understands that just as people seek immortality through their biological offspring, an alternate path to immortality is to preserve one's legacy.[25] Preserving Abel's (both his name and his profession) as well as leaving one of his own is Lemekh's innovation in the quest for immortality.

ADAM AND EVE TRANSFORMED

It is only after Lemekh that the story of Cain can find closure. Cain, as an individual, experiences life as Abel and ultimately learns from it. He builds a city, a model of cooperative living, and creatively learns to find meaningfulness in his new status. Cain's descendants find a different kind of meaning, even as they fear their own physical demise. They create legacies which outlive their own life spans and transform humanity in the process. As for Lemekh, he initiates the process by naming his children after Abel to immortalize him.

---

24. In the Hebrew, his craft is described as polishing the plow made of copper and iron.
25. This idea is captured magnificently in Is. 56:3–4:

> Let not the eunuch say, "I am a withered tree." For thus said the Lord: "As for the eunuchs who keep My Sabbaths, who have chosen what I desire, and hold fast to My covenant, I will give them in My house and within My walls a monument and a name better than sons and daughters."

This brings us back to the very opening of the story, where the Man and Eve seek their own immortality through their biological offspring. That initial effort is less successful, and in no small measure they bear responsibility. It is Eve who crowns herself as God's equal in the birthing of Cain, and both she and the Man contribute to Cain's narcissism and Abel's disenfranchisement. It is not surprising that the parents are absent from the entire story; it is emblematic of their parenting.

The story can achieve true closure only when they attempt to rectify their errors:

> Adam was once again intimate with his wife and she gave birth to a son. She called him Seth (*Shet*), because God gave (*shat*) me another child to replace Abel, for Cain had killed him. (4:25)

We notice how different Eve's words are with the birth of Seth. She is not the creator, God's equal, but the recipient of a divine gift. Furthermore, at Cain's birth, Eve's name is prominent while Adam is not present at all; he is still generic Man. Those roles are reversed for Seth's birth. Adam, for the first time, has a name as an individual, and Eve's name has disappeared. She has become "his wife." The subtle changes indicate an awareness that their approaches to raising both Cain and Abel were flawed and need to be adjusted.[26]

THE BIRTH OF MEANINGFUL HUMANITY

It is the sense of closure within both the story of Cain and its larger context of Adam and Eve that allows us to move beyond, to the next generation. Seth has a son named Enosh, Aramaic for "human," a cognate of the Hebrew *ish*.[27] With Seth imbuing his son with humane qualities as his own parents did for him, we begin the chain, immortalizing the human race. Enosh represents the beginning of humanity as we know it.

---

26. Abel is the "also" child, and is treated as worthless. Seth is described as an "also" child (4:26) as well, yet his "also"-ness does not diminish his status.
27. The plural of *ish* is *anashim*, preserving the Aramaic *enosh*.

This Enosh is identified not only with the beginning of humanity but with the beginning of humans seeking contact with God: "It was then that people began to call in God's name" (4:26).[28]

In our Introduction we spelled out the central theme of Genesis. God creates humans to have a relationship with them. Genesis 1 paints for us an image of God. Genesis 2–3 explores the fundamental nature of humanity and how we become the people we are. Genesis 4 examines people living with other people, mortality, the quest for immortality, and the search for meaningfulness. It is on this note that the Torah completes its first book of *toledot*. This section, which begins with the creation of the heavens and the earth, closes with humanity calling to God.

The legacy of God's creation is complex. It is fraught with danger and disappointment, as it yields Cain the killer. But it also yields Cain who can learn from his mistakes, Lemekh who seeks meaningfulness in leaving the world a better place than he found it, and ultimately the generation of Enosh which seeks out God. The legacy of Creation is also hopeful, as the path to meaningful human engagement with God, though filled with suffering as a result of Man's mistakes, including tragic ones, also allows him to grow from them.

---

28. Rashi, 4:26, and Maimonides, *Laws of Idolatry* 1:1, understand this verse as indicating that in the days of Enosh people began worshiping idols. This is based on their understanding of the verb H-Ḥ-L (which is used in the context of God's name) as referring to desecrating or profaning the name of God. The translation I presented understands the verb H-Ḥ-L as "beginning," so that the verse reads that people then began calling in God's name. The verb appears many times in the early chapters of Genesis – 6:1; 9:20; 10:8; 11:6 – and while each of those tolerates both readings, since this is a book of beginnings I prefer to see the text as presented to us as a series of "firsts."

The second part of the phrase, calling out in God's name, is, however, unambiguous. It too appears throughout Genesis – 12:8; 13:4; 21:33 – and is used exclusively to describe Abraham calling out in (or announcing) God's name. The explicitly positive references associated with this phrase lead me to conclude that the entire phrase is to be read as a positive statement about the generation of Enosh.

Genesis 5:1–6:8

Doom Looms,
Hope Flickers

Most people are not eager to read genealogical lists, and many wonder why such lists are included in the Torah at all. Close readings of those lists, however, often yield surprises with significant insights.

The first such list covers the descendants of Seth. On the one hand they are presented as real people, not typological people like Cain and Abel. They are born and they die, they have multiple children (both male and female), they have life spans counted in years. They are so real that one famous midrash creates a timeline based on the data included in this chapter.[1] On the other hand, their life spans are so exaggerated, so outrageous (with one exception, they all live between 777 and 969 years), that they seem to belong to a different reality.[2]

---

1. *Seder Olam Rabba.*

2. Cassuto, in *Commentary on the Book of Genesis,* 169–180, points out that many of the ancient Near Eastern cultures have similar genealogical lists of their founding ancestors, also with exaggerated life spans. One substantive difference is that those life spans are in the thousands, or tens of thousands of years, and those mythical ancestral figures were effectively the founding gods. By contrast, those in this list live nearly a thousand years, but none cross that threshold. According to the psalmist

If we contrast Seth's genealogy (Genesis 5) to that of Cain (Genesis 4), we are struck by how different they are. Cain's genealogy covers seven generations in a span of six verses, of which four are devoted to the story of Lemekh. Seth's genealogy covers ten generations but takes thirty-two verses. Each generation in Seth's genealogy follows a pattern:[3]

- A lived for *x* years and fathered B.
- A lived for *y* years following the birth of B and fathered sons and daughters.
- The sum total of A's years are *x* + *y*, and he died.

The genealogy of Seth describes each individual as having lived and having perpetuated himself through his children. There is a sense of celebration with each new generation as it completes a cycle of life. Cain's descendants are pursued by the dark cloud of God's curse, while Seth's descendants find closure in the completion of their lives.

Despite the dramatic differences in description, a closer look at the two genealogies reveals striking similarities between them. Names that appear in Cain's line of descendants reappear, albeit with minor changes, in Seth's progeny. In both lines there is a Ḥanokh and a Lemekh, Cainon parallels Cain, Metushelaḥ matches Metushael, Mahallalel is mirrored by Mehuyyael, and Yered echoes Irad (in the Hebrew they are identical, with the addition of a single letter in Irad's name). The chart below demonstrates the remarkable parallels.

It appears that the descendants of Seth are intentionally giving names to their offspring that mirror Cain and his line. If, as suggested in the previous chapter, there is a concern of some impending curse to Cain and his descendants, then it seems that Seth's line is determined to preserve their names. This, in fact, likely predated a similar attempt we

(90:4), a thousand human years is barely a day in God's eyes. In that light, the Torah might be trying to emphasize that the great human ancestors did not even reach a single day in God's eyes – they were not gods at all.

3. We will soon see that just as in Genesis 1, the breaks in the pattern are quite significant.

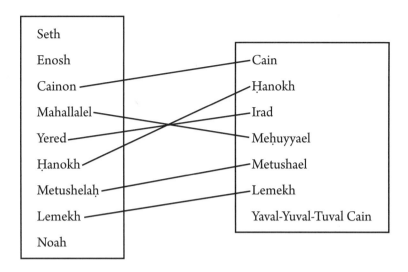

noticed in the previous chapter,[4] in which the children of Cain's Lemekh carry variations of Abel's name, seeking to keep Abel's name alive. Thus, it is Seth's (or Enosh's) inspiration which prompts Lemekh to redeem Abel as Seth's descendants were doing for Cain's line.

The two genealogies paint for us an image of six generations desperately seeking to counteract a divine curse. In this light, two generations stand out. First, there is no one in Seth's line carrying the names of Yaval/Yuval/Tuval-Cain, Cain's seventh generation. This is likely because those three are carrying Abel's name. They do not need redemption because they are redeemers themselves, not only in name but in profession.

The second name that stands out is Noah. He is the first in seven generations to carry his own name, unconnected to Cain's line. Moreover, we are offered an explanation for it: "This one will console us (*yenaḥamenu* – from the same root as *Noaḥ*) for our deeds and the pain[5] of our labor from the ground which God cursed" (5:29).

---

4. It is impossible to state this with certainty since there are no times associated with Cain's descendants. Nonetheless, it seems logical that the naming of Seth's third generation (Cainon) would have preceded the naming of Cain's seventh.

5. The Hebrew verb for pain (A-TZ-V) used here is identical to the one God used in His address to both the Man and the Woman at the end of Genesis 3.

The references to the curses of both Adam and Cain are clear, and so are the implications. After six generations of trying to rescue the line of Cain, Seth's descendants can begin to emerge from the shadow of the curse of Cain and commence their lives as their own selves. Noah represents their hopes for that life.[6]

THE END OF AN ERA

With Noah as the great hope, it turns out that there is another parallel between the two lists, but with a twist. Each list ends with the hero having three sons. Cain's Lemekh has Yaval, Yuval, and Tuval-Cain, while Noah has Shem, Ham, and Yefet. The irony in that parallel is that Lemekh's three sons are the first in that line to bear someone else's name, while Noah's three sons are essentially the first (excluding Noah) to *not* be named after someone else.[7]

There is yet another feature of the three sons in these two genealogies. In each, they are the last generation in the list. We hear nothing of the grandchildren of Cain's Lemekh, and the genealogical list which marks Genesis 5 concludes with the appearance of Noah's sons.

In Genesis, the appearance of three sons serves as a marker of the end of an era. The first instance of this is actually in Genesis 4, as Adam and Eve also have three sons. It is with the birth of the third son that the story of Cain and Abel finds closure, and his appearance marks the end of the first book of *toledot* in Genesis. The final example of this is evident in Genesis 11; the genealogical list of Shem concludes with Terah's three sons, Abram, Nahor, and Haran. Their births represent the end of the era of God interacting universally with all of humanity and the shift to a new era of God interacting through a selected individual or family.

The births of Noah and his three sons clearly mark the end of Seth's genealogy, and this is reinforced literarily as well. We pointed out the pattern in this chapter, beginning with "A lived for *x* years and fathered B." This pattern is first broken with the birth of Noah: "Lemekh

---

6. The mention of pain clearly references the curse of Adam (3:17), while the context of the names points to a concern regarding the curse of Cain. Yet it is hard to imagine they believed Noah would return them to the Garden.

7. See note 15 for further discussion on the significance of this.

lived for eighty-two years and fathered *a son*" (5:28). The name of that son, as opposed to all previous sons in that genealogy, is given only in the next verse, ostensibly so that the explanation for his name – with the hopes of humanity resting on his shoulders – can be presented as well. The same kind of pattern break is evident with the birth of Noah's three sons, not only by the appearance of three children but by Noah's age at their birth. Whereas all previous members of the genealogy father their child at an age ranging from 65 to 130 years, Noah's children are born when he is 500 years old. The comfortable pattern is ending; something new is about to happen.

MYSTERIOUS ḤANOKH

The struggle with impending doom drives Lemekh to attempt a rescue of Abel's legacy (which he hopes will, in turn, redeem Cain), and lead six generations of Seth's descendants to try to redeem Cain's line. The terrifying notion that an entire family, not just an individual, faces ultimate destruction becomes an obsession until the birth of Noah. Within the line from Seth to Noah, however, there is one mysterious individual who seems to challenge the very foundations of that fear.

Ḥanokh was sixty-five years old when he fathered Metushelaḥ. Ḥanokh walked with God, after fathering Metushelaḥ, for three hundred years; and he fathered sons and daughters. All the days of Ḥanokh were 365 years. Ḥanokh walked with God, but he was no longer present, for God had taken him. (5:21–24)

This strange passage clearly breaks the pattern of the genealogical list in multiple ways. First, Ḥanokh lives for only 365 years, as opposed to all his predecessors, who live 895 years or more.[8] Second, no death is mentioned for Ḥanokh; instead, the Torah mysteriously describes his "being taken" by God. Third, Ḥanokh is twice described as "walking with God," a phrase left undefined but with clearly positive connotations.[9]

---

8. Ḥanokh's grandson, Lemekh, lives for "only" 777 years.
9. In Genesis 6, Noah is also as described as walking with God, and in Genesis 17, God asks Abraham to walk before Him.

Medieval commentaries were aware of the anomaly of Ḥanokh, and some[10] offer a suggestion which objectively sounds bizarre but, within the context of the Bible – and especially the early Genesis chapters – makes sense. Like Elijah, who is removed from earthly existence with no indication of his dying,[11] Ḥanokh is similarly removed from this world. Thus the man whose life span appears to be less than half of his peers actually lived a perfect cycle of life. Three hundred and sixty-five years is a year's worth of years, 365 x 365. The man who "walked with God" is so perfectly in tune with God that he no longer belongs in an earthly existence. To put this into the language we've been using, Ḥanokh ceased to be a meaningful mortal and elevated himself into a meaningless immortal.

Ibn Ezra frames this interestingly.[12] As Man and Woman are sent out of the Garden, God places the *keruvim*, angelic (literally, "cherubic") figures, at the gate of the Garden, to block humanity's return to it. There is no going back to the previous existence. Cain's desire to return to that simpler life where there is no competition between humans is thwarted by the *keruvim*. Yet, Ibn Ezra suggests, it is possible to defeat those *keruvim*. This cannot happen by force, but by transforming oneself into a person for whom earthly existence is meaningless through complete submission to the divine will. According to Ibn Ezra, this is Ḥanokh's great achievement: he walks with God to the extent that he is no longer here.

IMAGINED DANGER, REAL DANGER

Earlier we witnessed (Cain's) Lemekh's attempt to overcome immortality by seeking the immortality of the collective and through leaving a legacy. Seth's descendants seek immortality for the group by attempting redemption of Cain's descendants. Ḥanokh seeks to restore the immortality of the individual, by reverting to a primeval version of humanity.

---

10. See Nahmanides, Lev. 18:4; Radak, Gen. 5:24; Ibn Ezra, Deut. 32:39. Rabbinic literature is split on the figure of Ḥanokh, with some sources viewing him as extremely beloved to God (Leviticus Rabba 29:11) and others seeing him as almost villainous (Genesis Rabba 25:1).
11. See the description of Elijah's disappearance in II Kings, ch. 2.
12. See his comment on Deut. 32:39.

The end of this section, however, reveals that those attempts may have been completely misguided.

The *toledot* of Adam closes with two brief narratives, one very clear and the other quite obtuse, but both of which indicate that there is something seriously awry with all of humanity. In the second of these, God explicitly declares the impending doom of all humans, but that catastrophe is not linked to the supposed curse of Cain. Instead, it is the behavior of people in that generation, not some old debt from a previous generation, which threatens their very existence:

> God saw that the evil of Man was increasing, and that the products of the thoughts in his heart were only evil, all day. God regretted that He had made the Man in the land, and He became pained in His heart. God said, "I will erase the Man which I created from the face of the earth – from Man to domesticated animal to crawling thing to the birds in the sky – for I regret that I created them." But Noah found favor in God's eyes. (6:5–8)

This passage closes the second book of *toledot*. If the first *toledot*, the legacy of Creation, is the emergence of hope (in Enosh and perhaps even in Cain) despite Man's missteps, this second book of *toledot* highlights the evaporation of that hope as any potential for good is drowned out by evil,[13] despite the individual sparks of light provided by Ḥanokh and Noah. The experiment called Man has failed, despite the early hopes for success. With Man undermining Creation itself, and with no realistic possibility for God to establish a meaningful relationship with Man, Creation no longer serves a function. Not only must Man be erased, with the absence of Man there is no value to Creation. God regrets the entire enterprise, to the extent that it will all be undone.[14]

God's emerging understanding that He must start again is described as bringing God "pain in His heart," contrasting with the evil

---

13. The "good and evil" of the Tree in the Garden have been supplanted by "only evil," and whereas in Genesis 1, God sees the "good," here God sees the evil in Man.
14. See the section "Un-Creation and Re-Creation" in the following chapter.

in the heart of Man. And the "pain" in God's heart echoes the language God invokes as He sends Man and Woman out of the Garden. Man can be creative and productive, but only with pain; Woman will bear children, and her produce will come to fruition only with pain. The irony is unmistakable: God's attempt to produce a human in His own "image" will also come to fruition only through His pain.

In retrospect, it turns out that the attempts to save humanity from the curse of Cain are misguided. We may never know God's intentions in His curse of Cain, yet it is ultimately irrelevant. It is the behavior of the present generation – not the feared curse of the previous one – which brings about its demise.

THE NEED TO RESTART

The narrative of God being "pained" in fulfilling His own "fruitfulness" is preceded by a most bizarre, albeit brief, passage (5:32–6:4). While a convincing and precise reading of that section is elusive, there are some clues which open up possibilities for a meaningful reading. But first a little background.

Philosophers throughout the ages have debated whether there is such a thing as natural morality. It appears that the Torah has something to say about this fundamental question.

God creates humans with some kind of divine "image" and presumes that this alone will suffice for humans to achieve their destiny. There are no instructions because, in theory, anyone created with the divine image needs no instructions. Hence God is disappointed with Cain for Abel's death, even though there is no specific prohibition to kill, because God assumes that the being created in His "image" does not need that to be explicated. Cain may not know about death, but he certainly should know that he should not do to others what he would not want done to himself.

While there certainly are some disappointments during those initial generations, there are many moments which confirm that God's hopes are not in vain. Thus, during the days of Enosh people begin calling out in God's name, and Seth's Ḥanokh "walks" with God with no explicit command to do so.

As we begin to explore this text we are immediately confronted with a verse which sounds like it has been borrowed from Genesis 1: "The sons of E-lohim saw the daughters of Man that they were good" (6:2). Let us recall one of the repeating phrases from Genesis 1, "E-lohim saw [what was created that day] that it was good." The problem is that God, seeing the actions of the "sons of E-lohim," apparently thinks that they are using their judgment poorly. The "sons of E-lohim," or those who are supposedly exercising their divine image – actually mimicking God of Genesis 1 – are getting it all wrong.

God thus declares, "It is insufficient that My spirit alone dwell within Man, for he is also flesh" (6:3).[15] God's reaction expresses the realization that implanting Man with a divine spark but without a set

---

15. It is thus fascinating that this incident essentially opens with, "As Man began (*heḥel*) to multiply on the face of the earth" (6:1), mirroring the earlier statement of the generation of Enosh, "Then they began (*heḥel*) to call out in God's name." This second "beginning," or *heḥel*, has undermined the former.

The rest of this passage remains mysterious, but one possible reading notices that it opens with the sons of Noah, the first people in seven generations to bear their own names, and closes with mention of "the people of the *name*," most likely referring to that same Noah and his sons referenced just five verses earlier. Furthermore, it is possible that the "sons of E-lohim" refer to those who were expected to act in accordance with their divine image – the descendants of Enosh who called out in God's name, including the legendary Ḥanokh – while the "daughters of Man" refers to the descendants of the cursed Cain. A similar possibility is raised by Ibn Ezra in his comment on 6:2.

If our above reading is correct, that the problem is the dilution of Enosh's genealogical line, it casts an entirely new light on a midrashic comment which has Noah marrying Naama, the daughter of Cain's Lemekh (4:22). There are many similarities between Noah and Naama. Both have fathers named Lemekh; the guttural *ḥet* in Noah's name is easily interchangeable with the guttural *ayin* in Naama's name (in fact, Noah's name is an abbreviated version of *neḥama*, which is identical to Naama's name with the *ḥet-ayin* switch); both names have similar connotations, Noah meaning "comfort" and Naama meaning "pleasantness." If Noah indeed marries Naama, and their children are Shem, Ham, and Yefet – the "men of the name" – then it turns out that Cain's line indeed achieves even biological redemption – but through the female side and not the male line!

The genealogical redemption through the female side is a recurrent theme. While the nations of Ammon and Moab are forbidden to marry into Israel, the rabbis limit

of instructions is insufficient to bring Man to make the right decisions, despite the limited successes in the days of Enosh and despite Enosh's descendant Ḥanokh. The experiment has failed. It will be necessary to restart it with minor tweaks to see if it will work on its next iteration.

The idea of creating a being endowed with a divine spirit is not a mistake, but it becomes clear that without guidance, Man will not achieve God's hopes. God is not angered by Man's failure to capitalize on that divine spirit,[16] but He is saddened, even pained, by it.

The two passages closing the legacy of Adam converge to paint a picture of God's disappointment with His creation. In the first passage we hear of God's frustration that Man needs more direction, while in the second we read of the divine pain in bringing His plan to fruition, much like the pain of childbirth. Man, as a whole, has disappointed, but there are sparks of hope. Enosh calls out in God' s name, Ḥanokh walks with God, and Noah finds favor[17] in God's eyes.

---

this to the males of those nations. Ruth the Moabite marries Boaz to become the ancestor of David (Ruth 4:18–22), and Naama (!) of Ammon marries Solomon to become the mother of all future kings of Judah (I Kings 14:21).

16. Nowhere in this prelude to the Flood does the text describe God as being angry.

17. In a delightful play on words, the Torah describes Noah as finding *ḥen*, favor, in God's eyes, the letters of *ḥen* – *ḥet, nun* – being the same as Noah's name but in reverse. Noah's name is his essence – favor. Later, in a parallel play on words, the character named Er (*ayin, resh*) is described as *ra* (*resh, ayin*), or bad.

The Great Confusion

T he epic commonly known as the Flood (or *Mabul* in Hebrew) is one of the most widespread stories throughout the ancient world. Multiple cultures have their versions of it, the most well-known being the epic of Gilgamesh. Those stories bear remarkable similarities to the biblical account and, as we might expect, some significant differences as well.[1] What interests us, however, is not the relationship between the biblical version of the story and the multiple other versions which are extant, or the question of which came first, but uncovering the meaning of the biblical narrative, specifically in light of the previous five chapters of Genesis.

In an odd twist, the Torah introduces the story to us twice. One of those we saw briefly at the end of our previous chapter; a second look reveals its intense focus on Man:

> God saw that the evil of *Man* was increasing, and that the products of the thoughts in his heart were only evil, all day. God regretted that He had made the *Man* in the land, and He became pained in

---

1. For a discussion of this, see Cassuto's introduction to this story. See also Nahum Sarna, *Understanding Genesis* (New York: Schocken Books, 1970).

His heart. God said, "I will erase the *Man* which I created from the face of the earth – from *Man* to domesticated animal to crawling thing to the birds in the sky. (6:5–7)

Four times in three verses, Man is blamed explicitly. It is Man's doing that pained God, necessitating God's decision to erase His creation – with the lone exception of Noah, who finds favor in God's eyes.

There, is, however, a second introduction to the story following the first, whose focus is profoundly different:

> The *land* became *ruined* before God; and the *land* became filled with corruption. God saw the *land* – that it had become *ruined* – because all flesh had behaved *ruinously* on the *land*. God said to Noah: "The end of all flesh has come before Me, for the *land* is full of their corruption,[2] and I will bring about their *ruin* together with the *land*." (6:11–13)

Perhaps the most remarkable observation is the absence of any mention of Man, which is the central theme in the first introduction. Instead of Man, his thoughts, and his actions, we find a dramatic shift to "all flesh" and the extraordinary focus on the ruin of the land (the land is mentioned six times in three verses; its ruin is mentioned four times).[3]

With two introductions that seem to have profoundly different interests, we are not surprised to find that each references God with a different name. The first, with its laser-like focus on Man, uses the name A-donai, echoing the story of the emergence of Man (chs. 2–3).

---

2. This is a loaded phrase. In God's initial blessing to people, He instructs them to "be fruitful and multiply and fill the earth" (1:28). This introduction to the Noah story is a pointed commentary on the human reaction to that blessing: instead of filling the earth with people it was filled with corruption. In a beautiful twist, the description of the Israelites in Egypt paints a picture of the fulfillment of God's instruction: "The Israelites were fruitful; they swarmed and multiplied and grew very, very strong, and the earth was filled with them" (Ex. 1:7).
3. At the beginning of the second introduction (6:9), Noah is described as "walking with God," reminiscent of Ḥanokh. In the Hebrew spellings of their names, the first two letters of Ḥanokh's name are the same as Noah.

That stands in contrast to the second, with its focus on the land and its ruin, which uses the name E-lohim, reflective of the opening Creation narrative (ch. 1).

It seems that these two introductions serve a dual purpose. On the one hand they function as an opening to the story of the Flood, highlighting that both from the perspective of the creation of humanity and from the perspective of the Creation in general there is a need for God to press RESTART. On a literary level, they function as bookends – a literary envelope – to the dual opening of Genesis. Genesis 1 opens with Creation, and the unit closes with God's declaration that the Creation has become corrupted. Genesis 2–3 discusses the emergence of humanity, and the penultimate passage of the unit seals that discussion with the decision to erase humanity. What this looks like structurally is A-B-B-A, pervasive in classical music and literature, in which two themes, A and B, are introduced, after which the second is developed and only at the end do we return to complete the first.

Why would the Torah choose to employ this kind of literary device here? Apparently, it serves a central theme of the story of "the Flood." This is not a story about an angry God unleashing His wrath on His disobedient subjects. Rather, it is a story of a pained God who is left with no choice other than to start again. This is not a story about destruction, but about a methodical deconstruction – or un-creation – of the world He created.

UN-CREATION AND RE-CREATION

The biblical narrative of the story of Noah is complex, filled with repetitions and internal contradictions.[4] Nevertheless, when viewed as a single literary unit, it neatly divides into two sections. There are many textual indicators pointing to this division, and, in fact, the two halves of the story often mirror each other. One simple example of this is the Torah's use of numbers in the story. In the first half of the story there is

---

4. See Breuer, *Pirkei Bereshit*, 136–205, where he demonstrates that the narrative is composed of two interwoven strands, each with its own focus. Unsurprisingly, those two strands begin with the dual introduction to the story and close with a dual description of the covenant of the rainbow at the end (9:12–17).

a seven-day waiting period, followed by a forty-day period of rain, and culminating with a span of 150 days of the waters rising. The mirror image of this is apparent in the second half of the story, in which we have a 150-day period of the waters receding, followed by a forty-day waiting period, and a seven-day span between Noah's sending of the raven and his sending of the dove.[5]

In light of what we said earlier, I would identify the first half of the narrative as the un-creation and the second section as the re-creation. The un-creation is summed up in a single verse (7:23): "[It] erased all that existed on the face of the earth, from human to domestic animal to crawling creature to the things that fly in the sky." Notice *what* is being erased and the *order* in which it is happening: human, animal, crawling creatures, and birds. This is reminiscent of the Creation narrative but in reverse order. Moving backward from humans, the last thing created on day six, to the flying things, created on day five, God is dismantling the initial Creation.

Even more striking is the Torah's description of the process. It is not just that the incessant rain inundated everything, but that "the springs of the great deep were split open and the storehouses of the heavens opened up" (6:11). The lower waters rise to meet the upper waters which are crashing down. Once again, the reader is invited to recall Genesis 1: on day two, God created the *rakia* as a separation between the upper waters and the lower waters, and our story describes the disappearance of the *rakia*/separator. This process continues as the waters cover the mountains (7:19), effectively erasing the separation between water and land that God put in place on day three.

To call this story a "Flood" contravenes its central message. It is un-creation. God is dismantling the world He created and restoring it to its initial state of *tohu* and *bohu* – undifferentiated matter brimming

---

5. Cassuto develops this idea. He suggests this story is written in a six-step chiasm (A-B-C-D-E-F-F-E-D-C-B-A), demonstrating its literary structure and unity. He further demonstrates the unity of the story through theme words repeated in multiples of seven through both strands of the text: God speaks with Noah seven times, the word *brit* (covenant) appears seven times, "water" appears twenty-one times, "flesh" appears fourteen times, "Noah" appears thirty-five times.

with potential that is not actualized.[6] In fact, the term for this event in the Torah is *"mabul,"* which literally means confusion, or mixing up. It is the returning of the world to its state of confusion, *tohu vavohu,* reversing the creative vector in Genesis which moved the world methodically from chaos to order.

If the first half of the story is un-creation, then we should expect to find evidence in the second half of re-creation and indeed, we do not have to look far. Genesis 8 begins the second half of the story, and already the first verse gives us a taste of what to expect: "God passed a wind over the *aretz* and the waters eased." This is reminiscent of the second verse of the Creation story, in which "God's wind hovers over the face of the water." It is in the second verse of Genesis 8, however, that we begin to get a clearer picture: "The springs of the deep and the storehouses of the heavens closed," precisely the inverse of the first half of our story in which they opened, beginning the un-creation. Reversing the un-creation is actually the beginning of the re-creation, as the *rakia* separating the upper waters from the lower ones is reconstituted.

If Genesis 8:2, the restoration of the *rakia*, represents the remaking of day two of Creation, then day three follows immediately afterward with the recession of the waters from the land. This is followed in succession by Noah's search for vegetation (8:8), reenacting the second half of day three; reintroducing flying animals into the world (8:12),

---

6. There are numerous midrashim in which God threatens to return the world to a state of *tohu*, reflecting a rabbinic understanding that the *Mabul* describes a reversal of the world to its initial state. In Ruth Rabba 1, God threatens that if Israel does not accept the Torah, He will return the world to *tohu*, midrashic language for un-creating the world. The version in *Otzar HaMidrashim* (p. 441) of the ten martyrs invokes the same "return the world to *tohu*" imagery. See also *Yalkut Shimoni* II:883.

There are conflicting rabbinic positions regarding what happened to the fish, which are not mentioned in the narrative at all and which, in theory, should have survived a flood of water. Some midrashic comments suggest that, indeed, the fish did survive (*Pesikta Zutreta*, Ex. 7:18; *Yalkut Shimoni* II:519), spawning a midrashic conception of fish being protected from the evil eye (*Pesikta Rabbati* 20; *Midrash Aggada*, Gen. 48:16). Others, however, suggest that the waters of the flood boiled and killed all the fish (Sanhedrin 108b). In our reading of the story, the entire world was un-created and subsequently re-created. Accordingly, fish would be part of that as well.

reenacting day five; and bringing forth the land animals and people (8:18-19), renewing day six.[7]

The idea that God is systematically undoing that which He had created in order to put it back together again is hinted to via the language used in the second introduction to this story: "God saw the land, that it had become ruined" (6:12). The focus is not what anyone or anything is *doing* but on what the result is – the land is self-destructing. God intervenes to stop that before it's too late. This enables Him to methodically undo the Creation in order to allow the possibility for its rebuilding.[8]

THEOLOGICAL IMPLICATIONS

There is a fascinating parallel to this in the world of halakha. On Shabbat, there are thirty-nine categories of forbidden labor. One of the defining features of these categories is that they are all forms of creative work, mirroring God's work in Creation. At first glance, some of these categories seem to defy that description: tearing, untying, destroying, erasing. Upon closer inspection, however, we see that many of these are formulated carefully: one who tears *in order to be able to sew*, one who erases *in order to be able to write*.[9] Disassembling with the intent of rebuilding is considered a constructive act – it is a necessary part of the building process – and hence is prohibited on Shabbat. God's disassembly of the world *in order to systematically rebuild it* is also essentially a creative act.

This is evident in the Torah's description of the rain lasting for forty days. In both biblical and rabbinic literature, the number forty represents birth or rebirth. In the Bible, Moses is on the mountain for forty days and emerges as a man reborn with a radiant face. The spies enter the land as princes and forty days later return with the self-image of grasshoppers. The Israelite nation spends forty years in the desert and is transformed from a fractured nation of refugees into a unified nation of conquerors. In the post-Joshua period, many Judges leave the land quiet for forty years, providing a chance for the people to "rebirth" itself (though these prove to be

---

7. We will later discuss why day four is notably absent from both the un-creation and the re-creation narratives.
8. Understanding this story as un-creation followed by re-creation renders any search for evidence of an actual deluge irrelevant.
9. Mishna Shabbat 7:2.

opportunities that they sadly never use). Certain types of sins make the sinner liable for forty lashes,[10] after which the individual may no longer be called a sinner. In rabbinic literature, there are forty-minus-one categories of prohibited (creative) work on Shabbat,[11] a child is considered to be "alive" in the womb after forty days,[12] and pregnancy lasts for forty weeks.

The immediate theological implication of reading the story as a re-creation rather than as a divine deluge reshapes many popular images of God in the Bible, not to mention emphasizes the contrast between the biblical description of the story and those of parallel cultures. God is not angry, vengeful, filled with wrath, or impetuous.[13] Indeed, absent from this entire narrative is any word of God's anger.[14] Just like the God of Creation, He acts with forethought and planning, carefully undoing so that Creation can be redone.

This follows a pattern we have observed thus far in Genesis: God's reactions to the missteps of people are designed as corrective measures. The expulsion of the Man and the Woman from the Garden is a necessary outcome of their new status as mortal, but significant, beings. Transforming Cain into a nomad is necessary for him to understand the gravity of what he did to his nomadic brother. Creation must be undone before it self-destructs, so that it can be redone.

MAN RENEWED

All of this points to a central question. Why does God think that in the second round of Creation things will be any better? What changes does God bring about to help ensure that the second attempt will be more successful than the first?

There is an interesting anomaly in the story of the *Mabul*. The narrative is rife with dates: the six hundredth year of Noah's life, the second month, the seventeenth day (7:11); the seventeenth day of the seventh

---

10. The rabbis limited them to thirty-nine, yet insisted on calling them forty-minus-one.
11. Mishna Shabbat 7:2.
12. Bekhorot 21b.
13. For a fascinating study of God's anger, see Deena Grant, *Divine Anger in the Hebrew Bible* (Washington, DC: Catholic Bible Association of America, 2014).
14. Throughout the Bible, God's anger is reserved exclusively for those who defy His explicit covenant with them.

month (8:4); the tenth day of the tenth month (8:5); the six hundred-and-first year, the first day of the first month (8:13); the twenty-seventh day of the seventh month (8:14). What makes this particularly unusual is that these are the only dates listed in all of Genesis.

Apparently, with Noah sealed in the ark there is no way for people to measure time. For humans, time effectively ceases to exist – and there is textual evidence for this. Following Noah's exit from the ark, God promises that "the planting and harvest seasons, the cold and the hot, the summer and the winter, the day and the night, will never again be suspended" (8:22), the obvious implication being that for the duration of Noah's stay in the ark both the cycle of the year and the cycle of the day were, in fact, suspended. Ironically it is God, for whom time is meaningless, who keeps track of time in the absence of the functioning of the luminaries.[15]

Contained in that womb of an ark in which time is suspended are the seeds of the new world God is planning. They are the transplants that will help bridge the world before with the world after. And to understand why God believes that the second attempt will be more successful than the first, we need to first explore how people, and their roles in the world, change.

In the initial Creation, God fashions a world into which He places the humans. There is nothing left for humans to do other than maintain that which is handed to them on a silver platter. By contrast, Noah spends an entire year caring for what is essentially the whole world. It is Noah who steps out of the ark onto a barren planet in need of restoration. It is Noah who reintroduces animal life to the planet; he may even be responsible for reintroducing plant life.[16] Noah undoubtedly emerges with an enhanced sense of responsibility for everything in his

---

15. The entire incident, beginning on the seventeenth of the seventh month and concluding a year later, on the twenty-seventh of the seventh month, lasted for one lunar year plus ten days. Assuming a lunar year of 355 days, the total length of the incident was one complete solar cycle.

16. On the one hand the Torah describes that the dove found an olive branch; on the other hand one of Noah's first endeavors is to engage in agriculture, planting a vineyard. Moreover, he carries with him onto the ark samples of all plant foods (6:21).

charge, and emerging from the ark he takes on a new role – he is God's partner in restoring the world to what it was.

Even assuming that nothing externally changes, people are now different.[17] The transformation of Man's self-image from a consumer into a co-creator is dramatic, and significantly alters his relationship to himself and his environment.

Perhaps the most dramatic of these changes, however, becomes evident in Noah's first act emerging from the ark: he offers animal sacrifices to God. The significance of this cannot be underestimated. This is the first time that animal sacrifices are offered,[18] and there are only two other instances of animal sacrifice in all of Genesis.[19] In fact, until this point Man is not permitted to eat animals; only vegetation is permitted for consumption.[20]

Noah's act is audacious, and indicates that he is not the same man who entered the ark. After a year of living in close quarters with the animals in the ark, he understands, on a visceral level, what God had implied in both the initial Creation epic and the creation of humanity – that people are qualitatively different from animals. In doing so, Noah replays the discovery made by the Man in the Garden that he is qualitatively distinct from the beasts. Noah demonstrates that insight, clearly drawing the distinction between man and beast, by performing the ultimate act: he kills the animal and offers it to God, demonstrating his understanding of his role as a partner in the re-creation. The "savory scent" which God smells is God's delight in Noah's discovery of that idea and his bold, defiant expression of it in his sacrifice.

---

17. There is some discussion among the commentaries regarding whether the physical world had changed. Some argue that prior to this incident light did not refract as it did afterward, so that the rainbow was a new creation. See Ibn Ezra, 9:14; Nahmanides, 9:12.
18. Abel brings an "offering" of his sheep, but we are not told how that offering is delivered to God. The same is true for Cain's offering of his produce.
19. Abraham's offering of the ram instead of Isaac (22:13) and Jacob's offering just prior to his descent to Egypt (46:1). Abraham built multiple altars as did Jacob, but there is no mention of sacrifices being brought upon them.
20. According to Nahmanides, 1:29, killing an animal prior to the story of Noah was tantamount to murder.

NEW RULES

As God prepares for the new Creation, He does not rely solely on the internal changes within people. We recall that at the end of the legacy of Adam there is an enigmatic passage in which God acknowledges that creating Man with His spirit implanted within is insufficient for him to achieve that which God had hoped for; it would not bring the masses of humanity to lives filled with morality and bonded with God (6:3). In fact, in a paradoxical twist, the innate human capacity for evil, which the Torah explicates as one of the central factors necessitating the *Mabul* (6:5), is cited afterward as the very reason God will never repeat the *Mabul* (8:21).

The essential nature of man does not change. It is the way God relates to that nature that must be adjusted. One of the key changes God makes is the introduction of a rudimentary set of rules for people to follow, which would provide basic guidelines to direct human activity. If man, endowed with God's spirit, is unable on his own to bring good to triumph over evil, then God will provide assistance.

In light of Noah's actions, we are not surprised that God's new rules emphasize exactly the same point: "Everything that lives," declares God, "will be for you to eat; like the grass I have given you all" (9:3). Man may now kill and consume animals. However, at the same time that God grants man permission to consume meat, there is a restriction: "But you shall not eat flesh with its lifeblood still in it." Not only from Noah's perspective but from God's as well, the formal relationship between man and beast is altered and nuanced. Man is permitted to eat animal flesh but must be humane in doing so. As the rabbis understood this, we are forbidden to eat meat that is taken from a live animal.

Were this not explicit enough, the next set of laws drives home the point. People may kill animals, but animals may not kill people.[21] The climax of this set of laws is a beautifully constructed chiasm. Both the transliteration and the translation emphasize the construction:

---

21. It is not clear what God means when He declares that He will demand accountability from any beast that kills a person (9:5), but it nevertheless expresses the hierarchy of Man-beast unambiguously.

(A) *Shofekh* (One who spills)
  (B) *dam* (the blood)
    (C) *haadam* (of a human)
    (C') *baadam* (by humans)
  (B') *damo* (his blood)
(A') *yishafekh* (will be spilled)

At the center (C and C') of this compact, tightly wound statement are humans, and by placing people at the core, God packs one of the essential messages of the new Creation: the death of a human is different from the death of an animal, and the killing of a person is different from the killing of an animal. God will demand accountability from animals that kill people. Furthermore, people absolutely may not kill other people, and humans are responsible for avenging the blood of those who do kill.

The "punch line" of the above sentence comes in its closure: "For in the *tzelem* of God did He make the Man." The distinction between humans and animals is not quantitative but qualitative. Man is created in God's image, or as Noah understands, man is co-creator with God.

This message to Noah and his family is actually introduced prior to the command. God blesses Noah and his family, and that blessing echoes the one given to humans in the initial Creation, with subtle but significant differences:

God's blessing to humans (Creation)	God's blessing to Noah (re-creation)
Be fruitful and multiply	Be fruitful and multiply
and fill the earth,	and fill the earth.
and conquer it. (1:28)	The terror and fear of you
	will be upon the beasts of the land,
	and upon the birds of the sky,

	upon everything which crawls on the ground,
	and upon all the fish of the sea;
	they are given into your hands. (9:1–2)

The two blessings begin identically, but instead of the command to "conquer the earth" of Genesis 1, God expresses explicitly that the gap between man and beast is unbridgeable. Man is to dominate the earth and even consume the animals. Beasts are to be subservient to – even fearful of – man.[22]

FIXING THE PROBLEMS

The repeated dual emphasis on the distinction between man and beast and the prohibition against murder are apparently part of God's corrective to problems that were rampant prior to the *Mabul*. The prohibition against murder is inspired by the story of Cain and Abel, while the separation between man and beast is less clear. It may be related to the conversation between the serpent and the Woman in the Garden or perhaps the enigmatic "sons of E-lohim" who took all that they chose. Indeed, rabbinic commentary adds a sexual overtone to both of those incidents, some suggesting that the serpent wished to kill the Man so that it could mate with the Woman,[23] and others suggesting that the "sons of E-lohim" mated with beasts as well.[24]

---

22. It is for this reason that land animals, which were not blessed to be fruitful in Genesis 1 (so as to avoid conflict with Man), are given that blessing following the *Mabul*. Man, after the *Mabul*, is permitted to hunt and eat the animals, hence they need the blessing of fruitfulness in order to maintain themselves.

23. Genesis Rabba 18:6.

24. *Midrash Tanḥuma* 33. According to rabbinic tradition, there are actually seven universal laws, known as the seven Noahide commandments. Within the text of the Torah one would be hard-pressed to find all seven, yet if we apply the principle that the Noahide laws are intended as some form of remediation for problems with the first Creation, we gain insight into the rabbinic mind. For example, one of the laws identified by the rabbis relates to the entire spectrum of sexual immorality. Another is the prohibition of idolatry, clearly linked to one reading of the calling

In fact, not only are these laws designed as correctives for earlier misdeeds, they may provide an insight into what precipitated the *Mabul*. Despite the repeated introductions to the story, we are left with only the vaguest of descriptions of the problems: the Torah writes that the products of man's thoughts were turning to become exclusively evil, yet we have no indication of what kind of evil; the earth is filled with corruption, yet we are clueless about what kind of corruption; the land is self-destructing, yet we do not know what is causing that. These laws, the correctives after the re-creation, provide the clues as to what the prior, insoluble problems were.

The issue of mixing between the species emerges from careful attention to a single word, *lemineihu*, mentioned seven times, which serves as a theme word in the opening of the *Mabul* story. Noah is instructed to take "of the birds, according to its species, of the animals, according to its species, from the crawling things, according to its species" (6:20). Later, when the rain begins, we are told that Noah entered the ark with his family and "the beasts, according to its species, the animals, according to its species, the crawling things, according to its species, and the birds, according to its species" (7:13). The focus on the preservation of the species identifies *lemineihu* ("according to its species") as a theme word.

The only other place we find *lemineihu* appearing seven times is in the original Creation story, where it emphasizes the need for preserving the natural order God creates.[25] The re-emphasis of the word in the *Mabul* story suggests that the natural order of the species is being threatened, and that threat may have contributed to the necessity of the *Mabul*.

(or profaning) of God's name in the days of Enosh. Yet another is the obligation to establish a court system, which emerges from God's instruction to humanity to avenge the killing of people. Added to the list is the prohibition against theft, clearly connected to the injustices leading to the *Mabul* and possibly as well to the "sons of E-lohim" who took "all that they chose."

25. The strange description the Torah uses for the animals as "Man and wife" (7:2) and the fact that the animals are to emerge from the ark as families (8:19) further reinforce the sense that sexual fidelity is an issue. This is further amplified by the bizarre story just prior to the *Mabul* about the mixing between the sons of E-lohim and the daughters of man.

The second half of the story also hints that species-mixing was one of the key problems leading up to the *Mabul*. After forty days of waiting for the waters to recede, Noah sends out the raven. Seven days later he sends out the dove, and at first glance it is hard to figure out why he switches birds. Upon closer inspection, however, it turns out that the two sendings of the birds are profoundly different.

Noah sends the raven	Noah sends the dove
He sent out the raven, and it went to and fro until the water dried up from the land. (8:7)	Noah sent out the dove to see if the waters had receded from the ground. But the dove did not find rest for her feet, so she returned to him, to the ark – for there was water on the face of the land – and he extended his hand, took her, and brought her to him into the ark. (8:8–9)

Noah sends the dove on a mission, and when she is unable to complete it, we get a slow-motion description of Noah lovingly bringing her back into the ark. When it comes to the raven, however, we do not know why Noah sends it, and when the raven can find no dry land it flies back and forth (for weeks) until the waters recede. It sounds as if the raven is not sent on a mission, but is expelled from the ark at the first opportunity.

Rabbinic commentary suggests that the raven was involved in some sort of sexual impropriety on the ark,[26] echoing concerns we saw earlier. Even the Hebrew for raven, *orev*, means "to mix" (reminiscent of the chaotic *erev* of Genesis 1). Once again, the hint of sexual impropriety hangs over the story, suggesting that it is one of the key problems God seeks to correct.[27]

---

26. *Midrash Aggada*, Gen. 8:6.

27. In one of the strange twists of phrase, when instructing Noah to take seven each of the "pure" animals, God identifies the animals as "man and wife" (7:2). On the one hand, the phrase suggests a particular level of fidelity; on the other hand, it blurs the very clear line between human and animal that the Torah has been trying to emphasize.

THE ARK OF SEPARATION

If mixing between the species was an element of the corruption, then we should expect to find additional indications of this. Indeed, we do, and there are some interesting twists. When God instructs Noah to enter the ark He clearly makes a separation between the men and the women: "You should enter the ark, you and your sons, your wife and your son's wives" (6:18). Lest we think this is a casual expression, the phrasing is repeated when Noah actually enters the ark (7:7) and again when the Torah recalls the entry into the ark (7:13). When it is time to exit the ark, God is just as careful with His instruction, but this time shifts the emphasis to men and women exiting as couples: "Leave the ark, you and your wife, and your sons with their wives" (8:16). Whether because it is intended as a corrective to improper sexuality prior to the *Mabul* or whether because it is inappropriate to be engaged in procreation when the world is falling apart, the time on the ark is to be a period of abstinence.[28]

The implication that the exit from the ark marks a return to healthy sexuality is soon made explicit. Speaking of the animals, God says, "Let them swarm in the land, and be fruitful and multiply on it" (8:17). When speaking to Noah and his family, He both blesses them (9:1) and commands them (9:7) to be fruitful and multiply, essentially renewing the blessing and instruction given in the initial Creation story (1:28). The emphasis post-*Mabul* is clear – God wants to reestablish the natural order which He designed in the original Creation and which had been corrupted.

Despite God's implicit and explicit directives and the emphasis on repopulating the world, it is striking that Noah begins the story with three children and ends the story with three children. There is no record of him fathering any others post-*Mabul*.[29] In fact, despite the precision in God's instructions for exiting the ark, Noah actually exits together with his sons, while his wife exits with his daughters-in-law (8:18).

---

28. See Maimonides, *Laws of Dispositions* 2:2, where he posits that the way to correct character deficiencies is to temporarily swing to the opposite extreme, until the individual finds a healthy equilibrium, what Maimonides calls "the golden path."

29. Perhaps this sparked the rabbinic opinion (Leviticus Rabba 17:5) that Ham castrated his father, rendering him unable to father any more children.

It seems that even though Noah is saved from the *Mabul* and saves the world along with him, and even though he intuits what changes need to be effected post-*Mabul*, he is nonetheless a casualty of the *Mabul*. He has been so traumatized, by both the cause and the event, that he can no longer imagine himself engaged in procreative activity.

THE COVENANT

God's faith in humanity is initially grounded in the fact that people are created in His *tzelem*. Despite His disappointment in man, God's faith in humanity is restored now that man is given some guidelines. God is so convinced that the change in humanity combined with the new laws guiding human behavior will be successful that He establishes a covenant: He will never again undo the Creation. That in itself is a profound statement of confidence in human character, an extraordinary expression of His renewed faith in humanity.

At this time it appears there is yet one additional element in the restoration of that faith: God establishes a covenant not only with Noah but with Noah's family. It is no longer the individual but the family who bears the responsibility of the divine mission.

That covenant is accompanied by a symbol, the rainbow. There is much to be said about the rainbow: its shape, its colors, etc. It also represents a united but diverse group, of which the family is perhaps the quintessential paradigm. The one, unified family that enters the ark emerges from it as discrete family units. The rainbow is the symbol representing God's new model of hope.[30]

There is one additional aspect of the rainbow I would like to briefly explore. Throughout the course of biblical history God reveals Himself in one of two ways – through fire or through water. The Splitting of the Sea is an example of revelation through water. Heavenly fire used to consume sinners, or a sacrifice, is an example of revelation

---

30. It should come as no surprise that the nations which emerged from Noah's three sons are described using the term "family" (10:5, 20, 31), with a final coda of, "These are the families of the sons of Noah" (10:32). We are similarly reminded of the language of family used to describe both the "pure" animals Noah is to take into the ark, and human man and wife (7:2), as well as with regard to the emergence of the animals from the ark following the *Mabul* (8:19).

through fire. Fire and water are basic elements or forces within nature. Harnessed properly, they enable our survival. But every so often we are given a taste of their awesome power which we are rendered helpless to contain and which yields a terrifying destructive capacity. Hurricanes, tsunamis, forest fires, and volcanoes are but a few of the examples which humble us, and help us recognize that there is a power in this world far greater than anything we can imagine.

The rainbow is essentially a combination of those two modes of revelation. It is the light from the sun, the most significant fire in our daily lives, refracted through the water vapor in the clouds. It is the luminaries, suspended during the *Mabul*, letting us know that they are still functional. The rainbow represents God's desire to restore the delicate balance between His two modes of revelation, lest one obliterate the other. It is His way of letting us know that He is committed to our continuity.

THE NEW WORLD

The epilogue to the *Mabul* is another of those mysterious Genesis stories. Noah makes wine from the vineyard he planted, becomes intoxicated, and unclothes himself in his tent. His son Ham sees him and tells his brothers, who modestly cover themselves with a cloth in order to avoid seeing their father as they enter the tent to cover him. In the morning Noah awakens, and when he realizes what happened, he curses Ham's son Canaan while blessing the other two children, Shem and Yefet.

While much of the incident remains shrouded in mystery,[31] I would like to focus on one aspect. Some rabbis read this story as a devastating critique of Noah – the first thing he does after the disaster of the *Mabul* is plant a vineyard so that he can become inebriated, burying his sorrow in alcohol.[32] (We will not address the amount of time it takes for a vine to actually produce grapes and for those grapes to transform

---

31. What exactly did Ham do that was so terrible? Why is Shem elevated over Yefet? Why does Noah curse Canaan when Ham exposed him? These questions have vexed commentators throughout the ages.
32. Genesis Rabba 36:3–4.

into wine.) If we consider that this is not a stand-alone incident but an epilogue to the entire *Mabul* epic, it opens up new possibilities.

Noah is a bridge figure; he lives in the worlds both preceding and following the *Mabul*. According to the chronology presented in the biblical text, both Noah's and Adam's lives overlapped at some point with Metushelaḥ's life, so that Noah, deeply involved in the re-creation, may have heard a second-hand account regarding the initial Creation. As Noah examines the re-created world he realizes that something essential is missing. There is no Garden of Eden, and with its absence there is only the dashed hope of a possible return to an idealized existence.

Noah cannot imagine a world without that Garden and the hope it represents. He seeks to create his own version of the experience of life in the Garden. How will that be accomplished? Life in the Garden is marked by a sense of carefree meaninglessness and an innocent nakedness. Getting drunk accomplishes both, as Noah's inebriety diminishes his inhibitions. Of course Noah is not stupid. He knows his tent is no Garden, but he is trying, in his own private domain, to re-create that experience, to find some hope for an escape to the Garden.[33]

Ham sees his father and mocks the old man's stupidity, exposing Noah's nakedness both literally and figuratively by ridiculing his private venture.[34] We do not know if Shem and Yefet have a different opinion of their father's behavior from that of Ham, but they take every precaution to protect their father's dignity. They cover themselves with a cloth and walk backward to avoid seeing their father's nakedness.[35]

---

33. It is no wonder that R. Yehuda b. Ilai identifies the grape as the forbidden fruit (Genesis Rabba 15:7).

34. The Hebrew words *gilui* (to uncover) and *erva* (nakedness, in plural *arayot*) are used in the opening of this incident. The combination *gilui arayot* in Leviticus has very specific connotation: an improper sexual act. Again we find a textual hint for a rabbinic comment, in this case the interpretation that Ham raped his father. Even according to our reading, while Ham did not assault his father sexually he nonetheless did violate his father's dignity and dreams.

35. A similar, though not identical, image describes the dismantling of the Tabernacle. As the priests enter the Sanctuary and remove the curtain separating the Holy from the Holy of Holies, they use that curtain to effectively shield their eyes from the Holy Ark – until they use that very curtain to cover it, protecting its dignity by ensuring that it never be exposed.

The Torah passes no judgment as to whether Noah's initiative or his reactions to his children's behavior are commendable or contemptible. We are left, however, with two significant outcomes. First, it is clear that there is no Garden.[36] That belongs to an alternate reality that is never replaced after the *Mabul*. All that remains as a collective memory for humanity is the story of the Garden.

Second, Noah leaves us with a family in which there is a clear hierarchical structure: Shem at the top, followed by Yefet, and Ham – especially the line of Canaan – at the bottom. On the one hand, Noah may have intuited the necessity to create such a structure in order to avoid the kind of internecine battling which ultimately led to Abel's death and untold generations of anguish. On the other hand, up until now no one other than God has issued either blessings or curses. Noah, as God's partner in Creation, takes that role seriously and makes it his responsibility to carry on God's work of distributing blessings and curses as he sees fit. Within the context of his family, and perhaps within the context of the family of humanity, Noah sees the necessity for hierarchy. That necessity, however, will also haunt humanity.

---

36. Let us not confuse the biblical Garden of Eden with later Jewish cultural references to the afterlife as *gan eden*.

Genesis 10:1–11:26

Exercising and Limiting the Divine Spark

arlier, we studied the genealogies of Cain and Seth, and found them rich with meaning essential to understanding the surrounding narrative. The same holds true for the next two genealogical lists.

The first list is commonly known as the Table of Nations. It comprises the proverbial seventy nations often referenced in rabbinic literature,[1] which are organized into the three major groupings of Shem, Ham, and Yefet. Ostensibly, this list is meant to answer a central question vexing many readers: If we are all descended from a single man and his three children, from where does all the diversity within humanity come? The Table of Nations provides the map of who came from whom.

More than merely a list, this genealogy is filled with anomalies which beg our attention and open up further exploration. For example, the listing of each of the three groups closes with a formulaic coda, along the lines of, "From these branched out the nations, each according to their own tongue." The descendants of Yefet are listed

---

1. For example, Sukka 55b; Genesis Rabba 66:14.

first, and rather briefly; only three verses are dedicated to them. This is likely because the nations listed play a minor role in the Bible, as they do not interact with ancient Israel until the late, post-exilic books of the Bible. As much as Yefet is blessed by his father, these nations are essentially irrelevant to the biblical reader. Interestingly, the coda for the Yefet nations is different from those of Shem and Ham, as it specifically identifies some of these as the island nations (possibly Crete, Greece, and others).

THE FAMILY OF HAM

Quite different is the family of Noah's cursed son, Ham. It includes some of the Bible's most significant antagonists to the Israelites, including Egypt, Babylonia, Canaan, and the Philistines. In essence, the text seems to be preparing the reader for the central biblical story – the battle between Noah's cursed son (Ham) and his blessed one (Shem).

Particularly glaring are the anomalies related to the families of Canaan. This passage is set aside from the surrounding text by two Masoretic breaks, and is literally at the center of the chapter (there are fourteen verses prior to the Canaanites and twelve following). Additionally, each of the peoples listed prior to the appearance of Canaan is listed as a single individual with whom the nation is later identified: Kush, Mitzrayim (Egypt), Sheba, etc.

When describing the descendants of Canaan, however, we are told about the Jebusite, the Emorite, the Girgashite, etc. One gets the sense that the Torah is preparing the biblical reader for the clash with these Canaanite nations. Moreover, the Canaanite peoples are the only ones for whom the Torah provides geographic boundaries. The Torah seems to be prefiguring the borders of the Canaanite lands, which will ultimately become the Promised Land of the Chosen People.

Aside from the foreshadowing of the clash with Canaan's descendants, there is a strange diversion provided by a certain Nimrod. He is not a nation, yet he receives more biblical real estate than any nation listed in the entire chapter. Here is the Torah's description:

Kush fathered Nimrod; he was the first mighty man on earth. He was a mighty hunter before God. For that reason it is said, "Like Nimrod, a mighty warrior before God." The beginning of his kingdom was in Babel, Erekh, Akkad, and Kalneh, in the land of Shinar. From that land emerged Ashur, who built Nineveh, Rehovot Ir, and Kalah. Also Resen, between Nineveh and Kalah – that was the great city. (10:8–12)

The reader is left puzzled. Why are we told about this man, who does not even belong in the Table of Nations? And what does it mean that he is a mighty warrior before God?

Undoubtedly, Nimrod is a formidable figure whom the Torah cannot ignore. It is also clear that Nimrod is the first person described explicitly as having a kingdom, that is, that he exercises dominion over other people. This is significant for two reasons. First, we recall the blessings/instructions that God gave to Noah and his sons upon their exit from the ark: people are to dominate the animal kingdom. Nowhere in God's words, however, do we find approval for people dominating other people. Nimrod seems to defy that sense of order envisioned by God.

Second, let us remember that Noah himself establishes a hierarchy among his children. Assuming that Noah is justified in doing so (and much of the rest of the biblical narrative seems to uphold Noah's vision), Ham is supposed to be subjugated to his brothers. Yet Nimrod, a descendant of Ham, turns out to found the first empire, in which he effectively overturns his ancestor's order.

We are therefore not surprised that rabbinic tradition looks unkindly upon Nimrod. They saw the "mighty hunter before God" as someone who defies and challenges God, attempting to supplant Him with a human who controls the rest of humanity. The rabbis were well aware that Nimrod's name literally translates as "let us rebel."[2]

---

2. See, for example, Genesis Rabba 23:7.

THE FAMILY OF SHEM

Shem's family, too, is pockmarked with oddities that grab our attention.[3] Already in the opening verse listing his genealogy, Shem is identified as the father of all the descendants of Ever. This is doubly bizarre: we have not as yet been introduced to Ever, and when he is ultimately presented we discover that he is Shem's great-grandson, which renders the identification of Shem as the father of all of Ever's descendants superfluous. As we continue through Shem's genealogy, the rapid movement from one generation to the next is interrupted briefly by the explanation offered for the name of a certain Peleg: "For in his days the world was divided (*niflega*)." We don't yet know what this means and we are left wondering why he alone would be named after an event which affected all mankind.

The loose ends apparent in this Table of Nations leave us wondering if we are not missing something, and indeed the Torah wastes no time in filling in the blanks. The continuation of this section, commonly known as the Tower of Babel, offers interesting opportunities for explaining the anomalies of Nimrod, Shem, Ever, and Peleg.

THE MYSTERY OF THE TOWER

The story commonly known as the Tower of Babel (11:1–9) is one of the most beautifully constructed and tightly organized passages in the Bible. It has a multilayered chiastic structure filled with wordplays. Here is one version:[4]

---

3. The birth order of Noah's three children is somewhat of a mystery. They are generally described as Shem, Ham, and Yefet, although in this chapter the order is switched, with Yefet first and Shem last. Moreover, the opening verse listing Shem's family describes him as the brother of Yefet the elder, while the story of Ham's incident in the tent describes Ham as "the youngest son."

4. Based on Jan P. Fokkelman, *Narrative Art in Genesis: Specimens of Stylistic and Structural Analysis*, 2nd ed. (Sheffield, UK: JSOT Press, 1991), 11–45. See also Cassuto, *Commentary on the Book of Genesis*, 158–159, and Joel S. Baden, "The Tower of Babel: A Case Study in the Competing Methods of Historical and Modern Literary Criticism," *Journal of Biblical Literature* 128:2 (2009): 209–224.

(A) The entire land was of one language
  (B) Let us make for ourselves a name (*shem*)
    (C) And they spoke, each man to his friend
      (D) Behold! Let us
        (E) build
          (F) the city and the tower
            (G) God came down and saw
          (F') the city and the tower
        (E') that the people had built
      (D') Behold!...Let us
    (C') each man, his friend's language
  (B') from there (*sham*)
(A') God confused the language of the whole land

This magnificent structure contrasts the people's plans ("behold," people speaking with their friends, "let us," "build," city, tower) with what happens after God's intervention at the very center of the chiasm. Every element of their conspiracy is undone and every twist of phrase included in their plot is referenced as God foils and unravels their undertaking. The result is a reversal of the story's opening: the single language is replaced by multiple languages, God's plan undoes the people's plan, and instead of the name (*shem*) people try to establish for themselves, they are scattered from there (*mi-sham*).[5] All this is enhanced by the multiple wordplays, yielding an elegant biblical formulation of the Yiddish aphorism, "Man plans and God laughs."

With all of this, however, we are left somewhat perplexed. What is it about their plans that God does not like? With what is God concerned

---

5. There is great irony in their quest to make for themselves a name, a *shem*. The next passage spells out the legacy of Shem, Noah's son. While these descendants of Ham were trying to make for themselves a name, the only true *shem* is one achieved through the qualities displayed by Shem. See also Mishna Avot 4:13, where after enumerating three types of achievable "crowns," the mishna adds a fourth – the crown of the good name, the *shem tov*.

There are multiple other wordplays as well. The root N-P-TZ (scatter) appears both in the people's plans and in God's response, and verse 3 is filled with multiple examples of doubled language: *nisrefa leserefa, nilbena levanim, halvana le'aven, ḥamar laḥomar*.

when He says: "Behold, they are one nation with a single language, and that was the beginning of their action; now nothing will stop them from everything they conspired to do?

LANGUAGE AND DIVERSITY

A second look at the text reveals some interesting clues. For example, while the story is colloquially referred as "The Tower of Babel," the word "tower" appears only twice in the narrative and is always coupled with the word "city." By contrast, "city" appears three times, and the Torah's description of God's success in foiling their plan says simply, "So they ceased building the city" (11:8) – without mention of the tower at all. Is it possible that God's primary concern is about the city, and only secondarily the tower?

Here is a second clue. The story opens and closes (see parts **A** and **A'** in the chiasm above) with a focus on language, and the concern with language is the first idea expressed by God in this incident: "Behold, they are one nation with a single language for all" (11:6). Why is language such a central source of consternation?

And one final clue. After introducing the fact that everyone speaks the same language in the opening verse, the text continues with a mysterious phrase: "and *devarim aḥadim.*" Most contemporary translators render this as some variation on "one set of words,"[6] which adds little to the narrative, while many of the classical commentaries interpret it as "united words."[7] The core of the debate revolves around the word *aḥadim*, which could also be understood as "few."

When we piece the clues together the picture that emerges is that language *is* the central issue. The lack of diversity in language in the story's opening yields limitations to creativity. This is understandable, as every different language – with its unique grammar, structure, and vocabulary – yields nuanced differences of tone, meaning, intensity, etc. This is especially true in the spheres of human expression, such as poetry and literature. Every translation necessarily involves at least a minimal level of interpretation, and the resulting diversity of ideas is minimized when everyone speaks the same language. Hence the Torah introduces

---

6. This is Alter's translation. JPS translates it as "the same words."
7. See, for example, the commentaries of Rashi and Radak on this verse.

the story by mentioning the uniformity of language, resulting in *devarim aḥadim* – few things being said.

If, in fact, the lack of diversity of ideas is a core concern, then we are led to an entirely new understanding of the construction project. As we saw above, the project has two foci – the city and the tower. The city is a means to concentrate people geographically, and the tower provides a vantage point for control of those people.

Imagine multiple generations of the survivors of the Great Confusion (*Mabul*) living in the flood plains in and around Babel. Whoever has the high ground establishes control; the higher the tower, the more control. A tower with "its head in the heavens" expresses the desire to control everyone, to be all-powerful.

No wonder the rabbis saw the attempt to build the tower as a rebellion against God.[8] It is God who has dominion over humanity. People are not to dominate other people. And certainly nobody should have ultimate control over all humanity, as the designers of the tower intended. Any attempt to do so is viewed as an attempt to supplant God.

This sounds familiar to us, and we are not surprised that the rabbis linked this story with the earlier tale of Nimrod. Both narratives take place in the lands of Babel and Shinar, and both revolve around the desire by the few to dominate the masses. In the rabbinic mind, Nimrod, the "mighty hunter before God," is metaphorically hunting God Himself, and the builders of the tower similarly challenge God's rule over people.

The human race has witnessed way too many times in its history the desire by the few to control the masses. One of the most terrifying threats to totalitarian rulers is the free dissemination of information, which is why, in the Western world, freedom of the press is such a core value.[9] It is only through the control of information that one can hope

---

8. Genesis Rabba 38:6.
9. I vividly recall visiting the repressive Soviet Union in the 1980s. Customs officials were most concerned about printed materials, lest Soviet citizens get a glance of life beyond the Iron Curtain. Soviet scientists were hobbled in their work by strict limitations placed on their access to scientific articles emerging from outside the Soviet bloc and by the lack of interaction with colleagues from beyond the bloc, and Soviet Jews were prohibited from emigrating out of the fear that the Soviet people would be dispersed upon the face of the earth.

to limit the emergence of new ideas, and it is only through the limiting of ideas that the power-hungry can imagine imposing themselves on the underrepresented.

Now we also understand the fear of the leadership – "lest we be scattered." God's intent is for man to fill the earth, while the leaders in Babel seek to undermine that by concentrating humanity in one place, the city with its control tower. Hence we understand the divine response, which leads to the scattering of peoples across the face of the planet.

What is more, we understand God's method. Changing the language of people is not simply a tool to confound their plans. It addresses the underlying cause of the problem and undermines the plot itself. On a technical level, the inability for neighbors to understand each other forces them to live apart. Conceptually, however, the diversity of language leads to an explosion of ideas, necessarily resulting in the collapse of the tyrannical regime as people discover, explore, and express a diversity of thought. As we saw back in the Garden and with the killing of Cain, God's reaction is not punishment in the classical sense, but an attempt to correct the cause of the problem. This is divine justice – measure for measure – in which the response repairs the error.

BABEL AND *MABUL*

This brief story focuses on the attempts by the few to contain and control the many, even at the expense of innovation.[10] The location of this incident is called Babel, meaning confusion, as God confused the languages. Interestingly, the *Mabul* was also a great, creative confusion, and the similarity between the words *Mabul* and Babel (indeed, they come from the same root), suggests a link between the two stories. More careful reflection, however, reveals that the similarity masks the profound difference between them.

The story of the *Mabul* is God's reaction to unfettered exercise of the human capacity to choose. The sons of E-lohim take whatever they want, with no limits. In response to humans overstepping their

---

10. Ironically, as the text points out, it is only through the scientific innovation of making bricks that the city-tower project could have been envisioned. Had the leaders been successful it may have been the last real innovation of that society.

boundaries, exercising their divine spark without restraint, God needs to bring about the *Mabul*. Quite different is our present incident, in which we are witness to the attempts to crush human creativity and limit expression of that divine spark.

These two stories stand as polar opposites expressing the limits, on both ends of the spectrum, of the acceptable expression of the divine spark. God endows humans with that spark so that it be exercised. On the one hand, we have no right to abdicate our rights to it. On the other, we must exercise caution in how broadly it is expressed. The *Mabul* is the result of the abuse of the divine spark; Babel is the response to the crushing repression of it. These two stories frame the boundaries of acceptable and desired human creativity. If God's initial experiment fails because of the lack of guidelines, He now provides those guidelines in the form of the two "confusion" narratives.

CONSTRUCTING A MEANINGFUL CHRONOLOGY

If the tale of Nimrod provides meaningful background to the Babel narrative, the lineage of Shem helps locate that incident within the biblical chronology. This lineage is chronicled twice. The first time it is included in the listing of the Table of Nations. Like his brothers, Shem also has descendants from whom emerge many of the families of Man. The second iteration of Shem's line, however, is quite different. It is headlined by its own *toledot*,[11] it provides us with ten generations of descendants (as opposed to a maximum of four generations for his two brothers), and most significantly, the Torah lists the life spans of each central figure as well as his age when the next-in-line is born.[12] Cross-referencing the two genealogical listings of Shem provides clues for the timing of the Great Dispersion in Babel.

In the first manifest of Shem we are told that Peleg, the fourth generation from Shem, received his name because "in his days the land was divided (*niflega*)." This is a reference to none other than the central

---

11. See the Introduction for an explanation of the significance of this.
12. In this regard, while the genealogical lists of Yefet and Ham are concise, reminiscent of the seven generations of Cain, the record of Shem's descendants echoes that of Seth, the son whom Eve bore to "replace" Abel.

event of the second ten generations of humanity, the division of the people into distinct nations and languages. We earlier asked why Peleg, of all people, should bear this name. There are two likely possibilities: the event coincided with his birth or it coincided with his death. It is highly unlikely that a mere four generations after the *Mabul* there would be enough people to be split into seventy nations. Most likely, then, is that the event is coterminous with Peleg's death. Indeed, one rabbinic midrash concerned with chronology[13] notes that, according to the biblical text (10:26–30), thirteen children of Peleg's younger brother were included in the dispersion of mankind, concluding that the dispersion coincides with Peleg's death.

The second genealogy of Shem puts Peleg's death at 340 years after the *Mabul*. Thus, while Nimrod's place among the descendants of Ham provides a conceptual reference for the story of Babel, Peleg's place in the parallel description of the descendants of Shem contributes a chronological reference to the story.

The significance of that chronology, however, is not merely for establishing a biblical version of history. The Bible is not concerned with history as a record of events, it is interested in understanding what those events mean in the larger scheme of man's relationship with God, and how any story interacts with the rest of the biblical narrative – that is, how other stories affect our understanding of this one, and how this one impacts on our understanding of other biblical narratives. If indeed the dispersion occurs with Peleg's death, then according to that chronology Abram is alive at that time! In fact, he would have been forty-eight years old, and fully aware of the events.

It is no wonder that numerous midrashim place Abram at the scene in Babel.[14] It is also not surprising that the rabbinic imagination

---

13. *Seder Olam Rabba* 1.
14. Genesis Rabba 38:13; 44:7; 63:2. From the perspective of this midrash, other elements in the biblical text begin to take on a new light. Abram's father, Terah, mysteriously leaves Ur Kasdim (Ur of the Chaldees, a.k.a. Babel) to journey to Canaan. We may never know why he intended to go to Canaan or why he decided to stay in Ḥaran upon his arrival there, but according to this chronology we now know why he leaves his home – because *everyone* was leaving there as a result of the Tower of Babel. Terah's journey is part of the great dispersion of man.

generates dialogue, or debate, between him and Nimrod: if Nimrod is identified as the tyrannical leader in Babel determined to supplant God by ruling over all humanity, as well as the driving force behind the attempt to crush human creativity in the construction of the city and tower, Abram, the first person in ten generations with whom God speaks, challenges Nimrod's arrogance and restores a sense of divine order. Listen to one popular version of an encounter between the two:[15]

> Nimrod: Bow down to the fire!
> Abram: And why not bow down to water, which can extinguish the fire?
> Nimrod: Bow to the water!
> Abram: If so, we should bow down to the clouds, which bear the water.
> Nimrod: Bow down to the clouds!
> Abram: If so, we should bow down to the wind, which can scatter the clouds.
> Nimrod: Bow down to the wind!
> Abram: And why not bow down to people, who can withstand the wind?
> Nimrod: You are taunting me with words! I bow down only to the fire. I will throw you into it – let the God you worship come and save you!

The rabbinic account complements the biblical one, picking up on the subtle clues within the biblical text. The story of Babel, with Nimrod at the helm, is indeed a form of rebellion against God, and Abram – later to become Abraham – is God's champion in that den of human hubris.[16]

Twenty-seven years after his arrival in Ḥaran, his son Abram receives a message from God to leave that place and continue his journey. By the time Abram arrives in Canaan, the Canaanites – who also left Babel – had already settled in.

15. Genesis Rabba 38:13. Numerous midrashic comments paint Abram as the counter-figure to Nimrod. See Leviticus Rabba 27:5; 28:4; Ecclesiastes Rabba 2, 4; *Midrash Zuta, Ecclesiastes* 2:14, 26; *Pesikta DeRav Kahana* 8.
16. This is implied in many midrashic comments and explicit in *Otzar HaMidrashim,* p. 135.

THE PRE-HISTORY OF THE WORLD

Even without midrashic commentary, the genealogical lists provide a
rich picture of the Bible's conceptual presentation of the pre-history of
humanity. With the interpolation of the story of Babel, that pre-history
is infused with even greater meaning. God's initial attempt to establish
a relationship with humanity falls short because there are insufficient
guidelines. Absent a code to direct their behavior, people degenerate into
chaos, and take the rest of the world with them. When God starts again,
He provides them with the basic protocols, but in their overreaction to
the chaos which reigned pre-*Mabul,* they establish so much order that
they crush the very humanity they were trying to protect.

With the boundaries of abuse clearly established on both ends of
the spectrum, God is prepared to try again. Perhaps the third attempt,
with the new modifications God will make, will yield a better result.

Part II

Covenantal Couples

Genesis 11:27–12:5

Choosing Abraham

T he fifth chapter of Mishna Avot contains the following insight:

> There were ten generations from Adam to Noah, to make it known
> how patient God is, for all those generations increasingly pro-
> voked Him until He brought on them the waters of the Flood.
> There were ten generations from Noah to Abraham, to make it
> known how patient God is, for all those generations increasingly
> provoked him until Abraham our father came and earned merit
> for them all. (2–3)

In this striking passage, the rabbis describe how over the course
of twenty generations,[1] God's hope to have direct interaction with all of
humanity is met with repeated, colossal disappointment, necessitating a
new approach. God will no longer strive to establish relationships directly
with all people and not even with one entire family. Rather, he will
choose one individual – later to become a family and ultimately a nation –
with whom He will communicate directly. That person-family-nation,

---

1. There were actually only nineteen, as Noah is counted both as the tenth of the first
   set and the first of the second set.

through personal example, teaching, and contact with others, will be the vehicle for communicating the divine message.

As part of this new approach, the standards for the chosen ones are raised, with greater expectations and challenges alongside enhanced rewards. By necessity, those different standards require the chosen emissaries to be distinguished in a number of ways, as would befit any ambassador or royal emissary.

One of the great mysteries surrounding Abram is why God chooses him. There is very little information in the text about him prior to the dramatic call of *lekh lekha* (Go forth! [12:1]). This problem is so troublesome that the rabbis tell a wonderful story about Abram to suggest that it is not God who chooses him but rather Abram who chooses God:

> Terah (Abraham's father) was an idol maker. One day he needed to travel and left Abraham to sell in his stead. A man entered the store seeking to buy an idol. Abraham asked him, "How old are you?" "I am fifty, maybe sixty," he responded. Abraham exclaimed, "Woe to the man who is fifty or sixty years old and wants to worship something which is one day old!" Embarrassed, the customer left. Next, a woman entered the store with a platter of fine flour which she wished to bring as an offering. Abraham took a stick and smashed all the idols, leaving the stick in the hand of the largest one. When Terah returned he asked, "Who did all this?" Abraham responded: "A woman entered and asked me to bring her flour-offering. The idols began to argue, 'I want to eat first!' and 'No! I want to eat first!' The largest of them picked up the stick and broke the others." Terah said, "Why are you mocking me? Are the idols capable of anything?" Abraham responded, "Your ears should hear what your own mouth is saying!"[2]

---

2. It is fascinating that this story is not purely the result of rabbinic imagination. Rather, it is a rabbinic adaptation of the story of Gideon (Judges 6:25–31). For an analysis of the parallels between these two figures, see Nathaniel Helfgot, *Mikra and Meaning* (Jerusalem: Maggid Books, 2012), 55–64.

The necessity the rabbis felt to tell that story accentuates what is absent from the text. In this chapter we will examine the evidence in the biblical text, both prior to and following Abram's selection, to better understand God's choice and its implications.

THE LEGACY OF TERAH

As we noted earlier, Genesis can be identified as a book of *toledot* – legacies. Only thirteen times in the Bible is a section introduced by the words "*Eleh toledot*" ("This is the legacy of…") or "*Zeh sefer toledot*" ("This is the book of the legacy of…"). Eleven of those are in the Book of Genesis. This literary element is so dominant that Genesis could easily be read as being comprised of eleven books of *toledot*, each of which ends just before the next one begins, with chapter 1 as an introductory chapter.

This insight leads us to a somewhat puzzling observation. There is a *toledot* Terah, but no *toledot* Abram or *toledot* Abraham, that is, no legacy specifically attributed to Abraham. In fact, it would seem that Terah leaves a legacy under which Abraham's entire life's work is subsumed. Given Abraham's prominence throughout the Bible and Terah's apparent lack of importance, this seems counterintuitive.[3] How are we to make sense of this?

A close examination of Terah's introduction to us reveals a surprising, perhaps even revolutionary, aspect of the man.

Terah is introduced at the juncture between the descendants of Seth and the emergence of Abram (11:26–32). Right from the start it is clear that he represents the end of one era and the beginning of a new one: each previous generation is introduced as having borne a single son (there were surely other sons, but they were apparently unimportant to the story), while Terah has three, fitting into the Genesis pattern in which individuals at critical junctures in the narrative have three sons.[4]

---

3. Rabbinic literature tends to portray Terah's essence as an idolater, likely because this is mentioned in Joshua 24:2. Within the Torah, Terah's name and story span no more than seven verses (11:26–32).
4. There appears to be a pattern within the three-son structure. One son is clearly outside of the main story line (Cain, Ham, Haran), one is the central figure from whom the story will continue (Seth, Shem, Abram), and one son plays a "supporting role" (Abel, Yefet, Nahor).

More interesting, however, is the Torah's excessive mention of familial relationships when describing Terah and his family, in exaggerated contrast to all prior generations. Listen to the description of the journey Terah initiates (11:31): "Terah took Abram *his son*; Lot *the son of Haran, his grandson*; Sarai *his daughter-in-law, the wife of his son Abram*." Every relationship mentioned in this verse is unnecessary. Just four verses earlier the Torah informs us that Abram is Terah's son and that Lot is his grandson from Haran; just two verses earlier the Torah mentions that Sarai is Abram's wife. The text could have easily been written succinctly as: "Terah took Abram, Lot, and Sarai," yet it repeats and accentuates the familial bonds. It seems the Torah wants to focus our attention on the paramount importance of family for Terah.

The very fact that Terah takes his orphaned grandson suggests a sense of responsibility for grandchildren (contrast that with Noah, who curses his grandson). That sense of responsibility, however, is even further highlighted by the use of the verb *vayikaḥ* – "he took." It is the same verb used in this very narrative with regard to Abram and Nahor, who took wives. Their "taking" of wives are apparently also acts of responsibility, as the wives they took – Milka and Sarai (most likely another name for Yiska[5]) – were their orphaned nieces. Orphaned nephews are adopted; orphaned nieces are married. That is how they are cared for.[6]

The value of family, with the associated responsibilities, is Terah's legacy. It is not surprising that the end of *toledot* Terah indicates this as well. As we saw earlier, each book of *toledot* ends just before the next one begins. *Toledot* Terah ends with the death of Abraham and his burial (25:8–9). It is the first time in the Torah that we have a man being buried by his children. The sense of family responsibility has been extended to children's responsibility for their parents. Moreover, both Isaac and Ishmael bury Abraham. Even the family torn by strife is unified by the sense of responsibility for parents.[7]

5. See Rashi, 11:29. See also Devora Steinmetz, *From Father to Son: Kinship, Conflict, and Continuity in Genesis* (Louisville, KY: Westminster John Knox Press, 1991), 166–167.
6. This may be why the rabbis suggest that Mordekhai was married to his orphaned cousin, Esther. See Megilla 13a and the comment of Ibn Ezra on Esther 2:7.
7. In this light it is not surprising that Terah's son Nahor bears the same name as Terah's father. Terah honored his father by bestowing his name on his own son.

TAKING WIVES

The careful reader of the Bible is startled by the marriages of Abram and Nahor. The first eleven chapters of Genesis describe twenty generations of men; not mankind, but *men*. With rare exceptions (Adam and Lemekh), we read chapter after chapter of men begetting men. While it is obvious that women played a central role in the proliferation of humanity, their absence from the narrative speaks volumes. It likely reflects the culture and mores of the times: a strictly patriarchal society centered on men, in which women's primary role is to carry the man's seed for the next generation of men.

Enter Terah's children. Abram and Nahor are the first individuals in the line of Seth to be described as taking wives. Moreover, it becomes clear early on that Sarai is barren. In a society in which women's function is to serve as incubators for men's seed, taking – and keeping – a wife who cannot bear children is nothing short of revolutionary. If such a revolution were to take place it would make sense for it to happen within the sphere of Terah, the man for whom family relationships, responsibilities, and commitments are ever present. The concept of a wife being more than a child-delivery system is new, and it is eminently appropriate to find this innovation in the household of the one who (at least in the Torah) effectively "invents" the family.

Ironically, we never hear of Terah's wife. This may suggest that his focus on family relationships and responsibilities is limited to blood relatives, and that it is his children, who *do* take wives, who extend the concept of family to include spouses.

ABRAM CONTINUES TERAH'S LEGACY

We earlier pointed to a curious observation that all of Abraham's life seems to be subsumed under the legacy of Terah. At least from one perspective, that puzzling insight is no longer so strange. If Terah's innovation is the centrality of the family, and Abram continues or even extends that value, then at least that aspect of Abram's legacy should be credited to his father. In fact, a careful look at the Torah's description of two journeys makes this link between Terah and Abram unmistakable, and the evidence is so compelling that Abram's initial mission can be formulated as the command to complete that which his father began. Let us look at two parallel verses written only five verses apart, one describing Terah's journey from Ur Kasdim and the other narrating Abram's journey from Ḥaran:

Terah's journey (11:31)	Abram's journey (12:5)
Terah took	Abram took
Abram his son	
Lot the son of Haran, his grandson;	Lot, his nephew;
Sarai his daughter-in-law, the wife of his son Abram.	Sarai, his wife;
	and all their possessions and the souls they acquired in Ḥaran.
They left together from Ur Kasdim	They left
to go to the land of Canaan,	to go to the land of Canaan,
but they arrived in Ḥaran and stayed there.	and they arrived in the land of Canaan.

Note that the structure of the two texts is identical. Even the unnecessary descriptions of the family relationships (how many times do we need to be told that Sarai is Abram's wife and that Lot is his nephew?) are copied in the description of Abram's journey. And just as Terah takes responsibility for his orphaned grandson, Abram takes that same lad, Lot – his orphaned nephew – under his wing. The key difference between the two descriptions is that while Terah plans to go to Canaan, he never arrives (he mysteriously stops in Ḥaran and never completes his journey), while Abram finishes the trek that Terah starts and makes it to Canaan.

Both literally, in terms of the arrival in Canaan, and figuratively, in terms of developing the notion of family, Abram completes Terah's journey. This provides an entirely new focus to Abram's life, to the mission with which God entrusts him, and to the challenges he will face. Unsurprisingly, most of the challenges Abram/Abraham will face revolve around his family: the command to leave his father; Sarai's encounters with Pharaoh in Egypt and with Avimelekh in Gerar; Lot in Sodom; Hagar and Sarai; the banishment of Ishmael and the Binding of Isaac – all involve sacrifices related to family. The man who champions the value of family will endure challenges to that core value.

WHY IS FAMILY SO IMPORTANT?

This brings us back to our opening question: Why does God choose Abram? Now we have a clue. God chooses him because of his deep commitment to the value of family. But that conclusion itself begs the question: Is that enough? Does Terah's value of family connection and responsibility justify the choice of Abram to be God's emissary? And if Terah's concept of family is so revolutionary, then why is Terah himself not chosen for the mission?

Terah's disqualification may be linked to his status as an idolater (Josh. 24:2). While Terah's innovation with regard to family is significant, to the extent that Abraham's entire life is subsumed under Terah's legacy, it is insufficient for him to become God's emissary because he worships multiple gods. But it is likewise insufficient to simply disqualify Terah. It behooves us to find a justification for the choice of Abram. That text does exist, but not where we expect to find it. It does not surface until Genesis 18, some twenty-four years after God's initial revelation to Abram, and immediately prior to the destruction of Sodom. It is there that we are privy to God's thoughts regarding why He decides to reveal the impending event to Abraham:

> Can I conceal from Abraham that which I am about to do? Abraham will become a great and mighty nation, and through him will come blessing to all other nations of the earth. Since I know that he will instruct his children and his household after him, that they will observe God's way in doing righteousness and justice – that is why Abraham will receive all of that which has been spoken about him. (18:18–19)

Two things stand out in God's words. First, the opening identifies Abraham as the one who will become a great and mighty nation and through whom will come blessing to all the other nations. This is a clear reference to God's first direct communication with Abram, where God instructs him to embark on his journey and promises that he "will become a great nation," and that through him will come "blessing to all the families of the earth" (12:2–3).[8] It is now clear that God links sharing Sodom's fate with Abraham to His initial choice of Abram. To paraphrase God, "The same Abram I chose initially is the one with whom I have chosen to share this privileged information."

Second and even more extraordinary is that God reveals here precisely *why* He chooses Abram in the first place. Abraham understands that the family is a powerful vehicle for transmission of values, particularly those of *tzedaka* (righteousness) and *mishpat* (justice), and Abraham, through the vehicle of the family, will endeavor to promulgate those values.

Abraham actually has two core values. One is the family; the other is the combination of *tzedaka* and *mishpat*.[9] The marriage of these two core values is the foundation for the choice of Abram. While Abram likely learns the value of family from his father, from where does he glean the values of *tzedaka* and *mishpat*? There are two possibilities: either Abraham creates them himself or they are part of a received tradition.

ABRAM'S INNOVATION

A midrashic tradition describes Abram as being a student in the "yeshiva of Shem and Ever." This loaded, anachronistic phrase needs to be unpacked. First, the word "yeshiva" is meant to evoke the sense of a

---

8. Now we notice that God's blessing will come upon the "families of the earth"; not only is the family the source of blessing, it is also the vehicle for *receiving* the blessing. The "families of the earth" refers back to God's unsuccessful attempt to interact with Noah's family and the subsequent dispersion of families.

9. This pair of words appears dozens of times throughout the Bible. Courts are enjoined to combine these two values (Lev. 19:15; 35; Deut. 1:16; 16:18), kings are judged by their ability to combine them (II Sam. 8:15; I Kings 1:9; Is. 9:6; 32:1; Jer. 22:13; Ps. 72:1; 99:4), society is judged by its valuation of them (Is. 1:21–27; 5:7; Jer. 22:3), and God is identified as the champion of them (Is. 5:16; Jer. 9:23; Ps. 9:8–9; 97:2; 99:4).

tradition transmitted from teacher to student. Second, the heads of this yeshiva are identified as Shem and Ever, Noah's son and one of Shem's great-grandchildren (11:14), respectively. Why would rabbinic tradition pick these two individuals?

Shem is the son upon whom Noah bestows a special blessing. Noah, identified as a *tzaddik* (a righteous man) in a generation marked by the absence of righteousness, saw something proper – even Godly – in Shem: "Blessed be A-donai, God of Shem … E-lohim should grant beauty to Yefet but dwell in the house of Shem" (9:26–27). Regarding Ever, we are introduced to him even before he is born. In mapping out the families of Noah's sons, the Torah describes the following: "And to Shem as well, there were children born; he is the father of all the descendants of Ever" (10:21). This is a striking introduction to Shem, particularly since we do not yet know who Ever is – he is born only three verses later.

Apparently, the Torah is suggesting that there is a profound link between Shem and Ever, and between Shem and all those considered "Ever-ites," or *Ivrim* (later to be translated as "Hebrews"). When Abram is later identified as an *Ivri*, the meaning is immediately clear – he is an Ever-ite, both by blood and because he bears the Ever-ite tradition. If we tie together the strands of this thought, the Ever-ite tradition Abram receives is the one of righteousness and justice first identified in Noah (the only righteous man in a corrupt world), recognized by Noah in Shem, and transmitted to Ever.

Assuming this interpretation is correct, we are once again perplexed. If indeed Abram carries a tradition of *tzedaka* and *mishpat* from Ever, which had been passed on through Shem (or, in rabbinic language, a tradition learned in the yeshiva of Shem and Ever), why are Shem and Ever not chosen by God for the *lekh lekha* command and blessing? Was the student worthy but the teachers not?

The answer, I believe, is that while Shem and Ever may be champions of those special values, they have no reliable vehicle through which to transmit them. Noah waits to see the potential in one of his sons before blessing him; Shem waits for three generations before he finds someone worthy to teach; Ever waits even longer before Abram comes along. Without a stable means for transmitting values, they need to wait until a worthy recipient of their tradition can be found. For an emissary chosen by God to be the bearer of His message, this is insufficient.

Abram presents a new model, as he marries the values of family he learns from his father with the values of *tzedaka* and *mishpat* learned from Shem and Ever. He understands that the family is the appropriate vehicle for the transmission of those values. Abram's model declares that ensuring the transmission of values requires the creation of a self-perpetuating system which embodies those values and actively pursues passing them along. That system is called the family, and Abram transforms the family from an end unto itself into a means to a nobler goal.

And so God chooses Abram, not his father Terah for whom family is its own goal, and not Shem and Ever, who carry the torch of *tzedaka* and *mishpat* but who are unable to transmit those values to their own children. It is this combination that God reveals to us, but only later, which explains God's choice of Abram: "I know that he will instruct his children and his household after him, that they will observe God's way in doing righteousness and justice" (18:19).

MOVING FORWARD

Returning to our opening mishna, God waits twenty generations for Abram to arrive. It is this man, with his unique combination of values along with the desire and plan to transmit them, who will be God's "point man" in His interaction with the rest of humanity. Unbeknownst even to himself, Abram carries on his shoulders God's hope for all of humanity and will "earn merit for them all."

Genesis 12:1–9

Seeking and Seeing

Lt is difficult to know precisely why Terah initially thinks to leave Ur Kasdim and move toward Canaan.[1] As we saw earlier, according to one version of the biblical chronology, the story of the Great Dispersion takes place when Abraham is forty-eight years old. If that is true, then it is not just Terah who is on the move; everyone is on the move! The initial choice of Canaan makes sense, as it sits at the crossroads of three major continents and would be a superb place to establish some kind of trading post.[2] If Terah's initial intention is to reach a major crossroads, then when he reaches Ḥaran and finds that it sits on the intersection of two continents, it serves as an excellent alternative without necessitating further travel.

In the previous chapter we demonstrated the connection between Abram's and Terah's journeys, and established that Abram is to complete

---

1. This question is likely one of the causes for Ibn Ezra, 11:31; 12:1, to suggest that God's command to Abram to leave Ur Kasdim actually preceded Terah's trip, and that it is Abram, not Terah, who initially moves the family from Ur Kasdim. See also Nahmanides' comment on 11:28 and 12:1 for a scathing critique of Ibn Ezra and a creative, albeit highly speculative, suggestion. In the next section we will offer an alternative to both Ibn Ezra and Nahmanides.
2. See Yoel Bin Nun, *Pirkei HaAvot* [Hebrew] (Alon Shevut, Israel: Tevunot, 2003), 37.

what Terah began. In this chapter we will demonstrate the profound difference between their journeys and discover that God's command involves a much more nuanced and complex mission. Here is the text of God's call:

> God said to Abram: Leave your *aretz*, your *moledet*, and your *beit av*, to go to the land which I will show you. I will make you into a great nation. I will bless you, and I will make your name great, and you shall be a blessing. I will bless those who bless you, and those who curse you shall themselves be cursed; through you shall come blessing to all the families of the earth. (12:1–3)

WHAT MUST ABRAM LEAVE?

Let us begin with an exploration of exactly what it is that God is asking Abram to leave. In the Torah it is described by three expressions – *aretz*, *moledet*, and *beit av*. The first is the easiest. *Aretz* is usually translated as land, and that is perfectly appropriate in this context. God wants Abram to relocate, to leave his current land and move to a different one.

The second term, *moledet*, is a bit more complex. It is often translated as birthplace, but that doesn't work here. After all, Abram's birthplace is Ur Kasdim, and he already left there when his father moved the family at the end of Genesis 11. The context therefore demands a new interpretation of *moledet*, and I believe that it is related to the concept of group or national identity.[3] It is certainly used that way in contemporary Hebrew, and in this context it means that as Abram relocates himself geographically God wants him to simultaneously eschew his group identity.

The third element, *beit av* (literally, "the father's home") likely refers to those values one learns at home. God also wants Abram to abandon some of the values he has learned in his father's house, probably referring to Terah's idolatry.[4]

---

3. See S. D. Luzzatto, 12:1, s.v. *umimoladtekha*, where he explains that *moledet* refers to national affiliation. See also Esther 2:10, 2:20.
4. Remember that Terah's idolatry is explicit in the Book of Joshua, where Joshua cites God as saying that He removed Abram from that idolatrous culture: "Your ancestors – Terah, both Abraham and Nahor's father – lived on the other side of the river, and they worshiped other gods. But I took your father, Abraham, from

When we put the picture together, God is essentially asking Abram to abandon three fundamental elements of his identity:[5] his geographical connection, his national affiliation, and even some of the core values he learned at home. The combination of these three elements form the core of one's identity vis-à-vis the external world. (This is not the identity of "Who am I?" but of "Who am I in context of?") Lest the reader think that this is too much of a stretch, this combination of expressions resurfaces by the one person identified in the Bible as leaving behind her origins to affiliate with the Hebrews, and by another identified by the rabbis as doing the same.

Ruth, surprised by Boaz's generosity of spirit, asks why he is so kind to her. His response is brief and to the point: "Boaz responded and said to her, 'I was told about all that you had done for your mother-in-law following the death of your husband; you left your mother and father and the *eretz* of your *moledet*'" (Ruth 2:11). The language of the father's home, the *eretz*, and the *moledet* unmistakably parallels the language used with Abram, and the meaning of that formula is clear: the renunciation of one identity and the adoption of a new one. As Ruth herself famously says to Naomi: "For where you go I shall go, where you sleep I shall sleep; your nation is my nation and your God is my God" (Ruth 1:16). Ruth's declaration of allegiance is her statement of trading in one affiliative identity for another – in rabbinic language, conversion to the Hebrew people.[6]

There is yet another biblical character who is considered in much of rabbinic literature to be a convert, but about whom certain questions

---

the other side of the river and caused him to traverse the entire land of Canaan" (Josh. 24:2–3). According to this reading, quite different from the midrash cited earlier, it is not Abram who discovers God but God who discovers Abram!

5. Eventually, God will even change Abram's name to Abraham. There are few statements more powerful with regard to identity transformation and selfhood than changing one's name. Ferdinand Tonnies, *Community and Society*, trans. and ed. C. P. Loomis (New York: Harper & Row, 1957), proposed that there are three essential elements to community: kinship, place, and mindset, paralleling the three elements God asks Abram to trade.

6. This is not the place to discuss the notion of conversion in the biblical era. Interestingly, Maimonides' codification of the conversion process includes a strong element of national affiliation and identification with both the history and the destiny of the Jewish people (*Laws of Forbidden Intercourse* 14:1).

remain. Moses' father-in-law, Yitro, greets him at Mount Sinai and expresses recognition of the Hebrew God as the greatest of all. Later, in the Book of Numbers, we find a conversation between Moses and his father-in-law,[7] in which the latter declares that he plans to return to his *aretz* and his *moledet* – ostensibly his geographical and national home in Midian – yet there is no mention of the third element, his *beit av*. It seems that following his own revelation of the truth of God, Yitro has no intention of returning to the religious values he learned at home despite his feeling that he has no place in Israel.

WHY MUST ABRAM LEAVE?

Assuming that our analysis is correct, what God is expecting of Abram is far more significant than relocation. He is asking that Abram abdicate core elements of his identity. This raises the challenge considerably and makes Abram's fulfillment of the command that much more significant, as God is not merely asking him to abandon his identity, He is offering Abram to replace it with a new one.

Let us again look at God's declaration. Regarding the land, God not only tells Abram to leave his *aretz*, He promises Abram a new *aretz*, the land that He will show him. Regarding national identity, He asks Abram to leave his *moledet* but offers to build him into his own nation, replacing the one he is leaving. And with regard to the religious values component, He asks Abram to leave the idolatrous relationships he had in Ur Kasdim and Ḥaran and offers to replace them with a unique relationship with the One God who can provide blessing and curse.

The question, of course, is why it is important for Abram to undergo such a transformation.[8] If we return to our opening mishna about Abraham's place in the world following twenty generations,

---

7. It is unclear whether the character in that incident is Yitro or his son. The specific identification is less significant than the identity issues raised. For more on this incident see Zvi Grumet, "Within and Without the Encampment: The Ambivalent Acceptance of a Biblical Convert," *Tradition* 27:3 (Spring 1994).

8. A note of caution is in place here. There are certain questions for which we can only speculate, and when it comes to suggesting a rationale for divine decisions, we must do so with the appropriate humility and the understanding that our explanations are mere speculations.

it appears that God has decided to change His approach in dealing with humankind. No longer will blessing and curse and the divine message come directly from God. They will now be channeled through Abram: "I will bless those who bless you, and those who curse you shall themselves be cursed; through you shall come blessing to all the families of the earth." God wants to bring blessing to all humanity, but will now operate through His emissary. Abram must be transformed to take on that role. He must become someone new.

The choice of an emissary, and particularly the manner in which it is being done, is somewhat paradoxical. For Abram to be God's emissary he must make a break from his past and from that which is familiar. He must adopt a new selfhood as he embraces a new land, fathers a new nation, and builds a new kind of relationship with God. Abram must break from his origins to be able to assume a significant role vis-à-vis the world. He and his descendants must become Other, and therein lies the paradox, for in their "otherness" they must build connections with the rest of humanity in order to be able to channel the divine blessing.

Moses, too, undergoes a traumatic dislocation, first from his birth home and then from his adopted one, in order to return to lead the people. When he returns he is able to bring a perspective unlike theirs and a vision of the possible, and it is precisely because he leaves their reality that he is able to achieve that. And just like Abram, Moses becomes Other[9] to the people even as he tries to reconnect with them.

Abram's role as God's emissary to the rest of humanity is likely the reason that God wants him to go Canaan. It is, after all, the crossroads of the biblical world. While Terah may have sought it out for its business potential, for God it is the place where Abram and his family will have the greatest number of opportunities to interact with the people who they are to impact and to whom they are to bring blessing. Canaan, the crossroads of Shem, Ham, and Yefet, is the optimal place

9. Moses' "otherness" is expressed in his hesitation to go to the people, with the claim that they will not listen to him (Ex. 4:1). It is perhaps for this reason that on his return to Egypt he needs to reconnect with his people through the act of circumcision (ibid., 4:24–25). Ironically, Moses will eventually achieve a permanent status of Other as he descends Mount Sinai with his face aglow, to the extent that he needs to wear a veil separating himself from the people (ibid., 34:29–35).

to create an outpost to spread God's word. To become God's emissary Abram must become distinct from the sons of Noah and from everyone else, yet in order to be that emissary, he must maximize his interactions with people.

ABRAM THE SEEKER

And so Abram begins his journey, but with one significant difficulty. He is not quite sure of the destination. While the reader who knows the end of the story is aware that his destination is Canaan, God does not reveal that to Abram. Instead, He tells Abram to go to "the land that I will show you" (12:1). For some inexplicable reason Abram journeys toward Canaan, perhaps seeking to complete his father's journey, and awaits God's message to tell him when to stop. Much to our surprise God never does tell him explicitly when to stop, and we never hear God tell Abram that he has actually arrived. What, then, does happen?

> Abram took Sarai, his wife; Lot, his nephew; all their possessions; and the souls they acquired in Ḥaran. They left to go to the land of Canaan and they arrived in the land of Canaan. Abram passed through the land until the place of Shekhem, until Elon Moreh; the Canaanite was then in the land. God appeared to Abram and said, "I will give this land to your children," and Abram built there an altar to the God who appeared to him. He moved from there to the mountain, east of Beit El, and pitched his tent, with Beit El on the west and the Ai on the east; he built there an altar to God and called out in the name of God. Then Abram continued journeying southward. (12:5–9)

The map of Abram's travels clarifies what is happening. Abram's first stop in the land is Shekhem, essentially the first city one encounters when crossing from the eastern mountain ridge (in present-day Jordan) to the western ridge. The ancient route is well known, using the river-cut wadis to descend and ascend the mountains. Abram follows the Yabok stream to descend from the mountain route he took from Ḥaran, crosses the Jordan at the ancient (and modern) Adam crossing, and continues

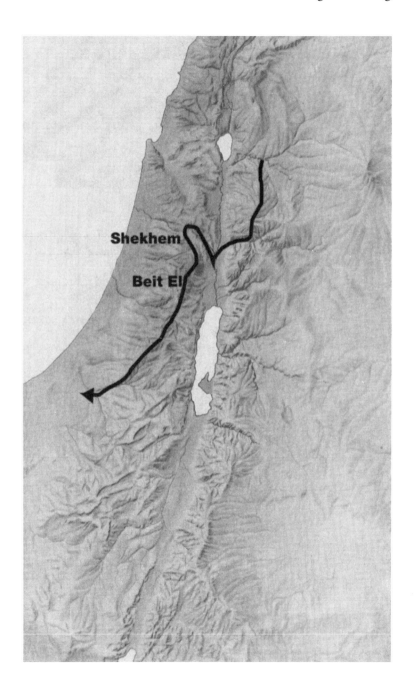

westward up the Tirtza stream, to arrive at the foot of the mountain route on the western side of the Jordan – at Shekhem.[10]

When he arrives in Shekhem he receives his second revelation from God, in which he is informed that this land will eventually be given to his children. While many of us assume this is God's way of letting him know that he has arrived in the right place, Abram clearly does not think so. He continues to journey southward on the mountain route.

Prior to continuing, however, Abram builds an altar to the God "who appeared to him." The purpose of that altar is far from clear, because Abram does *not* do what one usually does with an altar – offer sacrifices upon it. Abram builds the altar and moves on. It appears that the altar is to serve as a marker, a milestone for his descendants. When they arrive in the land to look for the place promised by God, they should look for an altar. And why does Abram choose an altar as his symbol? Because the altar is not merely a territorial marker saying, "I was here first"; those markers are well known throughout the world and even in the animal kingdom. The symbol Abram chooses indicates that his claim of the land comes from a higher authority. It is God Himself who promises it to Abram's children.

Construction of the altar notwithstanding, Abram continues southward, still awaiting a clear indication from God that he has arrived at his intended destination. When Abram does not receive that clear message, he calls out to God at Beit El, apparently asking for further instruction: "He built there an altar to God and called out in the name of God" (12:8). Much to Abram's chagrin, however, God does not respond. Abram, lacking a clear sign to stop, continues his journey even further southward.

The next time we find Abram he has traveled so far southward that he is in Egypt. Understanding this part of Abram's journey is complicated by the introductory line, "There was a famine in the land,

---

10. Jacob, upon returning from his sojourn with his uncle Laban in Ḥaran, takes the same route. His mysterious nocturnal wrestling match takes place at the Yabok crossing, he stops at Sukkot (where the Yabok meets the Jordan), and continues up the Tirtza stream until he reaches Shekhem. For more on Biblical routes see Yohanan Aharoni, *Eretz Yisrael BiTekufat HaMikra* [Hebrew] (Jerusalem: Yad Ben Zvi, 1987).

so Abram went down to Egypt to dwell there, for the famine in the land was heavy" (12:10). It is hard to know if his trip to Egypt is the result of his continued travels and waiting for God's word or a result of the famine – or some combination of the two. For example, it is entirely plausible that Abram sees the famine as a sign from God that he is in the wrong place and that he needs to move on.[11]

What is most interesting is what happens when Abram leaves Egypt. The Torah uses a bizarre phrase to describe his voyage: "He went according to his journeys, from the Negev to Beit El, to the place where he had previously pitched his tent, between Beit El and the Ai" (13:3). The phrase "according to his journeys" (in Hebrew it is a single word) is both ambiguous and unnecessary. The text could just as easily have said that he went from the Negev to Beit El. Apparently, the Torah is not merely describing a continuation of his trip, as it had done previously, but is pointing out that Abram is actually retracing his steps. He is traveling along the same path and taking the same journeys that he had traveled earlier, albeit in reverse.[12] Essentially, after reaching Egypt, Abram understands that he has traveled too far, that he has missed the place, that God *had*, in fact, showed him the place but he had somehow missed the cue. So Abram retraces his steps, both to find the place and to begin learning to recognize God's signals.

Where does he stop? At Beit El, the same place where he earlier hoped to hear God's word but did not, where he built an altar and called out to God, waiting for a sign. Ironically, it is in Beit El that Abram initially intuits that he needs to call out to God, but does not yet understand that his intuition is perhaps linked to or inspired by God's calling to him. It is only after having missed the place, and looking carefully at every place he stops along the way, that he begins to understand.

---

11. Classical rabbinic literature offers multiple explanations for the famine and Abram's response. For example, Rashi and Radak understand it as a test from God (will he question God because of the famine?) which Abram passes (he does not question God), while Nahmanides understands Abram's decision to go to Egypt as a tragic misstep (abandoning the Promised Land because of hardship) with cosmic implications.
12. Rashi understands this verse similarly, but interprets it very differently.

It is there, at Beit El, where God finally appears to Abram: "Lift up your eyes and see, from the place where you are, northward and southward, eastward and westward. For all the land which you see I will give to you and to your descendants, forever" (13:14–15). It is there, in Beit El, and only after Abram discovers the place on his own, that God explicitly confirms for Abram that he has found the place.[13]

God's initial command to Abram is neither to *go to* the place God instructed nor to *find* it, but rather, to *seek* it. Searching for the place is no simple task. Not only does Abram not have clear directions, he is not even sure how God will communicate with him. After trial and error and missed cues, Abram ultimately learns to read God's clues. The ambiguity in God's instruction is intentional, putting Abram on the path of becoming a seeker.[14]

Abram's search for the place is not a test of his obedience to God, it is an essential element of how he will become who he will become. The search for, and ultimately the discovery of, the land, is empowering. Abram is not shown the land; he must figure out how to discern it. Abram's quest, including the missed signals and the detour to Egypt, mirror the first Man's quest for a mate. Both involve a process of discovery, with trial and error, the result of which is a greater appreciation of that which they sought.[15]

---

13. Beit El has a long history of being a sanctified place for both non-Jews and Jews who deviated from pure divine worship, but for the normative Hebrew it is religiously insignificant. It never hosts the Temple or Tabernacle and does not function as a place of worship. We will discuss this later in the context of Jacob's encounter there. The description of the mountain "between Beit El and the Ai" has led many to identify this place as Mount Baal Ḥatzor. Topping off at 1,016 meters (3,333 feet) above sea level, it is the tallest mountain south of Mount Meron (in the upper Galilee), offering commanding views of almost the entire biblical Promised Land. When Abram arrives there initially, it may be precisely the height and the expansive view that lead him to believe that he has reached the right place and which inspires him to call out to God, but only upon his return does he understand that divine providence has brought him there.

14. Some argue that Abram's following an ambiguous directive was a far greater leap of faith than a self-explanatory instruction. See, for example, Gersonides, 22:2.

15. Rabbi Joseph B. Soloveitchik suggests another parallel between exploring the land and the search for a soulmate. See *Reflections of the Rav* (Jerusalem: World Zionist Organization, 1979), 117–126.

ABRAHAM THE SEER

A midrashic insight notes that Abraham's career on the biblical stage is bracketed by two calls of *lekh lekha* ("Go forth!").[16] The first was the subject of discussion earlier in this chapter. The second is God's call to Abraham regarding the Binding of Isaac. Here is the text of that second one:

> It happened after these things that the Almighty called to Abraham and said to him, "Abraham," and Abraham answered, "Here I am." He said, "Take, please, your son, your only son, the one you love, Isaac, and go forth to the land of Moriah. And bring him up there as a burnt-offering on one of the mountains which I will tell you." (22:1–2)

A quick read of the two passages reveals the similarities between them. Both involve a call of *lekh lekha*, both require a sacrifice (in the first Abraham must give up his past, in the second he must sacrifice his future), both involve a triple description of the sacrifice ("your *aretz*, your *moledet*, your *beit av*," in the first; "your son, your only son, the one you love," in the second), and both require a journey to a destination in need of further clarification ("to the land which I will show you," in the first; "on one of the mountains which I will tell you," in the second).

Any time there are two parallel passages, those parallels are designed not only to show the similarities and links between the two but to invite us to explore the differences. One of the significant differences between these two texts is how Abraham proceeds. We've already seen that Abraham's initial journey is filled with exploration and searching, to the extent that he initially misses his mark and needs to retrace his steps to discover what he overlooked. This lack of direction is noticeably absent in the second *lekh lekha*. Abraham is sure of his plan, and early the next morning he arises and gathers everything and everyone he needs for his mission. Then, "And it was on the third day, Abraham lifted up his eyes and saw the place from afar." There is no searching, no exploration, and no doubt in Abraham's mind. He sees the place and knows.

---

16. Genesis Rabba 39:9.

A midrash describes this poignantly:

> On the third day Abraham saw a cloud hovering above the mountain. He turned to Isaac and asked, "Do you see what I see?" Isaac answered, "Yes." He then turned to the two lads accompanying him and asked what they saw. "Nothing," they said. "Then you need to stay here," he responded, and went onto the mountain with Isaac. (Genesis Rabba 56:2)

The two lads see what anyone else would have seen – hills and valleys, a partly cloudy sky. Abraham, having spent decades in the service of God, has learned to see differently. He once misses God's cue; he sees the entire Promised Land but sees nothing at all. Abraham is determined not to let that happen again. This time he sees the cloud, and understands. Abram the seeker will ultimately emerge as Abraham the seer, but there will be many hurdles to overcome in the process.

Genesis 12:4–13:18

Lot, the Nephew

We are first introduced to Lot at the end of Genesis 11. His father, Haran, dies early, and leaves behind an orphan. Terah, true to his pioneering of family responsibility, takes Lot on the journey from Ur Kasdim. In Genesis 12, it is Abram who continues his father's tradition, taking his orphaned nephew under his wing as he continues the journey to Canaan – but here we find a surprise.

The Torah states that "Abram took Sarai, his wife, and Lot, his nephew," as Abram successfully leads the family to Canaan (12:5). Yet the previous verse says that "Abram went as told by God and Lot went with him." Two verses, one immediately following the other, describe Lot's journey. Once again the similarity (and the repetition) of the two verses begs an investigation of the differences between them, and it is in those differences that we begin to discover the complexity of the relationship between Abram and Lot.

At the core is the question of why Lot is traveling with Abram. Terah is still alive, and Abram has another brother, Nahor, who can take care of the orphan. The two verses provide two divergent answers to the question, both of which are correct and not mutually exclusive, but fraught with the seeds of tension. The earlier verse describes the initiative as Lot's; for whatever reason – the text shares no clues yet – Lot decides that he wants to go with his uncle.

On the other hand, the next verse focuses on Abram taking Lot, much as he takes Sarai, suggesting that Abram has his own reason for bringing Lot along independent of Lot's decision. Again the text provides no clues, but we do have a hint from earlier in the text: Sarai is barren and Abram is childless. From Abram's perspective, the adopted nephew may be considered his heir. Thus, while Lot has his own (as yet unspecified) reason for traveling with Abram, Abram has his own motive for taking Lot.

The disparity between Abram's motives and those of Lot may explain why the verse describing Lot's motives omits the family associations. Lot is not interested in the Terah-Abram value of family. From his perspective, Abram may simply be a convenient vehicle for getting what he wants, hence, "Lot went with him" without the family attribution. By contrast, the verse describing Abram's perspective is explicit in describing Lot as Abram's nephew, just as it describes Sarai as Abram's wife. For Abram, Lot is a significant family member for whom he bears responsibility and for whom Abram may have plans.

But why *does* Lot go?

SPLITTING THE FAMILY

The next time we encounter Lot, he is still journeying with Abram and they are on the return trip from Egypt. While we have not as yet discussed what actually happens to Abram in Egypt (that will be discussed in the next chapter), it is sufficient to note here that Abram leaves Egypt with great wealth: "Abram had sheep, cattle, and donkeys, male and female servants, she-donkeys and camels" (12:16); "Abram went up from Egypt – he and his wife and all his possessions and Lot with him – toward the Negev. Abram was very heavily laden with livestock, silver, and gold" (13:1–2). Lot, by traveling with Abram, has amassed a small fortune of his own as well: "And Lot, too, who was traveling with Abram, had sheep and cattle and tents" (13:5). Is the Torah trying to suggest that Lot's motivation is linked with what he perceives as a path to financial success?

It turns out that Lot has become so wealthy that he and Abram can no longer dwell together:

> The land could not support their dwelling together, for their possessions were great and they could not dwell together. There was strife between the herdsmen of Abram's flocks and the herdsmen of Lot's flocks. The Canaanite and the Perizzite were then dwelling in the land. Abram said to Lot: "Let there be no argument between me and you, and between my herdsmen and yours, for we are brothers. Behold, the entire land is open to you; separate from me. If you go left I will go right, and if you go right I will go left." Lot raised his eyes and saw the entire plain of the Jordan, that it was well watered – before God had destroyed Sodom and Gomorrah – like the garden of God, like the land of Egypt.... So Lot chose for himself the whole plain of the Jordan. (13:6–11)

At first glance this seems like a perfectly reasonable suggestion. If the land is too crowded, then the flocks need to be separated. Upon further consideration, however, it becomes apparent that both the scenario and the suggestion are actually absurd. Let us assume that their flocks were as numerous as one could imagine. Why could they not dwell together in Beit El (where Abram went upon his return from Egypt) and simply graze their flocks in different places? Abram's generous offer would have been no less generous were he to suggest that Lot choose either north or south of Beit El to graze his herds while Abram would graze his herds in the other direction so that the family could remain together in Beit El. Moreover, both Abram and Lot had shepherds tending their flocks; the family would be able to live in peace while they directed their shepherds to graze on different hills.

Even the assumption that the land cannot support the two herds is itself unreasonable. There are currently two other nations identified as living in the land, a land that will eventually be able support at least seven Canaanite nations and eventually hundreds of thousands or even millions of Israelites. Is it possible that the land is unable to support the flocks of two large clans, necessitating a dramatic geographical split between two parts of a united family? It appears that something else underlies this story.

Lot's motives are becoming clear. His primary priority is sheep. He sees the plains of the Jordan River valley, and despite the reputation of the Sodomites he chooses to dwell among them. The wealth he accumulates in Egypt, just by being in Abram's proximity, is his prime motivator, and it stands to reason that this has been driving him all along. In fact, Lot's newly acquired Egyptian wealth gives him a new appreciation for its associated culture. Looking out over the Sodomite plain, described as "like the garden of God, like the land of Egypt," Lot knows where he belongs.[1]

As for Abram, the man who values family above all, who adopts his orphan nephew in order to care for him – he seems all too eager to create a dramatic rift between them over grazing land. Abram seems to quickly give up on Lot as a potential heir. What could possibly cause him to shift so dramatically?

THE VIEW FROM HEBRON

Perhaps it is premature to conclude that Abram gives up on Lot.

As we just observed, Abram's suggestion to split seems extreme. Why should an argument over grazing land precipitate a complete separation, so that if Lot were to go south[2] Abram would go north, and vice versa? In fact, in the continuation of the story we find that Abram apparently breaks the deal he makes with Lot.

This incident begins in Beit El, just north of Jerusalem. Lot chooses to go to Sodom, which is southeast of their current location. According to Abram's suggestion, he should be traveling northwest, yet the next time we see Abram he sets up camp in Hebron, due south of Beit El and in the hills overlooking Sodom!

---

1. For an expanded version of this idea see Elhanan Samet, *Iyunim BeFarashat HaShavua*, 2nd series, vol. 1 [Hebrew] (Maaleh Adumim: Maaliot, 2004), 45–50. Samet argues that Lot was not materially motivated prior to the trip to Egypt but changed as a result of his sojourn there. See also Nehama Leibowitz, *Iyunim BeSefer Bereshit* [Hebrew] (Jerusalem: World Zionist Organization, 1975), 88–89, who apparently agrees with Samet's assertion based on a subtle textual shift describing Lot's travels prior to and immediately following the trip to Egypt.
2. In the Bible, the orientation is to the east. Directions to the right therefore mean south, while to the left mean north.

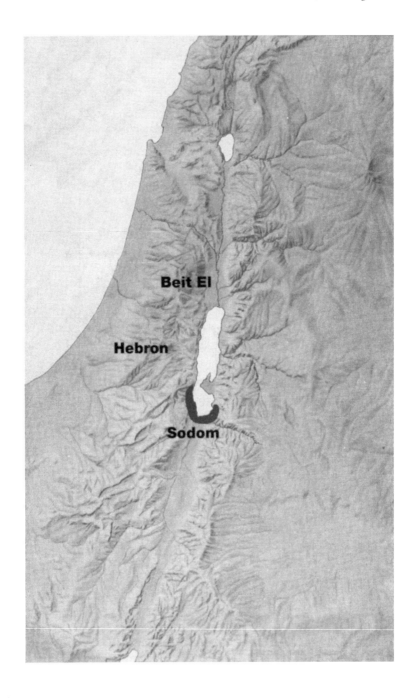

Apparently, despite what Abram *says* (that he will generate a significant distance between himself and Lot), what he actually *does* is follow Lot and keep watch from the hills of Hebron. Imagine a mother letting her child walk to school alone for the first time. She is likely to follow him from a distance to make sure that everything is okay, careful that he doesn't discover her subterfuge and discover that he is really not independent. Abram waits in Hebron – close enough to follow what is happening but far enough away so that Lot doesn't know that he's there – to give Lot his space, while keeping a watchful eye on him.[3]

In the next chapter Lot *does* get into trouble, as he is taken captive by four invading kings from the east, and Abram is called upon to rescue him (we will discuss this in greater depth later), vindicating Abram's intuition about Lot's choice. Not surprisingly, when Abram saves Lot (along with many other Sodomites) he is greeted as a hero and thanked by the king of Sodom and by Melchizedek (a nearby king), yet from Lot we hear silence. Lot's silence is revealing – to thank Abram would be to acknowledge his own error. Not only can Lot not confront Abram, he cannot confront his own failure in decision-making. So Lot offers not even a single word of thanks to Abram.

Lot reminds us of the overconfident teen who believes that he can make it on his own, and who bristles at the thought of adult involvement in his life (or even at the thought that an adult could be correct), but who does not know what to say when he needs the adult to bail him out of a difficult bind. Abram, on the other hand, is the cautiously optimistic guardian who wants to give that teen the opportunity to make his own mistakes while extending a safety net from afar.

This brings us back to Abram's exaggerated north-south response to the feud between the shepherds. The problem is not that the land cannot support the two of them, it is that *no land* can support them living together. Lot had amassed enough of his own wealth that he now needs to be independent of Abram. Abram understands that Lot needs

3. Lot's arrival in Sodom is marked by an odd verb, *vaye'ehal* (13:12), meaning he pitched his tent. Abram's parallel arrival in Hebron is distinguished by the same verb (13:18), again suggesting that he is shadowing Lot. These are the only two places in the Bible that the word appears in this form.

his space and he gives it to him, but takes the precautions to help ensure that the mistakes Lot makes will not be devastating ones.

Abram's encouragement of Lot to separate does not emerge from his giving up hope on Lot, but from precisely the reverse – from his desire to allow Lot to grow into his own independent person. He wants Lot to make his own decisions *and* feel like he is independent, while simultaneously keeping a close eye on Lot from Hebron.[4]

POSTPONING THE MISSION

Abram's care of Lot is yet another expression of the centrality of family and of responsibility within family. Yet Abram's decisions regarding Lot come at a price.

Terah, traveling from Ur Kasdim (Babel) after the Dispersion, intends to go to Canaan but never arrives. When Abram finally completes his father's journey, he finds that the Canaanites got there first: "Abram passed through the land until the place of Shekhem, until Elon Moreh; the Canaanite was then in the land" (12:6).[5] If that were not enough, as a result of Abram's initially missing the divine cue in Canaan and ending up in Egypt before turning back to find his intended destination, others settle in the land, for on his return we hear that "the Canaanite and the Perizzite were then dwelling in the land" (13:7). Each delay in Abram's claiming and settling of the land generates a vacuum which is filled by others who settle it first, complicating the fulfillment of God's promise to Abram and his descendants.

---

4. We will later discuss Lot's ultimate fate in the context of the destruction of Sodom.

5. Many have claimed this verse as a prooftext that the Torah was written at a time when there were no longer Canaanites in the land, postdating its writing to many hundreds of years after Moses. Ibn Ezra's cryptic comment on this verse suggested to many commentators, including the medieval R. Yosef ben Eliezer HaSephardi (fourteenth century) and Rabbi Moshe Almosnino (1518–1581), that Ibn Ezra held similarly. (The question of later additions to the Torah is beyond the scope of this book. For more on this, see Amnon Bazak, *Ad HaYom HaZeh* [Hebrew] [Tel Aviv: Miskal–Yedioth Ahronoth and Chemed Books, 1983]. See also Marc Shapiro, *The Limits of Orthodox Theology* [Oxford: Littman, 2004] and Menachem Kellner, *Must a Jew Believe Anything?* [Oxford: Littman, 2006].) According to my reading, this text cannot serve as a proof for that claim, as the verse is explaining that the Canaanite was *already then* in the land, that is, that their arrival preceded Abram's.

In our current story this apparently happens again. Abram pitches his tent in Hebron to keep an eye on his nephew Lot. Yet between Lot's departure and Abram's moving to Hebron there is another divine revelation:

> God had said to Abram following Lot's departure from him: Lift up your eyes and look from the place where you are – to the north and the Negev [south], and to the east and the sea [west] – for all the land which you see I will give to you and to your offspring, for eternity. I will place your offspring as the dust of the earth, so that if the dust of the earth can be counted so will your offspring. Rise up! Walk the length and breadth of the land, for to you I will give it. (13:14–17)

Two key observations leap out of this passage. First, it is now clear that from God's perspective, Lot is not Abram's intended heir. The text emphasizes that it is only "following Lot's departure" that the land is promised to Abram and his children. God wants to make it clear that He withheld that promise to Abram until Lot was out of the picture lest anyone think that Lot has a claim to the land as Abram's heir.

Second is that God commands Abram to walk the length and breadth of the land. In ancient times this was a way of demonstrating ownership, so that God is instructing Abram to effectively claim the land in fulfillment of the divine promise. Yet Abram's response is to set up camp in Hebron to keep an eye on Lot. Abram's trip to Hebron is not only a violation of his own word to Lot, it is also in defiance of God's explicit instruction to traverse the land and lay claim to it.

There is a price to pay for defying God and abandoning the land. Genesis 15 contains a central, if mysterious, text of the Abrahamic narrative. It involves a covenant God establishes with Abram accompanied by bizarre symbolism.[6] Our interest now is in the narrative at the end of that event, where the Torah tells us that God establishes a covenant with Abram regarding the land inhabited by "the Kenite, the Kenizzite, the Kadmonite, the Hittite, the Perizzite, the Refaim, the Emorite, the

---

6. We will discuss this later.

Canaanite, the Girgashite, and the Jebusite" (15:19–21). After Abram's delay in Hebron, his third delay already, the land is now inhabited by ten nations, not the one or two we saw earlier, and claiming that land is becoming increasingly challenging.

God chooses Abram because he possesses the core value of family. God promises him both his own offspring and the land in return for his reshaping his identity and joining God's adventure. While Abram does heed the call, he adheres to his core value, family, and in the process delays fulfillment of the divine promises – particularly that of the land. Each time Abram places family before land he creates another obstacle to the fulfillment of the divine command as more nations inhabit it and complicate the divine promise.

Given the choice between family and land, Abram – the champion of the family – chooses family.

Genesis 14:1–24

The Very First World War

Abram's commitment to Lot embroils him in a conflict unprecedented in biblical history. The battle, sometimes called the War of the Four Kings against the Five, ends up with the capture of Lot, which is ostensibly why it is included in the Torah text. Given that its apparent significance for the Torah rests on Abram's rescue of Lot, it is difficult to understand why the text provides such detailed background. Here is the opening narration:

> It was in the days of Amrafel, king of Shinar; Aryokh, king of Ellasar; Kedorlaomer, king of Elam; and Tidal, king of Goyim; that they did battle with Bera, king of Sodom; Birsha, king of Gomorrah; Shinav, king of Admah; Shem-Ever, king of Zevoyim; and the king of Bela, which is Zoar. All of them joined in the Valley of Siddim, which is [now] the Salt Sea. For twelve years they served Kedorlaomer, and in the thirteenth year they rebelled. In the fourteenth year, Kedorlaomer and the kings who were with him came and smote the Refaim in Ashtarot Karnayim, the Zuzim in Ham, and the Eimim in Shaveh Kiryatayim. Also the Hori, as they camped in Se'ir, all the way until El Paran which is above the wilderness. They swung back and came to Ein Mishpat, which is

Kadesh, and they smote the entire Amalekite region, as well as the Emorite in Ḥatzatzon Tamar. (14:1–7)

One must wonder why so much valuable Torah real estate is being devoted to the obscure background of a battle in which Lot is captured.

THE RIVERS OF PARADISE

In the era prior to the destruction of Sodom (perhaps marking the close of the era of pre-history), the known world can easily be divided into three main centers, each marked by an extremely fertile region fed by mighty rivers.[1] In the east is Babel, the land fed by the Tigris and the Euphrates; in the west is Egypt, fed by the Nile. Between those two mighty centers is the Valley of Siddim[2] – the land of Sodom and Gomorrah – fed by the Jordan. Indeed, when the Torah describes Lot's choice of Sodom in Genesis 13, the area is described as being, "like the garden of God, like the land of Egypt."[3]

A quick glance at the map below reveals that the four invading kings came from the east, from Babel. The invading coalition set their sights on controlling the bread basket at the center, in the Valley of Siddim. For twelve years the city-states of the Siddim valley paid tribute to the invaders from the east, who likely left behind some token bureaucrats and tax collectors while the kings and warriors returned home. When the Siddim Valley city-states rebelled by withholding their

---

1. We are concerned here not with historical and geographical accuracy but with a conceptual understanding of the world as presented in the Torah.
2. Although it would be a grammatical oddity, perhaps Siddim is a masculine plural version of the word *sadeh*, or field. That would render the Valley of Siddim as the Valley of the Fields, indicating its value as an agricultural center. The assonance between Siddim and Sodom cannot be overlooked, so that Sodom might be the principal city-state of the Siddim valley.
3. These four regions (i.e., the garden of God, Babel, Sodom, and Egypt) are the focus of significant biblical attention, primarily in Genesis but in Exodus as well. These areas are notable for their endowment of natural resources, so much so that very little effort is needed to produce food (see, for example, Deut. 11:10). The ready availability of food frees up time to invest in culture and scientific development, but in the biblical narrative inevitably leads to a descent into moral corruption resulting in a collapse of the civilization.

tributes, the Babylonian coalition returned with their military might to crush the rebellion.[4]

The route taken by the Babylonian coalition, described in painful detail, is quite unusual. Rather than choosing one of the well-traveled, direct routes to Sodom, they instead follow a circuitous route, wasting precious time and energy on their way to crushing a rebellion. Moreover, the Refaim, Zuzim, Eimim, and Hori with whom they chose to engage in warfare were known as mighty and fierce fighters.[5] Why do the invaders from the east intentionally get involved with difficult, unnecessary battles which could tire out their soldiers? Why would they choose a route which circumnavigates Sodom rather than a more direct one?

CONTROL, NOT DESTRUCTION

Apparently, while the Babylonian invaders are interested in subduing and subjugating Sodom, they are not interested in engaging it in battle. One can only conjecture as to why, but a strong possibility is because they want the Sodomites to continue paying tribute. Destroying the nations will leave the land fallow, undermining the whole purpose of the campaign.[6]

If so, this military endeavor is designed to intimidate the five kings of the Valley of Siddim so that they accept the yoke of the Babylonian coalition. As the invaders march down the mountain route east of the Jordan they systematically defeat one mighty and fearsome nation after another, sending shockwaves throughout the region. They pass Sodom but do not engage it, traveling southward to defeat the Hori in Mount Se'ir. They then swing around to Kadesh where they "cleanse" the Amalekite fields, and finally complete their circuit around the Sodomite area until they reach Ḥatzatzon Tamar (today associated with the oasis of

4. Throughout the biblical period there are two mighty empires, one in the northeast (Aram-Assyria-Babel-Persia) and the other in the southwest (Egypt). Those two empires constantly vie with each other for "global" domination, and the battlefield passes through the Promised Land, which sits at the crossroads.
5. See Deut. 2:10–22. There the Torah describes how God helps Ammon, Moab, and Edom defeat the mighty peoples who had previously inhabited their lands. These peoples are the very same ones mentioned in our story.
6. Ironically, this is what eventually happens to that region.

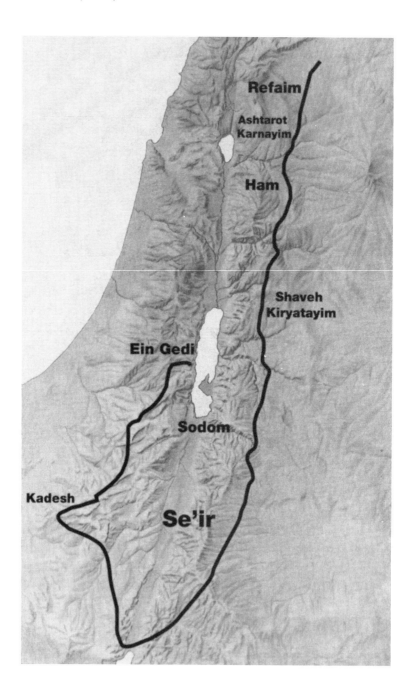

Ein Gedi). Having completely encircled the Valley of Siddim, they leave a wake of terror in the hope that they will have instilled enough fear in the five Sodomite kings that no battle will be necessary.

REPEATING AND REVERSING THE MARCH

One of the fascinating things about the route the Babylonian coalition takes is that it is familiar to careful readers of the Torah. It is essentially the same route later traveled by the Israelites in their fortieth year in the wilderness, but in reverse.[7] Numbers 20–21 and Deuteronomy 2–3 describe their departure from Kadesh, swinging around toward Eilat to circumnavigate Edom, Ammon, and Moab, and finally the battles with Sihon and Og. This route is as bizarre as the one in our own story. Given that the Israelites begin their trek at Kadesh, on the southern border, we must wonder why it is necessary for them to travel on a circuitous route and enter from the east, with all the attendant problems. Can God not help them defeat the Canaanite in the south just as He helps them defeat the mighty Emorite kings in the east?

Apparently the Israelite journey is designed to serve the same function as that of the Babylonian invaders. When the Israelites first leave Egypt they strike fear in the hearts of the Canaanite nations: "Peoples heard, they quaked; trembling seized Philistia's dwellers. Then the chieftains of Edom were shaken, shuddering seized the mighty of Moab, all the dwellers of Canaan melted. Terror and fear fell upon them" (Ex. 15:14–16). Word of the nation that humbles the mighty Egyptian empire and whose God splits the Reed Sea brings great fear to the entire region. That fear serves an essential function – it obviates the need to fight for every inch of the land: "I shall send My terror before you and I shall panic the whole people among whom you shall come, and I shall make all your enemies turn tail to you. I shall the send the wasp before you and it will drive out the Hivite and the Canaanite and Hittite before you" (Ex. 23:27–28). Under God's initial plan, the conquest of the Promised Land will be a quick, bloodless enterprise.

---

7. Y. Bin Nun, *Pirkei HaAvot*, 56–67, makes a similar observation but draws very different conclusions.

That fear, however, begins to dissipate with the Amalekite attack,[8] which demonstrates that the nation is not invincible. The Israelites' wandering in the wilderness for forty years makes the fear of them a distant memory for the Canaanite nations. How can the Israelites reinstate that fear, minimizing resistance to their entry into the land? God's answer, counterintuitive at first,[9] is to have them defeat a terrifying nation outside the land.

The plan, in fact, worked. We first hear of the Moabite terror: "Balak, son of Tzipor, saw all that Israel had done to the Emorite. And Moab was very terrified of the people" (Num. 22:2–3). Next we hear from Rahab, hostess to the Israelite spies, of the fear of the people of Jericho:

> I know that God has given the country to you, because dread has fallen upon us, and all the inhabitants of the land quake before you. For we have heard how God dried up the waters of the Reed Sea for you when you left Egypt, and what you did to Sihon and Og, the two Emorite kings across the Jordan. (Josh. 2:9–10)

Rahab's words are particularly revealing. The defeat of Sihon and Og rekindles memories of the Exodus from Egypt and the fear it generated throughout the region.[10]

ABRAM DEFENDS FAMILY

While the Israelite strategy is successful, it apparently fails when employed by the Babylonian invaders of Sodom. Eventually the battle does take place in the Valley of Siddim, and the Sodomite coalition of five kings loses. While the kings of Sodom and Gomorrah manage to flee, many of the inhabitants and their possessions are captured, including Lot.

Someone, an anonymous refugee, comes to tell Abram that his nephew (the Torah calls him Abram's brother) has been taken captive.

---

8. Ex. 17:8–16. See Rashi, Deut. 25:18, s.v. *asher karkha.*
9. The Israelites at the time certainly do not understand or appreciate God's plan. See Num. 21:4–5.
10. The fears continue to impact on the conquest of the land, inspiring the city-state of Givon to deceive Joshua into signing a treaty in which the Givonites will accept the yoke of the Israelites. See Joshua 9.

The Very First World War

The anonymity of the refugee indicates that *someone* knows Abram is nearby, that Abram cares, and that Abram might do something about it.[11] That says much about Abram and the impact of his presence in the area, so much so that the one who informs him could have been anyone at all.[12]

Many times I have asked people to provide descriptions for Abram. Various themes repeat themselves, but one which rarely comes up is "warrior." It is precisely because of this that Abram's rescue of Lot is so significant. It represents a side of Abram that seems to be out of character with the rest of our image of him. In fact, the strange background to our story helps highlight just how extraordinary Abram's rescue is.

Against a coalition of Babylonian kings so powerful that they defeat all the major powers in the region and think that they can easily intimidate the five kings of the Siddim valley, Abram does not seem to stand a chance.[13] Yet he gathers a small force of 318 men, including three local people with whom he has established some kind of covenant, and chases after the Babylonians.

What Abram doesn't have in numerical strength or military prowess he compensates for with strategy. Abram introduces two significant military strategies into his battle with the superior enemy. First, he continues his pursuit and the battle at night, highly unusual in the

---

11. Kass, *Genesis*, 262, writes, "Abraham enters political life as his brother's keeper." Interestingly, Abram is identified here for the first and only time as an *Ivri*, an Ever-ite, heir to an ancient tradition. The anonymous refugee is likely aware of this.

12. Genesis Rabba 42:8 suggests identifying him as Og, king of Bashan. Og is a figure favored by Midrash, and he surfaces repeatedly from before the Flood until his ultimate demise at the hands of the Israelites in their fortieth year of wandering. There is a midrashic preference to identify anonymous characters in the Bible as Og (see Isaac Heinemann, *Darkhei HaAggada* [Hebrew] [Jerusalem: Magnes Press, 1954], 21–26). On the non-midrashic level, it could be argued that those characters are intentionally anonymous to emphasize that their identity is irrelevant.

13. The four Babylonian kings originated from Abram's home region of Ur Kasdim. We earlier saw a midrashic tradition in which Abram feuds with Nimrod, king of Babel, before Terah moves the family. Some midrashic traditions identify Amrafel, king of Shinar, with that same Nimrod (Genesis Rabba 42:4; *Midrash Aggada*, Gen. 14:1). If we combine those traditions, the battle between Abram and the Babylonian kings is a replay of the feud between Abram and his nemesis, Nimrod. Abram's defeat of Nimrod and chasing him from the land is a demonstration that Nimrod and everything he stands for have no place in the Promised Land.

ancient world. Second, Abram splits his camp and attacks from two directions. The combination of these two strategies catches the Babylonians by surprise and scares them into thinking they are being attacked by a superior force, compelling them to flee.[14] Abram is not a mighty warrior, but a passionate defender of family who displays responsibility, courage, daring, and cunning.

ABRAM MEETS THE KINGS

It is not clear how many details of the battle are known in Abram's day. One thing that is clear is that he becomes a regional hero, and this raises his public profile considerably. If God chooses Abram and sends him to Canaan to position himself to influence those around him, one unanticipated outcome of his military campaign is that he now has an audience.

The first evidence for this emerges from within the incident. Upon his return from the battle Abram is met by two kings, the first of whom is the king of Sodom. Before the Sodomite king speaks, however, the encounter with Abram is interrupted by Melchizedek, king of Shalem – someone apparently not directly threatened by the Babylonian coalition but impacted upon by the entire incident. Melchizedek greets Abram with bread and wine and engages Abram in an interesting conversation. When Melchizedek is finished, we are returned to the story of Abram and the king of Sodom. Here is the text:

> The king of Sodom came to greet [Abram] after he returned from defeating Kedorlaomer and the kings who were with him, to the Valley of Shaveh, the valley of the king. But Melchizedek, king of Shalem, brought out bread and wine; he was priest to the El Elyon (Superior God). He blessed him and said, "Blessed be Abram to El Elyon, Creator of heaven and earth. And blessed be El Elyon

---

14. This same tactic is repeated by Gideon (Judges 7). Faced with an invasion of a numerically overwhelming enemy, he splits his army of three hundred men into three groups. In a surprise midnight offensive, his men attack from three sides, holding torches in one hand and jugs in the other to hide the flames. With his small band he sufficiently terrifies the enemy so that they flee in the one direction from which they saw they were not being attacked. Note that the midrashic version of Abram's early history paints him as prefiguring the character of Gideon; see p. 116, note 2.

who delivered your enemies into your hand"; and he gave him a tenth of everything.[15]

The king of Sodom said to Abram, "Give me the people, and take the possessions." Abram said to the king of Sodom, "I raise my hand in oath to El Elyon, Creator of heaven and earth: I shall not take from a string to a shoe-strap;[16] I shall not take from anything that is yours, lest you say, 'I have made Abram wealthy.' Nothing for me, only what the young men ate and the portion of the men who accompanied me, Aner, Eshkol, and Mamre,[17] they will take their portion." (14:17–24)

There are many fascinating observations to be made here, such as the choice of items brought by Melchizedek, or the dramatically different images portrayed by the two kings – one who owes nothing to Abram yet brings him an offering, the other who owes Abram everything yet wants to take for himself. Those discussions, however, will distract us from our focus on Abram.

The term El Elyon is first introduced in the Torah by Melchizedek. It is unclear who Melchizedek is or what his exact intention is when he uses that term, but that is less interesting than Abram's adoption of that very same language when speaking to the king of Sodom, declaring an oath to El Elyon! Abram, who is sent to influence others, is himself influenced by Melchizedek.[18] Not only does Abram adopt Melchizedek's language, he adopts his content as well. Melchizedek introduces God as

15. The ambiguous use of the pronoun "he" is intentional, as it reflects the ambiguity in the Torah text. While it is likely that Abram gave this priest a tithe, the meaning in the Hebrew remains open to interpretation.
16. I recall hearing Nehama Leibowitz suggest that the string refers to the cord used to affix the ancient headgear, much as Arabs use a cord to tie the keffiyeh. That would effectively render this statement to mean, "I will not take anything, from head to toe."
17. These three individuals were mentioned earlier as the local Hebronites with whom Abram had established a treaty.
18. Perhaps this would explain why *Midrash Tanḥuma* 19 associates Melchizedek with none other than Shem, son of Noah, Ever's partner in the chain of tradition from Noah to Abram. Who else could possibly teach Abram a lesson in theology if not one of his own mentors? This comment of Melchizedek has influenced the Jewish prayer book as well. The opening blessing of the *Amida* (the central, standing prayer)

the one who created and owns everything (the Hebrew verb *koneh* in its primary form means "to own" or "to acquire"). It is immediately following that encounter that Abram invokes the name of that same El Elyon, who created and owns everything, in his pronouncement to the king of Sodom that he wants nothing from the spoils because he does not want anyone to think that it is the Sodomite king who enriches Abram but God Himself, who owns all.

Ironically, it is when we see Abram influencing others that we are also witness to his being influenced by them. Abram, chosen by God to deliver His message, is beginning his work, and is growing in the process.

LOOKING BACK, LOOKING FORWARD

Our careful reading revealed that God's *lekh lekha* call is not so much an instruction to relocate as it is a plan for Abram to begin transforming his identity. Abram's embrace of that call leads him first on a path in which he needs to begin to understand God's message even absent clear, direct communication. We further observed the tension between God's instructions to Abram to claim the land and Abram's commitment to his extended family, and that the choices Abram makes complicate God's delivery of His promise. Finally, we noticed that Abram's responsibility for family takes him on a campaign which, in the short term, seems to complicate his achievement of the divine promise but in the long term brings him prominence, which enables him to influence and be influenced as he sets out to implement the divine mission.

With all the changes taking place in Abram and his deviations from God's instructions, we are left to wonder what God's response will be. Will Abram be rewarded for the sacrifices he makes or castigated for overlooking or ignoring divine instructions? In what ways is Abram progressing on his path to becoming the source of divine blessing for all the families of the earth?

---

contains the line, "El Elyon, Bestower of good kindness, Creator of everything," and one of the Friday night blessings includes the phrase, "El Elyon, Creator of heaven and earth."

Genesis 15:1–21

The Covenant between the Pieces

The Covenant between the Pieces is a seminal event in Jewish historical consciousness. It includes an outline version of Jewish slavery and redemption, along with the Jews' divine deed to the Promised Land; it is filled with an early form of divine revelation, a precursor to the Revelation at Sinai; it is accompanied by mysterious imagery and a profound statement of faith.

That statement is issued by none other than Abram, who is often portrayed as the quintessential man of faith. Heeding the call of God, he leaves everything behind and ventures to an unknown land armed only with his faith. Ultimately, he prepares to sacrifice his son in an act of supreme faith. In a series of popularized midrashic commentaries, the rabbis see Abram as the one who discovers God, hence his faith is unshakable.[1] Kierkegaard called Abraham the knight of faith,[2] and we expect the knight of faith not to falter.

---

1. Genesis Rabba 30:8; 38:13; 39:1; 64:4.
2. Søren Kierkegaard, *Fear and Trembling*, ed. Stephen Evans and Sylvia Walsh (Cambridge: Cambridge University Press, 2006).

Yet what if this image turns out to be too facile, unsupported by the text? It is remarkable that something as profound as discovering God should have gone unmentioned in the Torah. In fact, as we pointed out earlier, in the Torah text Abram does not discover God at all, but it is God who chooses him after he displays the rare combination of the values of justice and family. If so, then while Abraham may *ultimately* emerge as the knight of faith, we cannot reasonably expect that he has *always* embodied that remarkable character.

Aside from being a central pillar of the story of the Israelites, the narrative surrounding the Covenant between the Pieces presents Abram's faith seemingly to falter – not once, but twice. As we investigate this further we find ourselves facing startling conclusions about Abram, about faith, and about this central covenant in the Jewish narrative.

THE FIRST CRISIS OF FAITH

The opening section of Genesis 15 reads as follows (ellipses in the text do not imply omitted words but signify my suggested pauses):

> (1) It was after these things that God's words came to Abram in a vision, saying, "Do not fear, Abram. I am your protector; your reward is very great." (2) Abram said, "God, the Almighty, what could You possibly give me while I am childless,[3] and the one who takes care of my household is Eliezer of Damascus?" (3) Then Abram said, "You have not as yet given me children, and a member of my household will inherit me." (4) Behold, God's word had already come to him,[4] saying, "This one will not inherit you; rather, one who comes from your own loins shall inherit you." (5) He took Abram outside and said, "Look at the heavens and count the stars … if you can count them." … God then said,

---

3. This translation differs slightly from more standard ones. We will discuss this shortly.
4. Most translations render this as, "And then God's word came to him, saying." My translation is based on the Torah's usage of the past perfect, indicating that this is what God had *previously* said to him rather than being a description of God's present response to Abram's comment.

"So shall be your offspring." (6) He trusted in God, and He considered [that faith] [as Abram's] generosity.[5] (15:1–6).

Several fundamental observations are helpful in shaping our approach to this text. First, this event is connected to the previous one, Abram's battle to rescue Lot and his encounter with the two kings (14:1ff.). Second, this event opens with a new kind of divine communication: a vision, as distinct from all prior communication, which was aural (15:1). Third, it clearly comes to address a fundamental fear of Abram's, or perhaps more than one fear (15:2). Fourth, Abram seems distressed that he still does not have children, and it appears that an outsider to his family will inherit all that he has (15:4–5). Fifth, God tries to reassure Abram by showing him the stars (15:5). Sixth, Abram believes God's promise (15:6). Finally, God appreciates Abram's faith (15:6).

These observations should not be taken for granted. For example, the second one, which introduces us to a new form of communication which includes a visual element – more advanced than simple aural communication – represents an upgrade in God's connection with Abram.[6] It implies that Abram is doing something right. That "something" is presumably connected to the first observation, that God's enhanced revelation to Abram comes on the heels of his actions in the previous chapter. What is unclear is *what* in the previous chapter prompts this. Could it be Abram's bravery in saving his nephew, his commitment to family, his newfound status as a regional hero, the lessons he learns from Melchizedek, or something else as yet unspecified?

---

5. This verse is the subject of intense debate among the classical commentaries. Its interpretation is complicated by the use of multiple pronouns and by the fact that in Hebrew there are no capitals, so that it is unclear *who* is considering *what* to be generosity. Even the term "generosity" (in Hebrew, *tzedaka*) is the subject of great discussion. For a range of positions on this see the study guide of Nehama Leibowitz at www.nechama.org.il/pages/1231.html. It seems clear to me that the *tzedaka* (generosity) mentioned here is linked to the value of *tzedaka* which God later identifies as one of Abram's characteristics for which God decided to select him (18:19).

6. Throughout the Bible prophets are described as having visions, the highest form of which is experienced by Moses (Num. 12:6–8; Deut. 34:10).

Which brings us to our third observation. If God's appearance is to ease some fear of Abram's, of what is Abram afraid, particularly if he is the man of faith (15:6)? And if he is the man of faith, then why does he question God regarding the promise of the children – shouldn't the man of faith be more steadfast in his faith? Moreover, how does God's display of the stars placate him?[7]

Perhaps, as I suggested earlier, Abram is not *yet* the man of faith, but a man with good values whom God selects who embarks on a quest of faith and reaches a series of milestones on the way. Upon choosing him and sending him on his journey, God promises Abram both land and a multitude of progeny. As Abram begins his journey he makes choices to sacrifice his land, or at least delay claiming it, to protect his family. Pushing himself to his limits, Abram chases away an invading empire to rescue his wayward nephew, but receives no thanks from his kinsman.

God acknowledges Abram's bold actions in his rescue of Lot and reassures him, "Do not fear, Abram. I am your protector; your reward is very great." The root of the word for protector, M-G-N, clearly evokes the battle of the previous incident, in which Melchizedek blesses the One who M-G-N Abram's enemies into his hands.[8] On the simplest level, while Abram is successful in a sneak attack on the foreign bully, he is fearful of the opponent's return, upon which he stands no chance in an all-out battle.[9] God thus reassures Abram that He will protect him.

Abram receives this part of God's address well, but when God promises him a great reward he is taken aback. Think about this from Abram's perspective. At this point he is bereft. He has sacrificed his land for Lot, but it is now abundantly clear to Abram (much to his chagrin) that Lot is lost. Lot will not be his heir, for he is swallowed up by the Sodomite culture and God has made it clear to us readers that Lot is out of the picture. Abram leaves his family, sacrifices his land, and loses his heir – he is completely at a loss, with no future. And while God has promised him children, a number of years have already passed since that

---

7. Each of the Patriarchs needs to be reassured about his fear, Isaac in 26:24 and Jacob in 46:3. We will discuss these fears later.
8. See Sarna, *Understanding Genesis*, 121.
9. This is the approach taken by many classical commentators, including Rashbam, Nahmanides, Radak, Ibn Ezra, and Seforno.

promise without even a hint of God's delivering on it. Why should we expect Abram to be calmed by yet another promise when he is beginning to question God's ability or willingness to follow through on the previous one? Abram expresses his crisis of faith by lashing out at God (15:2). Here is what he says, interspersed with my interpretation of what he means: "What could You possibly give me that would be worth anything to me? Do You not see that I am childless, despite Your promise of children? Do You not see that my future has been terminated?[10] Do You not see that there is no one from my family whom I can leave in charge? Instead, all I have is Eliezer, whom I captured from my battle in Damascus (14:15)." Abram's point may be correct and his frustration justified, but the tone is certainly not.

In the Torah the root A-M-R ("to say") introduces a speaker. The next time the word is used it usually indicates a response from the other party. When it is used, however, to reintroduce the same speaker, it is never simply a continuation of the speech. Rather, it indicates that there is a pause after the initial comment, and that the speaker resumed speaking after that pause. (We will see another example of this, albeit with slightly different implications, later in this same chapter.)

After Abram's outburst he expects some response from God, but none is forthcoming. God is apparently displeased with his manner of expression and meets Abram's tirade with silence. When Abram speaks again he leaves the content intact but softens the tone: "You have not as yet given me children, and a member of my household will inherit me" (15:3). We no longer hear the cynical comment, "What could You possibly give me?" nor the disparaging of Eliezer.

GOD'S EXPERIENTIAL RESPONSE

At first glance it appears that once Abram reformulates his comments God has three responses (one in 15:4 and two more in 15:5), but a careful reading of the Hebrew text (which I tried to capture in my translation

---

10. The Hebrew word he uses to describe that he is childless is *ariri*. The two other places it is used in the Torah (Lev. 20:20–21) clearly refer to childlessness as a punishment, perhaps even with the implication that if there were children beforehand they too would die.

above) indicates something far subtler. In reality, God's words that "this one will not inherit you; rather, one who comes from your own loins shall inherit you" (15:4) are not a response to Abram at all but a reminder to the reader of what God had *already told* Abram.

Beginning with "I shall give this land to your descendants" (12:7) and again in "all the land which you see I will give to you and to your descendants" (13:15), God has repeatedly promised Abram children. Yet although God earlier says the words, Abram does not hear them the way God intends. Early in his biblical career, Abram is fixed on Sarai's barrenness and hence on Lot as his heir, so that when God refers to Abram's offspring Abram cannot imagine that it refers to biological children. Abram thus understands God's words as metaphorical. However, once it becomes clear that Lot is *not* the heir, the issue burns for Abram. If indeed it is now clear to Abram that Lot is not his heir, then the reality of the nonfulfillment of God's promise hits him forcefully.

This explanation is not as radical as it may seem at first. Let us remember that Abram initially misses the place God told him to go, ending up in Egypt and having to retrace his steps. If Abram's interpretation of God's geographical markers needs to be sharpened, is it beyond the imagination that there are additional areas in which Abram must learn to understand and interpret God's words?[11]

Only after the text clarifies to the readers that God had previously addressed Abram's concern about progeny is it prepared to describe God's present response to Abram's crisis, and that response is surprising. God takes Abram outside and has him look at the stars to try to count them – and then He waits, as if to give Abram the opportunity to try. How do we know that He waits? Because just as before, where the presence of two consecutive occurrences of the root A-M-R associated with the same speaker indicates a pause between the two speeches, here too we have two A-M-R words.

---

11. Interpreting prophecy – even by a prophet – should not be taken for granted. Many prophets need initial guidance in understanding their prophecies. Samuel is not even aware that he is experiencing prophecy (I Sam. 3), Jeremiah needs training in interpreting his visions (Jer. 1), Zechariah receives guidance in refining his understanding of his visions (Zech. 5–6), and Daniel receives direction as well (Dan. 10).

God's pause between the two speeches, however, is not because He is expecting a response but because He is waiting for Abram to realize that *there is no possible response*; he cannot, in fact, count the stars. It is only after Abram appreciates the magnitude of the moment, only after internalizing that the Creator of heaven and earth (something he only recently learned from Melchizedek) made the innumerable stars, that he is prepared to hear God's promise that his children will be as numerous as those stars.[12]

God's response to Abram is prefaced by a profound moment of discovery. Abram's experiential learning is contained within the pause between God's two A-M-R words, which makes what God says more believable to Abram, and in that pause Abram develops his faith in God. The Abram who did not discover God and who earlier did not understand God's words or subtle signals is now discovering his faith. God values that faith and considers it an act of generosity. After all, given Abram's circumstances, there is no rational reason for him to trust God, who has yet to deliver on His initial promise. Abram's newfound understanding of the divine, resulting from his experience with God's handiwork, opens the door for him to believe beyond the reasonable. Particularly in light of Abram's profound disappointment with the nonfulfillment of the existing promise, the trust he places in God is remarkable. It is truly an act of generosity.[13]

THE SECOND CRISIS OF FAITH

Abram's reinvigorated faith seemingly opens the door to God's comment, "I am God who took you out of Ur Kasdim to give you this land

---

12. In God's earlier promise to Abram, He indicated that Abram's descendants would be as the dust of the earth (13:16), whereas the imagery here is switched from the dust to the stars. While there is much homiletic hay to be made with this, it likely parallels Abram's newfound ability to lift up his eyes and see beyond his immediate surroundings, the stars being the farthest thing that a human being can see.
13. Rashi, Radak, and Seforno all express variations on this theme. My formulation is very close to that of Radak, who puts it this way: "God considered Abraham's complete faith as an act of generosity and uprightness of heart, for he and his wife were progressively aging and the [fulfillment of the] promise was substantively delayed – and despite that, he believed."

to inherit" (15:7). The power of this line cannot be overstated. The Ten Commandments begin with a similar opening: "I am God, your God, who took you out of the land of Egypt, from the house of slavery" (Ex. 20:2). In the context of the Ten Commandments, the language introduces a unique covenant between God and the Israelites. It stands to reason that the language has a similar meaning here, as God presents Himself to Abram as a covenantal partner.

Yet once again the reader is surprised. Abram has just found his faith and is rewarded with a promise of covenant, but his response to God's initiative sounds like insecure backsliding into a pre-faith mode: "God, the Master, through what will I know that I will inherit it?" (15:8). What happened to Abram's newfound faith?[14]

GOD'S MYSTERIOUS RESPONSE

If Abram's question is troubling, God's response to him is mysterious and obtuse. God asks Abram to gather four types of animals: a calf, a goat, a ram, and two birds (a turtledove and a pigeon).[15] Abram takes the mammals, not the birds, and cuts them in half, lining them up facing each other. Vultures descend on the pieces, but Abram chases them away. As the sun is setting, a deep sleep falls upon Abram, followed by a fearsome, great darkness. It is then that God speaks to him:

> You will know well that your offspring will be strangers in a land not their own, where they will be enslaved and oppressed for four hundred years. I will also judge the nation they will serve, and afterward they will emerge with great wealth. As for you, you

---

14. This question is particularly troubling for the classical commentaries, who tend to view Abram as the quintessential man of unshakable faith. For more on this see Rashi, 15:6; Nahmanides, 15:2; Radak, 15:8; Malbim, 15:8. According to Nedarim 32a and *Midrash HaGadol* 9, Abraham and his descendants are punished for his questioning God at this point.

15. There is a word attached to the three mammals, *meshuleshet* (likely related to the Hebrew word *shalosh*, meaning "three"), which baffles the commentaries. Bekhor Shor suggests it refers to the quality of the animal, Ibn Ezra and Gersonides think it means that the animals needed to be three years old, and Rashi and Nahmanides understand that he was to take three of each kind.

will go to your ancestors in peace; you will be buried at a ripe old age. And the fourth generation will return here, for the sin of the Emorite will not have been completed until then. (15:13–16)

Once the sun had set and the darkness had grown thick, a smoking oven and a flame of fire passed through the pieces. The narration concludes with the following:

> On that day God established a covenant with Abram, saying, "I have given this land to your offspring, from the river of Egypt to the great river, the Euphrates. [The land of] the Kenite, the Kenizzite, the Kadmonite, the Hittite, the Perizzite, the Refaim, the Emorite, the Canaanite, the Girgashite, and the Jebusite." (Genesis 15:19–21)

God's response is so puzzling it is almost overwhelming. What does it all mean? Here is just a sampling of the problems generated:

- This entire scene is apparently a response to Abram's question of "Through what will I know that I will inherit it?" yet we have little direction understanding *how* God's presentation addresses that question.
- God's message includes both aural (slavery and freedom, four hundred years, four generations, Abram's peaceful death, etc.) and visual (split animals, chasing away vultures, flame of fire, etc.) components, but much like bad dubbing of a foreign film, there seems to be little synchronization between the verbal communication and the images. Moreover, Abram receives no explanation of the images he is shown.
- Why are extended slavery and oppression suddenly introduced, and how can Abram "rest in peace with his ancestors" knowing that his children will endure great hardship?
- Just prior to Abram's question, God had promised Abram that the land would be given personally to him, but in this mysterious covenant God declares that the land will be given only to Abram's descendants.

- Just what is the "sin of the Emorite" and why should it impact on God's promise to Abram?

COVENANT AS PARADOX

It is possible that, like the mysterious apocalyptic imagery in the Book of Daniel,[16] the Covenant between the Pieces is meant to leave us with questions. If Daniel and Abram are themselves not provided a clear explanation, perhaps both experiences are meant to defy any specific interpretation. God has a plan for His people, but the enigmatic visions are left unexplained to allow for humans to help shape that plan. As Robert Alter writes, "All this is mystifying and is surely meant to be so, in keeping with the haunting mystery of the covenantal moment. It seems unwise to 'translate' the images into any neat symbolism."[17]

Despite the above caveat, there are hints of coherence in literary and thematic connections, both internal to this scene and as it connects externally to other passages. For example:

- The visual component consists primarily of three split animals and a fourth doublet which is not cleaved, while the number four features twice in the aural component to highlight the generation of redemption (the four hundred years of servitude and the fourth generation which will be returned).[18]
- Abram had asked how he will know (Y-D-A) that he will inherit the land. God's response includes the line, "You will know (Y-D-A) well," with that verb doubled for emphasis.

---

16. Dan. 7–11.

17. Alter, *The Five Books of Moses*, p. 76, n. 17. The great darkness which falls upon Abram reinforces the ominous and mysterious nature of this revelation, and is befitting a message in which Abram's descendants will descend into a terrifying, four-hundred-year darkness.

18. We are presented here with three "tripled" sets of animals followed by the birds (described in the text as a single animal). This parallels the popular presentation of R. Yehuda (*Sifrei*, Deut. 201) of the plagues in Egypt as coming in three sets of three, followed by a final one which is substantively different from the rest. This parallel is even more intriguing because the plagues in Egypt describe the beginning of God's fulfillment of the promise He makes here.

- Abram's vision, in which his destiny is permanently altered, is prefaced by a deep sleep (*tardema*) which falls upon him. This same deep sleep (*tardema*) befalls the first Man just prior to the introduction of the first Woman (2:21), which significantly alters the trajectory of his life.
- God promises that Abram's children will leave their land of oppression with great wealth. This is particularly ironic in light of the fact that Abram's desire for wealth is seemingly involved in his entanglement in Egypt (12:12–20), and his eschewing of financial reward is a hallmark of his interaction with the king of Sodom.
- Abram's descendants will end up as slaves to the Egyptians. Those Egyptians are the descendants of Ham (10:6), the very same Ham upon whom Noah had decreed that *he* would be a slave to Shem (9:26). The covenant with Abram suggests a reversal of Noah's decree.
- The smoke and the fire in this scene evoke the pillar of cloud and the pillar of fire which accompanied the Israelites from the moment of their liberation from Egypt (Ex. 13:22; Neh. 9:19) until the moment of their entry into the land, as God fulfills the covenant made here.

What do these observations tell us? First, that even though we do not precisely understand how, it is clear that this scene is God's direct response to Abram's question. Second, that this covenantal scene involves the charting of a new destiny, not the completion of a preexisting one. Third, that there is something in this covenant which indicates a suspension or reversal, if only temporarily, of an earlier blessing.

When we put this together, the picture which begins to emerge is somewhat startling – that this Covenant between the Pieces is *not* part of the initial divine plan but is a reaction to something Abram says or does. That is why the language of Y-D-A is used in response to Abram's invoking it; that is why it reverses Noah's blessing; that is why fulfillment of the promise will come only to Abram's descendants and not to Abram himself; that is why there needs to be an extended period of suffering before the promise is actually fulfilled.

It would be easy to argue that the catalyst for all this is Abram's questioning of God, but Abram's repeated delays in taking the land cannot be overlooked. To be sure, those delays result from conscious choices Abram makes, and early on we saw that the land is becoming increasingly difficult to claim as more and more peoples begin to inhabit it – first the Canaanite, then the Perizzite, and then the Emorite (with whom Abram establishes his own treaty [14:13]). Those consequences are not necessarily punishments, but they do demand recognition of the fact that choice involves sacrifice.

When God tells Abram that there will be a delay in the return to the land until the sin of the Emorite has completed its course, this may very well be a reference to Abram's treaty with that nation, that is, Abram's acceptance – implicitly or explicitly – of their rightful presence in the land. (Later this will haunt him, as he must negotiate with them to secure a burial place for his own family.) Yet this is the land which God had promised Abram, and Abram's willingness to formally affirm the presence of the Emorite nation carries with it the consequence that it will become more difficult for him and his heirs to take that land when the time does come. In essence, Abram's delay in claiming the land is met by God's delay in giving it to him. And when his descendants eventually do get the land, they will have to contend not with one or two or three peoples inhabiting it, but with the full complement of ten nations listed at the end of the covenant.

Paradoxically, along with the negative associations of this covenant, there seem to be many positive aspects as well. God's revelation takes on a new form, one which includes images. Moreover, in God's early promises to Abram there is no explicit, long-term commitment to Abram's descendants; it is Abram who would become great. With the introduction of this covenant, however, there is a profound sense of long-term commitment, whether lasting four generations or four hundred years. The pillar of cloud and fire introduced here become the symbols that the Israelites in the wilderness look to every day as a reminder of the depth of God's commitment to completing the journey with them to the Promised Land.[19]

---

19. The Israelite rejection of the land in the incident of the spies results in a forty-year extension of the four-hundred-year waiting period. Those forty years represent a microcosm of the patience necessary for maintaining the covenant. In this light, the presence of the symbols of the fire and the cloud throughout the wilderness experience take on a new dimension of security for the wandering people.

The Covenant between the Pieces introduces ideas which transcend simple reward and punishment. It is not a reformulated system of reward and punishment, i.e., Abram should follow God's command so that God will grant him children. Rather, it is a long-term relationship. For this reason, Abram's complaint about children is met initially with a riddle about counting the stars. He needs to be shaken from his prior mode of thinking.

God's response of covenant transforms Abram's past actions as God forges a new bond with him. Abram's sacrifice of the land is not the result of sloth or a lack of commitment but because he makes a conscious decision that the value of family supersedes that of divine blessing. God's covenantal response acknowledges both elements: there are consequences for the delay with regard to the land, and the nature of Abram's relationship with God takes on a new dimension precisely because of his prioritizing the value of family.

Abram's preparedness to forgo immediate rewards of the land is matched by God's commitment to a long-term process, the inherent message being that long-term covenants can outlive those who make them. Abram's patience in fulfilling the promise of the land yields a covenant whose fulfillment he will not live to witness, but he will rest peacefully with his ancestors confident that his descendants will be the beneficiaries of his patience.

Along with God's long-term commitment comes one from Abram as well. The man who complains that God has not fulfilled His promise of abundant progeny, and who wonders how he will know when God's promise will be fulfilled, suddenly finds himself in a covenant, the result of which he will not live to see fulfilled in his own lifetime – despite God's telling him that he will know when it is fulfilled. Even though Abram will live to a ripe old age, he will have to die holding on to the faith that God will, eventually, fulfill His commitments. The man who is impatient with God must learn eternal patience. If Abram's faith is unstable, God's response provides him with a long-term program to strengthen it.

Perhaps this is the essence of covenant. It is not hasty or impetuous or fleeting. It demands long-range thinking, fortitude for weathering the hard times in the hope for a better future, and a commitment beyond any other in the human experience. This message is the essence of God's response to Abram's request for a guarantee.

The paradox of the covenant extends even further. We wondered earlier what it was about Abram's prior actions that opened the door to enhanced communication with God. It seems like the most significant thing Abram does is demonstrate his profound obligation to his nephew Lot, which he pays for with the land. Yet Abram's very commitment to his nephew, much like his commitment to remain with his barren wife, signals that he is prepared for a deeper commitment to God as well.

DECONSTRUCTING AND RECONSTRUCTING

The duality of the covenant – the result of Abram's delaying his claim of the land as a consequence of his commitment to family – is actually embedded in the structure of the chapter. The chapter begins with God's communication to Abram, reassuring him not to fear and promising great reward. Abram initially challenges and ultimately questions God about the promise of progeny. This same pattern is repeated when God reaffirms the promise of the land. Abram again challenges God with a request for a guarantee or a sign that he will know when the promise is fulfilled.

Perhaps, however, Abram is not simply challenging God but interrupting Him. Could it be that God is not yet finished when Abram interjects with a concern that makes it pointless to continue until that concern is addressed?[20] If so, then it seems that Abram interrupts God not once, but twice![21] By mapping out the interruptions and God's responses to them as parenthetical comments, separating the interruptions from God's primary communication, we can reconstruct what God originally intended to say to Abram. Here is what the chapter would look like through that lens:

---

20. Moses, too, interrupts God. Exodus 3:7–10 is the beginning of God's instruction to Moses to free the Jews from Egypt. This instruction continues in the middle of 3:12, where God tells Moses that upon their exit from Egypt the Israelites should worship God at "that mountain." In the middle we have Moses interrupting God with his question of, "Who am I?" followed by a brief response by God before God continues with His initial message.

21. There is a common format for both interruptions. Abram uses the dual name of God, A-donai E-lohim, followed by a question of "What" (*ma*). God's responses to the two interruptions are also parallel, as they both contain a visual symbol to concretize the message.

God's intended message	Abram's interruptions and God's responses
(1) It was after these things that God's words came to Abram in a vision, saying, "Do not fear, Abram. I am your protector; your reward is very great."	
	Abram interrupts (and then reframes) with a challenge about nonfulfillment of the promise of progeny.
	God responds by taking Abram outside and letting him experience His power.
	Abram trusts God, and God values that trust.
(7) He said to him, "I am God who took you out of Ur Kasdim to give you this land to inherit."	
	Abram interrupts, asking for a sign.
	God responds with the Covenant between the Pieces, a second experiential response.
(19–20) "[The land of] the Kenite, the Kenizzite, the Kadmonite, the Hittite, the Perizzite, the Refaim, the Emorite, the Canaanite, the Girgashite, and the Jebusite."	

If we read just the left column – that is, we remove Abram's interruptions and God's responses to them – we get a reconstruction of what God had intended for that encounter: a reaffirmation of the promises of progeny and the land, along with a reassurance that Abram's dedicated courage and personal growth do not go unnoticed. It also points to God's intent (15:7) to give the land to Abram without delay, despite the presence of the ten nations which are already there.

The above outline of Abram's encounter with God graphically reveals that the boldness of Abram's character and his preparedness to confront God both necessitate and enable the Covenant between the Pieces. Abram is not the simple man of faith who, when asked to jump, responds with the question of, "How high?" That description would be more befitting a character such as Noah, who when told that there is going to be a flood makes no attempt to intercede or mediate God's intention. Abram is dynamic and does not follow blindly.

Furthermore, the outline suggests that had everything gone according to God's plan, there may not have been a need for the Covenant between the Pieces, for the dark and mysterious experience Abram has, or for the servitude and oppression in Egypt. Abram's challenges and questioning of God, however, highlight that the world God creates and the special individuals He chooses are not perfect. It is precisely because of their imperfections that not everything goes according to God's plan.

The interesting part of God's responses to both of Abram's challenges is that they have a substantive experiential component. In the first, Abram is asked to count the stars; in the second, Abram must split three sets of animals and encounter terrifying darkness. Whereas Abram earlier needs to rely solely on the verbal promises he receives from God, which are apparently insufficient, God uses an educationally more powerful tool to help Abram internalize the message.[22]

God does not get angry with Abram, but rather adjusts His ideal plan to the reality in which His people live. Perhaps this is what the rabbis mean when they write, "Wherever you find His greatness there you find His humility."[23] God's greatness *is* His humility – the

---

. Sarna, *Understanding Genesis*, 126, writes: "The awesome spectacle that generated the 'deep dark dread' had as its sole purpose the strengthening of faith in God."
23. Megilla 31a.

humility expressed in reshaping the divine plan to meet the humans where they are.

AN INTENDED COVENANT

In the previous section I suggested that this covenant is not part of God's initial plan but rather His response to choices Abram makes. It turns out, however, that there are multiple clues which suggest a dramatically different understanding. First, this chapter opens with a visual component to God's communication – in Hebrew, a *maḥazeh* – which Abram had not merited earlier, suggesting that God's intention is to intensify His relationship with Abram.

Second, God's opening words in that vision, "Do not fear," are surely meant to reassure.[24] A quick survey of Genesis reveals that those same words are used to reassure Isaac and Jacob as each faces a crisis of confidence in his own status vis-à-vis God. Isaac is told not to fear after his encounters with the Philistine Avimelekh, in which he jeopardizes Rebecca and is repeatedly repulsed from the land (26:24). Jacob is reassured as he packs up his life and begins his descent to Egypt (46:3).[25] Despite the apparent evidence that his place in the divine promise is threatened, God reassures him that there is in fact no danger at all. So too, with Abram: Following his military campaign he is reassured that he has not disqualified himself as God's messenger. This, however, is not a response to Abram's challenge but is God's initial message.

Third, in 15:7, God introduces Himself to Abram, "I am A-donai, who took you out of Ur Kasdim." As we saw earlier, this phrase is identical in framing to the opening of the Decalogue (Ex. 20:2): "I am A-donai, your God, who took you out of the land of Egypt." The parallelism suggests that just as the Decalogue is a covenant (opening with a personal introduction by God), so too, the *initial intent* of this

---

24. According to Rashi, Abram is concerned that his miraculous battle victory used up his merits. Rashbam, Nahmanides, Radak, Ibn Ezra, and Seforno suggest that Abram fears retaliation of the four kings. Nahmanides adds that Abram also fears he will die childless, a fear not connected to the prior story.

25. Rashi, 32:11, similarly suggests that Jacob earlier was fearful he had become sullied in Laban's house, thereby disqualifying him from the divine promise. Rashi makes a similar suggestion with regard to Abram on 15:1.

communication with Abram is to establish a covenant with him, which includes the period of travail for Abram's descendants followed by a glorious redemption.

According to this line of thought, Abram indeed interrupts God, but in no way do those interruptions impact God's fundamental message that He is establishing a covenant with Abram. This reading yields a dramatically different conclusion: the covenant is not God's reaction to Abram's challenge but a significant event designed to elevate Abram's relationship with God – a step forward in Abram's growth as Patriarch. Abram's interruptions are not the catalyst for covenant but rather introduce the need for minor adaptations in its expression, through concrete, symbolic acts of reassurance: stars for the first interruption; animals, smoke, and fire for the second. It is not surprising, then, that visual imagery introduced in response to the second interruption does not align completely with the aural message of the covenant. The aural message had been planned in advance, while the visual imagery is introduced to ease Abram's fears.

From the time Abram is called upon by God he is confronted by competing commitments, his commitment to family and his commitment to God to find and claim the land. Abram repeatedly adheres to family commitments, resulting in his distancing from the land. God demonstrates to him that there are consequences to the choices we make in life, even when the choice is the correct one. For Abram, choosing to cement his family commitments has made it that much more difficult to claim the land. There are ten nations currently dwelling in it, and Abram has established treaties with at least one of them.

As a result of Abram's choices there will be an extended delay in the fulfillment of the promise of the land. The great irony is that the fulfillment of the land will come to Abram's children, the very ones which he feared he would never have. The promise of the land and the promise of the children become inextricably bound. Faith in one will ensure the fulfillment of the other.

Genesis 12:10–20; 16:1–16

The Wife, the Maidservant, and the Boy

We have been following Abram from before God called to him through his search for an heir, yet it is difficult to talk about an heir that will emerge from Abram's own flesh without a discussion of the woman who is ostensibly to be the mother of that heir. The problem, of course, is that Abram's wife, Sarai, is barren.

By the time we are finished with the Covenant between the Pieces, Abram seems unperturbed by this technicality. He has declared his faith in God's promise. He does not know *how* God will fulfill it, but be believes with complete conviction that it will be fulfilled. Sarai, however, is considerably more practical. She apparently knows that Abram has been promised an heir and she also knows that she is incapable of producing that child. And so she proposes that Abram take her maidservant, Hagar, as a wife, to be an ancient version of a surrogate. Hagar will bear the child and Sarai will take the maidservant's child and raise him as her own:[1] "Sarai, Abram's wife, took Hagar, her Egyptian maidservant – after

---

1. For more on ancient surrogacy see Sarna, *Understanding Genesis*, 128, especially ns. 30–31.

ten years of Abram's residence in the land of Canaan – and gave her as a wife to Abram, her husband" (16:3). On some level it is difficult to imagine a nobler, more selfless act. Sarai shares her husband with another woman so that God's promise to Abram can be fulfilled.

While the Torah does say that Abram listens to Sarai, there are indications that Abram is more hesitant than she – for while Sarai's intention is for Hagar to become Abram's wife, Abram is apparently unprepared to take that step. Abram's relationship with Hagar is described in words indicating cohabitation, not marriage: "He came unto Hagar and she conceived" (16:4).

Abram's caution is prescient, as Sarai's plan goes awry when Hagar gets cocky about her pregnancy and her new status as the expectant mother of Abram's child: "When [Hagar] saw that she was pregnant she made light of[2] her mistress [Sarai] with her eyes" (16:4). For the first time we have conflict within Abram's home. The pregnant maidservant struts about the house flaunting her swollen belly in front of her barren boss. This is too much for Sarai to bear, and she lashes out at Abram, even invoking a call for divine justice: "The violence done to me is on you! I put my maidservant in your bosom and when she saw that she was pregnant I became light in her eyes. Let God judge between me and you!" (16:5).

Sarai's response is puzzling. Why blame Abram for her troubles – isn't she the architect of the entire scheme with Hagar? Could this simply be an irrational outburst from the humiliated woman of the house? Did she not anticipate the challenges such a complicated arrangement could bring? While it is possible that the answer to all these questions is yes,[3] a little background to this story sheds a different light on it.

---

2. To "make light of" is my translation of the verb *vatekal* (also related to *kelala*, curse). Its opposite is to take seriously, or to give weight to, which in Hebrew is from the root K-B-D, meaning "heavy."

3. Both Nahmanides and Radak express strong critique of Sarai's banishing of Hagar. Building on Nahmanides' comment, Leibowitz, *Iyunim BeSefer Bereshit*, 112, suggests that Sarai's failure results from her inability to anticipate her own jealousy of Hagar. Had she not tried to engage in the superhuman feat of suppressing natural jealousy so that she could give Hagar to Abram, none of this would have happened.

BACK IN EGYPT

Abram and his brother Nahor are the first people in twenty generations to be described as taking a wife. Until then, women are apparently regarded as merely necessities for reproduction. This new status is especially prominent in Abram's case, as his wife, Sarai, is identified almost immediately as being barren. Abram stays with her despite her inability to bear children, flying in the face of conventional norms.

This romantic picture of spousal love, however, is challenged almost immediately. As Abram's journey brings him within the vicinity of Egypt, he senses that there is going to be trouble with Sarai:

> He said to Sarai, his wife, "Behold, I know that you are a woman of beautiful appearance. When the Egyptians see you they will say, 'This is his wife!' and they will kill me but keep you alive. Please say that you are my sister, so that it may be good (*yitav* – from the root T-O-V) for me because of you and that I may live on your behalf." (12:11–13)

What Abram has in mind is not exactly clear, but the story unfolds in a most unsavory way:

> When Abram arrived in Egypt, the Egyptians noticed the woman, for she was very beautiful. Pharaoh's servants noticed her and praised her to Pharaoh, and the woman was taken to Pharaoh's house. And he was good (*heitiv* – from the same root T-O-V) to Abram because of her; he had sheep and cattle and donkeys and servants and female servants and she-donkeys and camels. (12:14–17)

Reading this story leaves one with the feeling that there are no redeeming characters. It appears that Abram allows – even plans – for his wife to be taken and is hoping to benefit from her dishonor. In fact, it seems like his plan works. He anticipates that the plan will be *tov* (good) for him and that is exactly what happens, as Pharaoh does considerable *tov* to Abram, making him quite wealthy. Pharaoh and his men fare no better on the moral scales: they see a beautiful woman and take her to

Pharaoh's harem without even asking about her status. Sarai is in an uncomfortable position. Abram has asked her to lie for him and it doesn't seem like she has much of a choice, although she may have been spared the indignity of lying by not being given an opportunity by Pharaoh's servants to say anything at all.

Many of the classical commentaries struggle with this incident. Rashi sees Abram and Sarai as victims of an immoral empire, while Nahmanides accuses Abram of compromising and endangering his wife. Seforno attempts a valiant explanation: Since the custom in Egypt was to respect the right of the father or brother to negotiate the betrothal of the unmarried girl (while a husband was seen as an obstacle to be summarily disposed of), Abram plans to present Sarai as his sister to generate a bidding war between potential suitors and then delay choosing one until the famine ends – at which time he will conveniently return safely to Canaan. His plan, suggests Seforno, is thwarted when she is taken to Pharaoh, effectively undermining any battle of suitors.[4]

Notwithstanding the bold attempts to justify or explain Abram's behavior, the inescapable conclusion is that despite his championing of the value of family, there is something lacking in the way Abram behaves toward his wife. How does all this relate specifically to our present story?

Remember that in return for Sarai, among the things that Abram receives from Pharaoh are female servants. One of those is likely Hagar, the Egyptian maidservant whom Sarai now gives to Abram.[5] When Hagar demeans Sarai, it brings back the painful memories of Sarai's being taken by Pharaoh, and Abram's significant role in that sorry incident. The violence to which Sarai refers in her complaint to Abram (16:5) is not her present mistreatment by Hagar but her previous degradation in Pharaoh's palace – and, by extension, at the hand of Abram. Sarai is not *over*reacting; she is finally *re*acting to the disgrace she has now suffered twice at the hands of Egyptians (Pharaoh and Hagar), and Abram's involvement in the first cannot be overlooked.

---

4. This explanation is challenged by Pharaoh's complaint to Abram, "Why did you say, 'She is my sister'?" 12:18), indicating that there was, indeed, a ruse perpetrated by Abram.

5. Genesis Rabba 45:1 suggests that Hagar is Pharaoh's daughter.

ABRAM WITHDRAWS AND SARAI ACTS

What is Abram's response to Sarai's plea? "Here, your maidservant is in your hands; do to her as you see fit" (16:6). Abram's inaction could easily be seen as an abdication of responsibility. Why would he want to get in between two bitter, bickering women? More likely, however, is that he sees himself as a nonparty to the feud. In his eyes, Hagar is not and has never been his wife. He views her as nothing more than the surrogate who remains Sarai's maidservant. If the maidservant misbehaves then she needs to be dealt with accordingly by her owner, Sarai.

The Torah describes that Sarai did what is called in Hebrew "*inui*" (A-N-H), usually translated as oppression. Sarai's behavior certainly warrants scrutiny, as it seems unbecoming for the matriarchal lady of the house to be vindictive.[6] In light of the cultural norms prevalent in the Near East at this time, however, Sarai's conduct takes on a dramatically different meaning. The Code of Hammurabi reveals a relevant example of those norms:

> If a man married a sacred woman and she gave a female slave to her husband and she has then borne children, if later that female slave has claimed equality with her mistress because she bore children, her mistress may not sell her; she may mark her with the slave mark and count her among the slaves.[7]

It is remarkable how parallel this text is to our own. A slave-woman claims equality, or even superiority, to her mistress because she can bear children while her mistress cannot. In response, says Hammurabi, the mistress may "mark her with the slave mark," ensuring that there is no confusion about the relative status of each in the family. It is likely that this is what Sarai does to Hagar, the presumptuous maidservant who demeaned her

---

6. Nahmanides, 16:6, castigates Sarai for her mistreatment of Hagar. Invoking his idea that the Matriarchs and Patriarchs created historical templates which follow their descendants, he goes so far as to suggest that the Israelite slavery and oppression in Egypt was the cosmic consequence of Sarai's mistreatment of Hagar.

7. Code of Hammurabi 146, with slight changes. From James B. Pritchard, trans. and ed., *Ancient Near Eastern Texts Relating to the Old Testament* (Princeton, NJ: Princeton University Press, 1969), 172.

mistress. Rather than branding her, as Hammurabi would do, Sarai makes Hagar work like a servant, reducing her to her former status. For a servant who tastes freedom to be reduced back to the status of servant is indeed oppression, so much so that Hagar feels the need to flee.

HAGAR MEETS THE ANGEL

It is not at all clear where Hagar, a pregnant, runaway servant, thinks she will go, but to her surprise, she is greeted by a divine messenger who questions her. The questions, however, are odd, since it is clear that the angel already knows the answers: "Hagar, Sarai's maidservant, from where are you coming and to where are you going?" (16:8). The very fact that he knows her name and status as Sarai's servant suggests that the question is a rhetorical one.

We've already seen that rhetorical questions asked by divine beings in Genesis are a form of rebuke. After the Man eats from the forbidden fruit God asks, "Where are you?" After Cain kills his brother Abel, God asks, "Where is Abel, your brother?" The rhetorical opening question posed to Hagar, then, is also a rebuke, as the angel's intention is to say, "Why are you not serving Sarai, your mistress?" That implied message is then stated explicitly in the first of three messages the angel delivers to the runaway servant:

> The angel of God said to her, "Return to your mistress and suffer oppression under her."
> The angel of God said to her, "I will greatly increase your offspring; they will be so numerous that they will be uncountable."
> The angel of God said to her, "Behold you are pregnant and will give birth to a son; you will call him Ishmael (literally, "God hears"), because God has heard your oppression. He will be a wild donkey of a man, his hand will be in everyone and everyone's hand will be in him; and he will dwell on the face of all his brothers." (16:9–12)

The first thing we notice here is that there are three distinct speeches by this angel, each with its own "*vayomer*" ("and he said"). This is quite striking, almost to the point of being awkward, and in this case it appears that the angel is not waiting for a response but allowing for each message to sink in before continuing. Let's look at this sequence of speeches carefully to get a better sense of the messages Hagar hears.

The first message is a continuation of the divine rebuke: "Go back to Sarai and endure her heavy hand." This message certainly offers no comfort to Hagar, who has just fled from Sarai, and she needs some time to absorb the idea that she must return. This is followed by a second message, which should offset the negative implications of the first one: the promise of progeny so numerous as to be uncountable is bound to engender a feeling that her suffering will be worth bearing.

The third message leaves us – and Hagar – wondering. Is having a son who is a "wild donkey" of a man a positive or negative message? Is the fact that his hand will be in everyone else's business and their hands will be in his a blessing or a curse? What is the implication of the idea that "he will dwell on the face of all his brothers?"

This might be a classic case of "Beware what you wish for." Hagar's flight from her mistress is a desperate cry for freedom. Above all, she desires to have no yoke of servitude limiting her. When we combine the three elements of the angel's response, the message is clear: she will achieve her coveted freedom but only for her child, the "wild donkey" of a man, and the price is for her to accept the yoke of servitude upon herself.

The "wild donkey" image is well known in the biblical world. Jeremiah (2:24) uses it to describe the animal that accepts no domestication and no master; it is completely free and independent. That freedom means the animal lives wherever it wants, but because it lives everywhere it has no home.[8] It moves freely into the territory of others but must suffer others pushing back. Hagar's sacrifice of her own freedom will bring the ultimate freedom to her son, Ishmael, but he will be a nomad. The ultimate wanderer, his life is intertwined with everyone else's as he journeys from place to place as a traveling merchant.[9]

---

8. Reminiscent of Abel.

9. It is no wonder that Ishmaelites are involved in the sale of Joseph, taking a piece of merchandise from one place and conveniently leaving it somewhere else. The talmudic name for an Ishmaelite merchant is *taiya*, literally, "wanderer," or "one who is lost." This becomes significant in Genesis 21, when Hagar and Ishmael get lost in the wilderness.

THE RIDDLE OF HAGAR

The three messages delivered to Hagar by the angel outline a dramatic moment. The second message, informing her of the multitude of her progeny, echoes God's promise to Abram. In the Covenant between the Pieces, God tells Abram that he will not get to see that promise fulfilled in his lifetime, nor will his children. There will first be an extended period of trials and suffering, and only after the suffering of the parents will the promise come true for the children. Based on the message she hears from the angel, Hagar can easily draw the conclusion that she is the parent of the covenantal child promised to Abram, as she will also endure suffering to bring God's promise to her child. In fact, there are three key prerequisites for the fulfillment of God's promise to Abram: being a stranger (*ger*) in a foreign land, being enslaved, and being oppressed (*inui*), and all three are used to describe Hagar's experience – in the exact same language. She is a servant to Sarai, she suffers *inui* inflicted by Sarai, and her name, Hagar, in the unvocalized text of the Torah, could easily be read as *hager*, "the stranger."

When Hagar hears the angel's second utterance promising bountiful progeny, the first of the angel's pronouncements demanding that she suffer takes on new meaning. For Hagar, Ishmael is the heir promised to Abram, and like Abram, she will endure so that her child can receive that divine reward. Even Abram might believe that Ishmael is the promised heir; didn't Ishmael fit all the criteria spelled out earlier? Doesn't Ishmael qualify as one who emerged from Abram's loins? Is his divinely ordained name, which Abram gives him as well (16:15), not Ishmael – literally, "God hears"? Hagar and Abram have every reason to believe that Ishmael is the promised heir, fulfilling Sarai's initial plan – despite the personal difficulties between Sarai and Hagar.

Indeed, were we to read only the angel's first two messages to Hagar we would likely draw the same conclusion. But despite the uncanny parallels between Abram's and Hagar's respective destinies, there is one dramatic – and fundamental – difference between them. The climax of the promise to Abram is *rootedness* in a particular land: "The fourth generation will return here" (15:16), while the climax of the promise to Hagar is the *rootlessness* of her "wild donkey" of a child, free to the extent of being untamable. The promises of progeny are parallel, but the relationships to the land point in opposite directions. Ishmael's descendants will be nomads, while Abram's children will forever be rooted in their land.[10]

Ishmael's ineligibility to be Abram's heir is further attested to by the subtle use of adjectives describing Hagar. Hagar is referenced many times in this chapter – by the narrator, by Sarai, by Abram, and by the angel – and, without exception, she is repeatedly referred to as "the maidservant," or "the Egyptian." By contrast, Sarai is identified as either Abram's wife or Hagar's owner. The child of the maid cannot be the heir, particularly when there is a woman of the house. Ironically, while we readers may be aware of these clues, the protagonists in the story may not be aware of them at all.[11]

There is yet a third subtle indication of Ishmael's disqualification, and this one, too, points to his mother. Earlier we noticed that Abram must learn to discover God's clues, to see that which others do not. Although initially challenged, Abram learns to read God's ways and "lifts up his eyes" to see what others do not. Hagar *thinks* that she can see like her master Abram – she even names the place of her encounter with the angel "Be'er Laḥai Ro'i," "The Well of the Living One Who Sees." In reality, however, she sees nothing at all. Fleeing from Sarai, she arrives at a well in the wilderness and does not see it.

This chapter is filled with wordplays on the sense of sight, or its absence. Three times the Torah speaks of eyes (*ayin* in Hebrew); four times the word *ani* (a play on the word *ayin*) is used to describe Hagar's suffering; twice the word *ayin* ("spring"; again a play on the word for eye, which is spelled the same way) is used to describe that upon which Hagar stumbles; four times Hagar describes herself as being able to see. When Hagar thinks she sees, it turns out to be nothing but a mirage, a product of her suffering – or simply a spring. Ultimately, the angel tells her to name her son Ishmael, "God hears." She does not see God and God does not see her.[12]

---

10. The land-centric covenant with Abram emerges in Moses' blessing to the people at the end of his life. See particularly Deut. 33:12, 28. I am thankful to my student, Aaron Kohl, who pointed this out.

11. This will be reinforced even further in our discussion of Genesis 21.

12. Ironically, when Hagar is later expelled from Abraham's house, she doesn't want to see Ishmael and cannot see the spring which is there (21:19). For more on this see

Abram starts off unable to see and he is aware that he needs to learn. As Abram moves from non-seer to seer, God grants him a vision (ch. 15). By contrast, Hagar believes she can see when in fact she cannot, and she remains a non-seer until she is banished from Abraham's home. The angel's message is clear: You are no seer; you are not Abram's partner. And Ishmael is not Abram's heir.

The careful reader of the Torah is given the tools to understand that which Hagar does not. But it is not just Hagar who is in error. Abram is also not afforded access to the text to which the reader is privileged. He, too, apparently believes that Ishmael is the promised heir, and the stunning scene in which God tells him otherwise unfolds in the next chapter.

Steinmetz, *From Father to Son*, 72–79. God's "sight" is highlighted numerous times in the Torah, and often refers to God's intervention in human history. See Gen. 6:5; 11:5; 18:21; Ex. 2:25. The emphasis on the sense of hearing with regard to Ishmael is evidenced strongly in this story and repeated when Ishmael is explicitly rejected as the covenantal heir (17:20), where God says that He hears Abraham's appeal concerning Ishmael.

Genesis 17:1–27

Transformational Covenant

When we last left Abram he was eighty-six years old and was finally gifted a child via Hagar. His travels and wanderings are done and his uncertainty about his future resolved. He did what God asked, and God delivered on His promise. For thirteen years Abram nurtures and teaches the young Ishmael, preparing him to be the promised heir.

After all of his trials and tribulations, Abram is convinced his journey is complete and he can finally settle down into his blessed life in his new land with his new family. Imagine Abram's surprise, then, when at the age of ninety-nine God suddenly appears to him yet again: "I am El Shaddai; walk before Me and be without blemish. I will set My covenant between you and Me, and I will increase you very greatly" (17:1–2). While it is not yet clear what God is asking of Abram, Abram is stunned by the message and falls on his face, perhaps fearful of what God will now ask of him (17:4). Confirming Abram's fears, God ups the ante:

Behold, here is My covenant with you. You will become the father of a multitude of nations. Your name will no longer be Abram; instead your name will be Abraham, for I have set you to be the father of a multitude of nations. I will make you exceedingly fruitful and you will become many nations – even kings will emerge from you. I will establish My covenant between Me and you and your offspring for their generations, an eternal covenant, to be a God to you and to your offspring after you…. Every male among you shall be circumcised. And you shall circumcise the flesh of your foreskin, and it shall be a token of the covenant between Me and you. (17:4–7, 11)

Any chance of living a quiet, peaceful life is replaced by what seems to be a grand mission – even his name is changed to reflect his new status. Abram (apparently a contraction of Av Ram, "exalted father," or Av Aram, "the leader of/from Aram") is now Abraham, the father of many nations (the extra "h" forms the Hebrew word for multitude). Abraham's future includes royalty, and the earlier promise that Abram will become a great nation is replaced by the promise that Abraham will become the father of many nations. As opposed to Abram, whose destiny is linked to his becoming a great nation, Abraham takes on a leadership role for the family of man. Private man Abram is replaced by universal Abraham.

NOAH AND ABRAHAM

Earlier we alluded to differences between Noah and Abraham. This new covenant is an appropriate opportunity to explore those differences, not because of what they say about Noah but because of what they say about Abraham. Before we examine the differences, however, we should point out the similarities.

Both Noah and Abraham are inducted into covenants with God and both are given a sign or symbol of that covenant: for Noah it is the rainbow and for Abraham it is circumcision. Both are told by God that He will establish, or uphold, His covenant (the Hebrew verb used is the same, from the root K-U-M). Noah "walked with God" and Abraham is told to "walk before God," and both "walkings" are described using an uncommon reflexive form of the verb H-L-KH (*hit'halekh*).[1]

---

1. The reflexive form of H-L-KH (to walk), *hit'halekh*, appears in five contexts in Genesis. The first refers to God, who was "walking" in the Garden. Ḥanokh is described as "walking" with God, as is Noah. With Abram the reflexive verb appears twice, and both times, it describes not what Abraham actually does but what God wants him

The parallels serve to highlight a significant point. If the covenant with Noah represents God's second attempt to connect with humanity as a family following the failures of the first five chapters of Genesis, this covenant with Abraham suggests the next step in that process, channeling God's contact with humanity through an individual first and then through his family.

Despite the similarities, Abraham is not Noah and their covenants are not identical. First, while Noah is described as walking *with* God, Abraham is told to walk *before* God. The switch is not just semantic; it opens the question of who is leading. Abraham is instructed to walk before God, to play a leading role. At the very least, Abraham's role is that of the harbinger of the arrival of the King. He is the advance party. He moves from being a follower to a leader. The Abram who is first introduced by the command to walk forth for himself (*lekh lekha*) is now Abraham who walks before God (*hit'halekh lefanai*). God's expectations of Abraham exceed those He has of Noah.

Second, there is a profound difference in the symbols chosen for the two covenants. Noah's symbol is a rainbow, and just as God's covenant with Noah is essentially one-sided (God promises to Noah but demands nothing in return), so too the symbol is one which comes exclusively from God: He, not man, makes rainbows. Abraham's symbol of circumcision is profoundly different. He must perform the act, carving the symbol of the covenant into his own flesh. The language used in introducing Abraham's covenant highlights this. When speaking of His own obligations, God twice uses the word *ani* (17:1, 4), which could be translated as "as for Me." Parallel language is used when God presents Abraham's obligation, *ve'ata*, "as for you" (17:9). For the first time in the Bible we find a two-sided covenant, with obligations for both parties. God's commitment to Abraham needs to be matched by Abraham's commitment to God.

---

to do: God instructs Abram to "walk" the length and breadth of the land (perhaps in a revised instruction of *lekh lekha*), and here God instructs Abraham to "walk" before Him. The final instance in Genesis is Jacob's proclamation that his father and grandfather walked before God (48:16).

THE COVENANT OF THE FLESH

God's increased expectation of Abraham is matched by His intensified commitment to him. God will maintain that special relationship with Abraham's descendants for all eternity, as long as they maintain their commitment to the covenant. The circumcision marks them as partners with the divine, much as a uniform (temporarily) or a tattoo (permanently) identifies members of a group who have made a commitment to it. The circumcision is the logo branded into the flesh of God's earthly partners.

God chooses the reproductive organ as the site for this branding. For a covenant to be eternal it must be transmitted from generation to generation. As we saw earlier with regard to Shem and Ever, the great challenge in any endeavor to transmit values is generating repeated commitment to it. The act of circumcision not only inducts the newborn into the covenant, it sanctifies his entire life and his future offspring into that covenant as well. Two generations are drawn into the covenant simultaneously, the father, who is obligated to have the circumcision performed, and the one being circumcised, generating a cycle that can repeatedly build upon itself. Circumcision as symbol is an integral component of the self-renewing covenant.

The commandment of circumcision is introduced with an ironic twist. God initially informs Abraham of the new covenant, adding the instruction that Abraham "be without blemish" (17:1).[2] Once again there is a pause, indicated by a second *vayomer* (17:9). As with the angel's messages to Hagar, God apparently wants the first message to sink in before pushing even further. Paradoxically, just as Abraham is internalizing the idea of being without blemish he is instructed to circumcise himself.

---

2. The Hebrew word for "without blemish" is *tamim*. This word appears multiple times in the Torah, mostly with regard to the requirement that animals brought for sacrifices be without blemish. Outside of that context, it appears only three times in Genesis (once describing Noah, in our text as part of God's instruction to Abram, and as part of the Torah's depiction of Jacob in his early years) and twice in Deuteronomy (the first, as part of the Torah's overarching statement to adopt a stance which shuns sorcery, and the second as characterizing God's work). The implication of all the non-sacrificial uses of the word are variations on "without blemish": perfect, complete, wholehearted.

Moreover, as Abraham is inaugurated into his universal role, he is to bear a mark on his flesh that will set him and his household apart from the rest of humanity as God's emissaries. The covenant of circumcision distinguishes Abraham and his clan even as Abraham's horizons expand. The resolution of this paradox maintains its inherent tension, for as God's emissary, Abraham will need to ensure that his increased interactions with a variety of peoples do not cloud his mission or focus. He will need to be vigilant to ensure that he impacts on them more than they impact on him, and he has an ever-present reminder of his status. The circumcision serves as a permanent reminder of his uniqueness even as his circles widen dramatically, and the circumcision of the infant is the child's induction into that covenant via the very organ that represents continuity.

THE COVENANTAL CHILD

Particularly surprising is that the new covenantal status is not limited to Abraham and his biological children:

> Every eight-day-old male shall be circumcised throughout your generations, even slaves born into the household and those purchased from foreign nations who are not from your seed. Those born in your household and those purchased must be circumcised. (17:12–13)

Let us remember that Abraham had previously complained about the absence of an heir who is his biological descendant, terrified that Eliezer of Damascus, a man of his household, would inherit him. At that time God reassured him that he would have a biological child as an heir. God now turns that upside-down, as nonbiological children are welcomed into the covenant as well.[3]

---

3. According to halakha, a non-Jewish slave owned by a Jewish household is obligated in most of the commandments, and upon being freed is considered a full Jew (Maimonides, *Laws of Prohibited Intercourse* 14:19). The servitude functions as a period of acculturation into the national identity. It is often the case, even today, that long-time domestic or healthcare workers employed in the home are considered part of the family.

The implication of this is clear. As Abraham's status shifts from individual to father of a nation, the definition of nation expands beyond family-clan lines. While the core of the nation may be the direct offspring, the covenantal nation may swell to include foreigners inducted into it. When we first met Abram he had accumulated much wealth, including people, in Ḥaran. Those people were outsiders, adjuncts to the family. With the introduction of this paradoxical covenant, the one which simultaneously makes Abraham both universal and distinct from the rest of mankind, the boundary between the family and its adjuncts, in the context of a national identity, suddenly becomes more porous.

This paradox is amplified by the broader context in which Abraham is being inducted into the covenant. The self-renewing covenant and its accompanying symbol of circumcision must precede the birth of the covenantal child. That child will be born into the covenant, not brought in from the outside. Ishmael, the son of the maidservant, is rejected as the covenantal child. That status is being reserved for a new child, Isaac.

The pace of the life-changing messages in this chapter is breathtaking. Abram becomes Abraham; private citizen becomes God's emissary to humanity; an eternal covenant binds Abraham's children with God, while the command to circumcise extends to all the males of the household. If that were not enough, God speaks yet again – before Abraham has a chance to respond to any of the above: "Sarai, your wife, shall no longer be called Sarai, for her name is now Sarah. I will bless her and also give you a son from her" (17:15–16).

It is at this point that Abraham finally responds – he again falls on his face and laughs. Could he, the ninety-nine-year-old man, father a child? Even more insane, could Sarah, the barren wife, give birth at the age of ninety? Indeed, what Abraham hears from God sounds utterly absurd. Could the barren, now post-menopausal Sarah bear a child? Moreover, is it necessary? After all, he is already raising Ishmael to be his heir. Why does God offer to needlessly violate the very laws of nature? And so Abraham musters the words to express what he is feeling: "If only Ishmael were to live before You" (7:18). From Abraham's perspective, the birth of another child is superfluous. Ishmael answers all of his needs.

This is the second time in this chapter of Genesis that Abram/ Abraham falls on his face. When God first appears to him he is concerned that the blessed life he has built is about to be interrupted. When he hears this second message about Sarah bearing him a child his greatest fear is confirmed. His life *is* being radically interrupted. Another child, one from Sarah, would ruin everything he has built for the past thirteen years. This is as challenging as his original *lekh lekha.* There he was asked to leave his father, while here he is being told to sideline Ishmael. So Abraham falls on his face and proclaims that he prefers to remain with only Ishmael.

God, however, persists, and presses the point further:

> But Sarah, your wife, will bear you a son, and you will name him Isaac (in Hebrew, Yitzhak, playing on the Hebrew root for "laughter," TZ-Ḥ-K). I will establish My covenant with him as an eternal covenant, and with his offspring after him. As for Ishmael, I have heard you. Behold, I have blessed him and made him exceeding fruitful; he will father twelve princes and I will make him a great nation. However, I will establish My covenant with Isaac, whom Sarah shall bear for you at this time in another year. (17:19–21)

God's response is clear. True, Ishmael may be your son. Also true that he will be blessed because he is your son. But that does not make him the covenantal child. That position is reserved for Isaac, whom only Sarah can bear. Despite Abraham's avowal that he is satisfied with Ishmael, God insists that Ishmael is outside the covenant. On a human level, God's message shatters Abraham's carefully constructed world.

THE COVENANTAL WIFE

Nothing could have prepared Abraham for the last part of God's triple message, that Isaac will replace Ishmael, yet a careful reading of the text suggests that there is yet another message, which may have been just as difficult for Abraham to swallow. It is not only Abraham's name that will change, but Sarah's as well. God has a message for Sarah, and when we lay it out next to His message for Abraham we discover that they are extraordinarily parallel:

God's message about Abraham (17:5–6)	God's message about Sarah (via Abraham) (17:15–16)
Abram becomes Abraham (add the Hebrew letter *heh*)	Sarai becomes Sarah (replace the Hebrew letter *yud* with the letter *heh*)
I will make you exceedingly fruitful	I will bless her
You will become many nations	She will become nations
Even kings will emerge from you	Kings of nations will emerge from her

Not only does God bless Sarah with a child, He bestows upon her the same blessings bestowed upon Abraham, even to the extent of changing her name. The implication is clear: just as Abraham is entering a covenant with God, so is Sarah. Her covenant will not be independent of Abraham's, but it will be fulfilled as she becomes Abraham's covenantal partner. From this point onward it will be impossible to speak of Abraham's covenant with God without speaking of Sarah's role in that covenant. It means that any discussion of an heir for Abraham is meaningless without including Sarah as the mother of the covenantal child.

Three times in this short passage about Sarah, God insists that the child must come from her (17:16, 19, 21). Not from Sarai but from Sarah. When Abraham avers that he would be satisfied with Ishmael, God's retort is revealing:

> But Sarah, *your wife*, will bear you a son, and you will name him Isaac.... I will establish My covenant with Isaac, whom Sarah shall bear for you at this time in another year. (17:19, 21)

What makes Isaac different from Ishmael is that Ishmael's mother is an Egyptian maidservant, while Isaac's mother is the covenantal wife. Sarah's prior barrenness is necessary to prevent her from bearing a child outside of the covenant; it is only now that both Abraham and Sarah become true partners in the divine mission that God blesses her to bear the covenantal child. Only the covenantal couple can bear the covenantal child,[4] one who will be the inaugural member of the child born into a self-renewing covenant.

The challenge for Abraham to grasp this cannot be overstated. Abram's taking of Sarai as a wife was nothing short of revolutionary, and his staying with her despite her barrenness was even more radical. Yet as we follow Abram it becomes clear that his concept of a wife falls somewhat short of an ideal. In Egypt, he is willing to pass her off as his sister, with all of the associated indignity. When she complains of Hagar's mistreatment of her, Abram responds not with compassion but with dispassion: "Here is your maidservant; do with her as you please," he says. Abram removes himself from the scene as a noninvolved party.

As God brings Sarah fully into the picture, He is trying to execute a course-correction for Abraham, insisting that he must change the way he relates to Sarah. She is neither an accessory nor an adjunct, but an equal. She, too, is God's covenantal partner, and Abraham must step back to make room for her to play her role. As he begins to figure out how to be God's covenantal partner, he must begin to figure out how to allow Sarah to be his.

Leon Kass writes, "Abraham is eager to be the founder of a great nation. But he has an incomplete understanding of how a nation becomes truly great." Kass continues:

> However manly the man, founding a great nation is absolutely dependent on woman, on her generative power. She holds the key to the future, not only by her natural capacity to give birth but also by her moral and educative influence over her children, an influence itself deeply rooted in the powerful mother-child bond imposed by natural necessity.[5]

---

4. Sarah's centrality begins to emerge in the previous chapter. It is she who initiates the relations between Hagar and Abram, it is she who challenges Abram afterward, and it is she who makes sure Hagar is put in her place as the maid.
5. Leon Kass, *Genesis*, 266.

Genesis 17:1–27

COVENANTAL PARADOXES

This chapter presents us with multiple paradoxes: being without blemish vs. physically branding oneself, exclusivity vs. universality, rejecting one son in favor of another, and readjusting one's relationship with God while navigating a new one with an old wife. For Abraham, these are not mere paradoxes but challenges to his very essence, demanding yet another transformation. The continuation of his story explores how he wrestles with them.

194

Genesis 18:1–33

Three Mystery Guests and ...

At the age of ninety-nine, Abram becomes Abraham as he circumcises himself and enters into a covenant with God. At the same time, Sarai becomes Sarah and is designated as Abraham's covenantal partner. With the first covenantal couple identified, God tells Abraham that the time is ready for Sarah to become the mother of the first covenantal child.

Soon afterward we find Abraham sitting at the entrance to his tent in the heat of the day. God appears to him, yet the Torah makes no mention of the content of that appearance. Abraham is then visited by three men carrying a divine message that Sarah will bear him a child. Sarah overhears the message and laughs in disbelief, and God seems upset by her laughter. Abraham is distressed by God's response, and when he confronts Sarah about her laughter she denies it. The men leave Abraham and continue on to Sodom, at which point God decides to reveal to Abraham that He is about to destroy the evil city.

This entire passage is puzzling. What is the purpose of a divine appearance absent a message?[1] Why is God angered by the laughter of

---

1. Maimonides, *Guide* 2:43, is so troubled by this that he posits that the entire encounter with the three visitors is actually a vision. Nahmanides, 18:1, is mortified by this suggestion and lashes out at Maimonides, exclaiming, "These words contradict the

Sarah, who hears about her impending pregnancy from three passing strangers, but not by Abraham's laughter in the previous chapter when he hears directly from God? And why is it necessary for three strangers to visit Abraham to inform him of his good fortune when God has just told him directly about Isaac's impending birth?

ABRAHAM'S REBUKE

A closer look at the Torah text will offer some significant clues:

> God appeared to him in the plains of Mamre, and he was sitting at the entrance to his tent in the heat of the day. He raised his eyes and saw – behold – there were three men standing upon him. He saw and ran from the entrance of the tent to greet them, and he bowed on the ground. He said, "Adonai,[2] if I find favor in your eyes, do not move on from upon your servant. Let there be taken some water – wash your feet – and rest under the tree. I will take a loaf of bread – eat to your heart's content – then you can move on, for this is the reason you have passed by your servant." They responded, "Yes, do as you spoke."… He was standing over them under the tree as they ate. They said to him, "Where is Sarah, your wife?" He said, "Behold, she is in the tent." He said, "I will return to you at this time next year, and Sarah will have a son," and Sarah was standing at the entrance of the tent which was behind him.[3] Now Abraham and Sarah were coming along in days; Sarah's womanly ways had ceased. Sarah laughed inside and said, "After I am worn out shall I be refreshed and have a cycle?

---

text. It is forbidden to even hear them and surely to believe them." As an alternative, Nahmanides suggests that the appearance was a visit to honor Abraham for having performed the covenantal circumcision.

2. It is unclear whether this is meant to refer to God or is a polite salutation ("My master") to his guest. The vocalization under the letter *nun* is uncommon, although in this narrative and the following one it appears multiple times, and by multiple individuals: 18:27, 30-31 (Abraham); 19:18 (Lot); and 20:4 (Avimelekh), many of them bearing the same ambiguity.

3. In the Hebrew this phrase uses multiple pronouns, leading to multiple possible interpretations.

And my master is elderly!" God said to Abraham, "Why is Sarah laughing, saying, 'Can I bear a child and I am elderly?' Is anything beyond God? At this time I will return to you next year, and Sarah will have a son!" Sarah denied it, saying, "I did not laugh," for she was afraid, but he said, "No, you did laugh." The men left there and gazed upon the face of Sodom while Abraham was walking with them to send them off. God had previously said, "Can I conceal from Abraham that which I am about to do? Abraham will become a great and mighty nation, and through him will come blessing to all other nations of the earth. Since I know that he will instruct his children and his household after him, that they will observe God's way in doing justice and righteousness – that is why Abraham will receive all of which has been spoken about him." God then said, "The cries of Sodom and Gomorrah are great, and their sins are very weighty. Let Me go down and see – if the cries which come to Me describe their actions, then they are finished – and if not, then I will know." (18:1–21)

It is odd that the three guests ask about Sarah's whereabouts (or even that they know who Sarah is), yet never request to speak with her. It is also curious that at the beginning of the scene Abraham is at the opening of the tent but later it is Sarah who is at the opening, while Abraham thinks that she is inside.[4]

When we put these observations together with our earlier questions there seems to be a single conclusion. The purpose of the visit is not to inform Abraham that Sarah will bear him a child, as Abraham already knows that. The purpose is also not to inform Sarah that she will give birth to a son, for there is no message ever directed to her (even though the three travelers are unusually curious as to her whereabouts). The purpose of this visit is to rebuke Abraham for not informing Sarah that she will have a son.

---

4. Perhaps it is because Abraham sees Sarah's place as in the tent that he does not invite his guests inside but rather serves them under the shade of the tree. It is curious that the tree is mentioned explicitly both in his invitation (18:4) and as he waits on them (18:8).

Abraham's ambivalence at initially hearing God's message necessitates God's repetition, insisting that "Sarah, your wife, will bear you a son, and you will name him Isaac. I will establish My covenant with him as an eternal covenant." Yet that does not anger God, as Abraham's ambivalence is understandable. Similarly, Abraham's laughter of disbelief in the previous chapter does not provoke God's anger, as it should not. Abraham is on a path to faith, but is not yet Kierkegaard's "knight of faith." Doubt is to be expected, and laughter is the natural reaction to a message which seems absurd. Once, however, God's message is unambiguous – regarding both Sarah and Isaac – it is inexcusable for Abraham to have withheld the news from his wife.

Had he shared that message, Sarah would not need to overhear it from three passersby. She would have laughed earlier, when Abraham told it to her in the name of God, and like Abraham, would have been justified in her laughter. Her laughter now is all the more reasonable because she hears the message for the first time from the three mysterious guests. So why does God rebuke her for her laughter? Actually, He does not, but He does rebuke Abraham for Sarah's laughter: "Why is Sarah laughing, saying, 'Can I bear a child and I am elderly?'" The rhetorical question God poses is directed at Abraham, not at Sarah. If Sarah is laughing it is because she is surprised by the news, because Abraham did not share it with her. And he should have.

That is why the three visitors inquire about her whereabouts. She is going to be the mother of the covenantal child; why is she not side by side with her husband? This rhetorical question posed by a divine figure is intended as a rebuke to Abraham for being unaware of his wife's status. Abraham had relegated her to the tent, where he instructed her, as he instructed the servant, to prepare a meal for the guests. When asked where his wife is Abraham responds that she is in the tent, behind the scenes, playing only a background role. But Abraham is wrong. She is not in the tent at all but at the opening of the tent, the same place occupied by Abraham at the beginning of the scene, taking her rightful place. Ironically, the three guests see precisely where she is. Only Abraham is unaware, as the opening of the tent is behind him (18:10).

Abraham is unaware of the need to change his approach to Sarah's status, so that even when confronted about Sarah's laughter – intended as a rebuke to him – all he can think of is to rebuke Sarah for her laughter, passing the blame on to her. Sarah's denial of her laughter reveals that she doesn't feel treated as Abraham's equal; she fears him. Leon Kass writes, "Proud men are not given to yielding to their wives. Before he can become a founder, and even a proper father, he must become a proper husband and appreciate Sarah as a wife."[5] Abraham needs to go beyond his initial revolutionary innovation of appreciating Sarah as a wife; he needs to welcome her as his full covenantal partner.

What does all this have to do with God's mysteriously silent visit to Abraham in the opening scene?

GOD INTERRUPTS HIMSELF

In the Covenant between the Pieces we learned that Abram interrupted God's speech, and only by separating God's initial intention from His need to respond to Abram were we able to make sense of the narrative. In this story I suggest that it is not Abraham who interrupts God but God who interrupts Himself, and the structure of the text which emerges will not only solve a riddle in the Torah but reinforce my point.

The story begins with God appearing to Abraham, after which our attention is diverted to the visit of the three travelers, and only when that tangent is finished do we return to our original narrative. Here is how the story without the interruption would read:

> God appeared to him in the plains of Mamre, and he was sitting at the entrance to his tent in the heat of the day.... God had previously said, "Can I conceal from Abraham that which I am about to do? Abraham will become a great and mighty nation, and through him will come blessing to all other nations of the earth. Since I know that he will instruct his children and his household after him, that they will observe God's way in doing justice and righteousness – that is why Abraham will receive all of which has been spoken about him." (18:1, 17–19)

---

5. Leon Kass, *Genesis*, 266.

God's initial appearance to Abraham is apparently to inform him of His intentions regarding Sodom. This is a very powerful statement, and flows directly from the circumcision covenant which precedes it. In that covenant Abraham is given responsibility for a multitude of nations as he becomes God's partner. He is the one chosen by God to be the conduit of divine blessing for all the families of the earth, a phrase hearkening back to God's initial call to Abram ("Through you shall come blessing to all the families of the earth"). As a partner, it is only appropriate that Abraham be apprised of God's intentions regarding one of the nations under his aegis. That is the message that emerges when we read the story without the interruption.

But the story *is* interrupted, and it is God Himself who interrupts it by bringing the three visitors.[6] Why would God do that? Because God's sharing of information with His covenantal partner, Abraham, should have been mirrored by Abraham's sharing of information with *his* covenantal partner, Sarah. Abraham, however, fails in that partnership, and God interrupts His own communication with Abraham to rebuke him. It is only after the interruption that God can continue where He left off, modeling for Abraham the appropriate way to share information.

God's interpolation of this scene within a scene is meant to inform Abraham that it is inconceivable for God to continue His new relationship with Abraham without addressing Abraham's attitude toward Sarah. The business of saving Sodom must take a backseat to the nature of the relationship between Abraham and Sarah. It is only after the censure is issued that our story can continue. In this light, it is particularly troubling that even as God rebukes him, Abraham continues to shift the blame to Sarah, censuring her – and not himself – for her laughter.

---

6. This sense of interruption is reinforced by the choreography with the three visitors. Abraham escorts them on their way to Sodom when he is confronted by God. His guests continue on their way while Abraham speaks with God. When God finishes telling him about Sodom, Abraham sees that this is exactly where his three guests have gone. It is only then that Abraham realizes that his thee guests were not ordinary travelers, and that God's intentions regarding Sodom need to be addressed immediately.

Three Mystery Guests and...

DOES ABRAHAM UNDERSTAND?

It is immediately clear that Abraham understands the nature of his covenant with God: no sooner does God finish telling him of His plan for Sodom than he launches into his valiant effort to save the doomed cities. Abraham, about whom God testifies that he is chosen for his values of justice (SH-F-T) and righteousness (TZ-D-K), immediately champions those values before God: "Will the judge (SH-F-T) of the entire world not do justice (SH-F-T)?" he confronts God,[7] and seven times during the negotiations over the fate of Sodom he describes the righteous using the same root word God uses to identify him, *tzaddik* (TZ-D-K). As God's partner, Abraham holds God to the same standards which God identifies as criteria for Abraham's partnership.

In Abraham's negotiations with God, there are a number of elements which stand out quite prominently. First, with great subtlety, Abraham shifts from asking, almost rhetorically, whether God will destroy the righteous along with the wicked, to using the righteous to save the entire city.[8] Not that God is fooled by Abraham's deft move, but the vigor with which Abraham tries to save a region for which he feels a sense of responsibility is noble. This energy is, no doubt, the direct result of Abraham's new role as "the father of a multitude of nations," which in his eyes includes the five Sodomite city-states.

Second, it is quite remarkable that not once in his attempt to save Sodom does Abraham mention Lot, the very nephew for whom he earlier risks his life in battle. It appears that for Abraham, Lot is at best one of those few righteous people and at worst a nephew who he once thought would be his heir and for whom he has now completely given up hope.

Third, Abraham asks God six times to save the entire city in the merit of a decreasing cadre of righteous people,[9] and each time God

---

7. The Hebrew "*vayigash*" literally means to approach, yet when used in the Torah it inevitably means a close-up, unmediated, face-to-face encounter. See, for example, Gen. 27:21–22; 33:6-7; 44:18; 45:4; Ex. 44:30–32.
8. We will examine this argument further in the next chapter.
9. Many are perplexed by the sequence of the number of righteous people Abraham proposes – 50, 45, 40, 30, 20, 10 – with the number 45 standing out. Note that Abraham never asks about 45; rather, he asks whether God would be prepared to "lose the deal" if the 50 were missing 5. Abraham was fishing to see whether he could

responds obliquely, promising to "not destroy" the city if He finds the requisite number – but at no point does God actually say that the required quorum cannot be found. That has two fascinating implications. One, that Abraham continues to negotiate without receiving a clear indication of the facts on the ground and the results of his previous request; two, that even when the negotiations are over, Abraham does not know if he has been successful in saving the city.

These last observations come back to haunt us the next morning as Abraham arises early and returns to where he earlier negotiated with God. Looking out over the region, he sees nothing but smoke (19:27–28); his first attempt at partnership with God apparently fails, as he is unable to dissuade his Partner from carrying out His threat. The irony in all this is that Abraham *is* successful, but precisely in the area in which he makes no effort: "It was, as the Almighty destroyed the cities of the plain, that He remembered Abraham, and sent Lot out from the upheaval" (19:29). Abraham had given up on Lot. He thought that his nephew had been swallowed up by Sodomite culture prior to its destruction and then consumed by God's ensuing wrath. Unbeknownst to Abraham, God saves Lot, perhaps through means that he cannot even imagine, which we will explore soon.

At least in his initial venture as God's covenantal partner, Abraham succeeds where he gives up and fails where he tries the hardest. This leaves us with two unanswered questions. First, just how does Abraham save Lot? Second, assuming that his attempt to save Sodom is an indication that he understands his new role vis-à-vis God and the rest of humanity, does Abraham finally internalize God's message regarding Sarah and her role?

---

find flexibility in any number that would be agreed to, so that 30 could become 25 and 20 could become 15. God does not yield to Abraham's attempt, stating simply that for 45, He would not destroy the city. My thanks to Rabbi Dr. Michael Berger for pointing this out to me.

Genesis 19:1–38

Lot in Sodom

All indications from the opening chapters in Abraham's career point to his failure regarding Lot, despite his noble intentions and valiant efforts. Soon after the unfortunate trip to Egypt, Abraham and Lot separate, Lot choosing to pitch his tent right up to Sodom (despite Sodom's well-known reputation). It does not take long before Abraham needs to rescue Lot from captivity in the first world war and it becomes abundantly clear that the ungrateful Lot will not become Abraham's heir. We fast-forward to Abraham's circumcision and new covenant with God – by now Lot is no longer camped at the entrance to Sodom but is an important resident with a position in the town square (19:1).[1] According to a rabbinic tradition, he even serves as one of the justices in Sodom.[2] Lot is a full-fledged Sodomite.

At the same time, Lot is clearly different from his neighbors. When two mysterious guests arrive in town Lot invites them in and persists in his invitation despite their initial refusal. When the townspeople want to Sodomize his guests, Lot protects them – at great personal risk.

---

1. In the ancient world, the city gate was the main gathering place where all important matters were discussed. See, for example, Gen. 23:10; Ruth 4:1.
2. Genesis Rabba 50:3.

While Lot may not be a paragon of the Abrahamic tradition, he certainly welcomes strangers into his home. A brief comparison of Lot's hospitality with Abraham's will highlight both the similarities and the differences between them.

Abraham's hospitality (18:2–8)	Lot's hospitality (19:1–3)
He raised his eyes and saw	Lot saw
ran to greet them	arose to greet them
and he bowed on the ground.	and bowed his face to the ground.
"If I find favor in your eyes,	
do not move on from upon your servant.	"Detour yourselves to your servant's home.
Let there be taken some water – wash your feet – and rest under the tree.	Sleep, wash your feet, arise early and continue on your way."
I will take a loaf of bread – eat to your heart's content – then you can move on, for this is the reason you have passed by your servant."	
They responded, "Yes, do as you spoke."	They responded, "No, we will sleep in the street."
	He persisted greatly,
	they detoured and came to his house,
Abraham hurried to the tent to Sarah and said, "Hurry! Three *seah* measures of the finest flour, knead them and make cakes."	he made for them a feast and baked matzot,
Abraham ran to the cattle, took a good, tender one, and gave it to the lad to prepare, and he hurried to prepare it.	
He then took butter and milk and the cattle which he had prepared and placed it before them – he was standing over them under the tree as they ate.	and they ate.

Like his uncle Abraham, Lot sees-greets-bows-invites-feeds his guests.[3] As with all parallel stories, the similarity between the two hospitality scenes highlights the profound differences between them. Abraham raises his eyes to look for guests and rushes to greet and feed them; first he offers a meager meal of bread and water but then prepares a sumptuous feast; he involves other members of his household in the hospitality; and he waits upon his guests. By contrast, all those elements are absent from Lot's hospitality, and he seems in a rush to have his guests leave his house before they are discovered.

On the other hand, Lot's situation is quite different. He is not performing a simple act of hospitality. He is providing refuge, and at great personal risk. He exaggerates the welcome by prostrating his face to the ground, pleads with the strangers to detour from their path, persists in bringing them into his home, and rushes to get his guests on the road at the crack of dawn for their own safety.

What is the message of these parallel stories, albeit with their multiple differences? I believe it demonstrates that despite our hasty judgment of how he does not reach the bar set by Abraham, Lot has learned quite a bit from his uncle and maintains it, despite and in defiance of the Sodomite culture. Lot stands out as one of the righteous people in Sodom whom Abraham sought, and it can be argued that Lot's preparedness to sacrifice himself – something he also apparently inculcated from Abraham's example – is precisely what earns him salvation from the destruction of Sodom. Abraham may be unaware of his impact on Lot, but it is that influence which ultimately saves his nephew.

There is great irony in the scene where Lot steps out of his house, closing the door behind him to protect his guests. It is just at

---

3. There are numerous other linguistic and thematic parallels between the stories. Sarah's laughter upon hearing her good news is mirrored by Lot's sons-in-law considering him to be a joker when they hear the impending bad news. Abraham's approach (*vayigash*) to God is reflected in the Sodomites' approach to Lot (*geshvayigshu*). Abraham sits at the entrance to his tent, while Lot sits at the entrance of Sodom. Abraham's guests ask about Sarah's whereabouts (*ayei*) and the Sodomites ask about the whereabouts of Lot's guests (*ayei*). Abraham has an opening (*petaḥ*) to his tent which remains open, while Lot's door (*petaḥ*) is a barrier to invaders.

that moment that the guests he tried to save actually save him from the raging mob, as they secrete him to safety and afflict the mob with some sort of limited blindness.[4] Lot's attempt to save them results in his own salvation, foreshadowing a much greater salvation to come later that evening.

Lot persists in his invitation to his guests, and it is that persistence which demonstrates his worthiness to be saved. In stark contrast, the townspeople persist in their desire to harm those guests, and it is their persistence which demonstrates the need for their demise. Strikingly, the same Hebrew verb for persistence is used for both.[5] One must wonder why the messengers refuse Lot's initial invitation.[6] While some may look to find fault with its contents, perhaps the strangers' refusal is to provide Lot with the opportunity to persist in it.[7]

It is fascinating that, without any effort from Lot, the messengers are prepared to save his married daughters and sons-in-law. The rest of the story indicates that they are far from righteous people, mocking Lot as he delivers the message of doom – their very mockery showing them to be full-fledged Sodomites and thus sealing their fate. The mere possibility, however, that they *could* be saved is apparently an expression of the principle that Abraham tries impressing on God – that the righteous can save not only themselves but others alongside them. It seems that God is even ready to accept Abraham's audacious request to save the wicked in the merit of the righteous with regard to Lot and his family.

---

4. Their blindness is focused on preventing them from seeing one particular thing. See also II Kings 6:18.
5. The verb for persistence (P-TZ-R) appears only one other time in the Torah; its primary use is in this story, accentuating its significance here.
6. Rashi, 19:2, sees their refusal as a sign of Lot's reduced status. By contrast, Ibn Ezra sees their refusal as the invitation for Lot to persist: "We will sleep in the street," they say, "*unless you insist.*"
7. It may be that testing Lot's worthiness is the meaning of God's initial statement to Abraham that He will "go down to see" if the cry of the city is as great as He hears (18:21). This is more than a fact-finding mission, it is a mission to test the true mettle of both the city folk and Lot. Are the former truly deserving of destruction and is Lot (and his family) truly deserving of salvation?

FLASHBACK TO ABRAHAM

Abraham's request to save the righteous is an expression of his dedication to justice, *mishpat*, while his argument to save the wicked along with the righteous demonstrates the value of righteousness, *tzedaka*. (We recall that it is these two values which God identifies just prior to this scene as His reason for choosing Abraham.) While *mishpat* seems perfectly reasonable, *tzedaka* is somewhat odd – why should the mere presence of some good people offset all the bad and save the evil as well?

Judging a collective involves a different set of considerations than does judging an individual,[8] and one of the key underlying questions that must be explored is whether the society as a whole has embedded within it a critical mass, a community of people who can impact positively on the collective.[9] If there is such an element then the general community has a hope of being transformed. If there is no such group, whether because it does not exist or because the community does not want it to be present, then the society is judged unredeemable. Thus, in the days of Noah, he is the individual who finds favor in God's eyes, while the rest of humanity exceeds the point of no return.[10] He can be saved, while the others cannot; he can't possibly impact upon them.

The essence of Abraham's argument is that if Sodom can host a critical mass of good people, then (a) by definition it cannot be judged an evil city, and (b) that critical mass can potentially impact upon the fundamental culture of the town and shift it toward the good.

If we continue the parallel between Lot and Noah, we notice one significant difference between them. Noah is saved, and along with him

---

8. Collective justice is pervasive throughout the Torah. Aside from the evaluation of individuals within the nation, the nation is judged as a whole. Throughout the sojourn in the wilderness the Israelite nation is treated as a single entity, and once they enter the land they are dealt with as a collective regarding rain, enemies, and exile. The Book of Deuteronomy is rife with national reward and punishment, both for Israel and for other nations.

9. This may be the foundation of Lot's argument for saving Zoar (see below, p. 210), because it was small. A small city may not need a critical mass to influence it; even a single righteous person can make a difference.

10. The rest of humanity descends into "only evil" (6:5) – the precursor of Sodom.

are his wife, his sons, and his daughters-in-law. While he is unable to change the human race, he is at least able to have an impact on those closest to him so that they are worthy of being saved. For Lot, however, his influence even on his family is more limited. His sons-in-law mock, and the daughters who are married to them are apparently not much better. They all perish along with Sodom.

LOT'S WIFE

The story of Lot's escape from the conflagration in Sodom becomes even more colorful with the introduction of the women in his life. When fleeing the burning city Lot is instructed not to look back – to do so would be tantamount to acknowledging that he misses Sodom and what it represents. For Lot to deserve refuge he needs to completely dissociate himself from that black stain on his life. Lot's act of heroism with the strangers is his first demonstration of the distance between himself and Sodom; not looking back confirms it.

While Lot is able to restrain himself, his wife cannot. As she turns around, looking wistfully at the world she is leaving, she becomes a permanent part of that world. Unlike Lot, she belongs in Sodom; she yearns for it. Lot can no better take his wife out of Sodom than he can take Sodom out of his wife. Lot's wife, however, is not really the focus of the story. We know nothing about her – not even her name – except for what happens in this one scene. Why is it necessary to include it in the Torah's narrative?

Apparently, just as Lot is the backdrop for a greater appreciation of Abraham, Lot's wife is the foil for understanding Sarah. It is hard to know whether Lot really thinks of his wife as his partner. Unlike Abraham's hospitality, which comprises the participation of Sarah and the lad, Lot does not include his wife in hosting the strangers. On the other hand, unlike Sarah, Lot's wife does not see herself leaping into a new beginning. She prefers to remain in Sodom. Sarah is prepared to leave the tent to become Abraham's true partner. The only obstacle she faces is Abraham's unwillingness to embrace her in that role.

LOT'S DAUGHTERS

When the townspeople demand that Lot hand over the two strangers to be Sodomized, Lot pleads with them, offering his virgin daughters for their pleasure instead. This extraordinary act of Lot's magnanimity is a grotesque perversion of the Abrahamic selflessness and generosity of spirit.

Circumstances in the following days take Lot's perversion and turn it on its head, so much so that we don't know whether to cheer or jeer. Hiding in a cave, Lot's daughters – the very ones he offers to the Sodomite mob – look at the destruction and are convinced that not only is Sodom destroyed, but that the entire world has ceased to exist. Instead of the world being obliterated by water it is now consumed by fire. They, too, decide that an act of selflessness is necessary – not to save their guests, but to save the human race. After all, as far as they know, the only ones to survive the destruction of the world are in that cave.

Knowing that their father will never consciously agree to their plan, Lot's daughters get him drunk and lie with him so that they may bear children and begin the repopulation of the world. Their choice stands in stark contrast to Noah and his wife, who after the *Mabul*, despite being commanded repeatedly to be fruitful and multiply, never have additional children. It is also reminiscent of the story of Ham and Noah, where there is also drunkenness following mass destruction, after which there is an act with sexual overtones. The difference between them, however, cannot be more pronounced. While Ham's actions are deemed selfish and condemned by Noah, Lot's daughters act selflessly in their attempt to save what they believe is all of humanity.[11]

Like Lot's selflessness, his daughters' selflessness is a perversion of Abraham's loving-kindness. Lot offered them and they now offer

11. The generosity of Lot's daughters reappears later in the Bible. The Torah explicitly forbids intermarriage with descendants of Ammon and Moab (the sons Noah had by his daughters), and explains that they did not greet the Israelites with bread and water upon their exodus from Egypt (Deut. 23:5). This makes sense only when we recall that the redeeming quality of their forebears was selflessness and they chose to suppress that quality when it came to the Israelites.

By contrast, Ruth the Moabite is brought into the Israelite fold as a mother of royalty, presumably because of her selflessness vis-à-vis her mother-in-law, Naomi. Moreover, Solomon's wife, who becomes the mother of the entire Davidic dynasty, is an Ammonite woman (I Kings 14:21). Rabbinic tradition also distinguishes between the males and females, maintaining the prohibition against intermarriage for the former but suspending it for the latter (Yevamot 76b–77a).

themselves. Lot teaches them to sacrifice themselves for a greater good and in the end, they do – although the greater good is not quite what Lot intended. Abraham's influence, albeit distorted, actually extends beyond his nephew to his nephew's daughters. Abraham thinks that he failed with Lot, yet little does he know how much impact he has had, on both Lot and his daughters. And Abraham's influence goes even beyond Lot's immediate family.

LOT SAVES ZOAR

When Abraham rises the next morning and sees the smoke rising from the Jordan valley, he is convinced that he failed miserably. But did he really?

Let us recall from the battle of the four kings against the five that there were five city-states of Sodom: Sodom, Gomorrah, Admah, Zevoyim, and Zoar (14:1–2). When Lot is instructed by his visitors to literally "run for the hills," he pleads with them to allow him to go to Zoar (19:19–20). Remarkably, one of the guests tells him that he will, indeed, do that for Lot: "Behold, I will grant you this too, so as to not overturn the city of which you spoke" (19:21). Indeed, many years later, when Moses describes a future destruction of the land, he describes it as "the overturning of Sodom and Gomorrah, Admah and Zevoyim" (Deut. 29:22). Zoar is not mentioned as being destroyed, because Lot saved it.[12]

Abraham's apparent influence on Lot and Lot's children inspires selflessness on their part (albeit quite different from Abraham's), which justifies their own salvation. Thus, not only does Abraham's initial plea to protect the righteous (Lot) from the destruction which consumes his environment succeed, it is possible that even his latter plea to save an entire city on behalf of a small number of righteous inhabitants is accepted.

Lot and his daughters are saved in their own merit, and Zoar is saved because of them.[13] But Lot is a secondary character in our story;

---

12. Genesis 10:19 also lists four city-states in the Sodom region; notably absent is Zoar.
13. Ammon and Moab are rewarded for their matriarchs' selflessness. Deuteronomy 2 identifies the lands that God gave to Ammon and Moab, Lot's children. It is likely that their lands are near both the site of their conception and Zoar, the city their patriarch saved.

after this incident he disappears from the central biblical narrative. Lot's wife and daughters are tertiary characters – they do not even have names. Their primary significance is that the daughters are the matriarchs of two satellite-cousin nations. They serve as foils through which to view Sarah and Abraham.

In the Masoretic text there are no breaks from God's appearance to Abraham just prior to Abraham's greeting of the three visitors through the story of Lot and his daughters, thus marking all of those narratives as one continuum. This block of text comprises the story of Abraham's partnership with God, including the challenge of making Sarah his true partner; Abraham's plea (as God's partner) on behalf of Sodom; and Abraham's unknowing deliverance of Lot and Zoar. The stories of Lot in Zoar and of Lot's daughters highlight Abraham as God's covenantal partner and inform us that Abraham's influence is far greater than he imagines.

Genesis 20:1–18

In the Land of the Philistines

Let us try to gauge Abraham's state of mind following the destruction of Sodom. He leaves his father's home and his very identity to pursue what he believes is a divine call. Desperately in search of a sign from God, he doesn't see that God has been pointing him to the heartland of Canaan. Going too far, all the way to Egypt, where he compromises his wife's dignity, he traces his way back until he discovers the place. But even before he can settle down to receive God's blessing he is confronted by the challenge of his nephew, the very one he thinks will be his promised heir.

Abraham likely believes that the separation from Lot it is a temporary, though necessary, stage, but after thanklessly rescuing Lot he ultimately mourns Lot's descent into Sodom and apparent demise in God's fiery wrath. Abraham may even blame himself for taking Lot with him from Ḥaran and allowing him to settle in Sodom. Little does he know that Lot is still alive and that in some bizarre way both Lot and his daughters carry some of Abraham with them.

Parallel to that, Abraham has been grappling with God's promises and covenants. For twelve years from the initial *lekh lekha* call, he waits, sometimes losing patience and mustering faith only with great effort, for God to deliver on the first of those promises. The pain of childlessness is eased when God finally gives him a child through Hagar, Sarah's surrogate, although that, too, comes with the near loss of that child when the expectant mother of the promised child is subjugated and flees the house.

After an additional (unremarkable) twelve years, Abraham is shaken from his placid life. God inducts him into a covenant which challenges him on three levels. First, Abraham needs to see himself as the head of a parochial clan with a universal vision. Second, Abraham needs to expand his vision to include Sarah as his covenantal partner. Third, Abraham must abandon the notion of Ishmael as the promised child, replacing him with the as-yet-unborn covenantal son, Isaac.

If these challenges aren't enough, Abraham is quickly put to the test. He takes his universal responsibility seriously, standing to defend the indefensible Sodom – but the morning after his valiant effort he wakes to the stench of an entire section of his domain incinerated. In his own eyes he is a failure, vis-à-vis both Lot and Sodom. He is unaware that in his merit, Lot, and by extension Zoar, have been saved. That is inconsequential, precisely because Abraham does *not* know.

After years of dwelling in Hebron to keep watch over his wayward nephew, Abraham leaves. But he does not go back to the place of divine revelation. In fact, he goes very far, almost back to the place of his first disgrace in Egypt: to Gerar, a Philistine city-state as far to the south as one can go without leaving the Promised Land, where he again anticipates trouble with Sarah similar to that which he encountered earlier in Egypt.

This trip, however, is enigmatic, especially when compared to his prior trip to Egypt. The first trip is motivated by Abram's search for "the place" and by the famine in Canaan. Under those circumstances we can understand why Abram goes to Egypt even at the cost of risking Sarai. The trip to Gerar, however, seems to serve no purpose, so why would Abraham again risk Sarah's dignity without a compelling need? We imagine Abraham would have learned from his debacle in Egypt and avoid repeating it, if possible.

Abraham's explanation justifying his behavior seems insufficient, and in fact, lame: "When God caused me to wander aimlessly from my father's home I said to her, 'Do this kindness for me; anywhere we go say that I am your brother'" (20:13). If this is indeed their standard practice, it is an unbecoming one. It should have ceased when God repeatedly impresses upon Abraham the need to include his wife as a covenantal partner. Abraham, who stands before God arguing the case for justice and righteousness, has better options from which to choose.

ABRAHAM'S DARK HOUR

All of this points to a lapse in judgment, perhaps precipitated by the crisis brought on by Abraham's sense of failure as God's partner. Sodom is lost, Lot is lost, he sacrificed the promise of the land and lost on the gamble, and Ishmael is displaced. Abraham's trip to Gerar is apparently an act of despondency, a flight from the very mission for which he was chosen. Abraham describes himself as "wandering aimlessly" (20:13), paralleling the description of Hagar's later disorientation in the wilderness of Be'er Sheba (21:14). Ishmael's ultimate expulsion causes Hagar to lose her way just as Abraham's sense of failure causes him to be lost.

Abraham's loss of focus is apparent in his conversation with Avimelekh, king of the Philistines. In the story, Sarah is taken by Avimelekh. God intervenes, afflicting Avimelekh and his household with some type of disease; appearing to Avimelekh in a nighttime vision; and demanding that Sarah be released, as she is Abraham's wife. In the morning, Avimelekh instructs all his people to keep their hands off Sarah, but he then confronts Abraham: "What did you do to us? What wrong did I do to you that you should bring upon me and my nation such a grievous sin? You did things to me that are simply not done!" (20:9). Abraham is so stunned by the charges that he is left speechless. He has no credible reply.

It is only after Avimelekh has scored his moral victory that he asks Abraham, "What did you see that you did this to us?" (20:10). He is no longer challenging Abraham but querying what it was that caused Abraham to act as he did. To that, Abraham musters a feeble response:

> Because I said that there is no fear of God in this place, and that they will kill me on account of my wife. And in truth, she really is my sister, from my father's side but not from my mother's side, and she became for me a wife. And it was when God caused me

to wander aimlessly from my father's home I said to her, "Do this kindness for me; anywhere we go say that I am your brother." (20:11–13)

Avimelekh charges Abraham with violating a basic moral code in addition to violating the hospitality of his host with his dishonesty. Abraham can say no more than that he was afraid, and the very fact that he offers multiple excuses for his behavior (there is no fear of God, technically she really is my sister, this lie is our standard operating procedure) suggests that he himself knows that none of his responses are adequate. In fact, not only is his initial deception reminiscent of his earlier encounter with Pharaoh, his response to being caught is similar. The problem, of course, is that the two situations are not analogous. In Egypt, Sarah is taken without being asked about her status, whereas in Gerar, Abraham announces that she is his sister, almost inviting the king to take her.[1] Moreover, while Egypt is indeed a den of immorality, the people of Gerar are, in fact, God-fearing (20:8). Avimelekh's outrage suggests that Gerar is guided by a moral code.

Abraham's resort to default mode – "that's what we've always done" – indicates that he is, in fact, in a personal crisis likely stemming from his sense of multiple failures. Abraham's default mode not only endangers Sarah, it is another sign of Abraham's ongoing struggle with welcoming Sarah as his covenantal partner, highlighting the question of his fitness to be God's covenantal partner.

Truth be told, Sarah's behavior is no less problematic than Abraham's. She participates in the deception, and of all people she should have known better than to agree to Abraham's ruse. Who suffers more than Sarah from the deception of Pharaoh at the beginning of their sojourn? Who endures greater grief from the presence of the Egyptian Hagar in their household? Avimelekh is well aware of Sarah's lapse, and just as he rebukes Abraham, he rebukes Sarah. When he sends them off he tells Sarah, "Behold, I have given a thousand pieces of silver

---

1. It was not considered immoral for a king to "requisition" an unmarried woman. See I Sam. 8:11–17; Esther 2.

to your brother" (20:16).[2] Calling Abraham her brother rather than her husband is a subtle, but powerful, snub. Sarah should have known better. She should have veiled herself as a married woman, and Avimelekh indicates this as well when he identifies the silver as providing "a cover for [Sarah's] eyes." As the future mother of the covenantal child, this entire episode could have – should have – been avoided. She, too, is held accountable for her complicity in this sorry incident.

THE REDEMPTION OF ABRAHAM

Abraham's redemption from his dark place comes at the hand of two unlikely partners – Avimelekh and God. God appears to Avimelekh in a nighttime vision in which He tells Avimelekh that he will die for taking another man's wife. Listen to Avimelekh's response: "O God, will You kill even a righteous nation?" (20:4). Avimelekh's words are almost identical to Abraham's argument on behalf of Sodom: "Will You consume even the righteous with the wicked?" (18:23). It seems that Abraham's message of the God of justice is rippling throughout the land of Canaan, subtly but significantly altering people's sense of right and wrong.

The great irony is that Abraham is completely unaware of his impact on the local peoples. He is shrouded in a self-perception of failure which, from the perspective of an outsider, is not grounded in reality. Just as Abraham impacts Lot and his daughters, he influences even the Philistine king of Gerar. Abraham could not have missed the irony in hearing his own words to God reflected back to himself from Avimelekh's mouth, so that Avimelekh's moral outrage of, "You did things to me that are simply not done!" assumes a fundamental moral code, one which we hear much later in Laban's comments to Jacob (29:26) and in the distress of Jacob's sons upon hearing about the rape and capture of Dinah (34:7). Abraham's discovery that the people of Gerar are God-fearing and morally upright must make an impression on him, so that Avimelekh plays an important role in Abraham's rehabilitation.

But Avimelekh is not the only one involved in this; God plays a significant role as well. After Avimelekh's protestations of innocence regarding Sarah ("I didn't know," "I didn't touch her") God responds: "I,

---

2. See Kass, *Genesis*, 283–288.

too, know that you did this out of a pureness of intention, hence I saved you from sinning against Me…. But now return the man's wife, for he is a prophet; he will pray for you and you will live" (20:6–7). Abraham may have given up on himself, but God does not give up on Abraham. Despite Abraham's performance in this story, God is covenantally committed to Abraham and uses the opportunity to bolster him. Avimelekh is instructed to implore Abraham the prophet to pray on his behalf. Not only does this reinforce the image of Abraham in Avimelekh's eyes, it likely helps Abraham see himself in a new light. His status as a man of God is restored in his own eyes, as his prayers heal Avimelekh and his household.

God, in partnership with Avimelekh, strives to restore Abraham's self-image as God's partner. Does this actually help Abraham?

ABRAHAM REESTABLISHES HIMSELF

There is no immediate response from Abraham to this episode, and that is probably a good thing. These kinds of messages need time to sink in, and pulling out of a personal crisis is rarely instantaneous. There is, however, a delayed epilogue to this incident.

At the end of chapter 21, Avimelekh and his chief military officer pay Abraham a visit looking to establish a treaty with him.[3] They say: "God is with you in all that you do. Now, swear that you will do no harm to me and my children and grandchildren; you should repay to me the kindness that I did for you and the land in which you dwelt" (21:22–23). Avimelekh's request of Abraham is packaged with a not-so-subtle reference to Abraham's previous dishonesty as Avimelekh attempts to capitalize on the moral high ground he achieved earlier. Abraham accepts Avimelekh's offer and swears to it, but immediately rebukes Avimelekh about some wells which Avimelekh's servants apparently stole from him. As before, Avimelekh protests his innocence: "I do not know who did this, and you did not say anything to me, and I heard nothing of it until this day."

---

3. The timing of this visit is unclear. The Torah introduces it with the words, "And it was in that time." In the one other place that this term is used to introduce a vignette (ch. 38), it clearly refers to events which had been developing for an extended period of time. See the comment of Ibn Ezra on 38:1.

In this scene the roles of Abraham and Avimelekh are reversed – Abraham rebukes while Avimelekh offers a triple defensive excuse. Avimelekh is exposed; he is apparently not as morally upstanding as he portrays himself, and Abraham reasserts his moral high ground. Moreover, as opposed to Avimelekh, who makes sure to gain as much advantage as possible from Abraham's (and Sarah's) moral weakness in the previous chapter, Abraham uses the opportunity to establish a relationship of mutuality. In fact, Abraham goes beyond Avimelekh's request for a one-sided oath, opting instead to institute a bilateral covenant: Abraham will no longer lie to or otherwise harm Avimelekh and his descendants, but Avimelekh must acknowledge Abraham's claim to the well.[4] The status of the stolen wells remains something of a mystery, but the place where they establish a covenant is not: Be'er Sheba, "The Well of the Oath,"[5] "for there they both swore" (21:31).

Abraham converts a moment of confrontation into a moment of covenant. He establishes treaties with local peoples. He regains his own moral high ground without rubbing it in the face of others. He even plants a tree in Be'er Sheba and builds an altar there, calling out in God's name, much like he does earlier in Shekhem and Beit El – returning to his initial mission of claiming the Promised Land. It appears that Abraham is rebounding from his crisis.

FOCUSING ON SARAH

As much as this story is about Abraham – his personal crisis and redemption – it is as much a story about Sarah, and Abraham's approach to her. The entire story revolves around her, from the expectation that the Philistines will take her, to her complicity in the ruse, to God's comments to Avimelekh about her which mention

4. Isaac later tries to deceive Avimelekh (apparently a descendant of the present one), and soon afterward we hear of the rejection of Isaac's claim to wells he digs.
5. The biblical text tells of seven sheep which Abraham presented to Avimelekh as part of this covenantal ceremony. Those sheep are a testimony that Abraham dug the well at Be'er Sheba. The Hebrew word *sheva* both means "seven" and is a play on the word for oath; the name Be'er Sheba is doubly grounded in Abraham's pun.

that Avimelekh's household is afflicted *al devar Sarah*, "because of the issue with Sarah."[6]

This incident stands as part of a series which begins with the covenant of the flesh. That chapter (ch. 17) ostensibly focuses on Abraham's new covenant with God, but the dramatic moment in that chapter is the introduction of Sarah as a covenantal partner who will bear the covenantal child. The focus on Sarah continues as the three guests visit Abraham's tent to rebuke him for not including Sarah, and her role is highlighted by the contrast to Lot's anonymous wife who rejects partnering with him. The focus on Sarah continues as they journey to Gerar, where Abraham again tries a wife-sister swap, and climaxes with the birth of Isaac. Despite God's repeated efforts, Abraham is still unprepared to welcome Sarah as his covenantal partner.[7]

No matter; Sarah's moment has arrived.

---

6. 20:18. Rashi's comment on this verse is particularly striking. Jumping off the word *devar*, which can mean either "issue" or "word" depending on context, Rashi cites a midrashic suggestion that the night Sarah was taken, she used her words to decree who should be afflicted by the plague.

7. After Abram's battle to rescue Lot, he refuses to take anything from the king of Sodom, lest the latter take credit for Abram's wealth. This stands in stark contrast to Abram's attitude in Egypt, where he has no hesitation about gaining materially from Pharaoh at Sarai's expense. It is certainly possible that Abram realizes that benefiting from Sarai's misfortune is problematic. The incident in Gerar, however, indicates that he still does not acknowledge the dubiousness of passing off Sarah as his sister.

Genesis 21:1–21

Sarah Takes the Reins

After decades of barrenness, Sarah conceives and bears Abraham a son, as God promised. If there is any chapter in the Torah which belongs to Sarah, it is this. It opens with a glorious, "God remembered Sarah as He had spoken" (21:1) and continues with Sarah's exultation, "God has made me joyous; anyone who hears will rejoice for me" (21:6). Sarah is the one who sees Ishmael's actions and demands that Abraham banish him, and when that displeases Abraham, God intervenes: "Whatever Sarah says to you, obey her voice" (21:12). For some Sarah is the villain, for others she is the heroine. Regardless, this is her moment. Despite Abraham's unpreparedness, Sarah becomes the covenantal mother. God redeems Sarah,[1] and she quickly takes her place of prominence in the family.

With Sarah at the center of the narrative, Abraham fades into the background, and this is not surprising. We recall Abraham's reaction to

---

1. The Hebrew verb used to describe God "remembering" Sarah is P-K-D. This verb means more than "to remember." It has implications of being remembered for a long-awaited destiny. See, for example, Joseph's dramatic double use of the word in 50:24 describing God's future redemption of the clan. Here, God finally brings Sarah to her destiny by granting her a child.

hearing that Sarah will bear him a child: "No," he says, "that is unnecessary; I have Ishmael" (17:18). He is so ambivalent about this new prospect that he doesn't even tell Sarah. Even more extraordinary, he allows
the future mother of the covenantal child – his child – to be taken to
Avimelekh's palace in Gerar!

Yet Abraham quickly moves from out of the background. Already
by the third verse he takes charge and pushes Sarah out of the limelight:

> Abraham named *his* son, the one born to *him*, which Sarah had
> birthed to *him*, Isaac. Abraham circumcised Isaac, *his* son, at the
> age of eight days, as God had commanded *him*. Abraham was one
> hundred years old when Isaac, *his* son, was born to *him*. (21:3–5)

Notice how prominent Abraham becomes in Sarah's story – seven times
in the span of just three verses, the text emphasizes that Isaac belongs
to *him*. Abraham seeks to own Isaac, the son he only begrudgingly
accepts, lest he, or his mother, disrupt the life Abraham has carefully
constructed with Ishmael.

If this were not enough, Abraham throws a lavish party on the
day Isaac is weaned. Nowhere in the Bible do we hear of a party for the
weaning of a child,[2] and even the brief description of the party as being
"large" is *sui generis* in the Torah.[3] It is worth taking a moment to look
at the verse describing that party:

> The child grew (G-D-L) and was weaned, and Abraham made a
> large (G-D-L) party on the day Isaac was weaned (21:8).[4]

The verse has a parallel structure within it. The opening phrase has three
elements: the child, growing up (G-D-L), and weaning. Those same three

---

2. The only other reference in the Bible to celebration connected with weaning is when
   Hannah brings the young Samuel to the Tabernacle in Shiloh. In that context, Hannah is bringing Samuel to hand him over to the care of the priest Eli (I Sam. 1:23–28).
3. It appears in connection to a party only one more time in the entire Bible (Esther
   2:18), where it describes an outrageous feast.
4. Interestingly, the word G-D-L appears three times in another short verse describing
   Isaac (26:13).

elements appear in the latter phrase of the verse. At the very center of this verse is Abraham. He takes center stage, and his great moment of celebration arrives when he can begin to separate Isaac from his mother.[5] Abraham's exclusion of Sarah stands in stark contrast to Sarah's inclusion of Abraham. Sarah bears a child *to Abraham* (21:2), and when Sarah sings her poem praising God she includes Abraham in it: "Who would have said *to Abraham*, 'Sarah is nursing children!' For I have borne a son in *his* old age" (21:7). Sarah's nobility of soul is marked by her understanding that her redemption is not only personal; it redeems Abraham too, and is strikingly contrasted with Abraham's inability to let Sarah stand by his side.

The moment arrives, however, at which God no longer suffices with implied or subtle messages to Abraham. In a climactic moment in this chapter, He issues a direct command: "Whatever Sarah says to you, obey her voice" (21:12). What has until this point been a suggestion of a mindset shift is now demanded of Abraham as an unequivocal imperative. And now, the directive to obey Sarah's words places Sarah not only as his equal but as his superior.

LAUGHTER, HAPPINESS, ISAAC

Isaac's name bears a particular irony. The root TZ-Ḥ-K means "laughter" or "happiness." There are few figures in the Bible for whom this name could be less appropriate.

There is little in Isaac's life that sounds happy. He is born to a father who is ambivalent about his arrival and who is prepared to hold a knife to his throat in response to God's request. He witnesses his older brother being banished from the home and likely understands that it is because of him.[6] He marries a woman who is brought to him from afar and endures twenty years of childlessness. He tries to follow in his father's footsteps

---

5. By contrast, the text gives no voice to Abraham in this story, while Sarah's voice is prominent. Even Abraham's objection to the banishment of Ishmael is a silent one.

6. The paintings depicting this event by Pieter Jozef Verhagen (1781) (https://commons. wikimedia.org/wiki/File:Verhaghen,_Pieter_Jozef_-_Hagar_and_Ishmael_ Banished_by_Abraham_-_1781.jpg) and Johann Conrad Seekatz (1761) (www. hermitagemuseum.org/wps/portal/hermitage/digital-collection/01.+Paintings/3 8510/?lng=) portray Isaac as the young observer of the scene.

by pretending that his wife is his sister but gets caught in the act when he forgets to pull down the shades in his room. He has twin sons destined to struggle for supremacy, and when he prefers one over the other both his wife and the other son conspire to deceive him. One son wants to kill the other, and both eventually move far from home with their children. (More on all of this later when we explore Isaac in greater depth.)

What, then, are we to make of his name?

Let us pause to reflect for a moment on laughter. We laugh at the unexpected, when we are led to think one way and are caught by surprise. We laugh at the ridiculous because it is the farthest thing from our minds. Abraham laughs when he hears that Sarah, at the age of ninety, will bear a child, because it sounds absurd. Sarah also laughs, and for the same reason – especially when hearing the news from passing strangers. Isaac is a surprise, unexpected. There is nothing natural or usual about his birth; he defies the normal patterns. His name is predetermined and fits him perfectly because he is a living example of the absurd.

But after he is born, Sarah chooses to repair his name. For the same root that means laughter can also mean happiness. She proclaims, "God has made me joyous; anyone who hears will rejoice for me," and the word she uses to describe her joy is the same one the Torah uses to describe her laughter at the ridiculous proclamation she hears from the three visitors. Joy replaces laughter, so that Isaac is not the ridiculous one but the one who brings joy.

It is in this context that we must examine the next scene. Sarah witnesses Ishmael doing something which is described using the same verb, TZ-Ḥ-K. We do not know exactly what Ishmael is doing[7] or which interpretation of TZ-Ḥ-K he is acting upon. In fact, it might not be relevant at all, for what Ishmael is doing could be literally translated as, "he was Isaac-ing." That is, that Ishmael is seeking Isaac's place.[8]

This should come as no surprise. Ishmael, who for thirteen years is the only son, understands that he is the son of the maidservant Hagar

---

7. Rashi, 21:9, following the lead of the Midrash, suggests that Ishmael was engaged in the three cardinal sins of idolatry, adultery, and murder. The midrashic comments are grounded in various uses of the verb TZ-Ḥ-K in the Bible.
8. See Alter, *The Five Books of Moses*, 103.

and that the mistress of the house has no warm place in her heart for him. That mistress now miraculously bears a child to the master of the house. Ishmael must realize that despite being the firstborn, the other child's lineage supersedes his. His days as the sole heir or even the chief heir are numbered. Ishmael's response is to become Isaac, and Sarah catches him "Isaac-ing."

BANISH THE WOMAN AND THE BOY

Whatever it is that Ishmael is doing, Sarah understands its implications. Ishmael wants to supplant Isaac as the primary heir, adding a new dimension to Sarah's comment, "For this son of the maidservant will not inherit together with my son, Isaac" (21:10). The focus is on the future, on who will be heir to Abraham's legacy, and takes on particular poignancy in light of the following passage from the Code of Hammurabi:

> When a man's primary wife bore him children and his female slave also bore him children, if the father during his lifetime has ever said, "My children!" to the children of the female slave, after the father dies the children of the female slave share equally in the goods of the paternal estate, with the son of the primary wife receiving a preferential share. However, if the father during his lifetime has never said, "My children!" to the children of the female slave, then after he dies they may not share in the paternal estate; the slave children are to be set free.[9]

Although the situations are not identical, banishing Hagar and Ishmael is apparently Sarah's way of demanding that Abraham declare Ishmael as "not his child" and set him free – stripped of any claim to Abraham's estate.

This demand pains Abraham greatly. Abraham has invested heavily in this son for thirteen years, and even circumcised him into the national covenant. The language used throughout this chapter highlights just how profoundly difficult this is for Abraham, but also how necessary it is. In Abraham's eyes, Ishmael is "his son" (see 21:11). By contrast,

---

9. Code of Hammurabi 170–171, in Pritchard, *Ancient Near Eastern Texts Relating to the Old Testament*. My thanks to Dr. Gavriel H. Cohn for pointing out this reference.

Sarah identifies Ishmael as "the son of Hagar, the Egyptian" (21:9) and "the son of the maidservant" (21:10). For Abraham, Ishmael is an insider; for Sarah he is an outsider. Ultimately, God affirms Sarah's perspective on Hagar and Ishmael (21:12–13), and only after He issues a direct command does Abraham learn to see him as "the boy" (21:14).[10]

Sarah understands the new reality and its implications while Abraham needs more time to learn to accept it, but Sarah believes that immediate action is necessary. Abraham sees the present while Sarah intuits the future, and through her intuition she becomes the architect of that future by insisting that Ishmael be disowned. The covenantal mother shapes the next generation, and in doing so becomes a true partner to Abraham, doing what he cannot. Sarah is not vengeful; she is ensuring the future of the covenant, and Abraham obeys God's command and, by extension, Sarah's word. As for God, He has been trying unsuccessfully for a while to tell Abraham that Ishmael is not the heir. Abraham's reticence in coming to grips with that only delays and exacerbates the pain. One can only imagine how things might have played out differently had Abraham spent those years preparing his family for the momentous changes in their future rather than pretending that they were not going to happen.

Isaac is the central focus of this story, but he is its object, not its subject. Isaac plays no active role, but his arrival changes everything. The real story is about Abraham and Sarah: Abraham does not allow Sarah to take her place of prominence, but God ensures that she does.

HAGAR

Sarah puts a quick stop to Hagar's earlier attempt to supplant her as the mistress of the house, and Sarah's position is reinforced by the angel that meets Hagar at the well. When Ishmael follows in his mother's footsteps and tries to supplant Isaac as the primary son, he is banished to protect Isaac's place, and neither Sarah nor Abraham will consider banishing the boy without his mother.[11] But neither the text nor God abandons Hagar and Ishmael.

---

10. It is fascinating that throughout this story, Ishmael's name is not mentioned. God refers to him as "the lad" (21:12) and "the son of the maidservant" (21:13).

11. There is a subtle difference between Sarah's and God's formulations of the need to expel Ishmael. Sarah tells Abraham to banish "this maidservant and her son," while

Abraham awakens early in the morning, prepares some food and a skin of water, and sends Hagar away with the child.[12] While Hagar is likely familiar with the region, having lived there for a number of years, she wanders aimlessly in the wilderness, using up her water supply and bringing both her and her son to the brink of death. She tosses her son under a bush, and moves "a bowshot away" so that she will not see the boy die.

An angel reveals a well to her and reassures her that God's earlier promise regarding Ishmael will still come true. She fills the skin and gives the boy to drink. He grows up in the wilderness and becomes a good shot with a bow and arrow. Later, his mother finds an Egyptian wife for him.

These scenes of the expulsion and its aftermath reveal much about Hagar and Ishmael. The text focuses on Hagar – the mother who cast her dying son under a bush lest she witness his death, and who moves away to avoid hearing his cries. The Bible is unequivocal in its damning description of Hagar and her callousness, particularly with the description of her being "a bowshot away."

In the history of warfare, the invention of the bow and arrow must have been a momentous event, as warriors could now kill their enemies without having to experience their deaths up close. It is the ancient equivalent of using a remote-controlled drone to eliminate an enemy target. The controller sits far away, pushing buttons – as if in a video game. The distance of a bowshot is the Bible's way of describing the depth of Hagar's disengagement from her son's fate.

God tells Abraham not to fret about "the boy and the maidservant." Sarah focuses on Hagar first and on Ishmael second, while God focuses primarily on the boy and secondarily on his mother.

Sarah's focus on Hagar, despite her being prompted to expel mother and son as a result of the latter's behavior, suggests Sarah has concluded that Hagar's rebellion against her did not end upon her return; rather, she is channeling it through her son. It is fascinating that Abraham follows Sarah's formulation of the banishment rather than God's.

12. The biblical text does not say "with the child," but that Abraham "placed the food and the water on her shoulder and the child" (21:14). The ambiguity of the text leads Rashi to suggest that Abraham placed the child on her shoulders. As we will see below, this is highly improbable.

In an ironic twist, God hears the boy's cries but not hers, even though the text records her cries but not the boy's. No wonder his name is Ishmael, "God hears." God listens to him, but not to his mother. She is again rebuked by a divine messenger asking a rhetorical question: "What is with you, Hagar?" The question sounds absurd, and it is, indeed, absurd. The angel continues, "God has heard the voice of the boy, as he is *there*." We can envision the angel pointing his finger at the distant lad abandoned by his mother, as if to say, "If he is *there* then why are you *here*?"

The angel's final words are of admonition to a callous mother: "Arise, pick up the boy and hold his hand." This scene focuses on painting the portrait of Hagar, who is rejected as the covenantal mother, and this epilogue to the story provides a clue as to why God sides with Sarah, insisting Hagar be banished.

Ultimately, Hagar – the woman who thinks that she can see but in reality does not even see the well that is right there – nourishes her child back to health and finds him a wife from Egypt. She returns to her own roots to guide Ishmael's future, and since that future is in the accursed descendant of Ham and not from the family of Shem and Ever, she confirms her son's fate. He is not part of the covenantal future. It is Hagar who decides his trajectory, as she is the most significant force in Ishmael's life.

The Torah later makes this even more explicit: "This is the legacy of Ishmael, Abraham's son, who was birthed by Hagar the Egyptian, Sarah's maidservant, to Abraham" (25:12).[13] Hagar charts the course of her progeny consciously by choosing for him a wife from her own land, and subconsciously by her own example of cruelty to him. Hagar steers her son out of the covenant.

ISHMAEL: HAGAR'S SON

Classical artistic renditions of the above scene portray Ishmael as a young boy, perhaps somewhere between six and eleven years old,[14] yet a quick

---

13. See also Rashbam, 25:19.
14. See the depictions of Pieter Lastman (1612), Rembrandt (1637), Abraham Bloemaert (1638), Jan Victors (1644), Gerbrand van den Eeckhout (1666), Pieter Jozef Verhaghen (1781), and Guernico (1886).

calculation reveals that Ishmael is at least seventeen years old.[15] Placing Ishmael as a grown young man makes it difficult to understand how his mother can "cast him under one of the bushes." How can Hagar toss a seventeen-year-old boy under a bush, and what child of that age would accept such a thing from his mother? Why does he not pick himself up and walk away?

It appears that Ishmael, who until recently believes that he is Abraham's heir, is devastated – not only by Isaac's birth and the wresting of his inheritance, but by the rejection of both his father and his mother. Abraham suddenly sends him out into the wilderness and his mother abandons him under a bush to die. The crushing blows dealt by that double abandonment could be enough to cripple the spirit of even the healthiest of souls. Perhaps this explains his name – "God hears," for God is the only one who hears his cries.[16]

It does not surprise us, then, to hear that Ishmael becomes a bowman; he learns from his own experience how easy it can be to kill from a distance. Ishmael becomes Hagar's son.

SARAH WINS?

Despite Abraham's struggle with the question of how to include Sarah as his covenantal partner, God fulfills His promise to Sarah and more. She bears the covenantal child to Abraham, and protects both the child and his status. Tenacious in her efforts, she ensures that neither Hagar nor Ishmael threaten the child's future, and she confronts Abraham just as Abraham earlier (18:23–33) confronts God. Sarah ensures the future of the covenantal child, which Abraham must accept against his own wishes.

What will become of Sarah, and Isaac, when God instructs Abraham to offer up this embattled covenantal child?

---

15. He was thirteen when Abraham was informed that Sarah would bear a child a year later. Add one year for Sarah to give birth and another three for typical weaning in the ancient world, and we have a seventeen-year-old young man. That calculation assumes that Ishmael's "Isaac-ing" and the banishment happened immediately after Isaac's weaning, and does not even allow for space between those two events.

16. The psalmist (27:10) captured this sentiment exquisitely: "Were my father and mother to forsake me, the Lord would take me in."

Genesis 22:1–24

The Binding of Isaac

W hen we first meet Abraham, the Torah introduces him as the champion of the family who also understands that the family is the primary vehicle for transmission of values. Throughout the opening chapters of his life we repeatedly find that he is prepared to forego divine commands and blessings to protect his family – with the notable exception of his wife. When, however, God inducts Abraham into the covenant, making Abraham His covenantal partner and making Sarah the covenantal partner of Abraham, we begin to notice a shift in Abraham's priorities. Abraham stands before God to plead on behalf of Sodom, which he sees as part of his covenantal duties, but makes no mention of Lot. He objects to the banishment of Ishmael, but only silently; we never hear his voice. When God instructs Abraham to heed Sarah's words, he obeys without complaint. The Abraham who argues, negotiates, debates with, and interrupts God seems to disappear, replaced by an Abraham who is compliant, and for whom loyalty to God trumps family bonds and responsibilities.

According to rabbinic tradition,[1] Abraham is tested ten times in his life. All of those pit his value of family against some other value he holds dear. In the early tests he chooses family over land and divine gifts;

---

1. Mishna Avot 5:4.

in the latter he chooses loyalty to God over family. Nowhere is this shift more apparent than in the climactic Binding of Isaac.

The Binding of Isaac – *Akedat Yitzḥak* in Hebrew, or simply, the *Akeda* – is one of the seminal biblical stories, playing a central role in Jewish thought, culture, and liturgy. It inspired Jewish victims of the Crusades to take their children's and their own lives. It is also one of the most problematic passages in the Bible, spawning enough discussion and literature to fill its own library.

Each generation of interpretation has grappled with different questions evoked by this story. For some, it is the problem of how God could command something only to later change His mind; for others, it is the question of why an omniscient God needs to test anyone; and for still others it is trying to understand how Abraham could agree to carry out an overtly immoral command. On these pages we will neither survey all the relevant literature nor explore the myriad questions which have been raised through the ages. We will, instead, look at the story in its own right and in light of the themes we have been exploring.

LEKH LEKHA X 2

Earlier we saw that the core Abrahamic narrative is framed by two calls of *lekh lekha* ("Go forth!") and the similarities between them. God's initial call to Abraham to leave his ancestral identity in search of a new one opens with "*lekh lekha*," as does the Binding of Isaac, which is God's final call to Abraham. As we've seen multiple times, parallel texts beg the question of the differences between them, and the differences here are quite profound.

The first *lekh lekha* is filled with promise. God promises to multiply Abraham's seed and make him into a great nation which will be a source of blessing for all humankind. God does not explain *why* He wants Abraham to follow this particular call, but He does inform him that it will be worth his while. Contrast that with the call to bring Isaac as a burnt-offering, in which there is neither explanation nor any promise of reward or benefit to Abraham. Abraham must obey simply because he is instructed to do so. The first *lekh lekha* asks Abraham to sacrifice his past for the promise of a better future, but the second asks him to sacrifice his future for no apparent reason. In fact, the second *lekh lekha* actually threatens the first. If Isaac is indeed the promised child, as God has repeatedly confirmed, then sacrificing Isaac challenges Abraham to abdicate ownership of that promise.

This formulation of the second *lekh lekha* raises a serious theological problem: can God renege on His promise? Some have suggested that God does not *demand* that Abraham obey but merely *requests* that he do so,[2] which only shifts the problem from a theological one to a human one: how can Abraham respect an absurd and patently immoral request if he has the option to avoid it?[3] Others suggest that since Abraham already forfeited the original promise by his very actions, delaying taking the land and signing away parts of it in his treaty with Avimelekh,[4] this story is God's way of saying, "You were cavalier in sacrificing the promise of the land; will you so easily sacrifice the promise of the seed?"

There is, however, another significant difference between the two *lekh lekha* calls which becomes clear only when looking more closely at the two texts together.

The first lekh lekha (12:1)	The second lekh lekha (22:2)
God said to Abram,	He said,
Lekh lekha from your *aretz*,	Take, please, your son,
your *moledet*,	your only son,
and your *beit av*,	the one you love,
to go to the land	Isaac!
which I will show you.	And *lekh lekha* to the land of Moriah.
	And bring him up there as a burnt-offering
	on one of the mountains which I will tell you.

---

2. Rashi, 22:2. This is based on the Hebrew "*na*," please: "Take, please, your son." See also Kass, *Genesis*, 336–338.
3. In a surprising twist, Gersonides understands that Abraham passed the test *because* he chose to interpret God's word as demanding his son when he could have chosen an easier alternative.
4. See Rashbam, 22:1.

Both *lekh lekha* calls include an instruction to go to an unspecified place, and both seem to identify the mission using multiple terms: *aretz, moledet,* and *beit av* in the first; "your son," "your only son," and "the one you love" in the second. Yet while *aretz, moledet,* and *beit av* apparently refer to three distinct entities, the identifiers in the second *lekh lekha* serve to progressively narrow the focus in order to leave no room for ambiguity, climaxing with the son's name – Isaac![5]

This unambiguous focusing heightens the crisis into which God corners Abraham. Let us recall that for Abraham, the primal son is Ishmael; Abraham is both ambivalent about Isaac's birth and reluctant to send Ishmael away. Abraham's subsequent relationship with Isaac is a matter for speculation – the text is silent about that (until they trek together to Mount Moriah). Yet God opens this story demanding that Abraham first acknowledge Isaac as his son, then acknowledge that Isaac is the *only* son (confirming Ishmael's expulsion as final), and finally to acknowledge his love for that only son.

One can easily imagine this call to Abraham in slow motion, with pauses in between each demand – or even as a process taking multiple years. It is only after Abraham makes the internal moves to accept Isaac's uniqueness and status that God commands Abraham to sacrifice the very one he has learned to love.[6] The challenge for Abraham is as much intensely personal as it is theological.

AMBIGUITY PURSUES ABRAHAM

The clarity and laser-like focus on Isaac in the second *lekh lekha* call stand in stark contrast to the ambiguity of what to do with him. This ambiguity is evident only in the original Hebrew text and is lost in any translation. God tells Abraham, "*Vehaalehu sham le'ola,*" using both the verb form

---

5. This difference between the two calls of *lekh lekha* is reflected in Abraham's actions as well. In response to the first *lekh lekha,* Abraham searches for the place and misses it, while in the second, Abraham "lifts his eyes" on the third day and finds it without hesitation. That same "lifting of the eyes" resurfaces later in the story: as Abraham is prevented by the angel from slaughtering Isaac, he lifts his eyes and sees the ram which will be Isaac's replacement on the altar.
6. This highlights that sacrifice (in its non-ritual meaning) entails giving up something held dearly.

and the noun form of the root A-L-H. Literally, that root means "to go up," so that the form of the first verb used here literally means, "Raise him up." That could certainly imply sacrifice, but it could also mean something as simple as "Bring him up to the mountain."[7]

To further complicate matters, while the meaning of the word *ola* (based on the same root, A-L-H) in sacrificial terms unambiguously refers to a burnt-offering, in Genesis that definition is less than clear since Genesis precedes the sacrificial order first presented in Exodus. In fact, prior to this incident, there is only one sacrifice mentioned in the entire Torah.[8] The ambiguities in both the noun and the verb lead the medieval scholar Rabbi Yosef Bekhor Shor to comment:

> The Holy One, blessed be He, spoke in unclear terms. Abraham thought that he was commanded to slaughter [Isaac] and completely consume him in the fire, which is why he brought wood and fire and a knife with him. But He had commanded only to bring him up onto the altar, and once he had done that, he would have completely fulfilled the divine command.

Bekhor Shor's comment is extraordinary in that he posits that Abraham misunderstands God's instruction. It is not clear why this would have been a great test for Abraham had he understood God's real intent. Nonetheless, the comment illustrates the ambiguity in the command.[9]

A similar attempt at exploring the ambiguity is expressed by another medieval thinker, the commentator-philosopher Gersonides, who writes:

---

7. The verb appears more than four hundred times in the Bible. Of those, fewer than thirty refer to sacrifices (Ex. 24:5; 32:6; 42:29; Lev. 14:20; 17:8; Josh. 8:31; Judges 20:26; I Sam. 7:9; 13:9–12; II Sam. 24:25; I Kings 3:4, 15; 9:25; II Kings 3:27; 12:29–33; Job 1:5; Ezra 3:3; I Chr. 21:26; 29:21; II Chr. 1:6; 8:12; 29:27).

8. Gen. 8:20, regarding the sacrifices Noah brings following the Flood. The popular notion that Cain and Abel bring sacrifices is not explicit in the text. The Torah uses the word *minḥa*, or gift, to describe what they brought, but does not specify the nature of that gift or how it was offered.

9. By contrast, Maimonides, *Guide* 3:24, uses this story as proof of the absolute clarity and unambiguity of prophecy.

The nature of this test, in my opinion, is that the prophecy came
to Abraham in ambiguous language. That is, the Exalted One said,
"Vehaalehu sham le'ola." This statement could be understood to
mean that [Abraham] should slaughter him and make him into
a burnt-offering, or that [Abraham] should bring him up [to the
mountain] when he goes to do the burnt-offering so that Isaac
can be trained in the divine worship of the burnt-offering.

When we add to these interpretations the observation that God does
not express this as a command to Abraham but as a request (*kaḥ na*,
"take, please"), the sense we have is that were Abraham to have access
to a decent library of biblical commentary he might find multiple loop-
holes to avoid the heart-wrenching drama.

Further complicating our discussion is that if Abraham believes
God's multiple promises that Isaac is the promised seed and Abraham's
name is to be continued through Isaac, then he should have nothing to
fear from this test as he knows that God will work it out; and if Abraham
does not believe the divine promises then he has no reason to follow
through on this request/command.

The fact that Abraham goes through with the trial leads to the conclusion that he *does* believe the previous divine promises, which is why
he adheres to God's word now. Abraham believes that God will somehow reconcile this instruction with His prior assurances, but Abraham
does not know *how* He will reconcile them.[10] If that is the case, then we
come back to that fundamental question: What is the test?

SACRIFICING THE FAMILY

The answer to our question lies not in the realm of faith but in the
realm of loss. Regardless of how God resolves the conflict between

---

10. The great irony is that it is not God who resolves the paradox but Abraham himself. When the angel commands Abraham to pull his hand back from Isaac's neck,
Abraham lifts his eyes and sees the ram. Note that God does not show Abraham the
ram (as the angel did with Hagar and the well), but like Mount Moriah, Abraham
finds it for himself. In Abraham's initial conversations with Isaac, both father and son
can think only of a sheep for slaughter, which they do not have. Abraham discovers
a new possibility in the ram, and thus resolves his dilemma.

His promise with regard to Isaac and His command to offer him, it is clear to Abraham that as a result of this trial he will likely lose Isaac, the son he now loves. That loving father-son relationship is emphasized early on in the story. When Isaac speaks, he prefaces by saying "Father" (22:7), and when Abraham responds he opens and closes his words with "My son" (22:7-8). As the pair journey to the mountain the text twice announces, "The two of them walked together" (22:6, 9). But that closeness and togetherness is absent at the end of the story. Abraham returns to the two lads who are waiting for him, but Isaac is no longer with him (22:19).

We can easily imagine the toll this incident takes on the relationship between the father and the son. Isaac, bound on the altar, looks up and sees his father prepared to bring that blade upon his neck. Can Isaac ever learn to trust his father again? Can Isaac return with Abraham as if nothing had transpired? Will that image of the father with the knife not become a permanent feature of the son's psyche?

A midrash exquisitely and graphically expresses the impact of this experience:

> When Abraham bound his son on top of the altar, the tears of the weeping angels' eyes dripped into Isaac's eyes and etched themselves there. When Isaac grew older, his eyes grew dim from those tears.[11]

According to this rabbinic insight, as Isaac lay on the altar the angels were weeping and their tears fell into his eyes. Isaac's vision, both literally and metaphorically, is forever clouded (hence his blindness later in life). Isaac's soul is seared by the experience; he cannot return home with his father.

Where does Isaac go? The next time we find him (24:62) he is returning from Be'er Laḥai Ro'i, the well associated with Hagar (16:14) as she flees the oppressive Sarai. It is the place where the rejected members of Abraham's family go, and one can easily imagine Isaac feeling

---

11. *Midrash Abkir*, based on Genesis Rabba 65:10.

that he and Ishmael have more in common than either of them would have believed.

Abraham's loss, however, is not restricted to Isaac. He also loses Sarah, his covenantal partner. Abraham has been living in Be'er Sheba (21:33–34) and after the *Akeda* he returns to Be'er Sheba (22:19), yet when we next find Sarah she is in Hebron, where she dies. Abraham is not with her at that time and he needs to travel to Hebron in order to mourn at her side and prepare for her burial (23:2). Again, it is not hard to imagine Sarah's reaction when she hears that Abraham has taken her only son, the one she waited for and whose future she protected like a vigilant lioness, to be slaughtered. After the Binding of Isaac, we never find Sarah and Abraham together again.[12]

Abraham's test is not that he thinks he will have to slaughter his son. It is that although he trusts that Isaac will not be killed and that God will find a creative solution to the conundrum of the conflicting divine messages, Abraham will lose his family in the process. There is no greater challenge for the champion of the value of family than to give it up for a different value. The irony is inescapable, for it is Abraham's value of family for which he is initially chosen, and he is now being rewarded for sacrificing that family.[13]

With Abraham's induction into the covenant of the flesh, he begins a process which results in a seismic shift. Whereas earlier, as Abram, he consistently chooses family over adherence to divine will, he now prefers the divine will to his family. As he does so he abandons Lot (who is probably already lost), banishes Hagar and Ishmael, and now loses Isaac and Sarah. Abraham has moved from one extreme to

---

12. One midrash (Genesis Rabba 58:5) suggests that Sarah dies when she hears that Abraham nearly slaughtered her beloved Isaac.

13. A minor difference between the two *lekh lekha* calls suggests the immensity of Abraham's sacrifice. In the first, the *lekh lekha* statement comes at the very beginning of the call, whereas in the second it appears toward the end. The call of *lekh lekha* is essentially a call to loneliness, to leave behind that which is dear. The first *lekh lekha* suggests that the initial loneliness will be rewarded with a replacement family, national identity, and homeland. In the second, Abraham is being asked to again pursue a path of loneliness, in which he will leave Isaac and Sarah behind – but there will be nothing to fill that void.

the other, and despite his growing closeness to God the results are personally tragic.

ABRAHAM'S REWARD

With all the loss involved, does Abraham gain anything from this trial? A cursory look at the message he receives at the close of the story indicates that he is awarded a blessing:

> The angel of God called to Abraham a second time from the heavens and said: "I swear," says God, "that because you did this and did not withhold your son, your only one, that I will bless you and increase your seed like the stars of the heavens and the like the sands on the seashore. Your seed will inherit the gates of its enemies. And through your seed shall come blessing to all the nations of the earth, in return for your listening to Me." (22:15–18)

While this certainly sounds like a wonderful blessing, a closer reading reveals that it is little more than a restatement of that which Abraham had already been promised. Decades earlier, God had assured Abraham that his children would be as numerous as the dust of the earth (13:16) and the stars of the sky (15:5), in addition to the generic promises that he would become a great (12:2) and numerous (17:2, 6) nation. Abraham had also been promised that he would be a source of blessing to the nations of the earth (12:3). Is his reward for this trial merely a reaffirmation of previous divine promises?

Lurking behind this narrative is the question of whether Abraham passes his test or not. The simple reading of the text, adopted by most traditional commentaries, assumes that Abraham's absolute fealty to God is the ultimate demonstration of faith. By contrast, many modern readers boldly assert that his preparedness to violate the most fundamental moral norms demonstrates his failure to understand God.

Perhaps, however, the question is wrong. What if this is not a PASS/FAIL test but one of values clarification? In the world of values clarification, competing values are pitted against one another to help clarify priorities. Which value will emerge supreme, and what weight do secondary and tertiary values have?

Initially, Abram prioritizes family; not to imply that his commitment to God is not important, just that it is *less* important. And Abram is *gifted* the promises as the champion of the family. After the covenant of the flesh, however, Abraham prioritizes his partnership with God, while his commitment to family becomes secondary. The trial of Ishmael's banishment is an important tipping point in accelerating that shift, leading to its apex in the Binding of Isaac. In both, we see Abraham stubbornly clinging to his family. He objects (albeit silently) to the expulsion of Ishmael, and we can feel his anguish as he must part from his only remaining son; yet in both he yields to God's wish. The *Akeda* represents the climax of that shift, after which Abraham is reassured that he has *earned* those promises for prioritizing his fear of God.

That tension Abraham experiences throughout the *Akeda* is brought out exquisitely in the text's use of a single word – *hineni*, "here I am." That word is used throughout the Torah to express a preparedness to be at the service of another, and is a powerful statement of commitment. When God calls to Abraham at the beginning of the *Akeda*, Abraham responds with "*hineni*." As father and son climb toward Mount Moriah, and Isaac, speaking in terms of endearment, asks for his father's attention, Abraham responds to him with the same "*hineni*."

Abraham is torn between two profound commitments, between two deeply held values, between two "*hineni*"s. Yet he must choose. The choice he makes is irreversible; there is no turning back after he holds the knife over Isaac's neck. Abraham neither passes nor fails his test, but he has demonstrated where he stands. Either way, God affirms that the initial *lekh lekha* promises remain in effect.

AVIMELEKH'S SHADOW

It is impossible to ignore the significance of context in our reading of this profoundly difficult chapter. Let us begin with a fascinating observation linking this chapter with the story of Avimelekh (the numbers in parentheses refer to the verses):

Avimelekh (chapter 20)	Binding of Isaac (chapter 22)
Avimelekh sent out (SH-L-Ḥ) and took (L-K-Ḥ) Sarah (2)	Abraham sent out (SH-L-Ḥ) and took (L-K-Ḥ) the knife (10)
God came to Avimelekh in a nighttime dream (3)	The angel of God called to him (11)
I, too, know (6)	Now I know (12)
I did not let you touch her (6)	Do not send your hand to the boy (12)
I held you back (Ḥ-S-KH) from sinning against Me (6)	You did not hold back (Ḥ-S-KH) (12)
Avimelekh arose early in the morning (8)	Abraham arose early in the morning (3)
What did you see (10)	Abraham raised his eyes and saw (4)
That you did this thing to me (10)	Because you did this thing (16)
Because there is no fear of God in this place (11)	You are a God-fearing man (12)
Swear to me (21:23)	I swear (16)

Both stories involve someone about to violate another individual, a divine instruction to desist, discovered or revealed knowledge, holding back before an irreversible act, and the fear of God. Why would the Torah deliberately write the story of the Binding of Isaac in the shadow of Avimelekh's near-violation of Sarah?

The story of the *Akeda* may be God's response to Abraham's involvement in that previous story. We recall that Abraham goes to Gerar because he judges himself a failure as God's covenantal partner. Moreover, he is sure that there are no God-fearing people in Gerar, but he is badly mistaken; he has no idea just how much impact he has had on Avimelekh. Abraham's questioning of Avimelekh's moral worthiness raises questions about the moral worthiness of Abraham, who prejudges Avimelekh and arrives at the wrong conclusion.

In response to Abraham's hypercritical eye – both of Avimelekh and of himself – God puts Abraham to the test, as if to say: "Who are you to be accusing innocent people of not fearing God? Are you yourself

God-fearing enough to stand in a position of judgment?" From this perspective, the trial of the *Akeda* is the mirror that God holds up to Abraham so that he can see himself, and others, accurately.

Both stories involve unconscionable acts – in one case adultery,
in the other, murder and child sacrifice. Together, these two stories
are informed by two of the three cardinal violations for which a Jew
is commanded to give his own life rather than violate. In each case a
divine message prevents the offending act at the last minute. As Abram
becomes Abraham and places God at the center of his universe he needs
to understand that there are limits to prioritizing God, that not everything is acceptable when placing God first.

The coveted fear of God that Abraham thinks will be a barrier
to sin turns out for Abraham to be the catalyst for doing the unthink-
able. Abraham's religious devotion nearly impels him to extremes just as
Avimelekh's lust would have, and both need to be stopped before they
cross the line. Paralleling the *Akeda* with the story of Avimelekh demonstrates the dangers of overzealous devotion to anything, even to God.[14]

Additionally, it is notable that God rewards Abraham and lauds
him for his *fear* of God, that which Abraham sees as a litmus test of
worthiness.[15] What is missing from the story and the blessing, however,
is any mention of Abraham's *love* of God. In fact, it could be argued that
this is a story in which fear and obedience trump love; that is, the fear of
God trumps the love for a child. That fear of God which Abraham considers the highest value has its counterbalance – love – which is absent.
Fear of God earns Abraham the same promise given to Abram decades

14. In this reading, the fact that Abraham doesn't receive any reward for the *Akeda* may
suggest that overzealousness limits the blessings we receive.
15. The text uses wordplay to highlight that Abraham's fear of God, Y-R-A, comes with
his increased ability to "see," R-A-H, God's messages. The two words have different
roots but appear similar and play on each other. On the third day, Abraham sees
(*vayar*) the place from afar, and at the altar Abraham again sees (*vayar*) – this time,
the ram which replaces Isaac. When Isaac asks Abraham about the missing sheep
for the offering, Abraham responds, "God will see (*yireh*) for Himself the sheep";
Abraham later names the place "God Will See" (*yireh*). Abraham's increased adherence to the divine will and his increasing fear of God are linked with his ability to
"see" what God wants, yet this God-consciousness comes at a great price.

earlier. We can only dream what he would have earned had he instead performed an act of love.[16]

AFTERSHOCKS

It is not difficult to imagine Abraham returning home after the traumatic moment on the mountain. His transformation vis-à-vis God is complete; he is the knight of faith, the one who declares his loyalty to and trust in God above all. He is triumphant in his spiritual quest. Exhilarated by his achievement and emotionally exhausted, Abraham is also humbled by his earlier lack of awareness with regard to how he has impacted upon others and by the subtle rebukes he receives in the process.

And, of course, Abraham must deal with his new reality. While the *Akeda* propels him forward in his relationship with God, it forces him to burn his bridges with his most beloved ones – Isaac and Sarah. He returns alone to an empty tent, accompanied only by the anonymous lads. His *lekh lekha*, his forced loneliness, is also complete.

Soon afterward Abraham receives news of his long-lost brother, Nahor, whom he left behind in Ḥaran. Nahor has twelve children, the typological number for the completed clan poised to become a nation.[17] One of Nahor's children is Kemuel, the "father of Aram" (22:21), suggesting that Abraham's position in Aram (as Av Ram, or the father of Aram) has been supplanted by his nephew. While Abraham has been busy cultivating Lot, trying to save Sodom, banishing one son and effectively chasing away the other, his brother has already succeeded in building the foundations of his nation. This hardly seems appropriate for God's human partner.

Or perhaps it is most appropriate. One of the core messages of the covenant is that working with God involves investing for the long term; one cannot expect to reap short-term rewards. Abraham's personal fulfillment will come only after many generations.

---

16. It is interesting that the books of Isaiah (41:8) and Chronicles (II 20:7) refer to Abraham as the one who loves God. This aspect of Abraham is picked up in the Midrash as well. See Genesis Rabba 41:8; 65:10; and especially 55:8.

17. Just like Jacob's clan of twelve, eight are from the wife/wives while the other four are from the concubine/maidservants. Note that Ishmael, too, fathers twelve tribal leaders (17:20; 25:12–16).

It could be argued that Genesis repeatedly presents two models within the Abrahamic family. One branch of the family remains outside of the covenant and is built quickly: Nahor has his complete clan, as Ishmael (25:12–18) and Esau (36:1–19) will soon also have. Even Lot's two illegitimate children are identified immediately as nation-founders (19:37–38). Not only do these families achieve status as nations almost immediately, each gets to settle in its promised homeland without delay. Nahor's family leads Aram, Lot's children inhabit the eastern plain of the Dead Sea (Deut. 2:9, 19), and Esau takes over the land of Se'ir (36:9–43).

By contrast, the covenantal branch of the family must struggle. Abraham struggles with his two sons and Isaac struggles with his twins, and both of these patriarchal figures end up with one son outside of the land and excluded from the covenant. Even Jacob, who also has the coveted twelve nation-founding sons, must struggle to hold the family together, and when he finally succeeds he finds himself and his clan removed from their homeland. Nowhere is this expressed more dramatically than in the Book of Joshua:

> I made [Abraham] travel throughout the land of Canaan, I multiplied his seed and gave him Isaac. To Isaac I gave Jacob and Esau; but while I gave Esau the mountain of Se'ir as his inheritance, Jacob and his sons went down to Egypt. (Josh. 24:3–4)

Nahor, who remains outside of the covenant, is ready to build his nation. Abraham, who enters into the covenant, must do some more internal work with his people before they will be ready. Now that he receives the news about Nahor he takes a step back. With all of his work becoming God's partner he has neglected the other critical building blocks – orchestrating the family's future and laying claim to the promised homeland. It is these concerns which will drive Abraham's remaining years.

Genesis 23:1–20

Sarah Is Gone

Genesis documents many generations of deaths, but the record of Sarah's death stands out in two significant ways: Sarah is the first person whose death is mourned, and she is the first person recorded as being buried. That does not mean to suggest that others weren't mourned or buried, but their mention regarding Sarah demands our attention.

Abraham's mourning for Sarah is not to be taken for granted. The deaths of two other Matriarchs, Rebecca and Leah, do not appear in the Torah, and despite numerous references to the burial of Jacob's beloved Rachel, there is no discussion of mourning. Moreover, the description of Abraham's mourning for Sarah is accentuated by his eulogizing her: "Abraham came to eulogize Sarah and to weep for her" (23:2). The only other person the Torah describes as being eulogized is Jacob.

ABRAHAM DISCOVERS SARAH

We may never know Abraham's intended audience for his eulogy, but we can make a reasoned speculation about the nature of what he said. Let us recall some of the details of their relationship.

Abram's marriage to Sarai is considered something of a revolution in biblical history. Prior to that, women were considered simply a means to bear the next generation. Abram stands beside his choice despite Sarai's barrenness; she is his wife, and nearly every reference to her reminds us of this. When Sarai recognizes her own barrenness she invites Abram to take her maidservant so that he may have children, and Abram listens to her while affirming that Hagar remains his concubine and not his wife.

This apparently mutually loving relationship, however, leaves much to be desired. On at least two separate occasions Abram/Abraham pretends that his wife is his sister, either to avoid personal harm or for material gain, risking her ultimate disgrace. Abraham never asks God to address Sarah's barrenness, and laughs at the prospect of her having a child, even when informed directly by God. Most significantly, Abraham struggles to internalize the notion that Sarah is to be his covenantal partner. Despite God's implicit and explicit messages, repeated in His reproach to Abraham for not telling Sarah about her new status, Abraham still cannot embrace it. It takes a direct instruction from God for Abraham to chase Ishmael away from the covenantal child which Sarah has borne him.

All of this passes through Abraham's mind as he eulogizes her: How he let her be taken by two foreign potentates, how he never thought about her bearing children and didn't rejoice for her when she finally did. How he never fully digested the idea that she alone was fit to be his covenantal partner and that her son was to be the bearer of the covenant after him. How she was prepared to sacrifice for him, whether by introducing Hagar to his bed or including Abraham in her joy in Isaac's birth, but he never sacrificed for her. And now, with her death, it is only in her absence that he recognizes who she really was; but it is too late.[1]

Thus Abraham not only mourns Sarah but eulogizes her as well. Perhaps his audience is the assemblage of local Hittites. Perhaps his audience is himself.

---

1. It can be similarly argued that the eulogy for Jacob takes place when his sons finally discover who their father really was.

PURCHASING THE PLOT

Sarah's death forces Abraham to deal with the things he could not or did not want to deal with in her lifetime. Abraham begins to reflect on the other significant decisions he has made which directed his path, such as prioritizing family over receiving God's gift of the land and focusing on his role in the covenant while repeatedly missing God's clues regarding Sarah's role as his partner. These concerns lie just beneath the surface as Abraham prepares to bury Sarah.

Even a cursory reading of the story indicates that Abraham does not want to just bury Sarah; he engages in protracted negotiations over the burial site – while her body lies waiting in state. It appears that Abraham is interested in more than just the burial site he is offered. What is it, and why is it important enough for him to delay Sarah's burial?

Abraham's roots in Hebron date back to when he is watching over Lot. He is not just a resident but has signed a treaty with some of the locals, and upon his return from defeating the four invading kings he is welcomed as a war hero. Both Melchizedek of Shalem and the Sodomite king greet him upon his return from battle (14:17-24). His status does not seem to have waned with the years; in his discussions with the Hittites of Hebron they call him *nesi E-lohim*, which minimally translates into "an exceedingly important man" and maximally would yield "a prince of God." Yet despite the Hittites' deep respect for Abraham, they still regard him as somewhat of an outsider, and Abraham knows this. He calls himself a *ger vetoshav*, a resident alien. It is within this tension of Abraham's being a highly respected person but nonetheless an outsider that the negotiations over the burial cave take place.

The Hittites are gracious to their honored friend, and they offer Abraham any of their burial sites in which to bury Sarah: "In the choicest of our graves bury your deceased; no man will withhold his burial site from your burying your deceased." A careful look at their language, however, reveals the gulf separating Abraham from the Hittites. They have *their* burial sites, which Abraham is welcome to use, but they will remain Hittite sites. Respected as he may be, Abraham is still an outsider. Ancient Mesopotamian law did not allow for handing over land to those outside of the local clan.[2] Sarah can be buried there, but the grave will remain Hittite. The land will not become Abraham's.

Abraham is aware of the Hittite restriction on land transfer, but is also aware of the exception to this rule – land transfer to an outsider is permissible if approved by the entire town. It is for this reason that Abraham doesn't turn directly to Ephron, the owner of the plot he wants to buy, but asks the townspeople to act on his behalf. Likewise, every step of the negotiations involves Abraham presenting himself to the Hittite leadership, and the sale happens "in front of the eyes of the Hittites." It is Abraham's way of ensuring that there will be no questioning of his title to the land. He wants the place to bear his name in perpetuity.

Abraham's desire for permanence is echoed through other elements in the Torah's recounting. Take, for example, the language Abraham uses throughout. While the Hittites offer a grave, Abraham seeks an *aḥuzat kever*, a permanent holding for burial (23:4). That is, he is not just looking for a place to inter Sarah but for a burial place that will be identified with him exclusively. This emphasis on permanence begins with Abraham's initial request and continues until the closing line of the scene, with an affirmation that "the field and the cave within it were upheld to Abraham as a permanent burial place from the Hittites" (23:20).

Another example of Abraham's focus regarding the field is with regard to the payment. While Ephron twice offers the field as a gift,[3] Abraham insists on paying for it. The four hundred silver shekels Abraham pays are not only an exorbitant sum, the number four hundred is a tenfold multiple of the typological number forty. We recall from the Noah story that the number forty carries with it the symbolic meaning of rebirth. The four-hundred-shekel price tag represents the idea that the field itself has a rebirth, a conversion of sorts, from being a Hittite area to an Abrahamic one.

---

2. See Robert C. Ellickson and Charles DiA. Thorland, "Ancient Land Law: Mesopotamia, Egypt, Israel," Yale Law School Legal Scholarship Repository, Faculty Scholarship Series, paper 410 (1995), http://digitalcommons.law.yale.edu/fss_papers/410.

3. Most classical commentaries read Ephron's comment (v. 15) as a request for money, although the text is far from explicit.

This idea is beautifully expressed in a midrashic comment. Notic-ing the verb *kam*, literally, "to rise" (see 23:17, 20), the midrash notes that as a result of the purchase the field is uplifted, raised into Abra-hamic land.[4] In fact, the verse affirming the finality of the land sale is repeated; it is expressed first in 23:17 and again, after Sarah's burial, in 23:20. Apparently, it is only after Sarah is interred that Abraham's hold-ing on the land is solidified.

Abraham's protracted negotiations to secure the land as his own become even more extraordinary when we consider the circumstances. Sarah has just died; her corpse awaits dignified treatment. Abraham's sense of urgency in finding her a final resting place is palpable: he speaks of Sarah lying "in front of him" (23:4, 8) and he repeatedly refers to "my deceased" (23:4, 8, 13). The Hittites as a whole and Ephron as an individual are also apparently agitated by the lack of finality for Sarah. They also repeatedly refer to Sarah as "your deceased" (23:6, 11, 15) and unhesitatingly offer Abraham a burial place as they sense the body await-ing its final resting place. Their words seem to cry out, "Take the grave and bury her already!" As Leon Kass writes, "The sight of the corpse before us is most distressing."[5]

Despite the urgency, it is not until after Abraham has secured the plot as his own that he buries Sarah, and it is only then that she ceases to be "the deceased" and her name and identification as Abraham's wife are restored: "*Only then* did Abraham bury Sarah, his wife, in the Makhpela cave" (28:19). For Abraham, the urgency to bury Sarah is superseded by a greater need – establishing his permanent holding in the land.

ABRAHAM LOOKS TO THE FUTURE

Abraham repeatedly passed up earlier opportunities to take the land, making family his priority instead. When he is with his father in Ḥaran,

---

4. Genesis Rabba 58:8. The initial discussion between Abraham and Ephron revolves around the cave, which Abraham wants to convert into a family interment site. By the time the discussion is finished, Abraham owns the field surrounding the cave, even its trees. It is also worth noting that Abraham offers to pay – not for the cave, but for the land.
5. *Genesis*, 363.

the Canaanites preempt his arrival; while traveling to Egypt, the Perizzites join the Canaanites; and while looking after Lot, another eight nations settle in to the Land of Israel.

Now, when Abraham comes to bury Sarah, he is struck by the fact that he has no permanence, and this raises questions about the stability of the future. A landless nation is the Ishmaelite model, not the model God intends for His covenantal family. When Abraham first enters the land he builds altars, quite likely as markers, to indicate to future generations that they have arrived in the divinely promised land. Later he plants a tamarisk in Be'er Sheba as a sign of ownership, and eventually digs wells (see 26:15). But altars in the Bible have a way of being dismantled, destroyed, or reappropriated for other gods; trees wither and die; and even wells can be stuffed up or sealed (as happens to Abraham). A grave with a body accords a sense of eternal grounding like no other monument. Ironically, it provides a profound rootedness in the land.

We will later see that Jacob understands this as well. On his deathbed, he twice insists on being buried in the Makhpela cave back in his ancestral home. Jacob, apparently concerned that Joseph will shift the clan's center of gravity to Egypt, wants to send a powerful message about where the roots of the family lie, and that there can be no real future for the clan if it is not firmly grounded in its past. In the end, Joseph appreciates that message as well and asks that his bones be removed from the land of Egypt and reburied in the land of God's promise.

Sarah's death and the need to bury her serve as the catalyst for Abraham to rethink his priorities as he confronts the reality that it may be getting too late for him to lay claim to his promised land. There is a convergence of needs – the need for permanence and the need to fulfill his destiny in the land. He cannot leave Hebron without coming to a resolution of those needs, and thus he is driven to ensure that his claim to the land is unassailable, even to the point of purchasing it at an exorbitant price and delaying the burial of his beloved wife.

There is yet another aspect to Abraham's refocusing his attention on the land. Abraham cannot forget that the first time he settled in Hebron he befriended and built bonds with three local Emorite inhabitants – Aner, Eshkol, and Mamre[6] (14:13). When he arrives in Hebron to bury Sarah, his old friends are nowhere to be found; instead there are Hittites to deal with. To bury Sarah properly, he needs to negotiate with the new claimants of the land. Abraham has lived in Hebron, but as he wanders to Gerar and Be'er Sheba any claim he may have to Hebron is erased. His self-inflicted dislocation from the land generates a significant obstacle to his ability to claim it, and the impact is dramatically demonstrated as the *nesi E-lohim* needs to prostrate and humble himself before these newcomers to bury his wife. Abraham understands that he should have been the owner of the land and is instead a resident alien pleading to purchase a plot.

It is interesting that God's name is nowhere to be found in this story. God has been trying for decades to give Abraham his promised land, but Abraham has been preoccupied with other matters. It is Abraham's responsibility to take that which God has been trying to give, and to ensure that the divine promise is fulfilled.

---

6. It is possible that the name Mamre is a biblical play on the root H-M-R, meaning to exchange. Hebron is the paradigm of Abraham's exchanging God's promise for his value of family, only later needing to trade back for it.

Genesis 24:1–25:11

Two Brides

Abraham accepts Sarah as his covenantal partner and Isaac as his covenantal son only after it is already too late for both. Sarah is dead and Isaac is gone.[1] It is hard to imagine Abraham's loneliness, not just on a personal level but existentially as well. Do his missteps threaten the future of the covenant? Abraham's belated appreciation of Sarah's importance makes him acutely aware of the need to find the covenantal partner for his covenantal son. In doing so, Abraham sets the standard for marriage for the covenantal family in Genesis as well as for the rest of the entire Bible.

Canaanite brides are simply off-limits. Throughout Genesis, taking a Canaanite bride is usually equated with writing oneself out of the covenantal family. Lot and Esau stand out most prominently, but even Judah's status is threatened when he marries an anonymous Canaanite woman, and later in the Torah we are warned repeatedly against marrying Canaanite women (Gen. 28:1; Ex. 34:15–16; Deut. 7:3). While the reason is never made explicit, it likely has its origins back in the story of Noah's violation by his son: "Cursed be Canaan; he is to be a slave's slave to his brothers" (9:25). The cursed family is not to be mixed with the blessed one.

---

1. We recall that Abraham went back to Be'er Sheba alone.

With father-son relations strained, Abraham needs a third party, his loyal servant,[2] to whom he entrusts this most essential task of finding Isaac a bride. Abraham, however, does not simply tell his servant whom to reject as a potential bride, he directs him to go to Abraham's homeland, and further insists that the bride be brought to Isaac and not the reverse. These two clauses are critical for Abraham. First, Abraham knows the culture in which he was raised and the values that dominate his ancestral home. It is those values which spark God's choice of Abram, and after the *Akeda* and Sarah's death Abraham begins to retrace his own path to reclaim those values. It is those values which he seeks for his son's covenantal bride.

Second, with Sarah's death, Abraham is increasingly aware of the need to focus more on permanence in the Promised Land. Abraham wants to ensure that his son can achieve the permanence that he previously undervalued, and so he insists that Isaac not leave the land:

> A-donai, God of the heavens, who took me from my father's home and the land of my birth, and who spoke with me and who promised me, saying, "I will give this land to your seed," He will send His messenger before you and you will take a wife for my son from there.... just do not return my son *there*. (24:7–8)

This is perhaps Abraham's most vivid acknowledgment of Isaac's special status. The covenantal child may not leave the covenantal land. Isaac is, indeed, the promised child. And in a reversal of his earlier life, in which he is regularly prepared to sacrifice the land and eventually even the child, Abraham now adheres to both.

THE MISSION

Abraham must be aware of the difficulty of the mission. It requires not only finding the right woman but also convincing her and her family to

---

2. According to tradition, this is Eliezer, even though his name is not mentioned anywhere in this story. The deduction is a logical one, particularly in light of Abraham's reference to him as far back as 15:2, which further strengthens the question concerning the absence of his name here. It will later become clear why his name is omitted.

allow her to marry an unmet stranger and to take her far from her family. Put into the context of Genesis, Abraham insists that Isaac's bride take her own *lekh lekha* journey, paralleling his. It is for this reason that Abraham affirms the need for her willingness to go (24:8) rather than to rely on a marriage contract with the males in her family. In fact, the language Abraham uses in his instruction to the servant is laced with the loaded words of his own journey: "Go to my land and my birthplace," he tells the servant. Those are the same words God uses in reverse, in His initial instruction to Abraham: "Leave your land and your birthplace."

In light of this, it is significant that Abraham omits one element from his instruction. While God demands that Abraham leave his "father's house," Abraham does not ask the servant to seek someone from his father's home. Earlier, when we studied the initial *lekh lekha*, we noted that the three terms used were actually code words for different elements of Abraham's identity that he is being asked to leave behind and replace with new ones provided by God. The "father's home" he leaves represents the idolatrous values present there. When Abraham sends the servant to find a wife for Isaac, he wants to make sure that she has the same family characteristics for which he himself was chosen by God, but he is not interested in someone who has completely absorbed the idolatrous aspects of Terah's culture.

THE SERVANT'S PRAYER

Abraham's servant departs for Ḥaran heavily laden with ten camel-loads of Abraham's finest possessions, as he will need to convince both the girl and her family of the worthiness of the family to which he wants to bring her. It is not only the wealth that is impressive but the camels themselves. Historically, the domestication of the camel at this period was not widespread;[3] bringing ten camels was a sign of both wealth and great sophistication.

The servant is equally aware of the difficulty. He arrives in Ḥaran toward evening, as the town's girls arrive at the well (apparently situated outside of the town) to draw water for their families. We should not underestimate the difficulty of this daily chore, which needs to be

3. Camels had been domesticated beginning in Egypt. Abraham's camels likely came from his sojourn there. See Bazak, *Ad HaYom HaZeh*, 258–263.

completed between the time the shepherds finish watering their flocks and nightfall. As he sees the girls approaching he turns to God for help:

> A-donai, God of my master, Abraham, please let happen before me this one time today, and do kindness for my master, Abraham. Behold, I am standing at the spring and the daughters of the townsfolk are coming out to draw water. Let it be that the girl to whom I say, "Please tip your jug so that I may drink," who then says, "Drink, and I will also give your camels a drink," will be the one that You have demonstrated to be for Your servant Isaac, and through her I will know that You have done kindness for my master. (24:12–14)

The servant's absolute loyalty to Abraham and Isaac is noteworthy, repeatedly referring to Abraham as his master. His prayer[4] is not for himself but for Abraham. Even more significant, however, is that he invokes the word *kindness* in both his opening and closing lines.

It becomes clear that the servant's prayer is as much a revelation of the qualities he is seeking within the girl as it is a request for divine assistance. He is looking for someone with the Abrahamic qualities of welcoming the stranger and offering kindness, and a sensitivity to needs beyond the immediate request. Identifying God's assistance as a *kindness* makes this explicit.

GOD ANSWERS THE PRAYER

What actually happens surprises the servant and surpasses his audacious request. No sooner does he finish his prayer than the Torah presents to us "Rebecca, born to Betuel, the son of Milka, who is married to Nahor, Abraham's brother." She is "very fine in appearance, a virgin, and no man knew her." The description is rich, and leads the reader with each successive descriptor. This is a fine example of the omniscient reader who knows more than the main characters in the narrative. Rebecca has

---

4. According to the rabbis, this is not a prayer but a request for a divine omen. The rabbis were generally displeased with people asking for such omens. See Leibowitz, *Iyunim BeSefer Bereshit*, 171–175.

many fine qualities and she is desirable – for her family, her beauty, and her chastity – but will she pass the servant's test?

The girl has but a single jug which she had filled in the spring.[5] The servant runs to her and asks for a sip of water from her jug. She lowers the jug from her shoulder and gives him to drink. "Drink, sir," she says, and when he finishes drinking she adds, "I will draw for your camels too until they are finished drinking." Quickly, she empties her jug into the water trough and runs to the well to repeatedly draw water until the camels' thirst is slaked. Surpassing the servant's hope that she would say, "I will also give your camels a drink," Rebecca labors considerably.[6]

The dumbstruck servant watches in awe as she runs back and forth between the well and trough, repeatedly emptying and refilling her jug. When she is finished he is sure that God has answered his prayer, and bestows upon her a very generous gift of gold jewelry. "From which family do you come?" he asks. "Is there place in your father's house for us to sleep?" Without knowing her pedigree, he is convinced that she is the right one and is bold enough to request lodging. When she responds that there is plenty of room as well as food for the camels, the servant bows and utters a second prayer, this one of thanks: "Blessed is A-donai, God of my master, Abraham, who did not abandon His steadfast kindness from my master" (24:27). The servant understands that his master's God of kindness has graced him with that kindness in finding a woman with qualities appropriate for the family of kindness.

Reading the above story, we understand why the Torah describes Rebecca's actions in such detail – they far exceed the servant's expectations. What is astounding, however, is that the Torah repeats the entire story, both the prayer and Rebecca's actions, as the servant recounts the events to Rebecca's family. That amount of repetition is highly unusual for the Torah, which is usually driven by an economy of words. We expect to read something like, "And the servant told them his prayer and

---

5. The text speaks of both a spring and a well. It would likely be much easier to draw from the well – all one has to do is lower the jug with a rope, while to get to a spring usually requires clambering over rocks and through vegetation.

6. She could have, alternatively, offered to lend him her jug so that *he* could draw water for his camels.

how it was answered." The amount of biblical real estate devoted to the detailed retelling demands our attention, and once again suggests that we compare the two accounts.[7]

THE ENTIRE SAGA, AGAIN

The first thing we notice is that between the original narrative and the servant's retelling there is a short passage in which Laban, Rebecca's brother, sees his sister's new jewelry, hears her tale, and observes the man with the ten camels. As far as he can tell, the man, with his lavish entourage, is a wealthy trader from afar who wants to marry Rebecca. Laban is all too eager to welcome the rich guest.[8]

Second, we observe that the servant's description of the events is framed by a sense of urgency. As he is welcomed into the house his hosts prepare a meal for the tired traveler, yet he refuses to eat before he can present his case to them: "I will not eat until I speak my words" (24:33). When he finishes telling his story he concludes with a need for an immediate answer. "So now, if you will do a steadfast kindness for my master, tell me, and if not then I will turn right or left" (24:49). In doing so the servant denies his hosts the opportunity to feed him unless they provide him with the answer he wants as he projects his singular focus on his mission.

With this framework in mind, let us turn our attention to the servant's version of the story:

> I am the servant of Abraham…. My master made me swear… "Go to my father's house and my family, and take a wife for my son." I said, "Perhaps the woman will not follow me." He said to me, "A-donai, in front of whom I walked, will send His messenger with you and ensure your success, and you will take a wife

---

7. Genesis Rabba 60:8 notices the lengthy repetition but has little to say other than seeing it as a tribute to the greatness of Abraham if even his servant's prayer is repeated so many times. Note that it is not just the servant's prayer that is repeated but the entire saga, beginning with the oath and concluding with Rebecca's actions.

8. Notice that in Laban's eyes the man is an important person, an *ish*. The confusion of the servant with his master is alluded to in Genesis Rabba 59:9, suggesting that the servant wanted his own daughter to marry Isaac.

for my son from my family and my father's house." Today I came
to the spring and I said, "A-donai, God of my master, Abraham ...
behold, I am standing by the spring. The young girl who comes
to draw and I say to her, 'Please give me some water from your
jug to drink,' and she says to me, 'You drink, and I will also draw
for your camels' – she is the one whom A-donai has chosen for
my master's son."

Even before I finished speaking in my heart, behold,
Rebecca emerges with the jug on her shoulder. She went down
to the spring to draw and I said to her, "Please give me to drink."
Quickly, she took the down the jug and said, "Drink, and I will
also give your camels to drink." So I drank, and she also gave
drink to the camels. I asked her, "'From which family are you?'
and she responded, 'I am the daughter of Betuel the son of Nahor,
whom Milka bore to him.'" And I placed the nose ring on her
nose and the bracelets on her hand. I then bowed to A-donai and
blessed A-donai, the God of my master, Abraham, who guided
me faithfully to take the daughter of my brother's brother for his
son. (24:34–48)

While some argue that the differences between the stories are merely
a literary device to make the repetition more readable, we notice that
the details between the servant's version and the one told in the initial
narrative differ both in tone and in detail. The evidence emerging from
those seemingly minor deviations points to a substantive and conscious
shift that the servant is trying to create. Below are some of the more significant changes the servant makes:

- The word *kindness*, so prominent in the initial narrative, is remarkably absent in the servant's version.[9]
- In the primary version of the story, Rebecca's actions are described
as far exceeding the servant's expectations – she waits for him to
finish drinking and runs repeatedly back and forth between the

---

9. Instead of kindness, when the servant describes the events to Rebecca's family, he
speaks of truth. In the Bible, truth is often contrasted with kindness.

well and the trough to water the camels until they are completely finished drinking. In the servant's version, Rebecca's actions match almost verbatim the servant's hope.

- In the first version, Abraham asks the servant to go to his home-land and birthplace[10] but omits any explicit mention of family. This is significant because homeland, birthplace, and family are the three components God asks Abram to leave behind (12:1) in the initial *lekh lekha*, yet Abraham mentions only two of the three. In the servant's version, however, he repeatedly emphasizes that Abraham asked him to go back to his family (24:38, 40–41, 48).
- In the initial rendition, the servant gives Rebecca the jewelry first and only then asks about her family, whereas in his rendition he reverses the order.
- In the servant's retelling he omits any mention of Rebecca's offer of hospitality, which is so significant in the original version.

Additionally, the servant's repetition of the story does not begin with his arrival in Ḥaran. He includes an abbreviated version of the entire prelude, including a narrative introduction and Abraham's charge to him:

> I am the servant of Abraham. God blessed my master exceedingly and he grew great; He gave him sheep and cattle, gold and silver, male and female servants, and camels and donkeys. Sarah, my master's wife, bore a son to my master after she was aged, and Abraham gave him everything that he had. (24:34–36)

The servant's opening words must surprise his hosts. Here is a man of apparently great wealth, whom they think is Rebecca's suitor. It turns out that he is actually only the servant of the real suitor.

Following that surprise he returns to the beginning of the Torah's initial narrative, but expands with great detail upon "God blessed

---

10. S. D. Luzzato notices this change and suggests that it is to make the marital match more compelling in the eyes of his listeners. See also Meir Sternberg, *The Poetics of Biblical Narrative: Ideological Literature and the Drama of Reading* (Bloomington: Indiana University Press, 1985), 133.

Abraham with everything" (24:1). The servant's description is quite impressive, and their ears are getting a taste of what their eyes already behold. He then adds a critical piece of information *not* included in the original narrative – that Sarah miraculously gave birth to a son to whom Abraham gave everything he has.

Abraham is not unknown to Rebecca's family (he is, after all, Betuel's uncle), and as we will later see, they apparently are aware of his covenant with God. With that in mind, the servant's tale can briefly be paraphrased as: "Abraham has a special covenant with God. Aside from material wealth, God blessed Abraham with a miraculous heir to that wealth and covenant – and indeed, Abraham passed it to that heir." The servant then continues, and I again paraphrase: "What is still missing is a wife for that blessed child. My task is to find that wife; and she must be from Abraham's family!"

As the servant presents it, God has a plan, and at every step of the way He ensures that His plan will bear fruit. When Abraham is missing a child, God provides (despite the laws of nature). Now that there is a need for a wife, God will again provide. It is only after that prelude that the servant continues with the story, and it is in this light that the differences he introduces take on particular significance.

Let us recall that the thrust of the original narrative focuses on Rebecca's character: Abraham is interested in someone with his ancestral values, the servant looks for kindness and thanks God for His kindness, Rebecca's kindness is far beyond what the servant envisions – even to the extent that she invites them into her home. Even her family connection introduces her as the child of Nahor and Milka. We remember Nahor and Milka; their marriage is the result of Nahor's kindness of marrying his orphaned niece. In the Torah's narrative, Rebecca is painted as nothing less than the female version of Abraham.

In the servant's version, however, all the evidence pointing to her character is modified. The word kindness does not appear. Rebecca's acts do not exceed the servant's expectations; rather, they match them almost verbatim. The servant is not searching for *a* girl with values but for *the* girl from Abraham's family in whom the preordained signs are realized. In his rendition, it is only after he finds out who her family is that he gives her the jewelry, for the signs have pointed him toward *this* girl. In this picture, Rebecca's offer of hospitality is irrelevant (and omitted), and the significance of Rebecca's pedigree is not her grandfather's act of kindness but the fact that her grandfather is Abraham's brother.

When we put this together with his introductory and closing remarks of urgency, the picture becomes quite clear. He is a loyal servant fulfilling the mission of a man closely associated with God. God gave him the omen he requested; God brought him to *this* place and to *this* girl, making the mission successful; the marriage is preordained from Heaven and must be settled immediately. After all, who wants to interfere with a divine, cosmic order?

It seems that the servant's ploy works. Laban and Betuel respond immediately: "This came from God; we cannot speak about it either good or bad" (24:50). They are moved – perhaps even frightened – by the servant's rendition, and offer Rebecca immediately and unconditionally. "Here is Rebecca before you; take her and go, and let her become a wife to your master's son *as God spoke*" (24:51). It is only at that point that the servant agrees to dine, effectively transforming a meal of hospitality into a betrothal party in which he gives betrothal gifts to the bride and dowry to the family.

FATE OR DESTINY

Exhausted from his trip and exhilarated by his success with Rebecca's family, the servant settles in for the night. By the next morning, when the excitement of the moment seems to have waned, Rebecca's family has second thoughts. They want her to stay with them for an extended waiting period. This is our first encounter with the biblical theme of the family holding the girl back, but it repeats in the next generation as Laban wants to prevent Jacob and his wives from leaving, and reappears in the story of the concubine in Givah (Judges 19) – with devastating results. In each of those cases the delay is repeatedly extended, and there is no reason to believe that Rebecca's family will release her at a later time without the same resistance. The servant reminds them of the urgency of acting immediately on a divinely ordained matter: "Do not delay me. God has made my path successful; send me and I will go to my master" (24:56).

It is at that point that two extraordinary things happen. First, the family suggests asking Rebecca for her opinion, convinced that she will not want to leave, especially on short notice. This alone is remarkable because asking a girl or a woman what she wants is almost unheard of in the Bible; women do not generally have independent voices, especially in the realm of marriage. When they call her, however, they are shocked to hear that she is prepared to leave immediately.

One must wonder why Rebecca agrees to go. While the narrative offers no explicit explanation it is possible that our explication of the story yields some clues. Rebecca is the only one other than the servant who witnesses the primary story, and she knows how the servant has modified the story and for what purpose. Listening to the servant, she understands that Abraham is the man of the covenant, that Isaac is the child of the covenant, and that she has an opportunity to become the covenantal wife. There is no hesitation on her part. Like Abraham, she will embark on her own *lekh lekha*, leaving behind the familiar to seek out a new destiny.

She also knows what the servant initially values in her – her character. After all, the servant asks about her family only after he gives her the jewelry. It is worth noting that Rebecca's actions mirror those of Abraham in greeting his three guests. He runs to greet them and she runs to greet the servant. Abraham exceeds the norms of hospitality, as does she. In the servant, she finds a culture of kindred spirits. She feels appreciated for who she is and for the values that are important to her. She values what the servant values in her, and she wants to join the family that sent him.

Even more surprising than Rebecca's willingness to go is her family's acceptance of her chosen destiny. As she prepares to leave, they offer her a blessing: "Our sister, you should become thousands upon ten thousands. May your seed take hold of the gate of its enemies" (24:60). We are struck by the similarities between their blessing and God's blessing to Abraham following the *Akeda*:[11] "I will bless you greatly and make your seed very numerous, as the stars in the sky and sands on the seashore, and your seed will take hold of the gate of its foes" (22:17).

---

11. See Rashbam, 24:60.

Abraham's destiny is apparently known to them and they bless Rebecca with success in joining it. To paraphrase them, "Your destiny should be Abraham's destiny." Rebecca is eager to join it, and the family blesses her with success in her quest.

This entire episode, with its repetitions and intricacies, is recounted in the Torah to shine a light on the nature of Rebecca's family and Rebecca herself – her values and her chosen path. With her eagerness to become the covenantal partner, the text leaves us in anticipation. Will she be successful where Sarah was not?

MARRYING THE DREAM

Rebecca achieves her dream of marrying into the covenantal family and even gets her family's blessing in doing so. Little does she realize, however, what she is getting herself into. Isaac is not the dynamic Abraham. The first time she sees Isaac, even without knowing who he is, she falls off her camel. Austere Isaac is returning from an unspecified evening encounter in the field and his appearance is so overwhelming that it literally knocks Rebecca down. It is only afterward that the servant reveals to her that the mysterious man is her intended. Humbled, perhaps even terrified by Isaac's presence, she covers herself in a veil.

Isaac, too, gets to marry his dream. He brings Rebecca into his mother's tent and is comforted. He sees in Rebecca the replacement for Sarah, the parent who always showed him love.[12] No words are exchanged in the narrative between Isaac and Rebecca, but Isaac is the first person described in the Bible as loving his wife. A beautiful language play highlights this: Rebecca lifts her eyes and sees Isaac from afar; Isaac, too, lifts his eyes and sees her from afar. As we saw earlier, the lifting of the eyes suggests an ability to see beyond what meets the eyes. Both Rebecca and Isaac see beyond the superficial, and it is the deep values they see within each that they learn to love. They each marry their dream, but in an idealized, almost depersonalized kind of way. Rebecca marries into a covenant for which Isaac is the gateway; that is all that matters to her. As for Isaac, he sees in Rebecca the mother for whom he could

---

12. After Sarah's death, Isaac takes solace in his mother's tent (24:67).

not properly mourn, and for whose death he could find no solace. They each love the *idea* that the other represents.

As for Abraham, through the agency of his trusted servant he completes his mission of marrying Isaac to an appropriate woman, assuring the future of the covenantal family. With this, his journey comes full circle. In his waning years, there is no record of further communication with God, even though he does pursue those things he overlooked for too long: discovering the covenantal wife, settling the future of the covenantal family, and securing a place in the covenantal land.

ABRAHAM'S EPILOGUE

We expect Abraham's story to end here. His journey is complete. He has secured the core components of his covenant with God. And yet we are told that he takes another wife, Ketura, and fathers another six children. After Abraham's longstanding commitment to Sarah and refusal to take even Hagar as a wife, we are left perplexed by his marriage (at a very advanced age!) and fathering of an entirely new family. Why it is valuable for the Torah to describe all of this?

Reading the names of Abraham's children reveals that at least two of them reappear later in Genesis: together with Ishmael, Medan and Midian are involved in the sale of Joseph, suggesting some sort of complicity between Joseph's brothers and their cousins. This, however, does not seem to be enough of a justification for including the strange Ketura segment of his life.

It appears that this seemingly unimportant short passage actually provides the coda to Abraham's life. First, whereas he marries another woman and has six children with her, he sends them all away with gifts because he has given everything he has to Isaac. This other woman is not Sarah, and even though Abraham has many children with her, she is not the covenantal wife and the children are not the covenantal children. Abraham has no better way to demonstrate this than by sending them away from Isaac, much as he does earlier to Ishmael. More significantly, whereas Abraham is previously reluctant to send Ishmael away and needs a direct divine command, he now understands on his own the uniqueness of both Sarah and Isaac, and the children of Ketura are sent away summarily. He finally internalizes about Sarah and Isaac what God tried telling him for many years.

Second, the text describes Abraham's death and burial in the Makhpela cave. This is the same cave which he stubbornly insists on purchasing for Sarah, and which serves as his permanent and final resting place in his promised land. Abraham's investment in the land, albeit late, comes to fruition, and his own burial in the land secures it as a covenantal holding for his children – more than any wells he dug or altars he built.[13]

13. With Abraham's legacy secured, we are witness to an unspoken bond between Isaac and Ishmael. Both sons come to bury their estranged father in his special cave. And Isaac settles into Be'er Laḥai Ro'i, The Well of the Living One Who Sees, the place associated with Hagar and Ishmael.

Genesis 25:19–26:33

Passing the Baton

God's initial selection of Abram is motivated by Abram's understanding that family can be a vehicle for transmission of values. Abraham's passing raises significant questions about the success of this new endeavor. Will Abraham's divinely chosen child carry the covenant with him, and if so, what will be Isaac's imprint on that covenant? Moreover, on the assumption that Isaac will bear his father's torch, will he be able to pass Abraham's dual legacy, of the family and of the covenant, to the next generation?

We are thrust immediately into these questions and left hanging with anticipation as the Torah presents Isaac. As opposed to Abraham's story, to which the Torah dedicates more than thirteen chapters, and later Jacob's story, which effectively spans almost half of Genesis, Isaac's story gets barely three chapters of attention, and even that is only if we include the narratives of the birthright and blessing. Isaac is a hidden, mysterious character; we know almost nothing about him, and the little that we do know is underwhelming. Perhaps a close reading of the spartan text will shed some light.

ABRAHAM MAKES ISAAC

One of the first things we notice in the Torah's introduction of Isaac is the phrase, "Abraham brought forth[1] Isaac" (25:19). This is particularly unusual because the beginning of that very verse opens with, "This is the legacy of Isaac, Abraham's son," rendering the second half superfluous.[2] The phrase stands out even more when viewed in contrast to the parallel phrase describing Ishmael: "This is the legacy of Ishmael, Abraham's son, who was birthed by Hagar the Egyptian, Sarah's maidservant, to Abraham" (25:12). These two introductions are meant to highlight an essential difference between Abraham's two sons, with the focus on who is the primary influence in their lives. For Ishmael, it is his mother, the maidservant, the Egyptian; for Isaac, it is Abraham.[3]

When we pause to ponder the nature of Abraham's influence on Isaac, a complex picture emerges. Abraham learns to love Isaac, ironically demonstrated in the language used in their conversation on the way to the *Akeda*: Isaac repeatedly refers to Abraham as "my father," while Abraham responds with "my son." Let us also not forget that powerful phrase both prior to and following that conversation: "They journeyed together," and Abraham's efforts in securing a suitable mate for Isaac.

At the same time there is enough evidence to suggest that Isaac's life in his father's house is not pacific. Abraham needs to be convinced by God that Isaac's birth is necessary, and even after Isaac is born it becomes clear that Abraham holds on to the hope that Ishmael can be Isaac's equal. God's forcing Abraham to banish Ishmael cannot endear Isaac to Abraham. We also recall the conclusion of the *Akeda*, in which Abraham returns to his waiting lads – but without Isaac. In fact, the only recorded meeting between Abraham and Isaac after the *Akeda* is when Isaac comes to bury his father.

---

1. Traditional translations read, "Abraham begot Isaac."
2. Rashi cites a midrashic interpretation suggesting that the Torah emphasizes Abraham's paternity – to the point that Isaac looks like his father – to silence the cynical claim that Avimelekh is, in fact, Isaac's biological father (see Genesis 20).
3. See Rashbam, 25:19. It is worth noting that Hagar brings her son a wife from Egypt, her place of origin, while Abraham arranges for a wife for Isaac from his own family back in Ḥaran.

Of course, we have the *Akeda* itself, during which Isaac sees the glint of the blade in his father's hand as Abraham is held back at the last moment by the angel before slaughtering his son. The traumatic effect of the *Akeda* on Isaac cannot be overstated. Isaac flees from his father, recoiling from the dominant and dynamic figure who towers over and nearly slaughters him. Isaac finds solace in the solitude of the desert of Be'er Laḥai Ro'i, where he develops into an intense, perhaps even terrifying, figure.

Indeed, it is Abraham who makes Isaac who he came to be – a dark, quiet, intense character. It is no wonder that we barely hear Isaac's voice throughout the narratives describing his life. Even when Isaac prays, we don't hear his words, only the narrative description, "Isaac prayed." This is dramatically different from Abraham, who has many interactions with both people and God, and whose words repeatedly reverberate throughout the text.

Like Sarai, Isaac's wife Rebecca is barren, but Isaac relates to it differently than does his father. Abram's reaction to childlessness is to complain to God about his own childlessness, but Sarai is not even mentioned in his complaint:

> Abram said, "God, the Almighty, what could You possibly give me while I am childless, and the one who takes care of my household is Eliezer of Damascus?" Then Abram said, "You have not as yet given me children, and a member of my household will inherit me." (15:2–3)

Notice that Abram neither speaks to or about Sarai. Rather, he speaks of God's unfulfilled promises to *him*.[4] Isaac, by contrast, takes a different approach. He is the first in the Torah described as loving his wife (24:67), and when he realizes she is barren he prays to God on her behalf and in her presence, literally, "facing her" (25:21).

Isaac experiences not only Abraham's ambivalence toward himself but Abraham's sidelining of his beloved mother, Sarah. Isaac wants

---

4. Let us recall our earlier discussions about Abraham's difficulty including Sarah as his covenantal partner.

to make sure that in his family, the relationship between himself and his wife will be different from the spousal relationship he witnessed as a child.[5] Indeed, the Torah cannot speak of Isaac's legacy without introducing his covenantal partner, Rebecca.

CAN ISAAC BEAR THE TORCH?

All this leaves us with a challenge. If Isaac is a traumatized man, comfortable in silence and solitude (as opposed to his dynamic father), can he really be the next link in the great covenant? I suspect that Isaac is also troubled by this question. He has two sons: one is outgoing, dynamic, and unafraid to encounter life-threatening challenges on a daily basis; the other is a *tam*, a tent-dwelling shepherd. It is difficult to precisely define *tam* – simple, unsophisticated, naïve. Whatever it means, it is intended as a contrast to his worldly and gregarious brother.

At first glance it would seem that Jacob is very much like his father, and we wonder why Isaac prefers Esau over Jacob. Upon further reflection, however, the choice makes perfect sense. Isaac sees himself faced with the choice of someone like himself or someone more like his father. If Isaac sees himself as a mere shadow of his father, unfit to be the bearer of the covenant, then his choice of Esau and rejection of Jacob makes sense. He sees in Jacob his own weakness, but in Esau he sees Abraham's strength. The bearer of the covenant, in his own mind, cannot be an introvert like himself, unable to confront the world, and so he prefers Esau for that role.

Indeed, a close look at the text points us in this direction. Isaac prefers (literally, "loves") Esau, for he "puts prey in his mouth" (25:27). Esau is what Isaac is not and can never be. Later, when Isaac decides to bless his chosen son, he asks for Esau to bring him some freshly hunted meat. Many have wondered why Isaac needs the food to give the blessing, but it now seems clear: it is not the food, but the hunt itself which inspires Isaac to see Esau's power and potential. This is most evident in Isaac's instructions to his son prior to the blessing: "So now, pick up

---

5. Ironically, Isaac's sensitivity to the status of the wife may be the result of the revolution which Abraham started but could not develop further. In the next chapter we will explore the figure of Rebecca.

your instruments, your quiver and your bow, and go to the field, and
hunt me a hunt" (27:3). The repeated references to Esau's profession
and his tools – the instruments, the quiver, the bow, the field, and the
double mention of the hunt – highlight Isaac's attraction to Esau. Isaac
is fascinated by what is beyond his own capacity.[6] Later, Isaac repeats his
affinity for Esau's ability to grapple with the world when he prepares to
deliver the blessing to the son standing before him: "Behold, the scent
of my son is the scent of the blessed field" (27:27).

ABRAHAM'S GIANT SHADOW

Despite Isaac's recoil from his father, it seems that he cannot avoid being
both overshadowed by Abraham and subconsciously-instinctively walking in Abraham's footsteps. And it is not just Isaac who sees himself in his
father's shadow; God apparently does as well. The following passage is the
first of the only two direct communications that Isaac receives from God:

> There was a famine in the land, aside from the first famine in the
> days of Abraham, so Isaac went to Avimelekh the king of the
> Philistines, to Gerar. God appeared to him and said, "Do not go
> down to Egypt! Dwell in the land which I shall tell you. Live in
> this land. I will be with you and bless you, for to you and your
> children I will give all of these lands as I fulfill my promise to
> Abraham, your father. I will increase your seed as the stars of the
> heavens, I will give to your seed all these lands, and all the nations
> of the earth shall be blessed through your offspring – because
> Abraham listened to My voice and heeded My instructions, My
> statutes, and My teachings." (26:1–6)

We are immediately struck by Abraham's ubiquitous presence in
God's inaugural encounter with Isaac. The famine is framed in reference to Abraham, the blessing given to Isaac is Abraham's blessing,

---

6. It is possible that Isaac's simultaneous attraction to these tools and inability to deal
with them himself is a result of his experience at the *Akeda*, where he saw the tools
of death being wielded against him. For a different understanding of the importance
of food to Isaac see Shmuel Klitsner, *Wrestling Jacob* (Jerusalem: Urim, 2006).

and Isaac's blessing is the result of Abraham's earning it. Even the language of the blessing is borrowed almost verbatim from God's blessings to Abraham.

God's messages to Abraham	God's message to Isaac (26:4)
I will greatly increase your seed (22:17)	I will increase your seed
as the stars of the heavens. (22:17)	as the stars of the heavens.
I will give to you and to your seed after you the land of your dwelling, all of Canaan. (17:7)	I will give to your seed all these lands.
The nations of the earth shall become blessed through your offspring. (22:17)	All the nations of the earth shall be blessed through your off-spring

Isaac's blessing is copied from that of his father and is inherited, not earned. Ironically, the language in this blessing to Isaac is borrowed almost exclusively from the blessing Abraham receives after the *Akeda* – implying that Isaac's passive role in the very event which shatters his relationship with his father is the one which "earns" him the right to inherit the blessing his father earned there. Once again, Isaac's passivity becomes his defining feature as he is overshadowed by his deceased father.

When we extend the comparison between Isaac and Abraham we notice that God's message to Isaac is actually the reverse of His message to Abraham: God tells Abraham *lekh lekha*, "Go forth!" while Isaac is told to stay put. Moreover, we earlier saw that in God's messages to Abraham regarding both the initial *lekh lekha* to leave his ancestral land and the final *lekh lekha* of the *Akeda*, the destination is left vague. While God wants Abraham to figure it out, God leaves no room for ambiguity with Isaac. He opens with, "Dwell in the land which I shall tell you," which is reminiscent of the unclear destination told to Abraham, but continues immediately with, "Live in *this* land." While God wants Abraham, the bold venturer, to seek and explore, He wants the shy Isaac to stay close to home.

If this were not enough, let us look at God's opening words to Isaac: "Do not go down to Egypt." Nowhere does it say that Isaac intends to go to Egypt; if anything, it says that his destination is Gerar, in the land of the Philistines. God's message seems superfluous, unless the point is to emphasize that Isaac should not even contemplate doing as his father had done.

All of this seems as if God were saying, "You are not your father, and don't even pretend to be. Nonetheless, I will bless you because of your father." Following in Abraham's wake cannot be helpful to Isaac's sense of worthiness.

FAILURE AND SUCCESS IN GERAR

If we wonder why God suspects that Isaac will simply repeat what his father had done, we need look no further than the continuation of the story. Isaac arrives in Gerar and settles in. When asked about Rebecca he tells them that she is his sister, just as his father had done twice earlier (each with unpleasant results). The problem with Isaac's attempt to deceive his hosts is twofold. First, he is traveling with two children; if Rebecca is his sister, then he has a lot of explaining to do. Second, he doesn't think to close the window shades and gets caught "playing"[7] with his wife (obviously in a manner that one would not play with a sister). Isaac mimics Abraham's actions but lacks his father's "street smarts" to understand how to make it work. He admires his father's success but he has no clue how to achieve it for himself.

This becomes strikingly evident in the epilogue to the wife-sister incident. After being discovered by Avimelekh, Isaac decides to do something radically different from his shepherd father – he plants. As we noted in our study of Cain and Abel this is not merely trying something new. It involves a radical lifestyle change from being a nomad to being rooted in a land. Even more remarkable is that Isaac chooses to farm the land during a drought! For the shepherd, the ability to wander is essential for survival, yet Isaac seems to be prepared to sacrifice that

---

7. In a brilliant play on words, the Hebrew word used to describe Isaac's "playing" with his wife, *metzahek*, is itself a play on Isaac's name (Yitzhak).

at the worst possible time. There is no logical reason for Isaac's business move to succeed, yet succeed he does, and dramatically so, beyond anyone's wildest imagination: "In *that* year Isaac reaped a hundredfold" (26:12). Isaac's success defies rational explanation, so the Torah provides a supernatural one – "God blessed him."

Left to his own devices, Isaac is a dramatic failure in his worldly interactions. Blindly mimicking his father's actions would have brought him to Egypt, and ultimately leads him to try deceiving Avimelekh without knowing how to make the ruse work. Isaac fails at being different from his father just as he fails at mindlessly mimicking him. The introverted, naïve Isaac is seemingly immune to earthly success. Only divine intervention saves him.

WELLS IN THE NEGEV

The opening scenes in Isaac's story paint a powerful, troubling image of the second Patriarch, who seems far from patriarchal. That image, however, is Isaac's starting point. Just as Abram needs time and experience to evolve into Abraham, Isaac must undergo his own transformation, complete with its own surprises. And given what we know about Isaac, we are not surprised when we discover that his transformation is hidden in a seemingly banal tale of digging wells. After all, Isaac is mostly a hidden character.

Isaac's miraculously meteoric financial success generates so much jealousy from his Philistine hosts that they ask him to leave. Isaac travels upstream along the Gerar wadi and discovers that, after his father's death, the Philistines plugged a series of wells Abraham had dug.[8] Isaac re-digs those wells and restores the names his father used to identify them.

---

8. We have no earlier record of Abraham digging these wells. They apparently serve a purpose similar to the monuments and altars Abraham builds but never uses; they are literally landmarks left behind as permanent signs of his presence. In this light, the Philistine plugging of those wells, an important resource for travelers, becomes meaningful: they are trying to erase the memory of (the now-dead) Abraham from the land, denying his claim. It is worth noting that they did not dare do that during Abraham's lifetime. It is also interesting that the Philistine actions are a clear violation of the covenant Abraham made with the Philistines (21:27–33).

Isaac's goal in digging these wells is not to fulfill a divine imperative but to uphold a filial responsibility. He aims to restore Abraham's
legacy in the land, so that passersby unfamiliar with the Philistine intervention would be unaware of Isaac's work, seeing only Abraham's wells
and their original names. Isaac leaves no mark of his own, illustrating
that at this stage he is still very much operating in his father's shadow.
This incident, however, points to a subtle but significant shift from his
earlier activity. Isaac is keenly aware of the Philistine attempt to erase
his father's landmarks, and it seems that his attempts to restore those
wells – with their original names – is a conscious effort to restore his
father's legacy rather than an instinctive aping of his father's actions.
Furthermore, it demonstrates that Isaac is no longer recoiling from his
father but is consciously prepared to embrace his father's legacy.

Following this incident Isaac sends his workers to dig completely
new wells, unrelated to Abraham's. Isaac is no longer simply renewing
Abraham's wells but digging his own. This is the next step in Isaac's emergence, as he not only restores his father's legacy but seeks to emulate
it. Isaac's attempts are valiant, but while his father manages to maintain
control of those wells throughout his lifetime, Isaac loses control of his
newly dug wells almost immediately:

> The shepherds of Gerar argued with Isaac's shepherds, say-
> ing, "The water is ours," so he called the well Esek (contention),
> for they contended with him. They dug another well but they
> argued about that one too, so he called it Sitna (hatred). So Isaac
> uprooted[9] himself from there. (26:20–22)

Isaac's attempts to leave his own mark on the landscape are hijacked
by the Philistine shepherds. It is not even clear if the names he gave
ever take hold. Isaac's attempt to interact with the world like his father
did is again met with failure. And unlike Abraham, who confronts
Avimelekh when his well is stolen (21:25), Isaac opts to move away

---

9. The verb *vayaatek* appears only twice in the Torah. Its first appearance describes
Abram's changing from the river wadi route to the mountain path on his initial *lekh
lekha* search for "the place" (12:8).

from conflict. He cannot hold his own in the face of the shepherds of Gerar.

What is interesting, however, is that Isaac tries yet again, moving farther and farther from Gerar until he finds a place that is uncontested: "He dug another well, and they did not argue over that one, so he called it Reḥovot (space, expansion), as he said, 'For God has expanded our space and we may be fruitful in the land'" (26:22). Isaac tests out different places and perseveres despite being twice rebuffed by the shepherds from Gerar. Although he prefers to leave rather than fight for his land, he persists until he finds a place that will be unquestionably his. Unlike his father, who often succeeds on his first attempt, Isaac doggedly presses on until achieving the desired result.

ISAAC THE PATRIARCH

The story of the wells is far from mundane. It is actually the veiled story of Isaac's emergence as a Patriarch, a metaphor for his transformation. Isaac has shifted from one who blindly repeats his father's actions to one who understands the value of consciously emulating his father's values. Rather than pushing to create some new model, Isaac is the archetype of the faithful transmitter and bearer of his father's mission. Isaac's patriarchal model is thus profoundly different from that of Abraham. The importance of this model cannot be overstated.

Revolutionary leaders, such as Abraham, make dramatic changes which alter the course of history. Their presence in the world divides history into two distinct eras, pre-revolution and post-revolution. This is true in all revolutions – political, scientific, cultural, etc. Yet revolutionary leaders often lack the skills to make their revolutions stick. Following the revolution, there needs to be a period of stability during which the dramatic changes effected can take root and become truly transformative as they replace the prior status quo. Had Isaac tried to be an Abrahamic figure, Abraham's revolution may never have taken hold. It is only because Isaac faithfully maintains his father's legacy that Abraham's legacy lives on.

This points to one of Isaac's great hidden qualities: his tenacity. Rejected by Avimelekh and pursued by the Philistine shepherds, he is undeterred by failure and persists until he can claim Reḥovot as his own. Unlike Abraham, who complains to God when the promise hasn't been fulfilled and who retreats into a personal crisis when he believes he has failed Lot and Sodom, Isaac faces repeated failures yet continues to push on with quiet resolve until he meets with success. It is precisely this quality which is essential for him as the faithful bearer of the Abrahamic tradition. Nothing will stand in his way as he ensures that the treasure he holds is passed forward.

Isaac is no longer running from his father or mindlessly following Abraham's script. He has chosen as his mission to be the solidifying link in the chain. Nowhere does this become clearer than at his next stop, Be'er Sheba. Upon his arrival God appears to him, for the second and final time. A careful reading of God's second message – the one after his sojourn to Gerar – reveals that it adds little to God's first communication with Isaac – the one prior to his arrival in Gerar – even to the point of referring repeatedly to Abraham. Why is it necessary for God to repeat the first message?

While the primary content of the two communications is essentially identical, the second message adds a particular formulation: "Fear not, for I am with you" (26:24). This same reassuring formula is delivered to Abram after his battle with the four kings (15:1), and later to Jacob as he prepares to join Joseph in Egypt (46:3). For each of the Patriarchs, the reassurance comes just at the time when they fear God's promise to them has been compromised. Isaac is greeted in Be'er Sheba with God's confidence in *him*: he is not the disappointment he imagines himself to be, God's promise endures despite his self-image as a failure, and his earned patriarchal role in that promise is secure.

God's initial message to Isaac assures the blessing in Abraham's merit. In God's second message to him, Isaac receives God's blessing because he chooses to be Abraham's successor, defining his own patriarchal role. Isaac, the Patriarch, receives his own patriarchal blessing. This is primarily evident in Isaac's first acts in Be'er Sheba (26:25): he builds an altar, calls in God's name, and pitches his tent in succession – precisely the same things Abram does upon entering Canaan (12:8). Once again, Isaac has chosen to be Abrahamic, and in doing so cements his role as Patriarch.

Isaac's transformation is recognized not only by Isaac himself as he emulates his father's entry into the land, not only by God as He renews the promise to Isaac as one who earns his place as the loyal transmitter of Abraham's covenant with God, and not only by the careful readers of the text, but by the Philistine king Avimelekh as well. Avimelekh comes to meet Isaac in Be'er Sheba with a delegation and a military escort. Avimelekh wants nothing less than to establish a treaty with Isaac, much as an earlier eponymous Avimelekh sought to establish a covenant with Isaac's father. Avimelekh proclaims, "We have seen that God is with you" (26:28), just as the earlier Avimelekh proclaims to Abraham (21:22). Isaac, the Patriarch, has arrived, recognized by outsiders as God's blessed one.

The accompaniment of Avimelekh's military general could easily have been interpreted as a threatening move. The pre-patriarchal Isaac would likely have cowered and moved on, fearful of confrontation, but patriarchal Isaac meets them forcefully: "Why did you come to me – you hated me and sent me away!" (26:27). Isaac's show of bravado is not natural; it may even be a mask for his fear,[10] yet he shows no external signs of that fear in the face of the king and his military entourage. Like his father, Isaac enters into a treaty with the Philistine. Unlike Abraham, who presents Avimelekh with seven sheep, Isaac offers nothing to pacify the local king. This treaty needs to stand on the word of its two protagonists, and Isaac no longer cowers before the regent.

BE'ER SHEBA

On the very day of Avimelekh's departure, Isaac's servants inform him of another well they dug. He names this well Shiva, and the Torah adds a fascinating coda: "It is because of this that the name of the city is Be'er Sheba [*sheva* is the Hebrew term for "Sheba"] until this day" (26:33). The Torah's attributing the name to Isaac is perplexing. Hadn't Abraham named the place a generation earlier, in *his* encounter with Avimelekh (21:31)?

Apparently, when Abraham named the place the name did not take hold. It isn't until Isaac comes that the name Be'er Sheba becomes

---

10. This is also likely the reason that Isaac finds it necessary to send his guests away the next day (26:31); Isaac still feels threatened by Avimelekh and needs to dismiss him quickly. This element is missing from Abraham's encounter with Avimelekh, where the latter leaves on his own. It is also missing from Jacob's confrontation and covenant with Laban (31:55).

its permanent name. Abraham's revolution is not guaranteed until it is reaffirmed and carried on for another generation. Isaac, as Patriarch, takes on that role – his naming of the place ensures that Abraham's naming of the place endures.

ISAAC CHOOSES HIS PATH

Isaac begins as the man who blindly copies his father's actions, not understanding why he does so, leading to sometimes comical and other times simply failed results. The farcical results are a reflection of Isaac's essence, embodied in his name. Isaac equals laughter, or mockery. Abraham laughs at the very notion of his birth, as does Sarah. Early Isaac does not know how to interact with the world.

It is only when Isaac acts completely illogically by planting during a drought – representing a break with his father – that he is successful. That is apparently the beginning of the emergence of the new Isaac. It still takes him some time, during which he regularly runs from conflict, but eventually he finds himself and his role – along with the strength to stand his ground and face Avimelekh. Bolstered by God's affirmation of his patriarchal status, Isaac concludes a treaty with Avimelekh and sends him off.

Ironically, Isaac arrives at his father's place, digs wells just like his father, and even names the place Be'er Sheba as did his father. But the new Isaac does so out of choice, not because he does not know better. When the early Isaac restores his father's wells, we are left clueless about Abraham's naming of those wells. When patriarchal Isaac renames a place with the very name his father used, the name of the place is attributed to him, not to Abraham.

Isaac thus defines his patriarchal role. He innovates nothing; rather, his role is to preserve his father's legacy and pass the covenant on to the next generation. This is no small task. It requires perseverance and self-restraint, allowing the credit to go elsewhere, and that suits Isaac well.

Abraham stands out as a revolutionary figure, blazing new ground with God, people, and morality. God chooses Abraham because of Abraham's innovation of marrying a set of values with a vehicle of transmission. Isaac is the epitome of the bearer of tradition and the self-submission necessary to ensure that the tradition is passed on – unblemished.

Genesis 26:19–28

Rebecca, the Covenantal Wife

Rebecca is first introduced when Abraham's servant travels to Ḥaran in search of a wife for Isaac. She surprises him with her Abrahamic hospitality, surprises her family with her eagerness to leap at the opportunity to leave with the stranger and join the family of the covenant, and surprises Isaac with the Sarah-like serenity she brings him.

With the narrative focus shifting from Abraham to Isaac, Rebecca is once again introduced to us. This is in itself surprising, as Sarah's importance does not emerge until halfway through the Abrahamic narrative. But Isaac is not Abraham, and Rebecca is not Sarah.

REBECCA OF ARAM

Perhaps the most interesting thing about the Torah's initial presentation of Rebecca in our present narrative is the focus on her background: "Isaac was forty years old when he took Rebecca, the daughter of Betuel the *Aramean* from *Padan Aram*, the sister of Laban the *Aramean*, for a wife" (25:20). Three times in this introductory verse Aram is mentioned, whether referring to the land of her origin or her family affiliation. Given Rebecca's enthusiasm for leaving her Aramean family, the Torah seems to be highlighting the gap between her and her background. While her childhood community and family are Aramean, she decides to leave behind that part of herself. Rebecca becomes who she is in spite of her Aramean origins. Like Abraham, she embarks on her own *lekh lekha* journey from Aram.

The Hebrew for Aramean is *Arami*. A slight orthographic alteration using the same letters yields the similar-sounding *rama'i*, meaning "deceiver." Our initial encounter with Betuel and Laban reveals a deceptive side, and Laban's deceit will later emerge as perhaps his defining characteristic. With the *Arami-rama'i* play, Rebecca of Aram is none other than Rebecca from the House of Deceit. She unhesitatingly takes the first available ride out of Aram, seeking to join the Abrahamic covenant, but the reader is left with a lingering question: What will she bring with her from the culture she was born into?

REBECCA THE PROPHETESS

Like Sarah, Rebecca is barren. According to the Talmud, God makes the Matriarchs barren because He adores their prayers.[1] Uriel Simon[2] says it differently: the Torah wants to emphasize that the births of the Patriarchs are miraculous; only divine intervention could have brought them about. As we saw in the previous chapter, as distinct from Abraham's treatment of Sarah, Isaac is acutely aware of his wife and makes her a partner in his prayers.

Rebecca's pregnancy is unusual. Something is happening in her womb which seems to far exceed the norm.[3] Rebecca is so anguished that she calls out, "If so, then why am I … ?" Perhaps her distress is so intense that she cannot finish her sentence; perhaps she holds herself back from finishing her sentence. Either way, she does not wallow in her pain but decides to do something about it: "She went to inquire of God" (25:22).

---

1. Yevamot 64a.
2. *Reading Prophetic Narratives* [Hebrew] (Jerusalem: Mossad Bialik, 1997), 43.
3. The Hebrew word describing this is *vayitrotzetzu*; its meaning is far from clear. Many of the classical medieval commentaries (Rashi, Rashbam, Ibn Ezra, Radak) understand it as an intense form of movement or running. Ḥizkuni understands it as smashing (see Psalms 74:14), indicating extreme turbulence in her womb.

Rebecca's "inquiry of God" opens up some disturbing questions. To where does she go to inquire of God, and why does she need to go anywhere? Isn't Isaac, who has an intense relationship with God, accessible?

What seems clear is that while Isaac makes efforts to include Rebecca in his relationship with God, Rebecca finds it necessary to establish her own. She seeks out God independent of Isaac and must "leave" his presence in order to do so. Moreover, Rebecca makes no effort to include Isaac in her communication with God, so much so that there is no indication that she shares God's subsequent response with her husband – in fact there are multiple indications that Isaac is completely unaware of her prophetic insight.[4] Rebecca may be Isaac's willing partner in the covenant, but she does not suffice with being a passive participant in *his* covenantal role. She insists on her own.

PROPHETIC AMBIGUITY

Rebecca's prophecy is itself worthy of significant attention:

> Two nations are in your womb, and two peoples shall emerge from your innards. One people will be stronger than the other, and *rav yaavod tza'ir.* (25:23)

The last three Hebrew words are usually translated as "the elder shall serve the younger," and it is clear that Rebecca understands her prophecy thus. When describing the parental preferences, the Torah indicates that Isaac's preference for Esau is based on the latter's hunting ability, but no parallel explanation is offered for Rebecca's preference for Jacob, apparently because none is necessary. Rebecca prefers Jacob because she believes, based on her understanding of the prophecy, that Jacob – the younger – is preferred by God.[5]

The problem is that Rebecca's interpretation of the prophecy is not uncontestable. While the word *tza'ir* clearly means young (or

---

4. Rebecca's withholding from Isaac parallels Abraham's withholding from Sarah. The male-female roles in Isaac's home reverse those of Abraham's.

5. Rashbam, 25:23, s.v. *verav yaavod tza'ir.*

younger), nowhere in the Bible do we find the converse of *tza'ir* being *rav*. For example, Lot has two daughters, the *tze'ira* (feminine form of *tza'ir*) and the *bekhira* (feminine form of *bekhor*, the firstborn). Similarly, Laban has two daughters, Rachel the *tze'ira* and Leah the *bekhira*. The word *rav* is not used to describe the elder in either case.[6] In fact, the word *rav* does not mean elder at all, it means large (or larger), great (or greater), powerful, or numerous. For example, Abram and Lot need to separate because their belongings had become very great (*rav*; 13:6); Pharaoh is afraid that the Israelite nation is becoming greater (*rav*) than his own (Ex. 1:9); Moses instructs the people to give a larger portion of the Promised Land to the larger (*rav*) tribes (Num. 26:54); the early trans-Jordan peoples are described by Moses as being "a large, numerous (*rav*), and giant-sized, tall people" (Deut. 2:21).

Given what the word *rav* usually means in the Bible, the last three words of the prophecy can easily be read as, "the younger will toil greatly,"[7] meaning that while Esau, the elder, will reach his destiny quickly, Jacob will achieve his only with great effort. This is, in fact, what is described later in the book. Esau creates a nation and settles into the land of Edom on the eastern shores of the Dead Sea, while Jacob endures long years of hard labor in Laban's house, followed by many difficulties with his children, followed by generations of servitude in Egypt – and only after an extended delay do his descendants reach their Promised Land. Read this way, Rebecca's prophecy is the perfect sequel to the Covenant between the Pieces, in which God informs Abraham that his children will endure hundreds of years of hardship before the divine promise is fulfilled.[8]

Even were we to ignore the unusual usage of the word *rav* and accept its popular rendering in this verse as "elder," God's prophecy to Rebecca is still ambiguous at best. In the Hebrew language, the

---

6. See also Gen. 43:33; 48:14; Josh. 6:26; I Kings 16:34.
7. See Ḥizkuni.
8. This perspective on the distinction between Esau and Jacob is expressed with great clarity by Joshua: "To Isaac I gave Jacob and Esau, – but while I gave Esau the mountain of Se'ir as his inheritance, Jacob and his sons went down to Egypt" (Josh. 24:4).

preposition *et* directs a verb to a specific noun. Its absence leads to inconclusive reading, so that in our case, the absence of *et* yields two alternate, equally plausible readings. One is the familiar, "the elder shall serve the younger"; the other is less familiar: "the elder, the younger shall serve."[9]

Earlier we saw that God's *lekh lekha* prophecy to Abram with regard to his destination is intentionally vague to allow for Abram to figure out God's intent. It appears that Rebecca, the second generation's Abram, is also the recipient of an ambiguous prophecy. Listen to R. Huna's comment in the Midrash: "If he merits, he will be served; if not, he will serve."[10] Apparently enticed by the grammatical anomaly of the missing *et*, R. Huna uses his midrashic license to capitalize on the absence of vowels in the Torah text to make his point that the prophecy is ambiguous, that the word "serve" (*yaavod*) can be vocalized to read "will be served" (*ye'aved*). Not only is the prophecy ambiguous, it may be intentionally so.[11]

SELF-FULFILLING PROPHECY?

The uncertainty about the meaning of Rebecca's prophecy opens up new possibilities for reading the entire story. Rebecca prefers Jacob because of her understanding of the prophecy, as a result of which she encourages Jacob to deceive his father and receive the blessing intended for Esau, and this results in the need for Jacob to flee. We can only speculate what would have happened had she interpreted the prophecy differently. Could Esau have been the preferred son? Could it be that there would have been no preferred son and both would bear the covenant, just as all of Jacob's own sons were heirs to the covenant?

Stimulating as the above questions are, the answers to them rest purely in our speculative imaginations. In the end, Rebecca's interpretation of the prophecy is self-fulfilling – she understands that Jacob is God's preferred son and acts accordingly, resulting in him becoming

---

9. See Radak; *Haamek Davar.*
10. Genesis Rabba 63:7.
11. *Haamek Davar* also argues that the ambiguity is intentional.

God's preferred, while Esau is shunted aside. As the Talmud says, all dreams follow their interpretations,[12] and dreams are a taste of prophecy.[13]

REBECCA, THE COVENANTAL MATRIARCH

While God may have answered Isaac's prayers, His response is wordless; Rebecca becomes pregnant, but there is no verbal communication from God to Isaac. Unlike Abraham, who hears multiple monologues from God and eventually engages in dialogues with Him, Isaac hears nothing. Rebecca, by contrast, is the Abrahamic figure in the family. She seeks God and receives a verbal response.[14]

Unlike Isaac, Rebecca is not born into covenant but chooses to become part of it. Unlike Isaac, who strives to include his wife, Rebecca sees her role not as working beside him but parallel to him, or possibly even in a leading role. In her eyes, Isaac is an awe-inspiring man but blinded by his own experiences, while she is the recipient of a prophecy which she deems her sacred responsibility to fulfill, even if it requires subverting Isaac.[15] Like Sarah, Rebecca understands that it is her role, not Isaac's, to ensure the future of the covenant. Rebecca evokes elements of both Abraham and Sarah; she is both patriarchal and matriarchal.

There is great irony in Rebecca's role in the covenant, as she, wittingly or unwittingly, draws on her own Aramean background of deceit, from which she flees, to fulfill her covenantal role. But it is not just her preparedness to trick her husband which she draws from Aram.

It is unclear to us, the readers, what Isaac's intention is regarding the blessing he offers to his eldest. What is the nature or power of that blessing? Is Isaac planning to determine the future bearer of the covenant? Does Isaac believe it is within his power to make that decision?

If we look back at Isaac's own background, one son is clearly the heir to the covenant while the other is not, but that situation is not

---

12. Berakhot 55b.
13. Ibid. For more on dreams, see Yaakov Medan, *Daniel: Exile and Revelation* [Hebrew] (Alon Shevut, Israel: Tevunot, 2006), 26–31.
14. And it is Rebecca, not Isaac, who is heir to the Abrahamic tradition of ambiguous prophecy.
15. It is possible she believes that Isaac will never accept her prophetic vision or its interpretation.

analogous to this. Ishmael is the son of Hagar, an Egyptian, a maid-servant, while both Esau and Jacob are the sons of the chosen wife. Even more, God instructs Abraham, against his will, to banish Ishmael and remove him from the covenantal family, and it is God who tells Abraham explicitly that Isaac is the covenantal child. Isaac, by contrast, receives no such divine communication or instruction. It is therefore entirely plausible that Isaac's blessing to Esau is not intended to have any bearing on the covenant.

What is clear, however, is Rebecca's understanding of Isaac's intentions. She certainly believes that Isaac is about to make a decision which will affect the future of the covenant, she certainly believes that Isaac is empowered to make that choice, and she certainly believes that the blessing has some kind of special power, like pixie dust, that even if sprinkled on an unintended recipient, will carry the same power and efficacy. In the Abrahamic family there is no precedent for such a concept, nor do we ever see such a concept again in the Torah. It is eminently possible that this idea is something Rebecca brings with her from Aram.

Rebecca is Isaac's covenantal partner, both because she chooses to be and because Isaac welcomes her into that role. Little does Isaac realize the significance of that partnership, or that Rebecca's perception of partnership is dramatically different from his own.

Like Sarah, Rebecca insists on her role in determining the direction and securing the future of the covenantal family. And like Sarah, once she accomplishes this, she disappears from the text. There is, however, one significant difference between Sarah and Rebecca. Sarah brings her demand about the choice of Isaac directly to Abraham, while Rebecca works behind Isaac's back. Perhaps that is why Sarah's death and burial are recorded in the Torah with great detail and fanfare, while Rebecca simply disappears. Her death and burial remain hidden. After this story, she will never be heard from again.

Genesis 25:19–34; 27:1–28:5

Birthright and Blessing

F
ew stories in the Bible have engendered fiercer competition for interpretation as the story of Jacob and Esau. For centuries, populist readings have portrayed Jacob as a serial thief. Some rabbinic midrashim, likely in reaction to the scathing critique of the Patriarch, engage in intense apologetics in an attempt to reverse the portraits apparently painted by the text. Take, for an extreme example, Rashi's portrayal of the two characters (sources cited below refer to both the text and Rashi's commentary).

In Rashi's eyes, Jacob is righteous even in the womb, eager to study Torah, while Esau runs to idolatry (25:22). As the boys grow into men, Esau engages in the three cardinal sins – murder, idolatry, and adultery. He is also deceitful (25:25, 27; 26:34), always trying to convince his father of his own righteousness, and a thief (27:5). Jacob, by contrast, is naïve, straightforward, and devout (25:27). When it comes time for Isaac to give the blessing, Jacob avoids lying, even when he says, "I am Esau your firstborn" (27:19). Isaac's confusion over who is standing before him emerges from his surprise that Esau is speaking politely and invoking God's name (27:20–22). Isaac, upon discovering the ruse, affirms that the blessing belongs to Jacob lest anyone think that it had come to Jacob improperly (27:33); Isaac appreciates Jacob's wisdom in attaining the blessing – it is not deceit at all (27:35); and in truth, the birthright really does belong to Jacob because he is actually conceived of Isaac's first seed (25:26).

Along with this story's potential theological implications, the radical disparity between the antagonists and the apologists highlights just how "loaded" the story is. Theologically based interpretations, however, do not allow for the texts to speak for themselves. What we will attempt in this chapter is twofold. First, we will separate two distinct stories – one about the birthright and the other about the blessing. Even though many conflate these two incidents, the Torah text itself carefully separates between them so that they are not confused with one another. Indeed, in Hebrew, birthright is called *bekhora*, while blessing is *berakha*. Confusing these two is easy, as they have the same letters (with the middle two transposed) and sound similar. Nonetheless, the play on words is meant to highlight linkage between two similar, but quite distinct, elements of the story. Second, we will engage in a close reading of each of these stories to discover *what* they are trying to tell us and about *whom* they are speaking.

THE BIRTHRIGHT

In a simplistic reading of the story, Jacob takes advantage of his compromised brother to extort from him the birthright in return for a bowl of lentil soup.[1] The astute reader, however, notices nuances in this brief incident which point to a more complex scenario.

The closing verse in this scene (25:34) provides a good example of this nuance. Most read the closing line as, "Jacob then gave to Esau bread and lentil soup." This reading, however, ignores the grammar indicating that the sentence is written in the past perfect, effectively rendering the verse as, "Jacob had already given to Esau bread and lentil soup." This subtle shift is quite significant, as it suggests that Jacob's

---

1. In an interesting twist, Alan Dershowitz, in *The Genesis of Justice* (New York: Warner Books, 2000), 142–143, turns the deceit into a positive quality, albeit one for which Jacob will ultimately pay a price. He writes, "Jacob is praised as a wily man, ready and able to employ guile and deception to navigate the dangerous waters of life… Jacob eschews the violence of his more physical twin, Esau, preferring brain to brawn. Guile is the great leveler between the physically unequal."

deal with Esau is concluded only after Jacob had already provided his brother with nourishment – contradicting the popular image of Jacob withholding food pending Esau's acquiescence to an unfair deal. In a larger context this makes even more sense than the conventional reading. After all, hadn't Isaac inherited considerable wealth from his father? It is inconceivable that Esau, upon returning home, would have died of starvation were Jacob to have denied him food – he could have simply gone into one of the other tents and eaten there.[2]

A similar approach is advocated by Radak, who suggests that the bowl of soup is not the price of the birthright but the traditional meal accompanying the close of a deal, the terms of which are not explicated in the Torah.[3] Note that Jacob never explicitly says that the soup is payment for the birthright as, by contrast, Rachel does when she offers Leah her night with Jacob in exchange for the mandrakes found by Reuben (30:15).

Esau's willingness to enter into the agreement is attested to by an oft-misunderstood exclamation. When Jacob asks Esau to sell him the birthright Esau responds by saying, "Behold, I am going to die, and what good is the birthright to me?" (25:32). If Esau's words cannot be taken literally, what were they meant to convey?

The birthright is likely something for which one must wait until the passing of the father. Under the law of primogeniture it refers to the passing of the leadership of the clan. Everything in the clan is transferred to the eldest upon the passing of the father, and everyone in the clan becomes subservient to him. "Cashing in" on the birthright, however, requires patience and long-term thinking. In a keen observation, Ibn Ezra and Rashbam point out that Esau, as a hunter, leads a precarious life – a wild animal, especially a wounded one, is quite dangerous. Each day might be his last, and he is well aware of that. The likelihood of his outliving his father is, in his eyes, minuscule. Therefore, when Jacob asks for the birthright it is truly meaningless to Esau, as he will not live long enough to benefit from it.

---

2. Ibn Ezra, 25:34, maintains that Isaac lost all of his father's wealth; Nahmanides rejects that assertion.
3. Similarly, the deal between Isaac and Avimelekh (26:30) and the agreement between Jacob and Laban (31:36) are concluded with shared meals.

The story concludes with the affirmation that Esau despises that birthright (25:34); it represents to him an approach to life antithetical to his own, one which requires years of patient waiting. Esau's agreement to the deal is not the result of duress or the immediate fear of starvation but the reasonable conclusion of someone who lives for the moment and truly believes that interminable waiting for his father's passing is incompatible with his character and lifestyle. For him, the birthright is irrelevant.[4]

What we have seen so far is sufficient evidence to conclude that in the sale of the birthright Jacob neither deceives nor extorts from Esau, and that there is a genuine sale of something which is useless to Esau but, for an as yet unexplained reason, meaningful to Jacob.

This sanitized portrayal, however, is incomplete. The incident opens with a description of Jacob's culinary exploits, and twice uses a word (once as a verb and again as a noun) with ominous overtones. The root N-Z-D appears six times in the Torah, of which three are in this scene, and in every instance describes nefarious intent.[5] The unique choice of that word draws our attention, particularly because of its closeness with Z-D-N (evil intentionality) and Z-U-D (sinister intent).[6] The choice of the word could not have been accidental, suggesting that Jacob's intent in cooking that stew is not innocent. If we preserve the idiomatic implications, a translation of the phrase, *"Vayazed Yaakov nazid"* (25:29), might yield, "Jacob cooked up a scheme."

In that light, one must wonder at the ease with which Jacob's request to buy the birthright slips off his tongue in response to Esau's request for food. How long has Jacob been waiting for precisely the right moment to make his request? When Esau readily agrees, Jacob anticipates that Esau will later regret the sale, so he makes Esau take an oath

---

4. Only when Isaac's demise seems imminent does Esau recognize that the birthright does have value (27:36).

5. Ex. 21:14; Deut. 17:13; 18:20. The word appears an additional four times in the Prophets, each time referring to a cooked food, and five times in the Writings describing evil intentions. Our story is the only context in which it is used with both connotations.

6. It is fascinating that the Hebrew root Z-U-D, describing Jacob's actions, is remarkably similar to the root TZ-U-D, used to describe Esau as a hunter. The two are similar phonically as well, one opening with a *z* sound and the other with a *tz*.

to ensure it – much as Abraham makes his trusty servant swear (24:3), and as Jacob later does with Joseph (47:31).

This combination of observations complicates our picture. While Jacob does not necessarily deceive or exploit his brother, acquiring the birthright has been on his mind for some time and he is waiting for the right moment to "pop the question." That time comes when Esau returns exhausted from and exhilarated by the thrill of yet again escaping death and vanquishing his prey. While Jacob may not be a deceiver, exploiter, or liar, he is certainly a schemer and plotter.

ISAAC MISSES JACOB'S CHANGE

The most important part of this analysis, however, does not come from the incident of the birthright itself but from its context. The Torah earlier records that as opposed to Esau, who is a man of the field, Jacob is a *tam*, a simple or naïve man. It now becomes clear that he is not as naïve as we had previously thought, or perhaps he is *no longer* as naïve as he was previously. Aside from what this tells us about Jacob, it tells us even more about Isaac.

The greater context of this incident is the story of Isaac (and Rebecca). In the Torah text there is no paragraph break from the marriage of Isaac to Rebecca, through Rebecca's pregnancy and the birth of the twins, to the birthright incident; it is all part of a single continuum. Only after this incident does the Masoretic text insert a break. And when the story continues, it is not about Jacob and Esau but about Isaac and Rebecca. This suggests that the primary function of the incident of the birthright is not to provide insight into Jacob and Esau but to tell us about Isaac and Rebecca. The story of the sale of the birthright reveals important information about the parents.

Rebecca prefers Jacob, ostensibly because of her understanding of the prophecy she received; Isaac prefers Esau because Esau is unlike Isaac, a man of the field, a hunter who is successful in his external encounters. Isaac sees himself within Jacob the *tam*, and cannot imagine that the covenant needs another generation of himself. What Isaac fails to realize is that Jacob has changed. Jacob is no longer a *tam*. His successful plot to buy the birthright points to the emergence of a different character. Jacob is far more worldly-wise than Isaac can imagine, but Isaac's assessment of Jacob is stuck in the past. Not only is Isaac unaware of Rebecca's prophecy, he is unaware of who Jacob is becoming. Had Isaac only realized....

THE BLESSING

If the story of the birthright is complex, the tale of the blessings is even more so. What is the nature or power of a parental blessing, and what do *they think* the power of that blessing is? What is Jacob thinking as he stands before his father? Why does Rebecca think that receiving the paternal blessing is important, even necessitating deception, when her prenatal prophecy foretold Jacob's supremacy? Whom does Isaac think he is blessing as he issues it?

Isaac Summons Esau

Were this story the direct continuation of the sale of the birthright, it would make perfect sense: Isaac, seared by his father, prefers Esau for the future leadership of the clan because Esau is what Isaac can never be. Inspired by Esau's hunt, Isaac now seeks to enshrine his preference through blessing his firstborn. The power of this moment is not lost on Isaac, as the language used in the opening dialogue evokes the *Akeda*:

> [Isaac] said: My son...
> [Esau] responded to him: Here I am!

In a previous lifetime that conversation happened in reverse, as young Isaac on the way to the *Akeda* summons his father, saying, "Father," to which Abraham responds, "Here I am, my son!" That fateful conversation changes the course of Isaac's life. Isaac now invokes the same language in a conversation he believes is fateful as well, hopefully in a more positive and constructive way.

The problem is that this is not the direct sequel to the birthright incident. There are two significant passages separating Isaac's initial preference for Esau from this story of the blessing. The first, longer narrative describes Isaac's encounter with Avimelekh in Gerar (26:1–33). We learn of Isaac's chosen path and how he no longer passively lives in his father's shadow but paves his own patriarchal identity. This Isaac should be able to see past the superficial lure of Esau.

The second passage, lasting only two verses (26:34–35), relates to Esau's marriage to two Hittite women who bring "bitterness of spirit" to Isaac and Rebecca. Given Isaac's transformation and Esau's improper marriages (essentially writing him out of the covenant), we are puzzled by Isaac's continued preference for and desire to bestow blessing upon Esau.

This leads us to two possible conclusions. The first is that Isaac has no intention of passing Abraham's legacy to Esau. Rather, he intends a completely different kind of blessing for him. The plausibility of this interpretation is supported by the blessing which Isaac actually gives – it is about the dew of the heavens and the fat of the land, not about the sands of the seas and the stars in the heavens and a promise of progeny, nation, and land. In fact, the Abrahamic blessing is not mentioned explicitly[7] until after the story is concluded and Isaac prepares to send Jacob away to Jacob's uncle Laban, at which point Isaac actually confers that blessing upon Jacob.

If this is true, then Rebecca's attempt to redirect the initial blessing to Jacob is completely misguided. In fact, Rebecca's actions ultimately bring no benefit whatsoever to Jacob, yielding instead only profound discord within the family. The repercussions are far worse than she can imagine. But there is a second possibility.

Isaac does undergo a personal transformation in terms of how he sees himself in light of his father, and Esau's marriages are indeed troublesome to Isaac and Rebecca. As Isaac ages, however, his vision dims and the path he earlier chose for himself is no longer clear. Let us recall the midrash that suggests Isaac's eyes dim because of his experience at the *Akeda*.[8] That event haunts him as he gets on in years; the emotional scars have not been erased. The aging Isaac feels vulnerable and turns to the son who represents strength, and it is that strength which inspires him,

---

7. Although it is hinted to earlier (27:29): "May those who curse you be cursed and may those who bless you be blessed," evocative of God's opening message to Abraham (12:3).
8. See p. 237.

regardless of Esau's flaws: "So now, pick up your instruments, your quiver and your bow, and go to the field, and hunt me a hunt" (27:3). Vulnerable Isaac is once again taken by Esau's strength and his hunting tools.

Isaac's sense of vulnerability is reflected not only in his weakness of vision but in that he perceives his death as imminent: "Behold, I am aging, I do not know the day of my death" (27:2). In fact, Isaac's sense of his impending death, which both opens (27:2) and closes (27:4) his comments to Esau, brings us full circle to the earlier story of Jacob and Esau, where Esau sees his own death as coming at any time ("Behold, I am going to die" [25:32]). The difference between the two, however, is dramatic. Esau's vulnerability, resulting from his perilous lifestyle, renders him incapable of thinking about the future. Isaac's vulnerability impels him to think specifically about the future. Ironically, Isaac's words are similar to Esau's but his conclusions parallel Jacob's – we need to always be thinking about and planning for the future.[9]

Rebecca Hatches a Plot

While Isaac's intentions regarding the blessing are unclear, it is obvious that Rebecca understands them as an attempt to deliver a divine blessing to Esau. Quoting what she heard from Isaac, she tells Jacob that Isaac's intention is to "bless you before God before I die" (27:7). Rebecca understands well Isaac's sense of vulnerability, repeating this need to pass the baton prior to his death, but whereas Isaac says to Esau, "so that *I* may bless you before I die" (27:4), Rebecca understands that the blessing is "before God."

We have only a single recorded conversation between Rebecca and Isaac, and that doesn't come until the epilogue to this story. Despite Rebecca's profound awe of Isaac as a man of God, she seeks her own channels and is rewarded with direct divine communication. With the two covenantal partners each having their own conception of perpetuating the covenant, we are not too surprised by the lack of

---

9. The irony is compounded when we consider Isaac's later words to the son standing in front of him: "The voice is the voice of Jacob but the hands are the hands of Esau" (27:22). Here, Isaac's voice is the voice of Esau but his actions (i.e., hands) are those of Jacob.

spousal communication – they each believe that they know what is best and that they are guided by divine inspiration. Rebecca is convinced that Isaac is in error, perhaps driven by the terror of his own mortality, and that it is her responsibility to avoid the emergence of conflict between her prophecy and Isaac's blessing with God's imprimatur.

Does Rebecca believe that Isaac's blessing will carry weight in the heavenly spheres? Very likely. Does Rebecca believe that diverting the blessing to Jacob can be effective? Probably.[10] What does Jacob think about all this? There is no indication one way or another, but he does object to her plan: "What if my father touches me?" Jacob is smooth; Esau is hairy. Jacob is afraid of getting caught.

Jacob's objection raises the question: What is Rebecca thinking?! Does she think that Isaac is so removed from reality that he will be unable to distinguish Jacob's voice from Esau's, and to differentiate between the taste and texture of wild game – which so inspires him – and the domesticated veal he will soon be served? Does she not consider that Jacob will need to speak in front of his father? Or does Rebecca naïvely believe that Isaac's state of vulnerability and eagerness to pass the baton will blind him to the contradictions facing him? Rebecca, born into the house of deception in the land of deception, is not very good at deception. While her quality of kindness is akin to Abraham's, her ability to design and execute a plot involving trickery is no better than Isaac's.

Jacob's objection to the plan is neither philosophical ("That won't work because he's thinking about Esau") nor principled ("That's stealing!"), but a practical one – "What if I get caught?" At this stage it is not clear if Jacob is concerned about getting caught but unconcerned by the ethical violations involved in stealing from his brother and deceiving his father, or if he hesitates expressing principled objections out of respect for his mother (it would be irreverent to tell his mother that she is acting unethically). If the latter, then his objection to his mother may be

---

10. An alternate explanation is that she does not really believe that a misdirected blessing would be effective but wants to remove any doubt within the family about which child was blessed, as *they* would believe that the misdirected blessing is valid.

multilayered. He is fearful of being discovered but uses that as an excuse to avoid his mother's ploy without embarrassing her.

The language Jacob uses in expressing his concern may provide a clue, as he says, "I will be in his eyes as a misleader (*metaatei'a*)" (27:12). The Hebrew root of this word means "to be lost," and its conjugation in our context refers to an individual who causes someone else to be lost. The word itself is unusual, appearing only one other time in the entire Bible (II Chr. 36:16), and the root is used only sparingly in Genesis. Abraham, in his comments to Avimelekh (20:13), refers to himself as someone who is (caused by God to be) lost, in search of a direction or destination, and Hagar, expelled by Abraham, gets lost in the wilderness of Be'er Sheba (21:14). Later it is Joseph, in search of his brothers, who is lost (37:15).

By contrast, Isaac is never described as being lost, as he is explicitly told by God not to wander or leave the land.[11] In light of this, Jacob's concern takes on an additional dimension. Subverting the blessing would not only be thievery, but a perversion of Isaac's essence – Isaac does not get lost, but deceiving him would make him lost, erasing a critical aspect of his distinctiveness. This offense, Jacob understands, is unforgivable.[12]

Perhaps the most striking part of this scene is the one in which there are no words. Rebecca does all the action, while Jacob is passive. Rebecca takes Esau's clothes; Rebecca dresses Jacob in Esau's clothes; Rebecca places the meal, literally, into Jacob's hand. There is a thundering, impending silence as Jacob is thrust into his mother's plan. Jacob's passivity paints a powerful portrait of a man who cannot refuse his mother but is profoundly reluctant to obey her.

Jacob (as Esau) in Front of Isaac

Jacob's discomfort is evident throughout the scene and expressed by the extraordinary economy of words. He says as little as possible, sometimes

---

11. Genesis Rabba 64:3 describes Isaac as a pure offering, unsullied by venture outside the sanctity of the Promised Land.
12. Rebecca does not understand this, as she believes Jacob's concern to be that he will be cursed rather than blessed (27:13).

resorting to single-word responses. Let us observe how this unfolds in the narrative.

We earlier saw that Isaac summons Esau with the fateful language of the *Akeda*. That same language is repeated in the opening dialogue between Jacob and Isaac, but with surprising twists:

> [Jacob] said: "Father."
> [Isaac] said: "Here I am! Who are you, my son?"

This conversation is a replay of the one between Isaac and Abraham on the way to the *Akeda*:

> [Isaac] said: "Father."
> [Abraham] said: "Here I am, my son!"

The parallel between these two stories is shattered by father Isaac's insertion of three words: "Who are you?"[13] Jacob has said only a single word and already Isaac is suspicious. Jacob, hoping that he will not have to say more than a single word, is confronted by a suspicious query: "Who are you?"

From this point on there is nothing Jacob can do to pacify his father's wariness. Five times during this brief scene Isaac seeks confirmation of the identity of the person standing before him, and even then he remains unconvinced.

> "Who are you?" (27:18)
> "How is it that you found [your prey] so quickly?" (27:20)
> "Come forward and let me touch you, my son, [so that I might know if] you are my son Esau or not" (27:21)
> "Are you my son Esau?" (27:24)
> "Come forth and kiss me, my son." (27:27)

---

13. Kass, *Genesis*, 393, also notes the replay of the *Akeda*, suggesting that Isaac's question of, "Who are you?" presents this scene as a parody of the *Akeda*.

Far from being naïve, as Rebecca believes Isaac will be, Isaac is cautious and skeptical. Robbed of his sight, he uses his other four senses – sound, touch, taste, and smell – to resolve his doubts, yet his senses confuse rather than clarify because the evidence is contradictory: "The voice is the voice of Jacob but the hands are the hands of Esau" (27:22).

Ultimately Isaac does issue the blessing, inspired by the smell of Esau's clothes. Isaac's final request for his son to approach him and kiss him is an attempt to use his last resource, his sense of smell. The reaction is immediate: "[Jacob] approached and kissed him. [Isaac] smelled the scent of his clothes and blessed him, saying, 'Behold! My son's scent is like the scent of the field which God has blessed'" (27:28).

Does Isaac Know?

All of this points to a key question: Who does Isaac believe is standing before him when he confers his blessing?

On the one hand, Isaac doesn't hold back the blessing and is later shocked – trembling greatly in terror – when he discovers that it is someone other than Esau who receives his blessing: "Who is it, then, who hunted game and brought it to me, and from which I ate and [then] blessed?" (27:33). On the other hand, Isaac struggles with the conflicting facts: "He did not recognize him, for his hands were hairy like the hands of his brother, Esau" (27:23). Isaac is unconvinced even after eating, prompting his request to smell his son. And when we look at the blessing itself, it is missing two of the core elements of the Abrahamic blessing – the progeny and the land, and has only hints of God's initial *lekh lekha* message to Abraham: "May those who curse you be cursed and may those who bless you be blessed" (27:29).

Let us assume for now that Isaac intends to issue the Abrahamic blessing (which he eventually does [28:3–4]). Isaac's confusion with regard to identifying the son standing before him may have been compounded by his doubts about Esau's suitability for that blessing. Immediately prior to this story, the Torah narrates Esau's choice of wives and the distress this brought Isaac. (Prior to giving Jacob the Abrahamic blessing, Isaac emphasizes the need to avoid Canaanite wives.) To overcome his wavering support for Esau he needs a powerful reminder of just why he believes him to be the appropriate candidate, prompting his request that Esau bring him hunted game.

At the critical moment, however, Isaac is both faced with conflicting evidence about the identity of the person standing before him and internally conflicted about his initial preference for Esau. When Isaac's ability to make a decision based on rational considerations is compromised, the sense of smell, perhaps the most powerful trigger for emotional memory,[14] tips the scale. Esau's scent overwhelms him with a flood of emotions and the ensuing blessing pours forth.

Yet even though Isaac issues the blessing it is clear that he is still holding back. We noted earlier that in the epilogue to this story, Isaac summons Jacob and confers upon him the Abrahamic blessing. Even if Isaac's initial intent is to confer this blessing upon Esau, the combination of the identity confusion and his own internal struggle with his choice of Esau causes him to withhold the Abrahamic blessing. Despite the emotions triggered by Esau's scent, it is precisely because Isaac knows that his decision-making is compromised that he does not issue the Abrahamic blessing, waiting instead for greater clarity before doing so.[15]

Isaac's Trembling

This complicates the story and forces us to dig a little deeper. When we consider the decision-making process we can divide decisions into roughly two categories. In the first category are the decisions made based on rational consideration which, for most rational people, includes most of the decisions we make in our lives. We weigh the pros and cons of the available options, consider generating alternative options, and move forward guided by our intelligence.

---

14. See, for example, C. Rouby et al., eds., *Olfaction, Taste and Cognition* (New York: Cambridge University Press, 2002); F. Schab and R. G. Crowder, eds., *Memory for Odors* (Mahwah, NJ: Lawrence Erlbaum Associates, Inc., 1995).

15. Even if Isaac's initial intent did not include the Abrahamic blessing, it is clear from the end of the story, when he bestows it on Jacob, that it is very much on his mind. As such, very little would change in the analysis of what transpired while Jacob is before him posing as Esau.

Some decisions, however – and these often include the most important decisions we make in life – are based not on rational thinking but on emotional considerations. Whom to marry, where to raise a family, religious commitment, and more, certainly may involve a checklist, but often those decisions ultimately require a leap of faith. That leap is based on forces deep inside ourselves, instincts emerging from our most hidden places, so much so that they often remain hidden from us long afterward.

Faced with conflicting rational evidence, Isaac knows he cannot rely on facts. His instincts, triggered by the smell of the field coming from Esau's clothes, allow him to release a blessing – not necessarily *the* blessing, but a blessing nonetheless. When he soon discovers that it is, in fact, Jacob who stood before him and not Esau, he is shaken to his core; his instincts have failed him.

This raises for Isaac the most terrifying possibility of all: was this a single lapse, or have his instincts been wrong his entire life? Was he wrong to prefer Esau the hunter? Is that quality enough of a reason to choose him as a successor? And what about Jacob – has he been wrong about Jacob all this time? Isaac finally realizes that Jacob the naïve, the *tam*, is not so naïve after all. In fact, whereas Isaac is unsuccessful in his attempt to deceive Avimelekh regarding Rebecca, Jacob does a far better job deceiving and under much more difficult circumstances. Could it be, thinks Isaac, that Jacob is eminently appropriate to be the bearer of the Abrahamic covenant and the future leader of the clan?

Few things are more terrifying than to realize you have missed the greatest opportunities in life, especially if it is the result of being guided by a fundamental error. Isaac's terror is not generated by the prospect that he had given the blessing to the wrong son, but as a result of living his entire life in error and *almost* giving the blessing to the wrong son. Isaac's shock is not at being misled by Jacob, but at being misled by himself – about both Esau and Jacob.

Splitting the Blessing

It is valuable to explore the blessing Isaac issues (believing that the son standing before him is probably Esau), which in fact turns out to be a dual blessing. The first part is a blessing of agricultural bounty: "May

God grant you from the dew of the heavens and from the fat of the land" (27:28). Esau is a hunter; he follows the prey and is unconnected to the land. Isaac's blessing is a directive that Esau stop living dangerously, that he settle down and establish roots in the land.[16] As the future leader of the clan, Esau needs more stability than a hunter, hence Isaac blesses him to engage in agriculture.

That same blessing is appropriate for Jacob the shepherd, a nomad, disconnected from the land, like Abel and Abraham before him. The initial blessing Isaac bestows is generic, equally fitting for both sons. And while it may serve as a precursor to the Abrahamic blessing with its emphasis on rootedness in the land, it is very much *not* the Abrahamic blessing.

The second part of Isaac's blessing is quite different. It establishes the leadership of the clan, something which is normally passed automatically to the eldest son: "Be a master to your brother, and your mother's children will bow to you" (27:29). Here Isaac clearly establishes the supremacy of one son over the other, echoing Rebecca's prophecy many years earlier when the twins were still *in utero*.

It is striking that even in this second component, the Abrahamic blessing is not included. Supremacy among the brothers and leadership of the clan has been unlinked from the Abrahamic promise. Isaac does not rule out the possibility of connecting them, but he does not assume that linkage automatically.

In other words, in a moment of doubt, even as Isaac makes an emotional leap of faith, he still holds on to the Abrahamic blessing because he is just not sure enough. Imagine Isaac's shock when Esau exclaims that he has been "Jacobbed" (i.e., outwitted)[17] twice, and that the right of the firstborn has already been taken by Jacob.[18] Not only does Esau confirm Jacob's right, but that same Jacob has long been capable of the craftiness Isaac would have valued.

---

16. Remember that Isaac, unlike Abraham, tills the soil and does not leave the land.
17. The root of Jacob, A-K-V, has multiple connotations throughout the Bible. It could mean "heel" (as in the birth story), it could mean "in return for" (as in 22:18; 26:5), but it could also mean "to be crooked" (see, for example, Is. 40:4; Hos. 12:4; Jer. 17:9, and most strikingly, Jer. 9:3).
18. Esau's exclamation justifies Jacob's earlier demand that Esau take an oath confirming the deal lest he later regret it.

It is only when the scene is completed, when he can contemplate the events and make sense of them, that Isaac knowingly bestows the Abrahamic blessing. He summons Jacob and leaves nothing to the imagination:

> May El Shaddai bless you, make you fruitful and multiply you, let you become a community of nations. May He give you the blessing of Abraham, to you and your seed after you, to inherit the land of your dwelling which God gave to Abraham. (28:3-4)

Esau's Blessing

The rapid unfolding of events – from Isaac's struggle to identify Jacob to Esau's entry (immediately upon Jacob's exit) to Esau's revelation of the pre-history of Jacob and the birthright – leaves Isaac in a state of shock. Isaac's terror, learning that his lifelong trajectory has been built on a misguided assumption, is followed by a brief affirmation of the blessing he had just conferred, after which he is emotionally spent. It is Isaac's inner turbulence that explains the ensuing bizarre dialogue (27:34–38):

> Esau: Bless me too, my father!
> Isaac: Your brother came deceitfully and took your blessing.
> Esau: Is it for naught that he is named Jacob that he Jacobbed me twice – he took my birthright and now has also taken my blessing?!
> Esau (again): Did you not save a blessing for me?
> Isaac: Behold, I have made him your master over you, and I have made your brothers his servants, and I have supported him with grain and wine. For you, then, what could I do, my son?
> Esau: Do you have only one blessing, my father? Bless me too, my father!

Three times Esau asks his father for a blessing. Isaac repeatedly seems to think that he has none to offer. In the middle of this scene there is even an awkward moment, as Esau's revelation that Jacob already possesses the birthright is met by Isaac's silence. Is it possible that Isaac has no blessing to offer his son? Particularly since the initial blessing focuses on agricultural bounty, is it inconceivable that both sons could be blessed with that bounty? This is, in fact, what eventually does happen – Isaac gives Esau a blessing that parallels the one given to Jacob:

Jacob's initial blessing (27:28)	Esau's blessing (27:39)
May God grant you from the dew of the heavens and from the fat of the land,	Your dwelling shall be from the fat of the land and from the dew of the heavens above.
and a bounty of grain and wine.	

We wonder why it takes so long for Isaac to realize that he can grant Esau a blessing parallel to the generic blessing offered to Jacob. Moreover, Isaac's responses to Esau's repeated requests are exactly the opposite of how we would expect a father to console his son. The explicit declaration to Esau that his brother deceitfully stole what is rightfully Esau's will hardly calm him, and neither will explicating to Esau the extent of the blessing which had just been illicitly snatched.

Perhaps Isaac's lapse in judgment is understood best in light of his utter disbelief at what has just transpired. He is so shaken by the dramatic turn of events that he is paralyzed, incapable of a constructive response to Esau. It is only after reconsidering that he realizes he can, in fact, bless Esau without compromising his earlier blessing. Isaac tells Esau that he can have nearly everything Jacob has received.

While the first half of the blessings are nearly identical, the second half clearly identifies the difference between them:

Jacob's blessing (27:29)	Esau's blessing (27:40)
	And you will live by your sword,
Be a master to your brother, and your mother's children will bow to you.	and you will serve your brother,
	but when you rebel you shall remove his yoke from your neck.

Jacob is the master, Esau the servant; so it has been decreed. Except that Esau has the power to reverse that. In the second half of the blessing, Isaac essentially tells Esau that the blessing is a self-fulfilling prophecy. If Esau believes in Jacob's superiority then Jacob will be superior, but if Esau decides to change his fate vis-à-vis Jacob, he has the power in his hands. Ironically, Isaac's blessings echo the divine voice heard by Rebecca decades earlier: "One nation shall triumph over the other." There is, of course, a profound difference between Isaac's blessing and Rebecca's prophecy. While Rebecca does not understand that her prophecy is left open to interpretation, Isaac says it explicitly.

One element of Esau's blessing does stand out: "You will live by your sword." This affirmation of Esau's chosen profession stands in stark contrast to Isaac's initial blessing, where he encourages his son to change his profession, moving from an itinerant lifestyle to one of rootedness in the land. That element is subdued in Isaac's blessing to Esau, as Isaac confirms Esau as primarily a man of the hunt. Isaac has long correctly identified Esau as primarily a hunter, but only now does Isaac realize how poor a criterion for leadership that is. It is in these scant words that we witness Isaac's deep understanding of Esau's unsuitability for the leadership of the family, something which both Jacob and Esau themselves recognized years earlier.

Esau is a tragic character. He is not evil, although he does make some poor choices. The hunter's life of immediacy makes him unfit for the Abrahamic blessing, which requires patience and long-term thinking. His choice of Hittite wives is unfortunate; in the Book of Genesis, Canaanite wives are the exit card from the covenant. Esau's loss of the Abrahamic blessing, with its divine, long-term mission, is inevitable.

JACOB THE THIEF?

Let us sum up this complex chapter. Does a parental blessing "work"? All the characters in this story apparently believe so, even when the blessing is erroneously bestowed upon the wrong recipient. Does Isaac know who is standing before him? Probably not. Although the scent of Esau's clothes moves him to issue a blessing, he holds back on the Abrahamic blessing. Instead, he delivers one generic enough to be meaningful for either son, and ultimately nearly repeats the blessing for the other son.

What about Jacob? Is Jacob a serial thief, stealing Esau's birthright and blessing? After careful analysis of the sale of the birthright, it turns out that Jacob is neither a thief nor or a deceiver, but he is certainly no longer a naïve *tam* either. The incident of the blessing, however, is far more multilayered. Jacob enters the scene as an unwilling participant who seeks excuses to avoid entanglement, but who cannot resist his mother's determination – ill-conceived as he knows her plan is. His mother cooks the food, brings it to him, and dresses him in Esau's clothes, while he remains passive. As he enters his father's tent he wants to speak as little as possible, avoiding conversation and offering only minimal answers. And when he is done, he runs out as fast as he can.

But Jacob does lie to Isaac, repeatedly, as he watches his handicapped father struggling to parse out what is transpiring. Jacob does take something that is not rightfully his. And even though Isaac later reaffirms the blessing and even amplifies it with the Abrahamic blessing, the initial blessing is the ill-gotten product of a cruel and selfish deception. Violating fraternal and filial trust as he actively participates in the deceit of his father and theft from his brother are burdens Jacob will need to carry with him for a long time.

Can we identify Jacob as a thief? Esau certainly thinks so. Isaac probably does as well, but may secretly be applauding Jacob's behavior as Jacob demonstrates how different he is from Isaac – rendering him fit for the covenantal blessing in Isaac's eyes. And Rebecca sees the fulfillment of her prophecy as justifying the means.

And what about Jacob – does he see himself as a thief, a liar, and a cheat for doing what he does in the story of the blessing? This may be the most important question of all, and for this we will need to follow his protracted and life-transforming journey to and from his uncle Laban's house.

The Struggle of Covenantal Couples

There are many tragic elements to the stories of the birthright and the blessing. Rebecca's prophecy does not necessitate that only one of her twins will be *the* covenantal child. After all, as opposed to Ishmael, the son of the Egyptian maidservant, both Jacob and Esau emerge from the same womb; both Esau and Jacob were born to parents who were covenantal "insiders" – one by birth and the other by choice. The sale of the birthright also does not demand Esau's exclusion from the covenant, only his displacement from future leadership of the clan.

Even the blessing does not automatically place the other son outside the covenant; that is Isaac's ultimate decision. Just as Rebecca interprets her prophecy in a particular – but not necessary – way, so does Isaac understand his role as faithful bearer of Abraham's legacy responsible for its transmission to the next generation. For each, their choice of interpretation begins a snowball of events with the now well-known results.

Aside from the individual impact Isaac and Rebecca each have, the way they play out their covenantal couplehood has consequences as well. Rebecca chooses to withhold her prophecy from Isaac, Isaac secretly plans to pass the baton to *his* chosen son, and Rebecca schemes to subvert Isaac's plan. Echoing elements of Abraham's relationship with Sarah, the communication gap – perhaps even mistrust – cannot create an environment conducive to fostering a covenantal family.

Even in the epilogue to the story, Rebecca is less than honest with Isaac. The deception of her husband, which she plots and Jacob implements, is never spoken of. Esau's plan to kill Jacob and the need for Jacob to flee for his life remain her secret as well. Instead she taps into the one area in which she knows that Isaac is disappointed with Esau, his choice of wives, and insists that Jacob not follow suit:[1] "Rebecca said to Isaac, 'I am disgusted with my life because of those Hittite women [i.e., Esau's wives]. If Jacob takes a wife from the Hittite women of this land, why should I continue living?'" (27:46).[2]

THE STRAINED DYNAMIC OF COVENANTAL COUPLES

Both Rebecca's actions and her words expose the role she sees for herself in the constellation of the covenantal couple: it is her responsibility to ensure the next generation in the covenantal line. And she does not stop with Jacob's receipt of the blessing. Rebecca understands that marrying a Canaanite woman leads to exclusion from the covenantal path. Esau's marriage confirms for Rebecca that Esau must be rejected. Isaac understands and struggles with this as well even as he plans to bless Esau.

With the blessing now formally upon Jacob, Rebecca presses Isaac on this point, and Isaac apparently accedes. In language reminiscent of Abraham's charge to his trusty servant to find a wife for Isaac from his family of origin, Isaac summons Jacob and instructs him: "Go to Padan

---

1. The selection of a wife from Rebecca's family strengthens Nahor's branch of the Terah family and assures its place within the covenantal nation. Three of the four Matriarchs descend from Nahor, while the fourth, Sarah (according to the midrashic tradition identifying her as Yiska), is the daughter of Haran, Terah's third son. The legacy of Terah, then, is comprised of Abraham playing the central patriarchal role, with Nahor and Haran playing supporting roles as they provide the matriarchal line.
2. Interestingly, our story opens with a rhetorical question by Rebecca ("Why am I?") and closes with a rhetorical question by Rebecca ("Why should I continue living?"). In the original Hebrew, both questions are punctuated by the word "why?" Ironically, Esau, in his rejection of the birthright, uses almost identical language (25:32).

Aram, to the house of Betuel, your mother's father, and take from there a wife from the daughters of Laban, your mother's brother" (28:2). Just as Abraham insists that his son's wife come from within the extended family back in Aram,[3] so does Isaac – at Rebecca's behest. Rebecca's words to Isaac drive home the point that Esau is the wrong choice (because of his wives), and that for Jacob to take his rightful place he must marry from the appropriate family. Rebecca ultimately helps Isaac understand that Jacob is the appropriate successor.

In this role, Rebecca has finally stepped into Sarah's shoes. It is Sarah, after all, who insists Ishmael be expelled from the house to make it unambiguously clear that he will not be an heir to the Abrahamic tradition. Abraham unwillingly listens to Sarah, and even then only after receiving an explicit instruction from God. The Patriarchs, with all their spiritual gifts, are unable to see clearly beyond their own roles in the covenant. It is their covenantal partners, the Matriarchs, who make sure the line is continued properly.[4]

COMMUNICATION AND RELATIONSHIP

The lack of communication in our story is not limited to the relationship between the couple Isaac and Rebecca; as parents they set the tone for the family. Not once do we find a direct communication between Rebecca and Esau, and only once, when finally conferring upon him the Abrahamic blessing, does Isaac ever intentionally speak with Jacob. Never does the text describe Esau speaking with Rebecca, or Jacob (when not pretending to be Esau) addressing Isaac.

This would not be so surprising were it not for the abundance of dialogue in the story of the blessings. It is even more surprising when we

---

3. The difference between Abraham's and Isaac's charges is just as striking. Abraham sends his servant because Isaac is not to leave the land; Isaac sends Jacob away because it is important that Jacob *not* follow Isaac's path, just as Isaac does not follow his father's.

4. In Rebecca's case, her later intervention to send Jacob away from his brother functions as a literary corrective to Eve in the story of Cain and Abel. In that story the parents are remarkably absent until it is time to "replace" the dead Abel with a new child. By contrast, in our present tale, Rebecca is intensely involved and actively saves her son from being killed by his brother.

consider the exaggerated number of family references within that story. The words "son" and "father" appear more than twenty times each, usually in the context of, "Esau, my son" or a direct address by one of the sons to Isaac. The word "brother" appears twelve times and "mother" nine times. Like the repeated earlier references to familial relations in Terah's and Abraham's families, we get the sense that the text yearns for a functioning family but cannot find it.

A closer inspection of these familial terms in our present narrative reveals that they are quite specific. For example, Isaac summons Esau, *his* elder son, and in the dialogues Isaac has with Esau (both when being fooled by Jacob and in his direct communication with him), Isaac repeatedly refers to Esau as "my son." By contrast, when Isaac summons Jacob to instruct him about his future spousal options and to give him the Abrahamic blessing, he does not call Jacob "my son" and the narrative text does not call him "his son."

Despite Isaac's ultimate conferral of the Abrahamic blessing upon Jacob, nowhere is the breakdown of the parent-child relationship between them more striking than in their reunion after Jacob's extended trip to Laban's house. After more than twenty years of separation, Jacob returns home accompanied by three wives (Rachel has just died) and thirteen children. The text describing their reunion is less than sparse – it is nonexistent: "Jacob returned to Mamre, Kiryat HaArba (literally, 'The Town of the Four'), which is Hebron, where Abraham and Isaac lived. Isaac's days were 180 years. Isaac expired and died" (35:27–29). Not a word is spoken, no questions are asked, there is no catching up. There is no mention of Isaac telling Jacob about his mother's death, of Jacob sharing his grief at the loss of his beloved Rachel, or even of the reconciliation between Jacob and Esau. Just silence. Awkward silence.

Isaac's exclusive use of the term "my son" for Esau contrasts with Rebecca's references to her children. For sure, Rebecca calls Jacob *her* younger son.[5] But while Rebecca is never mentioned in the text as

---

5. The powerful relationship between Jacob and Rebecca becomes clear through a phrase repeated in the opening and closing of the story. When Rebecca first tells Jacob of her plan (about which Jacob had his misgivings), she says, "And now my son, listen to my voice" (27:8). When the plan eventually "works" it has disastrous

speaking *with* Esau, she does speak *about* him, and with an interesting surprise – she repeatedly refers to Esau as *her* son. We first hear it as she is misappropriating Esau's clothes to place them upon Jacob: "Rebecca took the beloved clothes of Esau, *her elder son*" (27:15). We hear it a second time when, after the theft of the blessing, she becomes privy to Esau's intent to kill Jacob: "Rebecca was told of the words of Esau, *her elder son*" (27:42). We hear it a third time in a most bizarre place: "Isaac sent Jacob, and he went to Padan Aram, to Laban, the son of Betuel the Aramean, brother of Rebecca, *mother of Jacob and Esau*" (28:5).

The identification of Rebecca as the mother of both Jacob and Esau draws our attention, as it is both superfluous and textually awkward. It powerfully attests to Rebecca's view of her children. Both are her children, both are beloved, even though only one will lead the clan. Her prophetic, matriarchal duty is to create that hierarchy even as she maintains her love for both.[6]

COVENANTAL FAMILY DELAYED

Isaac and Rebecca continue the struggle of Abraham and Sarah for the covenantal family. Abraham is unable to include Sarah as a covenantal partner until after her death. Abraham loses his heirs – Lot, who leaves for Sodom, Ishmael, whom he expels – and Isaac, whom Abraham finally embraces as his heir, never returns home after the *Akeda*. In the next generation, Isaac wants to include Rebecca in his covenant, but she seeks her own path. Isaac embraces Jacob as the covenantal son just in time for Jacob to leave home, much as Isaac did to his own father. Ironically, Esau retains his affinity for Isaac even after the blessing (28:8–9), and

---

side effects. As Jacob prepares to flee, Rebecca again instructs Jacob with the same words, "And now my son, listen to my voice" (27:43). Despite everything, Jacob places his trust in his mother and obeys her command.

6. In the Hebrew language there is a word which does not exist in English. *Shekhol* is used exclusively to describe the experience of a parent losing a child. It is therefore quite striking that when Rebecca hears of Esau's intent to kill Jacob, she tells Jacob to flee, explaining, "Why should I experience the *shekhol* of both of you on the same day?" (27:45) For Rebecca, the loss of Esau would be no less an experience of *shekhol* than the loss of Jacob.

Rebecca tries to remain the mother of both sons even as she sacrifices her relationship with one[7] to ensure that the covenant cleaves to the other.

If Abraham is chosen because he can transmit his values to the next generation, then Isaac has done the same. Both families fall short in that those values are transmitted only selectively. Passing on the covenant is an exercise of exclusivity; all those deemed unfit are peeled away from the central narrative. Ishmael is given his own *toledot*, distinct from the main line of the story. Esau, too, is given his own *toledot* – in fact, even two – as his branch of the family leaves the land to settle in the eastern hills and he integrates his clan into Edom (ch. 36). Ishmael is out; Isaac is in. Esau is out; Jacob is in.

This exclusivity provides an element of "quality control," but at the same time considerably limits the impact of the covenantal messenger to become the source of blessing for all the families of the earth. A single covenantal messenger in each generation won't get very far.

The era of the covenantal couples is marked by Abraham's struggle to accept a covenantal partner and by Isaac's and Rebecca's struggles to understand how to operate a partnership within that covenant. The struggles of the covenantal couples prevent the emergence of the covenantal family, necessary for God's message to spread. And the covenantal family will face its own set of challenges as well.

---

7. Esau never refers to Rebecca as his mother. Even when he takes Ishmael's daughter as an additional wife, he does so because he saw that the Canaanite women "were bad in his father's eyes" (28:8). His mother's eyes are apparently irrelevant.

Part III

Covenantal Family

Genesis 28:10–29:11

Jacob the Refugee

Imagine Jacob just prior to his mother's urging him to take his brother's blessing. Jacob is the apple of his mother's eye. We know little of his relationship with Esau, but there is not even a hint of tension between them even though they are dramatically different from one another. Most important, Jacob has made a long-term investment securing the future leadership of the clan through the purchase of the birthright from Esau, and he is prepared to wait patiently, for as long as it takes, to make good on that investment after his father's passing. In fact, he has probably already waited a considerable amount of time.[1] All he needs is more patience.

Now imagine his state of mind as he leaves his parents' home for the foreign land of Aram. Following his mother's imploring and ignoring his own sensibilities, he has fomented a deep animosity with his brother, has violated his father's trust, and is separated from his mother, the one who always looked out for his well-being. Moreover, all the years of patient waiting to take his rightful place at the head of the clan have just

---

1. Assuming that the biblical chronology is meant to be taken literally, calculating backward from Jacob's arrival in Egypt at the age of 137, he is 85 years old when he receives Isaac's blessing! According to a rabbinic tradition (Megilla 17a), he is 77 years old. The sale of the birthright apparently happens much earlier, before Isaac's journey to Gerar.

317

been laid to waste. He is distanced from his home and does not know if he will ever return. "Don't call us, we'll call you," his mother tells him as she sends him off. Jacob is severed from all that is familiar, and must flee for his life, traveling alone with only what he can carry on his back and without even a donkey to ride. He has lost everything – his brother, father, and mother – his past, present, and future.

To make things worse, Jacob must struggle with himself. How could he have violated his father's dignity by lying to him? How could he have violated his own dignity by pretending to be his brother, even wearing those clothes which must have felt so unnatural on his skin? How those words, "*anokhi Esav bekhorekha,*" "I am Esau, your firstborn," must be haunting him the way they have made readers squirm for thousands of years. No wonder that when he is startled awake in the middle of the night he blurts out, "*Anokhi lo yadati*" (clearly a play on "*anokhi Esav*"), which can easily be read as, "I don't even know who I am." Jacob's loneliness is beyond words; he has lost even himself.

It is this Jacob who finds himself scrambling for a place to rest on the road when he suddenly notices the setting sun. No wonder he takes a rock and places it next to his head;[2] he needs some kind of protection should a bandit or wild animal approach in the night. It is also this Jacob, finding himself with no earthly support, who dreams of coming under some kind of divine protection. His vision is of something rooted on earth but reaching the heavens, with angels rising and descending.[3] There is no

---

2. The Torah describes him taking "from the stones of the place" and placing it *mirashotav*. This uncommon word is used in I Samuel 26:7 to describe Saul sleeping with the sword at his head. A parallel to this word is *margelotav*, meaning "at his feet"; see Ruth 3:4.

3. The Torah describes this link as a *sulam*. In post-biblical Hebrew this means "ladder," yet *sulam* is a *hapax legomenon*, and appears only once in the entire Bible. Its precise meaning is not known. Hence, in our context, it can refer to anything linking the earth to the heavens above – a ladder, a ziggurat, a prayer, or even Jacob himself.

   The rest of the dream is equally ambiguous. Whose head reaches the heavens, that of the *sulam* or of Jacob? Are the angels or Jacob himself climbing the ladder? Is God standing atop the ladder or above Jacob? (Genesis Rabba 69:3). Given that the dream is a product of Jacob's mind, not God's, it need not make perfect sense. This may be, in fact, why the word *sulam* is used; it is inexplicable, the product of Jacob's imagination, disconnected from human reality.

necessity to assume that this part of his dream is divinely inspired (even though later in the dream, God speaks with him). This dream is the product of Jacob's deepest yearning. In his abject loneliness, he reaches out to God.[4] It is to this Jacob that God speaks.

GOD'S DUAL MESSAGE

God's communication to Jacob has two distinct elements, the second of which reads: "Behold, I will be with you. I will protect you wherever you go and return you to this land, for I will not leave you until I do what I told you" (28:15). It is here that God addresses Jacob's current state of mind:

- "Behold I will be with you": no one else is with Jacob, but God will be with him;
- "I will protect you": this responds to Jacob's deep sense of vulnerability;
- "and return you to this land": this assuages Jacob's worry regarding whether he will ever return home.

God's message is one of reassurance. Jacob is not alone; God will be with him, protect him, and return him home.

What is God's first message?

I am God, the God of your father Abraham and of Isaac. The land upon which you lie I will give to you and to your seed. Your seed shall be like the dust of the earth; you shall burst forth to the west, east, north, and south. Through you and your seed will come blessing to all the families of the earth. (28:13–14)

---

4. *Midrash HaGadol*'s introduction to this story (29:1) draws a parallel between Psalm 121 and Jacob's experience during this trip. Jacob lifts his head unto the heavens (as in, the ladder reaching the heavens and the ascending angels carrying his prayers) asking from whence will come his help. His help comes from God, as God speaks to him in the dream. Jacob can sleep because the Guardian of Jacob (Israel) will not slumber. See the midrash for the full explication of the psalm.

This message – with its focus on the land, the children, and the family as the source of blessing for the rest of humanity – is an unambiguous reiteration of the Abrahamic blessing. But did Jacob not just receive that blessing from his father?

Let us explore two possibilities. First, it is never established that Isaac is empowered to deliver that blessing. After all, Abraham is not given a choice regarding whom he will pass his blessing to. By what right should we think that Isaac is invested with that authority? According to this understanding, God needs to bless Jacob because Isaac's blessing is meaningless. This suggestion renders Rebecca's ruse and Jacob's complicity tragically useless. The chasm between Jacob and Esau and Jacob's subsequent flight from home could have been avoided altogether.

The second possibility is that God is not conferring the blessing on Jacob but affirming it.[5] Regardless of whether Isaac is authorized to transfer that blessing to the child of his choosing, Jacob needs God's reassurance. He has just engaged in ethically problematic behavior and may be questioning whether or not he actually deserves that blessing at all. Together with his profound sense of loneliness and vulnerability, Jacob is likely struggling with existential doubts about himself and his worth. *Anokhi lo yadati* – "I don't even know who I am."[6] If so, then God's dual message to the frightened Jacob, who reaches out to Him in a dream from the depths of his being, is a dual reassurance: (a) "the blessing is yours," and (b) "you are not alone; I will help you return home."

THE MIDDLE OF THE NIGHT

No doubt God's message has a profound impact on Jacob. He bolts awake and proclaims, "Indeed, God is in this place, and I did not know."[7] Yet immediately afterward he is gripped by terror, exclaiming:

---

5. The Torah text seems to distinguish between Jacob's vision, which is not necessarily a product of divine inspiration, and God's addressing Jacob. It is possible to read God's speech as part of Jacob's self-inspired vision, so that Jacob may also be imagining that God is blessing him. This would fit well with Maimonides' approach to similar incidents in the Torah (*Guide* 2:43). We will address this shortly.

6. In rabbinic tradition, many of the Patriarchs were fearful that a sin they committed caused them to lose the covenant. See Nahmanides, 28:20; Rashi, 32:11.

7. This is the plain meaning of the phrase "*Anokhi lo yadati.*"

"How awe-filled (or terrifying) is this place! This is none other than the
house of God; this is the gateway to the heavens."

When we look beyond Jacob's terror into his words, we notice
that he uses the Hebrew word *makom* (place) in each of the two sen-
tences. The word appears six times within the larger context of the narrative, functioning as a theme word, and the place is repeatedly referred
to as *the* place or *that* place (using the definite article), suggesting that
the place itself has some special quality:

> He encountered **that** *makom* and slept **there**. (28:11)
> He took from the stones of **that** *makom*. (28:11)
> He slept in **that** *makom*. (28:11)
> He called the name of **that** *makom* Beit El. (28:19)

The surprising thing about Beit El is its lack of importance in the rest
of the Bible. It is mentioned in the Bible forty-six times, and aside from
Jacob it has no religious significance – except, of course, for the despised
cultic site established by Jeroboam over which the prophet informs
him that he will lose his throne.[8] Equally bizarre is that although Jacob
changes the name of the place from Luz to Beit El, that very place is
repeatedly referred to as Luz afterward, even by Jacob himself (48:3),
and later in the Bible the name is changed back to Luz (Judges 1:23, 26).

It appears that while Jacob believes he has stumbled upon a very
special place, the gateway to heaven, he has mistaken his own profound
insecurity and search for safety for the holiness of an otherwise ordinary
place. Beit El is no different from anywhere else in the land – even the
name change to Beit El is repeatedly reversed in the Bible – but Jacob,

8. I Kings 13:1. Perhaps it is the Bible's negative associations with Beit El which prompt
Rashi (28:11, 17) to suggest that Beit El had somehow "folded itself" into Mount
Moriah (or Mount Moriah "moved" to Beit El), so that Jacob is actually in Jerusalem
at the time. Judges 20:26-27 mentions that the Ark was in Beit El, but it is unclear
if that suggests that the Tabernacle was located there temporarily or if the Ark had
moved there for the purpose of taking it into battle against the Benjaminites of Givah.
In rabbinic tradition, the Tabernacle never settles in Beit El; see Mishna Zevaḥim,
ch. 14. See also Sarna, *The JPS Torah Commentary,* 398–400, for a discussion of Beit
El in the Bible and Jacob's identification of it as *the place.*

who in his profound distress takes comfort in God's response to his nocturnal plea, feels that he has found **the** *makom,* **the** place. Ironically, while Jacob thinks the *place* is special, God's message to Jacob is that it is *he* who is special.

THE MORNING

Jacob's startled reaction to the dream and the divine message notwithstanding, he is exhausted from his travels and falls back asleep. When he awakens in the morning he sees the rock of his protection and, recognizing that it is no longer necessary (as God has promised to be his protector), he anoints it and dedicates it to God. The presence of God, who is *nitzav* (standing) over him in his dream, is now represented by a *matzeva,* an upright stone monument.[9] God is now Jacob's Rock.[10]

What comes next, however, is particularly troubling.[11] Jacob makes a conditional vow to God, and his conditions seem to refer to the very things God has just promised in the dream:

God's nocturnal promise (28:15)	Jacob's vow (28:20–22)
I will be with you,	If God is with me,
I will protect you wherever you go,	and protects me on this path which I take,
	and gives me food to eat and clothes to wear,[12]

---

9. Jacob seems fond of the *matzeva* as a monument or marker. He sets one up to mark his agreement with Laban (31:45) and another as a grave marker for Rachel (35:20). Later, Moses uses *matzeva* stones to symbolically represent the twelve tribes (Ex. 24:4), but by the time we reach Deuteronomy (16:22), the use of the *matzeva* for religious symbolism is explicitly prohibited and despised by God.

10. This is the first time in the Bible that God is imaged as a rock of stability and salvation. The image appears numerous times afterward. See, for example, Deut. 32:18, 37; II Sam. 22:32; Is. 17:10; 30:29; Ps. 19:15; 62:8.

11. For a brief survey of traditional commentary dealing with this issue from the rabbinic period through the premodern era, see Leibowitz, *Iyunim BeSefer Bereshit,* 212–215.

12. We see here the depth of Jacob's insecurity even more; he is afraid that he will have neither food nor clothes to survive the journey.

and return you to this land	and returns me peacefully to my home,
until I do what I told you.	and He will be God to me,[13]
	then this stone which I set as a *matzeva* will become a house for God,
	and from all that You give me, I will tithe to You.[14]

Jacob's vow is deeply problematic. How can he take what God just promised and make that the condition for his belief and worship? Does he not trust that God will fulfill His promise? Is he, like Abram, seeking some kind of heavenly sign?[15]

It seems to me that we are once again privy to a window into the soul of a budding prophet. Let us return to the opening scene. Alone and terrified, Jacob dreams of reaching up to the heavens for safety and succor. His dream moves from the ground to the heavens and from angels to God. God's message is comforting, reassuring, and even elevating. (Indeed, Jacob later "lifts up his legs" as though he were walking on air as he continues his journey.) The drama of his nocturnal vision awakens him in the

---

13. The various clauses of Jacob's vow are expressed in the Hebrew by the letter *vav*. While that letter is usually translated as "and," it has multiple other possible connotations, including "then" and "however." This vow is clearly formulated as an "if... then" statement, but there is no conclusive determination that *vav* represents the transition from the "if" to the "then" clauses. I will leave it to the reader to experiment with the possibilities. I have chosen to place the "then" clause at the beginning of the sixth line of the vow because it is the first that does not refer to something God promised. Alternately, one can easily argue that the clause, "and He will be God to me," is the beginning of the "then" clause. See www.nechama.org.il/pages/564.html.
14. It is curious that Jacob, in this last line, switches from the third person to addressing God directly.
15. This question appears in Genesis Rabba 70:4 and is addressed by many medieval commentaries. The possibility is not completely unreasonable: Abraham asks for signs (ch. 15); Moses asks for signs (Ex. 3); Gideon asks for multiple signs (Judges 7–8). Jacob's vow can be understood as the request for the fulfillment of God's promise to be his sign.

middle of night, and the startling appearance of God jolts Jacob into a state of fear, as he confronts coming to a holy place unaware and unprepared.

In the morning, however, it seems that Jacob is not quite sure of what happened during the night. Was it actually a prophetic message, or does Jacob want so much to hear from God that he imagines the whole thing? Was it just the ladder or the entire divine oration that was a product of his imagination?

Some dreams are so vivid that we wake in the middle of the night and check our surroundings to verify our reality. But in the morning, what was so real in the middle of the night is just a blurry memory. Jacob has no way to verify his dream-prophecy, so he takes a vow: "If, indeed, it is God who came to me…. If God really did promise to protect and care for me…. If the God of my fathers indeed chose me to be their successor and will hence be my God[16]…then I vow to reciprocate." Jacob does not doubt whether God will fulfill His promise; he doubts whether God ever made such a promise. And only time will tell.

LEAVING FROM, GOING TO

While Jacob grapples with his dream-prophecy, the reader wonders who Jacob is and what will become of him. Will his guilt over deceiving his father and stealing from his brother define him, or will he soar with the blessing he receives from God? Jacob's question and the reader's question may be two halves of the same question, and the answer may not be in God's hand but in Jacob's. Will he transform his dream into a prophecy fulfilled by God, or will he remain limited by the baggage he carries with him?

This question is introduced even before Jacob's momentous dream: "Jacob left Be'er Sheba and went to Ḥaran" (28:10). None of this is new information. We already know that he has been living in Be'er Sheba, we already know that he leaves his home, and we already know that he is off to Ḥaran (28:5–7). Yet the Torah repeats it all, perhaps to frame our entire story. We recall that both Rebecca and Isaac send Jacob to Ḥaran, and that each presents the necessity of the trip differently.

---

16. God introduces Himself to Jacob as "the God of your father Abraham and the God of Isaac." Jacob may very well be questioning whether he is, in fact, the next in line.

Rebecca instructs Jacob to flee Be'er Sheba so that Esau doesn't kill him, while Isaac orders him to go to Ḥaran to find an appropriate wife. Jacob is thus charged with a dual mission: to leave his current home and to build an alternate one.[17] This duality reflects the tension we discussed above. Will Jacob be trapped eternally in his refugee status, looking over his shoulder to see if someone – or his own reputation – is following him, or will he find himself a suitable spouse and build a covenantal home?

As is evident in both his actions and his words, Jacob starts off in survival mode, fearing Esau, the dangers of travel, his unknown path, and perhaps even himself and what he has done. "Jacob left Be'er Sheba" is a statement of Jacob the refugee – he must get away. His nocturnal encounter with the divine is designed to show him that he can transform himself from the person "leaving from" to the person "going to." He needs to become the one who goes to Ḥaran for the right reason: to fulfill a goal, a charge.

At first glance it appears that he indeed makes the switch. Following his conditional vow, he names the place where he had his dream-prophecy "Beit El" and anoints a stone as a *matzeva*. When he continues his journey the Torah describes the new bounce in his step: "Jacob lifted up his legs." Jacob is uplifted; he is no longer looking backward but forward, at the opportunities awaiting him in his uncle's home. But Jacob will quickly learn that personal transformation is not instantaneous. It is a process fraught with pitfalls and challenges that he cannot imagine.

JACOB ARRIVES IN ḤARAN

When Jacob arrives in Ḥaran[18] it seems that he is once again the *tam*, the naïve lad. His feet carry him to Ḥaran but he is not even aware that he has arrived: "From where are you?" he asks a group of shepherds

---

17. This is, effectively, Jacob's *lekh lekha*.
18. The Torah describes him as going to land of the "Kedemites." This word can be understood as "the land of the people who dwell in the east," but it can also be read as "the land of the people who came before." If taken as the latter definition, the description paints the picture of Jacob returning to his ancestral land, the place of Abraham's origin. Jacob is retracing Abraham's journey, but in reverse. It is worth pointing out that with the exception of Isaac, all the Matriarchs and Patriarchs had particular connections with this land.

gathered around a well. Jacob is not far from the town – there he will soon meet Rachel, who easily runs home to tell her family of the cousin's arrival – yet Jacob has no clue where he is.

A more thorough reading of the story reveals even more of Jacob's naïveté, evident in the dialogue between him and the shepherds.[19] Here is a paraphrase of that dialogue:

> Jacob: My brothers, from where are you?
> Shepherds: From Ḥaran.
> Jacob: Do you know Laban, son of Nahor?
> Shepherds: Yup.
> Jacob: Is all OK with him?
> Shepherds: Yup. Here is his daughter Rachel coming with the sheep.
> Jacob: There is much time left in the day; is it not time to gather the sheep? Give your sheep to drink and go graze them!
> Shepherds: Not until all the flocks gather and we can roll the stone from atop the well, and only then can we give the sheep to drink.

The conversation, if it can be called that, is almost comical. Jacob sounds like an innocent farm boy meeting the toughened city folk for the first

---

19. Interestingly, they are never identified as shepherds. That appellation is reserved in this story for Rachel alone. Even more fascinating is the Torah's description of the events, which focuses on the flocks, even though the narrative is clearly interested in the shepherds. Read the following text – the bracketed words are missing in the Torah's narrative!

   > He saw, and behold, there was a well in the field, and there were three flocks of sheep crouching upon it, for from that well [the shepherds] would give the flocks to drink, and the rock upon the mouth of the well was large. The flocks would gather there and [the shepherds] and would roll the stone from the mouth of the well and would give the sheep to drink, and then would return the stone to the mouth of the well. … They said, "We cannot until all the flocks gather and [the shepherds] roll the stone from the mouth of the well." (29:2–9)

   While we hear the shepherds' voices, they themselves are completely excised from the narrative. This perhaps points to their complete identification with their sheep – they live through, and for, them. Sheep are the local obsession.

time. They are not interested in the stranger, even after he opens the dialogue with them. He greets them as his brothers[20] and wants to engage them in conversation, while their answers are brief – in the original Hebrew, no more than two words. They extend their speech for the first time to get him to stop peppering them with questions: "Here's Rachel, go talk to the girl." Jacob still doesn't understand why the well is covered. After all, he is also a shepherd and understands shepherding culture. Where he comes from, keeping the water "locked up" to prevent strangers from accessing it is completely foreign. In an innocent voice he probes the elephant in the room: "Why aren't you out shepherding?" That innocent probing, however, is rather annoying, particularly when coming from a complete stranger. Naïve Jacob is unaware of the impropriety of the question.

The inhospitality of Ḥaran, reminiscent of Sodom, presents an image which reverses the expectations of his grandfather's servant when seeking a wife for Isaac. In quest of extraordinary graciousness, the servant finds even more, while Jacob expects ordinary courtesy and cannot find even that.

JACOB MEETS RACHEL

If Jacob's encounter with the local shepherds isn't enough to convince us of his state of mind, his meeting Rachel does. Read the description as he awaits Rachel's arrival:

> When Jacob saw Rachel, daughter of Laban, *his mother's brother*, and the sheep of Laban, *his mother's brother*, Jacob approached and rolled the stone from the mouth of the well and gave drink to the sheep of Laban, *his mother's brother*." (29:10)

Jacob is not motivated by amorous passion but by the sense that after an endless and lonely trek he has finally found his mother's family. His uncle's sheep and daughter move him to a superhuman feat. Jacob's initial

---

20. Jacob's greeting them as "brothers" may be his way of seeking companionship after a long and lonely journey. It foreshadows Joseph's comment of, "I seek out my brothers" (37:16).

attraction to Rachel is influenced by her profession and, strangely enough, her name; in Hebrew, a *raḥel* (Hebrew for Rachel) is a sheep. Jacob's frustrated desire for kinship with the strange shepherds is replaced by the overwhelming relief that he has finally arrived at some sort of home: a shepherd girl, like himself, who bears the name of her charges, and, given that she is from Rebecca's family, reminds him of his beloved mother.[21]

Overcome not by love at first sight but by the sense of finding home, Jacob kisses Rachel and erupts in tears. That crying is the outpouring of all of the conflicting emotions which have been churning within him ever since the fateful day of deceiving Isaac: the loss of his family, his home, and his previous life; the hopes raised by his extraordinary dream and his own doubts of its veracity; the excitement of having arrived in Ḥaran only to be greeted by a cold, unwelcoming, and altogether foreign culture. In multiple ways, Rachel represents home, and in that his heart is captured. She is the symbol of his solace from the turbulence in his life. She is the refuge he desperately seeks.

HAVE ISAAC'S FEARS COME TRUE?

Jacob's simplicity and fragility resonate throughout his journey from Be'er Sheba. We observe it in his anxious dream, his nighttime reaction to God's message, and his doubt-plagued morning-after as he utters his vow. We witness it again as he approaches Ḥaran, unaware of how close he is, and as he is overcome by the relief of his rescue by his shepherdess cousin who reminds him of home.

Jacob's return to being a *tam* raises for us, the readers, a critical question. If he is really reverting back to who he was even before

---

21. The Hebrew reveals a delightful wordplay highlighting Jacob's attraction to Rachel's "sheep-ness." After rolling the oversize stone off of the well, Jacob gives the sheep to drink, *vayashk*. Just six words later he kisses Rachel, and the word used for the kiss, *vayishak*, is spelled in Hebrew identically to the one used to describe his caring for the sheep. The word, in its various forms, appears seven times in the story, identifying it as a central theme word.

"The stone" is itself another theme word, appearing seven times in this story – twice in the post-dream scene and five times upon Jacob's arrival in Ḥaran. Jacob takes the portable stone in the dream scene and makes it permanent, while in the scene at the well he transforms the immovable stone into one which is portable.

purchasing the birthright from Esau, then were Isaac's fears about him founded on a deep understanding of his son – that Jacob amounts to nothing more than a replica of himself?

This is the essential question with which the text leaves us hanging. Will Jacob remain the refugee, following his mother's instruction and continually running from Esau and his own shadow, or will he establish a home and a name for himself following his father's directive? In other words, will Jacob successfully emerge from this uncertainty, having shed his naïveté in healthier ways than he did initially in his father's home, or will he remain frozen in his reverted state – challenging his suitability for being God's chosen link in the chain?

Genesis 29:11–31:18

In Laban's House

Jacob is overwhelmed by the hospitality he receives in his uncle Laban's house. Having endured the profound insecurity and loneliness as only refugees know, and initially greeted in Ḥaran by a cold indifference which must have been disheartening, the sight of Rachel – his little sheep – along with the reminders of his mother and home, and topped off by Laban's welcoming embrace, melt the months of pain he has suffered *en route*.[1] At last, he is home.

Laban's warm welcome makes Jacob comfortable telling him "everything" (29:13). He is able to unload all of what had transpired, likely including the theft of the blessing, Esau's threat, his father's Abrahamic blessing, his terrifying yet uplifting dream, and the ordeal of his trip. While no doubt therapeutic, all of this "unpacking" also makes him quite vulnerable. Jacob's past misdeeds are exposed. Even more, he is in great need of Laban's hospitality, for he has nowhere else to go.

Laban invites Jacob into his home as a family member and Jacob begins to share in the family chores, doing what he apparently does best – tending the flocks. Laban welcomes him literally as "my bone

---

1. If Ḥaran is the equivalent of Sodom, then hospitable Laban is apparently the equivalent of Lot. Interestingly, like Lot, Laban also ends up offering his two daughters.

and my flesh" (29:14), the same language used by the Man in the Garden to describe the Woman (2:23), perhaps even as a hint that Jacob marry into the family. Laban, aware of Jacob's multiple blessings, wants to benefit from them.

But while Jacob is accepted as a family member he remains an outsider, as Laban offers to pay him for his services: "Do you think that because you are my brother you will work for no pay?" (29:15). That seemingly generous move by Laban actually places Jacob just outside of the family circle and plays on his need for a home. Jacob's response is clear – he wishes to formalize the family embrace, moving his way into the inner circle of Laban's family and cementing his place there. Driven by his love for Rachel (29:18), he requests her hand in marriage in return for seven years of labor.

The Torah (Ex. 21:2) limits servitude by one Hebrew to another to six years. Seven years is an eternity to which no free person should be subjected. Jacob, in an attempt to demonstrate his loyalty to Laban, offers himself to Laban as a servant for a period exceeding the six-year limit. Dependent on Laban's hospitality, Jacob does not arrive in Ḥaran as a free person, and he is now even less free than he was when he arrived. The price for Jacob's success in securing his place in Laban's house is his freedom. This is even more striking in light of his mother's instructions that he remain in Laban's house for a few years[2] until she calls for him. Jacob indentures himself to Laban and prepares to be absorbed into Laban's family, apparently despairing of his birth home and abandoning those memories as he prepares to build a new life for himself.[3]

Jacob's absorption into Laban's house certainly serves his purpose, as he has a home and a family and has fulfilled his father's mission. But that absorption serves Laban's purposes at least as much. Laban has carefully manipulated the situation so that Jacob sacrifices his autonomy to become part of that family. Laban wants to own Jacob (and his blessings), and very quickly makes considerable progress toward that end.

---

2. 27:45. The text says "a few days," but the term "days" in the Bible often means years.
3. Jacob's actions prefigure Joseph's absorption into the Egyptian culture, where he too seeks to forget his birth home. *Pesikta Rabbati* 12 and *Aggadat Bereshit* 71 are critical of Jacob for his twenty-two-year absence from his father, suggesting Joseph's twenty-two-year absence from home is punishment for Jacob's absence for the same time span.

JACOB MARRIES, TWICE

Jacob's dependency on Laban becomes even more apparent when it is time to marry. Jacob fulfills his vow of servitude (which for him feels like the "few years" of which his mother spoke[4]) but Laban seems to be in no rush to fulfill his part of the deal, forcing Jacob to request his "payment" of a wife. Even more striking is that Jacob makes no mention of going free or returning home after he marries – in his mind, there is no road back. This is now his home.

It is hard to imagine how Laban succeeds in deceiving Jacob on the wedding night and how much work is involved in that scam. Beyond Laban and Leah, no doubt there are many others involved in the switch – perhaps even everyone[5] – except, of course, Jacob. Imagine Jacob's humiliation. He has been in town for seven years and his desire to marry Rachel is no secret. Jacob hears the laughter outside his wedding tent and thinks that it is communal joy. Little does he realize that it is the entire town mocking him.

Jacob's protestations to Laban the next morning are met with Laban's cynicism: "In *our* place [as opposed to where *you* come from!] such a thing is not done, to place the younger before the elder" (29:26). Those words mortally wound Jacob and leave him utterly speechless; Laban exposes and exploits Jacob's vulnerability as a refugee fleeing from an act of deceit in which he, the younger, usurps the place of the elder. Jacob, who toils for seven years to clear his name, falls into Laban's trap: "Work for another seven years," says Laban, "and this one [i.e., Rachel] shall be given to you as well" (29:27). Jacob's servitude to Laban is now doubled. He has no recourse, and enslaves himself twice over.

The self-doubts which plague Jacob when he flees from home and which he thinks he escapes now imprison him in Laban's home. Jacob leaves home feeling like a thief, so every accusation of dishonesty – or even a hint of an accusation – cripples him. Jacob's history is his Achilles' heel. Even more, now that he has eaten from the forbidden fruit of

---

4. The phrase *"yamim aḥadim"* ("a few years") used in the Torah clearly links the years of Jacob's servitude to Rebecca's words.

5. Indeed, according to a rabbinic tradition (Megilla 13b), Rachel participates in the deception as well.

deception, he can no longer return to the innocence of the *tam*. Jacob cannot go back to who he was, nor does he know how to move forward. Laban's familiarity with Jacob's history and weakness enables him to turn that to his own advantage, preying on vulnerable Jacob and subjugating him. Jacob is securely trapped in Laban's web.

SORORITY TENSION

Laban's entanglement increases dramatically with Jacob's marriage to both of his daughters. There is a reason that the Torah later forbids such marriages, calling the two sisters *tzarot*,[6] or nothing but trouble to each other. On the individual level, it is not hard to imagine Jacob having a strained relationship with Leah, an active participant in Laban's marital deceit. The word used both by the Torah and by Leah herself to describe her status in Jacob's eyes is "despised." Even were the word to be attenuated and read as "less loved," that in itself sets up a powerful tension between two sisters (not just two wives) competing for one man's heart.[7]

It is this tension which drives the story of the births, in rapid succession, of twelve of Jacob's children. Leah names her first three children after her desire to be loved, or at least attended to, by Jacob. Rachel, jealous of her sister's prolific womb, demands that Jacob provide her with children as well. Jacob's response to his beloved is less than loving or sensitive: "Am I in place of God who denied you fruit of your womb?" (30:2). Jacob's insensitive words betray his frustration.[8] He simply has no energy to deal with squabbles between sisters and certainly not to deal with requests that are out of his control.

Perhaps it is that lack of control – of his wives, his children, and his situation – which best describes Jacob's present state. Caught in a power struggle between feuding sisters, his ability to produce children for them or their proxies (whom they plant in his bed without so much as consulting him) determines in their eyes the winner of Jacob's favor.

---

6. Lev. 18:18.
7. Jacob's love for Rachel is attested to unambiguously in 29:18 and repeated in 29:30.
8. Jacob does not pray on Rachel's behalf the way Isaac prays for the barren Rebecca.

Reversing the trend of the first twenty generations in Genesis, in which women are viewed essentially as incubators for producing children, Jacob is reduced to a machine that provides seed for implantation. Jacob is emasculated by the women in his life, who are engaged in a battle of procreation possibilities. Listen to the following story:

Reuben, Leah's firstborn, comes home from the field having picked some flowers for his mother. His motives may have been innocent, or may have been a response to his awareness of his mother's distress at being unloved by Jacob. (Later, Reuben will engage in more serious behavior, taking vengeance against his father for snubbing his mother.) Barren Rachel sees the flowers and desires them – likely because in the ancient world it was believed that they had aphrodisiac or fertility powers.[9] Rachel asks for the flowers from her sister, who responds cynically, "Is it not enough that you took my husband that you should now also want my son's flowers?" (Let us remember that it is *Leah* who took *Rachel's* husband, and not the other way around!) Rachel's response is astounding: "Therefore let Jacob lie with you tonight in return for your son's flowers."

Whatever the flowers really mean to Reuben, Rachel, and Leah, imagine poor Jacob who returns home from a long day in the fields to discover that his sexual services have been traded between his wives like a commodity. Jacob has no say about with whom he shares his bed. Jacob is not only Laban's servant; his wives claim whatever Laban doesn't control.

Jacob has become pathetic, manipulated by his father-in-law and his wives. He even has no say in the naming of his children; they are all named by either Leah or Rachel.[10] Perhaps Isaac is right – perhaps Jacob does not have what it takes to stand up and take charge. Jacob has become even more passive than Isaac himself. What we witness is not Jacob, the *tam* of his father's house, but Jacob who is completely controlled by his adopted family. Is this the patriarchal figure upon whom both his father and God bestow the Abrahamic blessing?

---

9. See Rashi; Radak; Seforno.
10. Later, Jacob-Israel will rename Ben-Oni as Benjamin. See p. 380.

JACOB TRIES TO LEAVE

After the birth of twelve children over the second seven-year period,[11] specifically the birth of Joseph (30:25),[12] and what by now must seem an eternity of servitude, Jacob decides it is time to leave. He summons the courage to request permission from his father-in-law: "Send me away, so that I may go to my place and my land" (30:25). Notice how little of the Abrahamic language remains – the word "my place" replaces the more dramatic identity phrases used for Abraham. Jacob understands that it is time to go, but he can barely remember why or to where. He must simply get away: "Give me my wives and my children for whom I served you; you know how I served you" (30:26). For Jacob to ask permission to leave may be understandable, but to ask permission for his wives and children betrays his inability to assert himself and demand what is rightfully his. So crushed is his spirit that he doesn't even assert his right to his own family. In the Hebrew, this is even more striking, as the root *eved* ("to serve" or "to be a servant") appears three times in a single verse of Jacob's request.[13] Just as a servant owns nothing, as Laban's servant, whatever Jacob owns is Laban's.[14]

Laban's dual response reveals both his method and his true motives. He begins with flattery, seemingly ceding control of the situation to Jacob: "If I find favor in your eyes...I have engaged in divination, and God has blessed me on account of you." Laban is, and has been, interested in the prosperity Jacob brings as the blessed one. Once he has Jacob's attention he speaks again: "Name your wages, and I will pay it." Handing Jacob a blank check is both intensely empowering and

---

11. Jacob does not marry until he completes the initial seven years. His youngest, Joseph, is born at the end of the second set of seven years. Ibn Ezra, 30:23, calculates how all twelve were born in that time frame.

12. "It was when Rachel gave birth to Joseph, Jacob said to Laban, 'Send me that I may go to my place and my land.'"

13. It is almost as if Jacob has read Exodus 21 and interpreted it in Laban's favor: "If [the servant] came in [to servitude] unmarried he leaves unmarried; if he was married before, then his wife goes free with him. If his master gave him a [servant] wife and she bore him sons and daughters, the woman and her children remain the master's while he goes free alone" (vv. 3–4).

14. Pesaḥim 88b offers the halakhic formulation of this: "Whatever a servant acquires belongs automatically to his owner."

a masterful ploy; Laban makes Jacob an offer he cannot refuse. Since, for Laban, controlling Jacob is of paramount importance, the pay is irrelevant. It will all come back to him eventually anyway. As for Jacob, how can he turn down Laban's seemingly unlimited generosity and the opportunity to become independently wealthy?

The reader of the Hebrew text is alerted not only to Laban's methods and motives, but also to a powerful wordplay. The last time Jacob was invited to name his price he ends up serving Laban for fourteen years in order to marry Rachel. In Laban's present proposal, he says *nakva sekharkha*. The word *nakva* is a play on the word *nekeva*, meaning female. Even as Laban puts Jacob in the driver's seat he reminds Jacob of his previous request and how, blinded by his desire for a woman, he loses himself to Laban. Jacob will never be able to leave; he might as well make the best of his situation.

JACOB TRIES TO DEFEAT LABAN

Jacob cannot resist the offer, unaware of the danger involved in remaining with Laban. As with Lot following Abraham, Jacob sees this as an opportunity to become self-sufficient, a significant stepping stone to leaving on his own terms. He devises a complex plan involving separating the white sheep from the colored ones so that ultimately the white sheep remain Laban's (Laban in Hebrew is *"lavan,"* meaning *"white")*, while all the others will be Jacob's wages. With the flocks separated and Jacob tending the white sheep, Jacob engages in strange breeding practices involving striped sticks he places in front of the sheep during mating. There is much debate about these practices, with some arguing that they actually work,[15] while others suggest that Jacob is using a form of selective breeding using his understanding of genetics to increase his spotted and speckled herd[16] – and the sticks serve only to deceive Laban into thinking that Jacob possesses magical breeding powers.

---

15. Ibn Ezra, 30:39, and Seforno, 30:38, argue that Jacob's tricks are based on known medical practice.
16. See Judah Feliks, *Nature and Man in the Bible* (London: The Soncino Press, 1981), 6–12.

Regardless of Jacob's intention, a divine dream reveals to him that his actions had nothing to do with his success. It is all God's doing: "If [Laban] would say that my pay is the spotted ones, then [directed by God] all the sheep bore spotted ones. And if [Laban] would say that my pay is the splotched ones, then [directed by God] all the sheep bore splotchy ones" (31:8). Jacob's acumen in breeding or sorcery is irrelevant. Only divine providence brings his wealth.

Jacob again mirrors his father. Isaac, the man who is unsuccessful in most of his earthly dealings, becomes successful only when unwisely investing in farming during a drought. Isaac's success does not result from his keen business acumen or tactics but from God's intervention. As Jacob's success with the sheep is not the product of his craftiness but of divine intervention, Isaac's fears about Jacob being just like himself seem to be confirmed yet again.

Jacob's nocturnal vision of the sheep represents a profound setback in his development. Fleeing from his home, Jacob seeks out God and dreams of reaching up to the heavens with angels. That same Jacob, after just six years of focusing on building his fortune, now dreams of mating sheep. Jacob is now one with Ḥaran and its culture. Laban's takeover is complete.

Equally troubling is that Jacob is engaging in precisely the same kind of behavior he engaged in while in his father's home. It is there that he uses his wits to purchase the birthright from Esau and employ deception to get his father's blessing. In Laban's house he engages in practices – whether grounded in medical science, genetics, or sorcery – to outwit Laban. The specific methods may be different but the *modus operandi* is essentially the same. Rather than meeting Laban face to face and demanding what is rightfully his, he goes behind Laban's back, just as he and his mother had done to Isaac. Even worse, after deceiving his father, Jacob at least struggles with who he is becoming as he exclaims "*Anokhi lo yadati*," "I don't even know who I am" (28:16). In Laban's house, deception comes too easily. He loses his moral compass and is not even aware of how his quest for wealth has driven him to engage in dubious practices. And just as his actions in his father's house estrange him from his brother, his actions in Laban's house estrange him from his brothers-in-law, his adopted family: "Jacob heard Laban's sons speaking, saying, 'Jacob took all that which was our father's, and from what was our father's he made for himself all this glory'" (31:1). Not only does Jacob not regain his dignity, he is no longer aware that he has lost it.

Now more than ever before, Jacob seems unfit for the Abrahamic blessing.

A DIVINE PUSH

Jacob's increasing wealth impacts not only on him but on his adopted family and their relationship with him. He overhears his brothers-in-law complaining about how he has stripped their father's wealth and become rich at their expense. Even Laban, who wanted Jacob around for the blessing he brought, no longer looks at him the same way. Despite the signs that he needs to move on, Jacob does not. He is too caught up with increasing his flocks. Ironically, what initially draws Jacob into Laban's house is the promise of joining a family to replace the one he lost. Now, despite being rejected by that very family, Jacob cannot bring himself to leave. Were it not for a divine directive, Jacob would have ignored his adopted family's rejection and stayed to further increase his wealth.

Using the same terms that moved Abraham from this very place two generations earlier, God tells Jacob that he must uproot himself and return to his true family and identity: "Return to the *land* of your *fathers* and your *moledet*; I will be with you" (31:3). As with Abraham, the journey involves more than a geographic relocation; it demands a shift in identity. Jacob, who has become an Aramean,[17] needs to restore himself within the Abrahamic tradition.

Abraham is told to find himself a new home; Jacob undoes Abraham's *lekh lekha*, returning to Abraham's origins in Ḥaran, where he loses the ability to find his way back home. Like Abraham at his lowest point, Jacob is lost. He accepts two seven-year cycles of servitude to Laban, and just one year before completing a third cycle – ensuring his permanent enslavement – God pushes him to leave.

Jacob reacts to God's push, but still finds it hard to leave. He summons his wives and tells them his tale. He apparently feels the need to

---

17. See Deut. 26:5: "My father was a wandering Aramean who descended to Egypt with very little, but he became there a large, numerous, and mighty nation."

convince them of the justness of his cause. Despite God's push, without their approval Jacob may not be able to make the move:

> Your father doesn't look at me like he used to, but my father's God is with me. You know how I worked for your father with all my strength, yet your father mocked me and changed my wages ten times over. (31:5–7)

While Jacob labors to convince his wives, it turns out that they've been aware of this for a long time and have been waiting for him to take initiative. Led by Rachel, the two sisters respond in a single voice:

> Do we have any portion left in our father's estate? We are considered by him as strangers; he sold us, and then ate up the proceeds. Any wealth which God has reclaimed from our father rightfully belongs to us and our children. Do all that your God has instructed. (31:14–16)

Jacob's wives are acutely aware of what their father has done to him and, by extension, to them. They were initially complicit in stripping Jacob of his dignity; since then, they have powerlessly watched their husband's selfhood get systematically crushed.

JACOB FLEES, AGAIN

While Jacob gets the message that he needs to leave Laban's house and return home, he seems to miss the bigger point – his orientation needs to change. *He* needs to change, to seek out his selfhood, his *anokhi*. His entire presentation to his wives is one of victimhood. He takes no responsibility for allowing himself to become victimized or for the things he did earlier in life which set him up for victimization. It is all Laban's fault, and the only solution Jacob can envision is to get away from him.

Rather than learning from his mistakes, Jacob repeats them, but without the subsequent soul-searching. Twenty years after he runs away from Esau, he deceitfully sneaks away from Laban. Packing his things hastily in the middle of the night, Jacob takes his family and flees. The language used in the Torah is unmistakable: "Jacob stole the heart of

Laban the Aramean" (31:20). He arrived in Aram as an unwilling thief; he leaves Aram as a willing one.

And it is not just his family that he takes. Three times in a single verse (31:18), the Torah uses the root K-N-H, alternately meaning "flocks" or "acquisitions," to describe what he takes with him. Just as Jacob dreams of sheep (31:10), what concerns him now are his many acquisitions. We shudder to imagine what Jacob would have become were it not for God's push.[18]

Jacob's midnight flight raises the terrifying thought that he has learned nothing from his twenty years in Ḥaran, or worse – that he learned only the wrong things there, becoming completely absorbed into Laban's culture. Jacob is a son who jeopardizes the covenant into which he is born.

When Jacob earlier awoke from his divine vision in Beit El, he was unsure of whether God had really spoken with him. As we saw then, whether God will be with Jacob is very much dependent on Jacob himself. And at this point, it does not look good.

---

18. The Passover Haggada suggests a picture of what would have happened. Laban, it declares, was worse than Pharaoh; Pharaoh decreed only that the males be killed but Laban tried to uproot everything. I believe that the Haggada is referencing Laban's attempt to own Jacob, not just his work but his very essence. Laban crushes Jacob and almost transforms him into an Aramean. Just as in Egypt, divine intervention was necessary to prevent the ultimate disaster.

Genesis 31:17–32:3

Confronting Laban

J acob's first attempt to leave Laban's house is met with an offer too tempting to refuse. Jacob falls into Laban's trap and gets absorbed into the culture of Ḥaran, so much so that he ignores all the signs of his disaffection from the family. Six years later, only a direct divine command saves him from being completely swallowed up.

God does not tell Jacob to flee but to go back to his roots. This is not supposed to be a "leaving from" but a "going to." Nevertheless, Jacob flees. After consulting his wives, he gathers "his sheep and all the possessions he acquired, the purchases he had purchased which he acquired in Padan Aram," and runs away under cover of darkness. Three times in the span of three verses, the Torah describes Jacob as B-R-Ḥ, fleeing. We understand his need. He doesn't think that he can face Laban, afraid that his father-in-law will find some way to lure him yet again to stay. He has no choice but to escape.

When Laban hears of Jacob's escape he follows in pursuit, catching up with him in the mountains of Gilead:

> What did you do? You stole my heart and led my daughters like captives by the sword! Why did you flee, in hiding, rob me, and not tell me? I would have sent you in joy, with song, drumbeat, and harp! You didn't even allow me to kiss my sons and

daughters – now you have acted foolishly. I have the power to be malevolent to you, but the God of your fathers came to me last night and instructed me, saying, "Take heed not to speak with Jacob either good or evil." And now, you have left because you so desired your father's house. Why did you steal my gods?! (31:26–30)

Indeed, Laban, the master manipulator, once again tries to draw Jacob into returning using a crafty combination of rhetoric. Twice he employs rhetorical questions, designed to make Jacob feel guilty. He mocks Jacob, accusing him of needing to be in his father's house, like a frightened child running for parental protection. Most powerfully, he opens and closes with an accusation of theft, once of his heart and once of his gods. In Laban's brief speech, he invokes the root G-N-V (theft) three times. Laban knows Jacob's sensitivity and exploits it to the fullest.

Perhaps most troubling is that Laban's ploy seems to work. Jacob's response is not one of a dignified person protecting his rights and his family but of a humbled runaway struggling to save face:

Because I was afraid. Because I said [to myself], "You would rob me of my daughters." With whomever you find your gods, that person shall not live![1] In front of your brothers, identify[2] what is with me [that is yours] and take it. (31:31–32)

---

1. As we will see, this scene a has profound impact on Jacob's children who witness it, and is replayed a generation later. Joseph plants a goblet in Benjamin's sack and accuses the brothers of theft, chasing them down like Laban does to Jacob. Both Laban and Joseph's servant describe the owner of the missing item as engaging in divination (N-Ḥ-SH), and when the accusation of theft is leveled at Joseph's brothers they respond as did their father: "The one of your servants with whom it shall be found will die and we shall all becomes slaves to our master" (44:9). Moreover, their suggestion that they become Joseph's servants points to their understanding as young children of what would have been their father's fate: were Laban's *terafim* to be found, it would result in permanent servitude to their grandfather. Of course, Joseph refuses to accept their servitude, as that would be immoral, a scathing critique of how he understands Laban's intent.
2. The Hebrew is *haker* (H-K-R), the same word used to describe Isaac's inability to identify Jacob because of the hairy skins on his arm (27:23). This word haunts us through the rest of the Jacob-Joseph saga. See 37:22; 38:25; and the quadruple play on the root in 42:7–8.

Jacob's first two statements begin with "Because," a defensive acknowledgment of wrongdoing accompanied by an excuse based on
fear.[3] Jacob's fear impels him to suggest the death penalty (a grossly
disproportional response) for the thief. Moreover, in an effort to demonstrate his innocence, Jacob suggests that Laban search through his
possessions for what Laban claims is stolen. It is hard to imagine any
self-respecting person inviting such an invasive search, including that of
his personal belongings and his wives' private domains, just to prove his
innocence. Yet in the face of Laban, and especially faced with allegations
of theft, Jacob is not quite self-respecting. He has spent twenty years trying to shake the reputation of being a thief, and the public accusation
of theft drives Jacob to do the unimaginable to clear his name. Laban's
speech is quite effective. Jacob is again on the defensive.

JACOB'S RAGE

It is only after Laban's thorough search yields nothing that Jacob explodes
in rage. In his passionate oration, the first time he ever confronts Laban,
he retells the story of twenty years of his own honest, hard work and how
it is Laban who has been guilty of dishonesty. Jacob's rage overpowers
his fear, and he holds nothing back:

> Jacob was incensed and was confrontational with Laban. Jacob
> responded and said: "What is my crime, what is my sin, that you pas-
> sionately chased me down? You put your hands[4] all over my things;
> what did you find of all your household goods? Put it here, in front
> my kinsmen and yours; let them determine between the two of us!
> These twenty years I am with you, your sheep[5] and goats have
> not lost any young, and I have not eaten the rams of your flock.

3. In this, Jacob is mirroring his father's response to Avimelekh's accusation of deception regarding Rebecca (26:9).
4. The Hebrew verb is M-SH-SH. Indeed, this word is used to describe Laban's searching
but is the same verb used to describe Jacob's concern that Isaac will feel him and
discover that he is not Esau (27:12). It is also the word used to describe what Isaac
actually does to try to determine who is standing before him (27:21–22).
5. The word Jacob uses for sheep, *reḥeleikha* is a play on Rachel's name (*Raḥel*), as if
Jacob were saying, "I did not even leave your barren daughter, Rachel, childless."

I have not brought anything torn by a beast – I swallowed that loss, you can demand it of me – whether stolen by day or by night! By day I was consumed by parching heat and at night by frost; sleep escaped my eyes.

These twenty years I served you in your home – fourteen for your two daughters and six for your sheep – yet you switched my wages ten times over. Were it not for the God of my father Abraham and the Fear of Isaac who was with me, you would have sent me empty! God has recognized my oppression and my exertion, and demonstrated it last night." (31:36–42)

Jacob unleashes a torrent of pent-up fury, the result of twenty years of injustice done to him (note that he twice references "these twenty years"). He learns from Laban, spicing his comments with rhetorical questions as well. A careful comparison of his comments with Laban's reveals that his responses to Laban's charges are woven throughout:

Laban's charge	Jacob's retort
You stole my heart	What is my crime, what is my sin?
Why did you steal my gods?!	What did you find of all your household goods? Put it here, in front my kinsmen and yours; let them determine between the two of us!
[you] led my daughters like captives by the sword	These twenty years I served you in your home – fourteen for your two daughters
I would have sent you in joy, with song, drumbeat, and harp!	you would have sent me empty!
the God of your fathers came to me last night	God has recognized my oppression and my exertion, and demonstrated it last night.

Line by line and accusation by accusation, Jacob turns the tables on Laban. He exposes Laban's repeated treachery and lies, holding him accountable for false allegations. Jacob finally understands how Laban has manipulated him and systematically crushed his spirit, and explodes in a rage of righteous indignation against him.

From where does Jacob derive the inner strength to stand up and face down his oppressor?

RACHEL AND THE *TERAFIM*

In our retelling of the tale, there is one detail which we skipped. As Jacob prepares his family to flee Laban's house, "stealing" Laban's heart by sneaking out, Rachel is doing some stealing of her own – of her father's *terafim*. The text says nothing to explain Rachel's theft; suggestions include that she desires them as fertility gods,[6] that this is her attempt to assert that her family will continue as the line of Laban,[7] that it is an attempt to save her father from idolatry,[8] or that it is an attempt to prevent Laban from divining their location.[9] The context and repercussions of her theft, however, suggest a different possibility.

Jacob's wives had long known that he was being manipulated and taken advantage of by their father. Just as we, the readers, are troubled by Jacob's vulnerability to Laban's machinations, his wives, who are acutely aware that Laban is using and abusing Jacob, are even more troubled by it, as they have to live with it.

Rachel has her own frustrations with Jacob, blaming his passivity for her childlessness. But Rachel, who is the first in the family to meet Jacob and knows of his tribulations journeying from his parents' home, also knows about the dark cloud of his past and how it haunts him. His reputation as a thief and trickster makes him especially vulnerable to Laban and susceptible to Laban's repeated manipulations, and it is also Jacob's fear of that reputation which she is counting on.

---

6. See Steinmetz, *From Father to Son*, 181.
7. Ibid., 107.
8. Rashi.
9. Rashbam.

Rachel steals the *terafim* knowing full well that her father will pursue Jacob for them and accuse him of theft. She believes that the accusation, when proven false, will push Jacob beyond what he can tolerate, and will embolden him to finally stand up to her father. It is no accident that Rachel is prepared for her father's visit, sitting on the *terafim* after secreting them in the camel cushion, feigning menstrual frailty to derail her father's search.

Rachel has carefully orchestrated a complex plan in the hope that it will finally enable Jacob to become a free man.[10] If Jacob finally breaks out of his passivity and challenges Laban, it is because Rachel has made it impossible for him not to. Laban is almost successful at drawing Jacob back into his clutches; Rachel's theft saves Jacob from Laban, and from himself.[11] Jacob, provoked by Rachel, finally confronts his oppressor.

Imagine the story had Rachel *not* taken the *terafim*. Laban chases Jacob and accuses him of stealing his heart by sneaking out and not letting him even kiss his daughters and grandchildren – and in that, he is correct. Jacob's response to this charge is already recorded: he submissively apologizes. Even more, if Jacob is guilty of "stealing" Laban's heart then he needs to "return" it, by returning in shame to Laban's house. There is no accusation of the theft of the *terafim*, no humiliating search of Jacob's intimate spaces, and no outburst of righteous rage. Jacob will return with Laban even further humiliated, with no chance of rising. Rachel's theft of the *terafim* prevents Jacob's return to servitude and facilitates his own move toward reclaiming his self, his *anokhi*.

---

10. Rachel is the archetype of the schemer of impossibly complex plans. Indeed, in the Bible, complex plans like these are typical of Rachel's descendants. Joseph devises an impossibly complex plan to reunite with Benjamin, Ehud ben Gera (Judges 3:12–30) conceives one to penetrate and escape the king's palace after assassinating him, Mordekhai invents one to gain power in the Persian royal court (Esther 2:5–23), and Esther devises an unrealistic one to bring about Haman's downfall (Esther 5:1–7:10).

11. Rachel's theft of the *terafim* and subsequent deception of her father echo Jacob's theft from and deception of his own father, rendering Rachel as the soulmate of the Jacob who fled from his father. Counterintuitively, it is Rachel who emulates the "old" Jacob and who is the catalyst for the emergence of a new Jacob. In this incident she demonstrates her role as Jacob's covenantal partner.

JACOB STANDS HIS GROUND

Laban is unfazed by Jacob's stand, and lays claim – at least in principle – to his daughters and their children: "The girls [i.e., his daughters] are mine and the boys [i.e., Jacob's sons] are mine and everything you see is mine" (31:43). Recognizing, however, that he is dealing with a new situation, he offers to establish a treaty with Jacob. Far from being a peace treaty, it is more like an amicable divorce. Laban draws a virtual line to serve as a boundary between himself and Jacob that none may cross, and demands that Jacob desist from taking additional wives.

Three things stand out in Jacob's response. First, Jacob once again sets up a *matzeva*, an upright stone, as well as gathers together a pile (*gal*) of rocks. The stone and the pile presumably represent Jacob on the one hand and Laban on the other, yet it is far from clear which represents whom.[12] Laban calls the stone pile Yegar Sahaduta, which is Aramaic for "The Pile of Testimony." Jacob will not have Laban take control of the ceremony or the place, insisting that the Hebrew name, Gal-Ed,[13] be used rather than the Aramaic, and in the very next verse Laban accedes.

Second, as Laban sets out the terms of the agreement, he calls upon "the God of Abraham and the god of Nahor, the god of their fathers," to judge between them. Paralleling Abraham's God with Nahor's is a subtle attempt to co-opt Abraham's unique status and to place Laban's own theological lineage on equal footing with that of Jacob. Jacob, however, will have none of that, insisting on swearing only on the "Fear of Isaac, his father," unquestionably distinct from Laban's ancestral theology.

Third, Laban attempts to define the essence of the treaty, primarily in limitations on Jacob, but Jacob does not respond to that initial proposal; he no longer allows Laban to dictate to him. One can imagine Jacob standing silently, with his arms folded. It is Jacob's silence which impels Laban to redefine those terms, suggesting a dramatically different, more egalitarian agreement in which the stone pile and the *matzeva*

---

12. This is similar to, although substantively different from, the covenant ceremony Moses sets up in the beginning of Exodus 24. In that ceremony there are twelve *matzeva* stones (representing the tribes of Israel) and an altar (representing God).

13. "Gal-Ed" is apparently the origin of the place's later name, Gilead (Gil'ad in Hebrew). In unvocalized Hebrew they are spelled identically.

stand as boundary markers separating Laban from Jacob; neither may cross those markers with malicious intent,[14] and Laban has no claim to Jacob's family life. It is only after this reformulation, in which there are equal, mutual obligations, that Jacob agrees.

The covenant demonstrates Jacob's resolute commitment to repel any of Laban's attempts to exert control over him, whether in naming the place, identifying Abraham alone as God's chosen, or insisting on mutuality in the agreement.[15] Jacob listens to Laban's words with a keen ear, pushing back at the hint of Laban's exercising control. Jacob no longer cowers before Laban.

CLOSING THE CIRCLE

Jacob's saga in Ḥaran is a single, closed literary unit; in the Masoretic text there are no breaks in the middle. His time there is like a black box into which one Jacob enters and another exits. This sense is strengthened by a number of literary devices employed by the Torah.

On his way to Ḥaran Jacob has an encounter (P-G-A), and on his way out of Ḥaran he has an encounter (P-G-A); on his way to Ḥaran he meets angels and on his return from Ḥaran he meets angels; on his way to Ḥaran he comes to *the place* (*hamakom*) and on his return he comes to a different *place* (*hamakom*); on his way to Ḥaran he sets up a *matzeva* stone and on his return he does the same. These parallels form a set of "bookends" which bracket the story and delineate it as a unit.

At least one rabbinic commentary suggests that Jacob emerges from Ḥaran the same as he went in, unscarred and untainted by the experience.[16] Our reading of the narrative, however, understands that the Jacob of the beginning of the story is dazed and left adrift by his adventure with deceit and theft, and that his absorption into Laban's

---

14. The covenant between Aram and Israel is first abrogated by Balaam (Num. 33:7; Deut. 23:5) and later by Kushan (Judges 3:8–10). From then until the end of the biblical period, Aram and Israel battled often.

15. Although Jacob is the one who sets up the stone markers, Laban takes credit for it (31:51) and Jacob does not react. He apparently has decided to not take Laban's bait to argue about every detail, but limits himself to the areas he considers most significant.

16. See Rashi, 33:18, s.v. *shalem*.

family is transformative, but not in positive ways. He begins to reclaim himself only when God pushes him out and when, provoked by Rachel's behind-the-scenes machinations, he confronts Laban. The Jacob who emerges at the end of his twenty years is beginning to rebuild his identity and reassert himself, reclaiming his *anokhi*. The sojourn in Laban's house, difficult as it may have been, serves as a significant catalyst for Jacob's emergence as a new man.

On the way to Ḥaran it is Jacob who encounters the place, but on the return it is divine angels who encounter him. On the way to Ḥaran he sees the angels only in a dream, while on the return he encounters them fully awake. On the way to Ḥaran he thinks he has encountered a special, hallowed place – the permanent yet hidden gateway to heaven; on the return he realizes that God can encamp anywhere and that it is not the place which is significant but the encounter. On the way to Ḥaran the *matzeva* is a religious symbol representing God, but on the return the *matzeva* is a symbol representing either himself or Laban.

We thus come to understand that Jacob's journey not only involves reclamation of his self but reformation of his conceptions of God, place, and holiness. The dark tunnel of Laban's house is where Jacob hits rock bottom as he continues the path he begins in his birth home. The crisis of selfhood he experiences there is what spawns his emergence from Laban's house – not back to where he once was, but on the path to a completely new selfhood.

Jacob's sojourn to Laban's house represents a critical step in his development. He learns to stand up for himself, reversing his earlier Isaac-like qualities (which rear up repeatedly in Laban's house). He also apparently relieves himself of his doubt regarding who he is, as he ultimately leaves Laban's company with a clear conscience toward his kinsmen and with God as his witness.

Jacob, however, has still not confronted his true challenge – himself. He *did* deceive his father and steal from his brother, he *did* lie repeatedly, and he was probably appalled by his actions. Jacob's courage to confront Laban is praiseworthy, but until he faces those core inner challenges, he is not complete. And those challenges are not long in coming.

Genesis 32:4–33:20

Confronting Esau, Confronting Self

Leaving Laban behind, Jacob has a chance to reflect on that envelope in time he spent in Laban's house. He fled home with nothing and is now returning with four wives, twelve children, and enormous wealth: "With nothing more than my staff I crossed this Jordan and now I have become two camps" (32:11).[1] Emboldened by his ability to successfully stand up to Laban, he now prepares for the next critical step of his odyssey – confronting Esau. His journey begins with a flight from Esau; to complete it he will need to stop running from Esau.

Jacob prepares for the encounter by sending an advance party with a message to Esau, now living in Edom:[2] "Thus says your servant,

---

1. The two camps here reflect his splitting of his camp in case of an attack by Esau, but echo the two camps he names earlier after being met by God's angels (32:3).
2. The account of Esau's departure from Canaan is initially told four chapters later. Notice how closely the language and themes used to describe Esau's departure from the land because of an abundance of sheep and material possessions parallel that of Lot's departure from Abram (13:5–11):

    Esau took his wives, his sons and daughters, all the people in his household, his sheep and cattle and possessions which he acquired in the land of Canaan, and

Jacob: 'I have sojourned with Laban and have tarried until now. I have oxen, donkeys, male and female servants, and I am sending [this delegation] to you to find favor in your eyes'" (32:5–6).

A careful read of Jacob's message suggests that he is trying to tell Esau that their father's blessing did not work. Isaac had blessed Jacob to be the superior of the brothers, yet Jacob humbles himself as Esau's servant; Isaac had blessed Jacob with agricultural success – the dew of the heavens and the fat of the land – but Jacob has succeeded only in his old craft of shepherding. Jacob's attempt at reconciliation hinges not on his actions but on their results, as if to say, "It didn't make a difference in the end."

When the messengers return with news that Esau is on the way to meet Jacob accompanied by four hundred men, Jacob is terror-stricken, believing that his estranged brother is readying to attack. Preparing for the worst, he splits his considerable caravan in half: "Should Esau come and strike one camp, the other one will [have a chance to] escape" (32:9). What happened to the new Jacob, the one unafraid to face his demons?

THE IRONY OF JACOB'S ERROR

Even more disturbing than Jacob's backpedaling is his strategy for dealing with Esau's impending attack: splitting his wives and children into two camps. Is Jacob really prepared to sacrifice half of his family to save the rest? How will he decide which half will live and which will be sacrificed? Is this the same Jacob who confronted Laban demanding his wives and children?

At the same time as he prepares to be slaughtered he turns to God:

> The God of my father Abraham and the God of my father Isaac, the God who told me, "Return to your land and your *moledet* and I will do good for you"…save me, please, from my brother, from Esau, for I fear that he will strike me, mother with sons. You said, "I will do good with you and make your seed as the sands of the sea, that they will be too numerous to count." (32:10–13)

---

went to the land because of Jacob, his brother. For their possessions were too great for them to settle together, and the land of their dwelling could not bear them because of their sheep. (36:6–7)

This is the first time Jacob actually speaks with God (unlike when he flees Esau, where he turns to God only in his dream). Yet Jacob's plea is problematic, as he seems to blame God for his predicament – is it not God who tells him to leave the safety of Laban's house? And now, because he listened to that directive he faces an unimaginable tragedy. If we listen carefully to Jacob's words we are privy to a paradox: on the one hand he invokes God's promise of protection, while on the other hand his fear indicates that he does not really believe it. Jacob's desperation is replacing his earlier confidence.

As opposed to Abraham, to whom God responds verbally, and Isaac, to whom God responds through action (Rebecca's pregnancy), God does not respond to Jacob – verbally, silently, or otherwise. While Jacob seems to be both laying blame on God and turning to Him for salvation, God's silence suggests that it is not God who needs to act but Jacob himself.

The ironic tragedy in this entire scene is that while Jacob's messengers report Esau's imminent arrival, there is no indication of Esau's intent to do harm. (In fact, as the story unfolds, Esau greets Jacob, embraces and kisses him, and offers to provide him with protection.) It is entirely plausible that Jacob is misreading the entire situation.[3] If so, then it would mean that Esau has long forgotten and forgiven Jacob for what happened and is now bringing a national delegation of four hundred men to facilitate the merger of the two brothers into Esau's new Edomite nation in Mount Se'ir.[4] Esau, the mature brother, has put that nasty incident behind him and moved on with life. By contrast, Jacob – who carries the guilt of that incident for twenty years, allowing it to cripple him in his dealings with Laban and nearly resulting in his permanent entrapment in Ḥaran – is still stuck in the past.[5]

---

3. See Rashbam. Rashi presents a dramatically different perspective in which the evil Esau plans a revenge attack on Jacob and is thwarted only at the last moment.
4. This is prefigured by Abraham, who spends decades building his covenant with God while his brother Nahor has built a proto-nation with twelve children. Later, Moses indicates that the land of Edom has been vouchsafed for Esau and that Israel is forbidden to engage them in battle because their land is protected by God. See Deut. 2:5.
5. This scene plays itself out in the next generation. Joseph has forgiven his brothers, but they still carry the guilt of what they had done along with the fear of his retribution. The brothers' suspicion of Joseph is painful for him to hear after all he does to take care of and reassure them. See 50:15–20.

JACOB REVISES HIS STRATEGY

Jacob tries to sleep that night but cannot. Whether or not he is mistaken about Esau's intentions, he understands that preparing to be slaughtered is not a plan at all, and faced with divine silence he is forced to rethink his strategy. Believing that Esau is still intent on killing him and convinced that his earlier effort to make believe that nothing ever happened is a failure, Jacob decides to send a series of gifts to Esau. His gifts are exceedingly generous: two hundred female goats with twenty males, two hundred female sheep with twenty males, thirty nursing camels with their suckling young, forty cows with ten bulls, twenty female donkeys with ten males. Moreover, he instructs the servants handling the gifts to space themselves apart so that the gifts arrive in waves.

According to at least one traditional commentary, Jacob's instructions to put space between one flock and the next is an attempt to slow Esau down in order to give Jacob time to flee.[6] Jacob's bribery, or delay tactic, leaves us disappointed. Even if the tactic works, what would it say about Jacob? That Jacob is still one to run away from conflict, to disappear in the middle of the night, unable to acknowledge his own responsibility and face his accuser, or even to face himself.

Extraordinarily, the Torah shares with us Jacob's thinking (32:21): "I will cover his face [i.e., placate] him with the gift going before my face, following which I will see his face; perhaps he will lift up my face [i.e., forgive me]." Jacob is not simply trying to buy favor in Esau's eyes, he is attempting to use surrogates for the meeting with Esau. The goats and sheep and camels and donkeys will pass Jacob's face and cover Esau's face; they will represent, and mask, Jacob in his encounter with his brother. As opposed to the Jacob who at first initiates the encounter with his long-lost brother, this Jacob does everything he can to avoid the face-to-face meeting, hiding his own face and "covering" Esau's. In a dramatic about-face, Jacob hides his face from Esau's.

We, who have been following Jacob's descent in Laban's house and rise as he confronts his oppressor, had high hopes for Jacob as he reaches out to his brother. But whatever Jacob thinks initially has now dissipated in the face of his growing fear.

---

6. See Rashbam, 32:21, 25.

JACOB WRESTLES WITH ...

Jacob again attempts to sleep, but cannot. He gets up in the middle of the night and begins transporting his family across the Yabok stream. This sets the scene for a most mysterious incident.

At one point during the night Jacob is left alone, and a "man" wrestles with him until daybreak. The "man" is unable to defeat Jacob, but wounds him in the hip, leaving Jacob limping. With the breaking of dawn the "man" asks Jacob to release him, but Jacob refuses until the "man" blesses him. Before the "man" acquiesces he asks Jacob for his name, after which he tells Jacob that his name will become Israel (*Yisrael* in Hebrew), for he successfully struggles (*yisra*) with God (*El*) and man. The "man" refuses to provide his own name, but ultimately does bless Jacob.

Who is this mysterious man? Figures like these – who appear out of nowhere only to disappear afterward – are often understood as some sort of divine messenger.[7] Indeed, Jacob asks his antagonist for a blessing, and is so inspired that he "saw God" that he calls the place Peniel – "The Face of God." That being said, this "man" with whom Jacob struggles is his equal, as neither can defeat the other. Adding to the puzzle is the profusion of pronouns in this scene, to the extent that it is sometimes difficult to distinguish between the protagonists. Take, for example, "He saw that he could not defeat him" (32:26). Who saw that he could not defeat whom? Or, "Release me, for the dawn is rising" (32:27). We do not know who is asking to be released until the response: "I will not release you unless you bless me." It is as if the text is trying to generate an image of an intense wrestling match in which the two are so intertwined that it is difficult to tell them apart.

Furthermore, while Jacob ultimately wants this "man" to bless him, we are clueless about this "man's" motive. Is it to wound Jacob, to change Jacob's name, or perhaps simply to force Jacob to fight back?

As we revisit the scene we find Jacob – in terror of Esau – deciding yet again to flee. In the dark of night, however, he is gripped by the realization that he flees too easily, first from Esau, then from Laban, and now again from Esau. Will the rest of his life be driven by continually running away from his problems?

---

7. Rashi, for example, suggests that this is Esau's guardian angel.

In this specific moment Jacob's conundrum is sharpened. On the one hand, he has his father's blessing, which he wants to hold on to. On the other hand, that blessing has turned him into someone other than who he wants to be: deceitful, hiding, evasive. Holding on to the blessing will forever condemn Jacob to lose his sense of self, the *anokhi* he sacrificed by declaring to his father that he was Esau; but to regain that sense of *anokhi* he needs to forfeit the blessing, freeing himself of what has become his curse.[8] Running from Esau will allow him to cling to his purloined blessing. Facing Esau – and his own wrongdoing – necessitates giving it up.

This decision, or struggle, pits Jacob against himself. It is no wonder that in the wrestling match, neither can win. The antagonists are a matched pair because Jacob is both protagonist and antagonist. This internal struggle continues through the night but must come to closure: Jacob has only until the morning, when Esau arrives, to decide.[9]

Jacob asks the adversary, his alter ego, for a blessing. He doesn't want to let go of it; after all, he has already paid for it dearly. The adversary is prepared to grant the blessing, but only after presenting him with the alternative – to become Israel. To be sure, the name *Yisrael* comes from the word "to struggle with God" (or "to be engaged in a divine struggle"), but it also plays on the word *yashar*, "to be straight." Jacob needs to choose between the blessing and the name change, between remaining the crooked Jacob with the stolen blessing and becoming the straight Israel. Nowhere is this dichotomy expressed as clearly as in Isaiah 40:4: "The crooked (*he'akov*, based on Jacob's name, Yaakov) will become straight (*mishor*, playing on the name Yisrael)."[10] Jacob struggles with himself throughout the night, and it is unclear which of

---

8. Jacob's subconscious intuition foresaw this happening. Encouraged by his mother to take the blessing, he responds, "And I will bring upon myself a curse, and not a blessing" (27:12).
9. For a variation on this approach see Fred Blumenthal, "Who Wrestled with Jacob?" *Jewish Bible Quarterly* 38:2 (2010): 119–123. Maimonides, *Guide* 2:42, suggests that the entire incident is part of Jacob's dream.
10. Note that a biblical variation on Israel is Yeshurun, from the Hebrew *yashar*, or straight. See Is. 44:2.

the gifts of his internal struggle he will choose, the blessing or the new identity. But choose he must; he cannot keep both.

There is but a single clue during that struggle as to which way Jacob is leaning. Jacob wounds himself in the hip, rendering running impossible. The desire to keep that ill-gained blessing will cripple him.[11] Jacob finally realizes that he cannot continue as he has, and that to reclaim himself he must first confront Esau and take responsibility for what he has done to him. Indeed, the next day, after Esau's embrace, Esau asks about the multitude of livestock which came his way. Jacob offers it to him and Esau politely refuses: "I have much; my brother, let what is yours be yours" (33:9). Jacob's response is astonishing: "Take, please, my blessing, which has been brought to you" (33:11). What Jacob previously calls "an offering," even as recently as the previous verse, he now calls his blessing. "Take the blessing," he urges Esau.[12] He openly acknowledges that he must return what is not rightfully his before he can move on.[13]

As part of this dialogue Jacob refers back to the "face" that he mentions the night before, and the contrast to the previous night is striking: "I have seen your face like the face of God, and you have been appeased by me" (33:10). When initially sending the gifts to Esau, Jacob intends for them to "cover" Esau's face, that is, to mask the divide between the brothers, sweeping the past away with a generous gift. The next day, however, Jacob is no longer interested in hiding from his brother. He wants to see Esau face to face and without intermediaries, return what he took from him, and go forward.

---

11. The Torah indicates that as a result of this incident, Jacob's descendants refrain from eating the sinew of the thigh. That sinew represents Jacob's realization that he must accept responsibility and stop running. When Jacob arrives at Shekhem (33:18), he is once again whole and limps no more.
12. It is significant that twice Jacob refers to his wealth as an undeserved gift from God, implying that he did not benefit from the blessing.
13. See *Pesikta Rabbati* 13. Maimonides, *Laws of Repentance* (2:9), writes: "Offenses committed by one person to another, such as one who wounds, curses, or steals from his fellow, or anything similar, are not forgiven [by God] forever until he gives his fellow what he owes and appeases him."

In his confrontation with Laban, Jacob, through Rachel's manipulation, begins a process of self-redemption.[14] Jacob's new self-respect when facing Laban, however, is forced by the false accusations of theft; it disappears as he anticipates Esau's arrival, as he defaults to his familiar response to flee. But in the darkness of night, Jacob struggles mightily and profoundly with himself to recover his *anokhi*, ultimately choosing a path that frees him of the blessing which has held him back for so long. Jacob leaves his father's blessing behind and, in the process, liberates himself. He is on the path to becoming Israel.

MEETING ESAU, LEAVING ESAU

The next morning, as Jacob prepares anew to meet Esau, he again divides his family, but not into two camps. The children are joined with their respective birth mothers. None are going to be sacrificed. All will be presented to Esau. And this time, rather than buffering his meeting with gifts that "cover his face" as in the previous day, Jacob is at the front of the family delegation meeting Esau (33:3).[15]

The conversation between them, however, leaves us with some discomfort. Esau invites Jacob to join him in his new nation: "Let us journey onward, together, and I will go by your side" (33:12). Jacob declines politely, but not quite honestly:

> My master knows that the children are tender and the sheep and cattle burden me, and should they be pushed to move quickly they will all die. You, my master, should go ahead in front of his

---

14. The verse explaining the name Israel, "For you have struggled mightily (*sarita*) with men and you prevailed" (32:29), is remarkably parallel to Rachel's explanation for the name Naphtali (from the Hebrew root P-T-L): "I have grappled mightily with my sister and prevailed" (30:8). However, the Hebrew root Y-S-R, translated as "struggle," appears only three times in the Bible: twice in this episode and once in Hosea 12:5 in reference to this same episode. This leaves room for uncertainty regarding its precise meaning, but suggests its uniqueness to Jacob's struggle.

15. Jacob leaves Rachel and Joseph as the last to meet Esau, perhaps because he has begun to understand that Rachel is the force behind his new discovery of self. While each of the mothers goes before her children, Rachel follows Joseph. With Jacob at the front of the delegation, he trusts only Rachel to close the group from the rear.

servant, and I will go slowly, at the heels of my task and my children, until I reach my master in Se'ir. (33:13–14)

Jacob clearly does not want to go with Esau. Even when Esau offers his men to help, Jacob declines. We understand Jacob's reticence; he just narrowly escapes being swallowed up by Laban, and he has no interest in being swallowed by Esau. What is more, Esau has chosen a path diverging from Jacob's: Esau has left the ancestral homeland and the covenant, while Jacob needs to return to his promised land in pursuit of the covenant. We even understand why Jacob would not want to bring this up right now. This is not the time to tell Esau that God identified Jacob as heir to the Abrahamic promise. But the lack of transparency leaves us, and perhaps even Jacob himself, discomfited. The redeemed Patriarch is not yet fully redeemed.

JACOB STOPS AT SUKKOT

Esau returns home. Jacob, by contrast, does not. Despite God's instruction in Laban's house, and despite his apparent commitment to the covenant, Jacob travels a short distance to Sukkot,[16] where he builds a house for himself and *sukka* shelters for his sheep. This raises numerous questions: Why does Jacob not continue on his way and complete the journey he started? Why does Jacob build shelters for his sheep, which normally graze out in the open? And why would he name the place Sukkot after the sheep shelters?[17]

It seems that after twenty years of wandering – initially as a homeless person, then as someone completely dependent on and subservient

---

16. Sukkot is located on the eastern side of the Jordan; see Judges 8. It is one of the towns punished by Gideon for their lack of support in his battle against the Midianites. The other, interestingly, is Peniel, where Jacob wrestles with himself. This is not the same Sukkot mentioned in Exodus, which is on Egypt's eastern boundary.

17. Compounding the questions is that *sukka* shelters are not temporary shelters but permanent buildings in which one dwells only temporarily. Typically, farmers would build a *sukka* in the fields where they might rest during the heat of the day and stay during the harvest season to protect their crops (see Is. 1:8). These structures stayed up all year long and can still be seen in some Israeli landscapes. The *sukka* is distinct from a tent, or *ohel*, which is a temporary structure in which nomads live permanently.

to Laban, and then as a refugee running in terror of his brother – more than anything else, Jacob needs a place to call his own. He builds a house for himself, and extravagantly, *sukkot* for his flocks. No traveler builds a house on the road, and even people who are settled do not build *sukkot* for their animals, but that is precisely what Jacob does. He is spent from his running and from his confrontations, he needs a sense of security and stability, a place that he can finally call his own home. Even though he will not stay long in Sukkot, nothing for Jacob expresses the relief of the end of his flight as does a permanent place, even for his livestock.

Jacob needs that stop in Sukkot; it represents the peace of mind he seeks. But it distracts him from his goal. In Laban's house, God tells him to return to his covenantal home, and Jacob delays.[18] He is not yet ready to step into his covenantal role.

After his nighttime encounter, Jacob believes that he has been reborn as Israel. Following his stop in Sukkot he continues on to Shekhem, where he builds an altar to the Almighty God of Israel. Indeed, Jacob takes some dramatic steps toward becoming Israel. He faces Esau, begs him for grace, and offers him the blessing. On the other hand, Jacob is less than honest when he declines Esau's offer, suggesting that he will join him later even though he has no intention of doing so. His stop at Sukkot puts his quest to find his destiny on hold. Despite his nocturnal renaming and the altar he dedicates to the God of Israel, the Torah text still does not refer to him as Israel. Jacob takes important steps toward becoming Israel, and he may even think that he has earned that name, but the reader knows what God knows – he is not there yet.

---

18. This is reminiscent of Abraham's delay in taking the land.

Genesis 34:1–31

Shekhem

Jacob's trek from Ḥaran back to his ancestral land retraces Abraham's *lekh lekha* journey with one substantive difference: while Abraham has to figure out the destination, Jacob knows precisely where he needs to go. After crossing the Jordan, Jacob, like his grandfather, arrives at Shekhem as he climbs into the hill country, and just as Abraham stops in Shekhem, so does Jacob. There is, however, a significant difference between their stops. Abraham stops to build an altar and call out to God, apparently looking for a sign, after which he moves on. Jacob also builds an altar, but his stop is an extended one. He purchases a plot of land and settles in, despite his own promise and God's explicit instruction to return home.[1]

Jacob names the altar *El Elohei Yisrael*, the Almighty God of Israel, recalling his mysterious nocturnal encounter in which Jacob names himself Israel – the straight, the fighter – rather than Jacob the crooked (or, the heel). As Jacob stops in Shekhem he seems prepared to embrace and internalize his new identity. Equally important is that he identifies God as *his* God, partially fulfilling his vow at Beit El: "He will be God to me." Given these two indications of a seismic change

---

1. Perhaps Jacob stays in Shekhem to avoid facing his father, much like he initially avoids Esau's "face" and does not honestly decline Esau's offer to join him in Se'ir.

in Jacob, his delay in returning to Beit El to complete the rest of his vow is even more surprising.

Jacob's extended stay in Shekhem costs him dearly. His daughter, Dinah, goes out to meet the local girls. Instead of meeting the girls, however, she is taken by the eponymous Shekhem – son of the local chieftain, Ḥamor – who rapes her and holds her against her will.[2] Following the rape, Shekhem the captor is himself captivated by the girl and tries to win her heart.[3] As the story unfolds it sheds significant light on Jacob's understanding of his own transformation.[4]

GENERATIONAL DIVIDE

"Jacob heard that [Shekhem] had violated his daughter while his sons were with the flocks in the field, and Jacob kept silent until their return" (34:5). By contrast, "Jacob's sons returned from the field and were saddened – extremely distressed" (34:7). Jacob's silence throughout the opening of the incident draws our attention. Is this a display of weakness by the man who has just declared himself Israel? Or perhaps it is apathy – after all, it is *only* Leah's daughter who is taken.[5]

Equally likely, however, is that Jacob's silence comes from a desire to encounter Ḥamor and Shekhem from a position of strength. He does not rush to confront the chieftain and *his son*, waiting for *his own sons*

---

2. The Hebrew word is *inui*, which is an intense form of servitude. It is the same word used to describe Sarai's treatment of Hagar prior to Hagar's flight. See Gen. 15:13; 16:6; Ex. 1:11–12.
3. As opposed to Amnon, who after raping his half-sister despises and disposes of her (II Sam. 13), Shekhem's desire for Dinah only increases. In his quest to marry her, his actions match what the Torah (Deut. 22:28–29) will later demand of a rapist.
4. Our focus here is on Jacob, as he is the central protagonist of the greater narrative. Dinah's plight is the concern of many contemporary commentaries and popular works. For scholarly works, see www.iccj.org/redaktion/upload_pdf/201212141625570. Lost_Voice_Of_Dinah.PDF, and http://research.library.mun.ca/9318/; for a popular work see Anita Diamant, *The Red Tent* (New York: St. Martin's Press, 1997). Yet Dinah is not the focus of the biblical narrative. In the Torah's telling, what happens to Dinah is the event that generates the story, but is not the story's focus. Neither her plight nor her role is central in the biblical text.
5. The opening of the story emphasizes that she is the daughter of Leah, the unloved wife.

to return home first so that he can present his entire clan, not just himself as an individual. Moreover, he is waiting for Ḥamor to come to him on his own turf, turning the tables of power (compensating for the fact that Shekhem is still holding Dinah). In fact, it seems that Jacob plays his cards just right, as Ḥamor does come, making a very significant offer.

As important as understanding Jacob's silence is examining how his sons read the scene. They see themselves, and especially Dinah, as the children of Israel – not Jacob. After years of watching their father squirm in the face of Laban and Esau, and finally proudly watching him stand up to both and declaring himself Israel, they are deeply offended that the daughter of that same Israel has been defiled: "For [Shekhem] had disgraced Israel by lying with Jacob's daughter, and that is not to be done" (34:7).[6] Their distress that what Shekhem does to Dinah "is not to be done"[7] echoes Laban's cry of impropriety at marrying the younger before the elder (29:26). Israel's sons will not tolerate a violation of their newfound pride, just as Laban defends his daughter's dignity.

The difference between Jacob's approach and that of his sons continues beyond their initial reactions, and is mirrored by the reactions of Ḥamor and his son. Ḥamor, responding to his son's pleas to "get me this girl as a wife," visits Jacob to negotiate the marriage: "Shekhem, my son, craves your daughter. Please give her to him as a wife" (34:8). There is no expressed shame in Shekhem's actions or acknowledgment of her continued captivity in Ḥamor's house, but as Ḥamor the tribal leader sits in the tent of the leader of the newly arrived clan, this unspoken problem is the elephant in the room. Ḥamor, using diplomacy, suggests that the recent turn of events presents a new opportunity to

6. In the previous incident, none of his children object when Jacob is initially prepared to let half his family be slaughtered, while in this incident one daughter is taken captive and Jacob's sons are prepared to take extreme measures to avenge her defilement. Perhaps they are too young at the time of the meeting with Esau.

7. The text may be subtly hinting that Jacob's sons have reversed the moral order by playing Laban's hand. Alternatively, the text may be suggesting that unlike their father under Laban's control, they will not tolerate being stepped on as he was. The impact of their witnessing their father's confrontation with Laban becomes evident later, as both of Judah's grand orations, one to Jacob and the other to Joseph, evoke Jacob's speech.

circumvent the problem and strengthen his entire clan as the established clan merges with the new one: "You will take us in marriage; you will give your daughters to us and you will take our daughters for yourselves" (34:9).[8]

Before Jacob has a chance to respond, Shekhem himself interrupts the conversation, undermining his father's attempt to salvage or capitalize on the situation: "Let me find favor in your eyes – whatever [price] you say, I will pay. Name a very high bride-price and gifts to the family – whatever you say I will give – just give me this girl as a wife" (34:11–12). One can easily detect Shekhem's impetuous heat in his attempt to legalize what he has already illicitly taken. In his childish attempt to convince them of his abundant desire for Dinah, he turns his father's offer of a merger into a lopsided purchase.

Shekhem's offer of an exorbitant bride-price unknowingly raises Jacob's hackles, as Shekhem's too-good-to-be-true offer must remind Jacob of Laban's similar offers. Jacob suffered greatly as a result of taking that bait and he is unlikely to fall for it again. But Ḥamor is not the only one who is upended by the younger generation; even before Jacob can respond to either Ḥamor's or Shekhem's offer, his sons interrupt and take command of the conversation. Enraged by the violation of their sister, they devise a plot and speak deceptively to the violator. It would be a disgrace for their sister to marry an uncircumcised man, they declare, and all the males in the town must undergo the procedure (particularly since Ḥamor is proposing a multi-marriage merger). If not, then they will take their sister and go.

The scene which unfolds portrays two seasoned elders, armed with experience and perhaps wisdom, trying to figure out how to navigate a volatile situation and make the best out of it for both sides. Their children, however, hot with passion (either amorous or vengeful), undermine their fathers[9] – with devastating results.

---

8. Ḥamor's words, focusing on who gets to give and take the other's daughters, is a subtle attempt to normalize what his son did to Dinah. He is essentially offering Jacob's clan to do as Shekhem had done.
9. Ḥamor's undermining is likely unintentional, while that of Jacob's sons is calculated.

DECEIVING THE DECEIVERS

Ḥamor's proposal seems like a stroke of political brilliance. Instead of maneuvering through the crisis, he proposes a merger of the two clans. The problem will become an internal matter resolved through traditional means, avoiding the clash of cultures which will inevitably emerge from two separate clans living in close proximity.

A careful look at Ḥamor's words, however, reveals his craftiness. He proposes one deal to Jacob's clan but presents it quite differently to his own. The italics in the chart below highlight the key differences:

Ḥamor's proposal to Jacob's clan (34:9–10)	Ḥamor's proposal to his own clan (34:21–23)
You will take us in marriage	These people will be *one with us.*
You will give your daughters to us and *you will take* our daughters for yourselves.	*We will take* their daughters as wives and *we will give* our daughters to them.
You will live with us – *the land will be open to you.* Live and do business upon it, entrench yourselves firmly in it.	They will dwell in the land and do business upon it…their flocks, their possessions, and all their animals – *they will all be ours.*

In the version of the merger that he proposes to Jacob, Ḥamor suggests that Jacob's family will be in control; it is they who will be doing all of the giving (you will give your daughters to us) and taking (you will take our daughters for yourselves). Even Ḥamor's choice of words in his opening line is quite deliberate: "*Hit'ḥatenu otanu*" does not mean that we shall marry together (which would have been the case had he instead said *itanu*), but that you will take us in marriage.[10] When proposing the deal to his own townspeople, however, Ḥamor suggests that it is *they* who will be in control; they will be doing the giving (we will give our daughters to them) and taking (we will take

---

10. Ḥamor's choice of phrase carries the same tone as the one used to describe Shekhem's taking of Dinah: "*Vayishkav otah*" describes that he lay with Dinah as an object – "he bedded her." Had it been a more mutual act the text would have used "*itah*," "with her."

their daughters as wives). Moreover, his pronouncement that their possessions will be absorbed into Shekhem reveals that Ḥamor's goal is not a merger but a complete takeover of Jacob's clan. Ḥamor's proposal to his people is so convincing that they are prepared to undergo the painful procedure of circumcision, not so that Shekhem can marry his sweetheart but so that they can significantly expand their clan as it swallows the newcomers.

It is hard to know if Jacob's sons are aware of Ḥamor's duplicity when they respond to his offer with their own deception. It is also difficult to determine if all the sons are involved in the deception or just Simeon and Levi, and what the nature of the deception is: are they hoping that the threat of circumcision will be enough of a deterrent so that they avoid the marriage of Dinah to Shekhem, or are they already plotting the massacre of the city made vulnerable by circumcision? Or perhaps their counterproposal is a test of Ḥamor's intentions – insisting on circumcision of all the men of Shekhem is their way of demanding that Shekhem be absorbed into their clan rather than the other way around – rendering their own deceit as a means of exposing Ḥamor's duplicity.

JACOB SPEAKS OUT

Regardless of how we understand the brothers' intentions, a number of critical elements stand out. First, they cannot tolerate Jacob's approach to the issue and thus take matters into their own hands. Second, the intensity of their reaction is explicitly linked to their outrage at the defilement of their sister.[11] Consequently, their response is an explicit

---

11. Interestingly, when they first hear, they are distressed by what happened to "Jacob's daughter" (34:7). As Jacob's sons take charge of the situation, she is repeatedly called their sister and they – particularly Simeon and Levi, also Leah's children – are referred to as her brothers. Finally, when they remove Dinah from Shekhem's house and bring her home she is again described as "their sister" (34:27). The description of Dinah as Jacob's daughter fades. Even Ḥamor, in his initial proposal to Jacob, refers to her as your (in the plural) daughter.

The ostensible justification for their behavior, that Shekhem defiled (T-M-A) their sister, is mentioned both when they hatch their deceitful plan (34:13) and when they loot the city (34:27). The Torah already anticipates this by using the same phrase to describe the justification for Jacob's silence (34:5), suggesting that the brothers' response is not justified by the severity of the offense.

and principled rejection of Shekhem's offer; their sister is not for sale at any price. Finally, their looting of the city may very well be provoked by their understanding that Ḥamor's intention is ultimately to do the same to them, albeit through nonviolent means.

As much as this story is about Simeon and Levi, it is really about Jacob, the main protagonist of the broader narrative. In Laban's house, Jacob is submissive until provoked beyond his breaking point; with Esau, Jacob learns to accept responsibility and give up his ill-gotten gains, but still falls short of acknowledging his wrongdoing to his brother or honestly declining his offer to merge the two families. In this story, we earlier suggested that Jacob's initial silence results not from a position of indifference or weakness but from an attempt to position himself strategically in an effort to redo the imbalance created by the rape and seizure of his daughter. His sons do not see this. They see him as sliding back into submissive Jacob, while they are ready to stand up as the sons of Israel.

Ironically, prior to this incident God is not yet prepared to call him Israel, but immediately afterward, as Jacob completes his circuit in Beit El, God does identify him as such (35:10). It seems that this story helps Jacob complete his transformation by redefining the name Israel. Earlier, Jacob defines his new name as related to fighting. Indeed, that is the way his sons see themselves, as children of the fighter. For them, the transition from Jacob to Israel is about the transformation from victim to victor. But Jacob here apparently introduces the other meaning of Israel, of being *yashar*, straightforward and honest. This is the piece that Jacob has been missing, particularly in his dealings with Esau, and which he finally completes.

It is not surprising, then, that Jacob unequivocally condemns his sons' deception and ensuing massacre:

> You have sullied me, making me disgusting in the eyes of the inhabitants of the land, the Canaanite and the Perizzite. I am small in number; they will gather together against me to smite me, and I along with my family will be destroyed. (34:30)

Moral injustice cannot be righted by another moral injustice. The wrong of taking a woman captive cannot be righted by a revenge-taking of women as captives (34:29). And looting the city robs the act of vengeance of any morality it claims to have.[12]

Jacob's rage at his sons is not simply an expression of fear, even though fear is likely a factor; it is deeply personal. Jacob is incensed that his sons' violent duplicity revives the question of his honesty. Having invested untold energies over the course of twenty-plus years to demonstrate the uprightness of his character and dispel the dark accusation of being a trickster, Jacob once again faces the prospect of being labeled a cheat. Let us recall his expression of outrage to Laban:

> These twenty years I am with you, your sheep and goats have not lost any young, and I have not eaten the rams of your flock. I have not brought anything torn by a beast – I swallowed that loss, you can demand it of me – whether stolen by day or by night! By day I was consumed by parching heat and by night by frost; sleep escaped my eyes. (31:38–39)

The line "whether stolen by day or by night" in the original Hebrew is quite powerful. Jacob coins a word which he uses twice, *genuvti*. This word, constructed from the root G-N-V, meaning "to steal," is conjugated with a suffix so that it could easily be translated as, "I was robbed." In his passionate retort to Laban, who has accused him of thievery, Jacob proclaims his innocence and throws the accusation back at his tormentor: "I was robbed [by you] by day and I was robbed [by you] at night." Through Jacob's strident accusations we hear the pain that he carries over his own sullied reputation (which Laban repeatedly wields against him).

When working for Laban, Jacob goes to great lengths to demonstrate his straightforwardness. In his confrontation with Laban, he tries to clear his name; by returning the blessing to Esau and choosing to become Israel, he again tries to cleanse his reputation. Jacob wants to

---

12. By contrast, in the story of Esther, Haman's decree allows the killing and looting of the Jews' property. While the counter-decree of the king allows the Jews to do the same to their enemies, when the Jews actually defeat their enemies they lay no hands on the spoils – a point repeatedly emphasized in the biblical narration (Esther 9:10, 15–16). Refraining from looting their enemies demonstrates the morality of their self-defense.

return to Canaan with a new name and a new standing. His sons here undo two decades of work.

Even the argument that his sons are merely mirroring Ḥamor's own dishonesty, as in "Act crookedly with the perverse" (Ps. 18:27), provides no solace for Jacob. Jacob has himself fallen into that trap with Laban, when he tries outwitting Laban with the bizarre breeding practices to increase his own herd of marked sheep. Jacob's attempt to beat Laban at his own game results in his stooping to Laban's level, potentially becoming no better than his oppressor.[13] Jacob shudders at the thought of again going down that route, and excoriates his sons for opening that door. So mortified, and shaken, is Jacob by their actions that on his deathbed many years later, it defines his final "blessing" to them:

> Simeon and Levi, the brothers, tools of violence are their trade. In their secrets I did/will[14] not partake, in their gathering was/will my presence not be found. For in their fury they slaughtered men. (49:5–6)

Jacob does not forgive them, even on his deathbed, leaving them with an anti-blessing.

CONFRONTING THE FAMILY

It is quite significant that Jacob is substantively more forceful with his own children than with his adversaries. To explore this further, let us look at a parallel example, King David.

David is a larger-than-life figure in the Bible, the founder of a dynasty which lasts for fifteen generations, spanning more than four hundred years and in which, after his own death – extraordinarily – there

---

13. The looting of the city of Shekhem, including taking its women and children as captives (34:29), replays Shekhem's taking of Dinah, rendering her brothers no better than her oppressor. Exodus 21 warns us explicitly about this trap. The very first instruction God gives to the Israelites following the Revelation at Sinai focuses on the ethical treatment of slaves, countering the tendency of freed slaves to become as cruel as their previous masters.

14. Jacob's blessings on his deathbed are both retrospective, reflecting back on the past, and prospective, projecting into the future.

are no battles challenging the line of succession.[15] David the musician, the conqueror, and the unifier of the tribes under a single umbrella has inspired the imaginations of Jews ever since and is enshrined in Jewish tradition not only as the father of *the* Jewish dynasty but as the father of the Messiah, the ultimate redeemer of the Jewish people. That same David, however, struggles with his own family.

When Amnon, David's firstborn, rapes and subsequently despises his half sister Tamar,[16] David does not rebuke him. David's silence enrages Absalom (Tamar's full brother), who waits for the opportune moment and kills Amnon in revenge. David is personally devastated by the death of his firstborn and publicly mourns Amnon's death. While Absalom fears David's wrath, there is no response from David – not even a verbal one, only silence; and while Joab, David's general, tries to negotiate a reconciliation between David and Absalom, there can be no reconciliation where there is no communication. The events ultimately spiral out of control as Absalom rebels against David and even succeeds in temporarily deposing his father from the throne.

David's inaction and silence in the face of Amnon's violation of Tamar, Absalom's murder of Amnon, and even Absalom's putsch, reflect an area of weakness. Despite his successes in nearly every other sphere, David is challenged in his own home and seems powerless. This is repeated at the end of his life when Absalom's younger brother, Adoniyah, tries to wrest the throne from his aging father (I Kings, chs. 1–2). The Bible's description of Adoniyah is telling: "His father never saddened him by saying, 'Why did you do this?' He … was born to his mother after Absalom" (I Kings 1:6). The association between Adoniyah and Absalom coupled with the revelation that David never rebukes him sheds light

---

15. This does not intend to minimize the significance of the split of the kingdom by Jeroboam, but stands in stark contrast to the northern Kingdom of Israel in which no family stays on the throne for more than three generations.

16. The vulgarity of Amnon's actions are contrasted with those in our present story, in which the rapist Shekhem becomes even more enamored by his victim Dinah and wants to marry her. These two stories are linked literarily as well. Both Shekhem's and Amnon's actions are described as a "*nevala* (disgrace) in Israel" which "is not to be done." This event and its aftershocks span chapters 13–19 in II Samuel.

on David's failure to discipline his own children, leading to two of the major crises in David's reign.

When we compare David and his Achilles heel with Jacob, Jacob's sharp condemnation of Simeon and Levi – and its repetition many years later – stand as a mighty testament to who Jacob has become. Not only is Jacob prepared to be reactive to his oppressor, and not only does he take steps to be proactive in restoring his relationship with Esau, he is prepared to stand up to his own children when he feels that they have crossed the line.[17]

THE EMERGENCE OF ISRAEL

Jacob's rebuke of his sons becomes even more dramatic in light of his family history. Nowhere do we find Abraham rebuking either of his sons, even though Ishmael's behavior toward Isaac certainly warrants it. Isaac never rebukes his own children, even though Jacob's deception and theft are worthy of condemnation. Perhaps it is not surprising that both Abraham and Isaac have children who are excluded from the covenant. By contrast, Jacob does not let his own children's behavior go unnoticed. As he will later do again with his firstborn, Jacob takes a stand against behavior he deems unacceptable. In doing so he begins to lay the foundations for a family in which all members become the heirs to the covenant – unprecedented in the biblical narrative.

This Jacob is prepared to become Israel – but a different one from that which he envisioned in his nocturnal struggle. He has come to understand that without the personal dignity of being forthright, standing up for oneself leads to arrogance and immorality, not stature and greatness. Being Israel demands that defending one's dignity must be married with the dignity of being a *yashar*, a straightforward person of unquestionable character. Jacob's sons don't understand that, but Jacob finally does. He has transformed himself into Israel, and God is almost ready to confirm that for him.

---

17. Simeon and Levi reject the rebuke, responding with, "Shall we allow our sister to be considered a harlot?" The illusion of the Torah giving them the last word is shattered on Jacob's deathbed.

Genesis 35:1–36:43

Two Nations

RECONNECTING WITH GOD

Perhaps God is waiting for Jacob to stand up to his children before calling upon him to return to Beit El, the place where they first meet and to where Jacob vows to return. Or perhaps the incident at Shekhem is intended to be a wake-up call to Jacob, who for some inexplicable reason stops there rather than continuing to Beit El and home. Either way, God needs to instruct Jacob to leave Shekhem: "Rise up, go to Beit El and live *there*. Make *there* an altar to the God who appeared to you as you fled your brother Esau" (35:1). Jacob may have recovered, or discovered, his selfhood, but he also needs to reconnect with God.

Remember that Jacob's initial journey begins with a question: Does God really appear to Jacob, or is all of that part of Jacob's hopeful imagination? Ever since Jacob's dream about the sheep (31:10), there has been ample evidence to conclude that the divine promise is real. When God later tells Jacob explicitly to leave Laban's house the answer should have been clear, and when Jacob turns to God prior to his encounter with Esau, he reveals that on a primal level he understands, or at least hopes, that the dream at Beit El was indeed a revelation, requiring him to fulfill his promise and return there. Jacob needs to acknowledge that God does, in fact, keep the promise He made him at Beit El, and Jacob must live up to his – including accepting God as his God.

It is not surprising, then, that after God instructs him explicitly to return to Beit El, Jacob immediately instructs his family to cleanse themselves and purify the household of foreign gods.[1] The evidence for the journey to Beit El as a "reunification" with God leaps out of our current text. In a span of just eight verses the two Hebrew letters *aleph* and *lamed* (together spelling God's name) appear together no fewer than fourteen times, including in wordplays on the names of two trees playing prominent roles in the narrative, an *elah* and an *alon*.[2] It is also not surprising that this encounter with God prefigures the Israelite encounter with the Divine at Sinai, especially regarding the preparations for that encounter – purification, changing clothes, and removing foreign gods. [3]

Jacob's internal work in becoming Israel, both as a fighter and as a straightforward person, focus on the first three letters of his new name, the Y-S/SH-R. The last two letters of his name, however, are God's name: E-L. In God's eyes, for Jacob to become Israel he must take one final step and bond himself once again to God in fulfillment of his vow.

RETURN TO THE PAST OR LEAP INTO THE FUTURE?

On further reflection, were Jacob to have immediately returned to fulfill his promise in Beit El and then continue home to his mother and father, he would likely have been judged a dramatic failure, as he would have learned nothing from his extended exile. The Jacob who is exiled from his home, his land, and his family is in dire need of repair; a return without self-reflection and change would leave him unfit to continue as God's covenantal partner. By contrast, the Jacob who struggles with Laban, reaches out to Esau, fights to recover his integrity, refuses to stand by

---

1. Regarding the presence of those gods, most classical commentaries (Rashi; Rashbam; Radak; Seforno) suggest that they are from the spoils of Shekhem. Alter suggests that they may be the *terafim* that Rachel took, or similar items taken from Ḥaran by other household members. Interestingly, these items include earrings, which are also used to fashion the Golden Calf (Ex. 32:3).
2. Excluded from this count are two references to *elohei nekhar*, foreign gods, which, precisely because they are foreign, Jacob commands be removed from his entourage.
3. The first two are revived in Exodus 19 as part of the preparations for the Revelation at Sinai, the third is explicated as part of that revelation in Exodus 20.

idly when his children cross the line, and declares himself to be Israel – with its multiple meanings – is a redeemed Jacob.

When he ultimately does arrive in Beit El, God finally confirms what Jacob has been trying to achieve: "God said to him: Your name is Jacob; you will no longer be called Jacob. Rather, your name will be Israel. And He called his name Israel" (34:10). God doesn't need to explain the name Israel; Jacob already knows what it means to be Israel: to confront both the external and internal devils, to stand up for himself while maintaining his dignity and integrity, to stand firm even against his own children without chasing them away, and to do all of the above while accepting a partnership with God. From the time of his nocturnal struggle until his return to Beit El, he calls himself Israel and his children think of him as Israel, but the Torah does not refer to him as such until now, when God confers that new name upon him.

Jacob is not the first biblical character to have his name changed. His grandfather Abraham's name is changed by God as well. A careful look reveals striking similarities between those two events, resulting in what appears to be a formula. For both Abraham and Jacob, God introduces Himself as El Shaddai (17:1; 35:11), both Abraham and Jacob are informed that they will become a nation and a community of nations (17:5; 35:11), both are promised the land for their descendants (17:8; 35:12), and both are promised that among their descendants will be kings (17:6; 35:11). For Abraham, this formula is part of his induction into the covenant of circumcision; we have every reason to believe that it has parallel significance for Jacob.

The strong similarities between the two name changes, however, invites an exploration of the differences between them. For Abraham, once his name is changed from Abram he is never again referred to by his former name. The change of Abram's name to Abraham is intended to mark a significant milestone in a journey which begins with *lekh lekha*. Abraham's journey is distinguished by leaving his past behind to build for himself new personal, national, and religious identities.[4]

---

4. Abraham's new name is not radically different from his old one, suggesting that even with his radical transformation, his new identity is built upon the foundations of his former self.

By contrast, Jacob's new identity does not erase his old one. Jacob and Israel coexist; God affirms his old identity ("Your name is Jacob") just prior to conferring upon him a new one, and throughout the rest of the narrative he is referred to alternately as Jacob and Israel. Sometimes, in fact, the Torah refers to him using both names in the same or adjacent verses, yielding a complex and multifaceted character, Jacob-Israel.[5] Jacob is not supposed to become a completely new person. Rather, his identity as Israel is meant to complement the preexisting character. Abraham's covenant of circumcision seals the distinction between himself and the rest of his ancestral family; Jacob's "covenant" binds him to his ancestral family. Abraham's destiny is to permanently leave home, while Jacob's is to return home as a new person.

THE IMPORTANCE OF LOSS

We understand that Abraham's leap forward is inextricably linked to his ability to leave his ancestral clan. This move echoes the Torah's commentary on the first couple in the Garden: "Therefore must a man leave his father and mother and cling to his wife" (2:24). The ability to bond meaningfully with a spouse is bound with the ability to define an identity independent of parents.[6] The move forward is facilitated by leaving something behind.

Jacob, too, experiences loss as he becomes Israel, even beyond his earlier relinquishing of the blessing. Upon his arrival in Beit El he loses Devorah, his mother's nursemaid. We know nothing about this woman; she is neither mentioned prior to this passage nor subsequent to it. We do not even know if she is the woman who nurses Rebecca herself or who serves as the nursemaid for Rebecca's twin boys. Either way, she is part of Jacob's childhood, and her passing deeply saddens him. He buries her under an oak tree and names it the Oak of Weeping.[7]

---

5. A midrash explicitly identifies God as the God of Israel, claiming that Jacob's image is carved into the divine throne (*Midrash Sekhel Tov* 33:17; *Midrash Yelamdenu* 129), suggesting perhaps that Jacob's complexity is a reflection of the divine image. This is reminiscent of the divine male-female complexity in which humans are created.
6. Judith Viorst, in *Necessary Losses* (New York: The Free Press, 2002), highlights the developmental significance of leaving behind parts of one's self to enable moving forward.
7. According to rabbinic tradition, her death hints to Rebecca's death, yet why the Torah would intentionally hide Rebecca's death is unclear.

Just as Abraham's *lekh lekha* represents a loss of his birth family, Devorah's death marks for Jacob the loss of his childhood.

The second loss is even more profound, as Jacob suffers the death of his beloved Rachel immediately following his encounter with God in Beit El:

> They were still some distance from Efrat, Rachel gave birth, but her delivery was difficult. In her difficult labor the midwife said to her, "Fear not, for this one is also a son for you." As the life force left her she called him Ben-Oni, but his father called him Binyamin [Benjamin]. Rachel died on the road to Efrat, that is, Beit Leḥem. Jacob erected a monument (*matzeva*) on her grave, that is the monument of Rachel's grave to this day. (35:16–20)

The loss of both a mother figure and his beloved wife are profound. These two deaths sandwich Jacob's encounter with God at Beit El.[8]

Much as Jacob toils for years to earn the name Israel, moving forward requires him to be severed from his past, and there is one additional loss he endures. Jacob finally returns to his father's house without a mention of the reunion and without dialogue. The only thing mentioned is Isaac's death. Rebecca, Jacob's mother, dies without mention; Jacob cannot even mourn her loss. The symbols of love in Jacob's life are stripped from him. Unlike his early tentative promise to God, Jacob-Israel's unambiguous covenant with God cuts the umbilical cord to his past as he builds his future.

THE EMERGENCE OF JACOB-ISRAEL

We do not have to wait long before the complex figure of Jacob-Israel surfaces. We recall that the early Jacob, indentured to his father-in-law

---

8. Devorah's death is later followed by Jacob's setting up a monument stone in Beit El. That scene is marked by three variants on the Hebrew word for monument: "Jacob erected (*vayatzev*) a monument (*matzeva*) in the place where God spoke with him, a monument of (*matzevet*) stone" (35:14). The same three variants on the word appear in the narration of Rachel's death: "Jacob erected (*vayatzev*) a monument (*matzeva*) on her grave, that is the monument of (*matzevet*) Rachel's grave to this day" (35:20).

and manipulated by his wives, does not even have a say in the naming of his children. How different is Jacob-Israel! Rachel names her son Ben-Oni, "child of my misery," but his father names him Benjamin, "child of my strength" (literally, child of my right [hand]). Benjamin is the only child in this family named by his father, who insists on playing an active role in the naming. Jacob-Israel tries to preserve the sound of the name given by Rachel, while transforming his name from one of bitterness and negativity to one of strength and positivity.[9] Just as God changes his name, he changes the name of his son; and just as Jacob does not let Laban's Aramean influences and beliefs taint the name of the place of their agreement, he will not let Rachel's bitterness taint the name of his new son.

It is quite telling that Benjamin's older brother is also named twice, both times by his mother. Reacting to his birth, Rachel announces, "God has gathered (*asaf*) my shame," providing an etymology for his name, Yosef. In the very next verse, however, she maintains the name Yosef while changing the rationale for it: "God should add (*yosef*) to me another child." Rachel herself recognizes that her initial explanation for the name is an expression of thankless negativity, and changes the etiology to reflect a more positive attitude. With the birth of Benjamin, Rachel's initial reaction is again driven by bitterness, but Jacob refuses to let his son carry the scar of his mother's pain in his name and changes it to reflect strength.

If renaming Benjamin expresses the activist side of Jacob-Israel, his lack of reaction to a highly unusual and cryptically described incident suggests that he has more than a single *modus operandi*: "As Israel dwelled in that land, Reuben went and lay with Bilhah, his father's concubine, and Israel heard…" (35:22).

What are we to make of Reuben? Is he, like Shekhem, an impetuous young man unable to control his desires? Possibly. More likely, however, is that Reuben's act is more akin to that of Simeon and Levi – yet

---

9. A secondary reading of Ben-Oni would mean "son of my strength" (see 49:3). According to this understanding, Jacob insists on changing the name to one which is unambiguously positive, redeeming Rachel's legacy in the process.

another attempt to challenge Jacob's control of the family. Like Absalom, who beds David's concubines after claiming the throne (II Sam. 16:20–22) and Adoniyah, who seeks to marry Avishag the Shunammite (who had shared David's bed; I Kings 2:13–25), bedding the king's women is more of a political power-grab than an exhibition of unrequited sexual desire.

What could motivate Reuben to do such a thing now? Rachel's death certainly provides an opportune moment, particularly in the personal toll it takes on Jacob. Reuben may be angered by Jacob's intervention in naming Benjamin, another child of the beloved Rachel and hence another potential rival for leadership of the family;[10] he may even have been frustrated that Simeon and Levi leapfrog him in their attempt to take control. Regardless of the reason, Reuben decides that the time is ripe to wrest the leadership of the clan from his father.

Reuben fails miserably. Israel hears and, like his response to the rape of Dinah, is silent. But just as Jacob's silence in the face of Dinah's rape is not necessarily a sign of weakness, neither is his silence in the face of Reuben's brutish misadventure. Jacob sees Reuben as both immature and premature, his behavior hasty, primitive, and ill-conceived. While we hear nothing of Jacob-Israel's response here, as with Simeon and Levi we do hear his response on his deathbed. As he bestows blessings upon his children, Jacob-Israel opens with harsh words for his eldest:

> Reuben, you are my firstborn, my strength and the first fruit of my manhood; you had extra rank and extra power. But because you were impetuous and unstable as water, you will have nothing extra, for you mounted your father's bed; you profaned where I lay as you climbed on it. (49:3–4)

10. According to Genesis Rabba 98:4 he was avenging his mother's honor at being denied Jacob's love. Remember that it was Reuben who brought his mother the mandrakes. Yair Zakovitch, *Jacob: Unexpected Patriarch* [Hebrew] (Or Yehuda: Dvir, 2012), 142, suggests that Reuben's bedding Bilhah defiled her, making her unfit for Jacob and forcing Jacob to move his bed next to Leah's.

In the eyes of Jacob-Israel, Reuben's very attempt to prematurely claim leadership of the clan disqualifies him for that very position.

JACOB THE NATION-FOUNDER

Perhaps the clue to understanding Jacob-Israel's response lays in a bizarre anomaly in the text. The Torah's account of Reuben's act is brief, spanning less than a verse: "Reuben went and lay with Bilhah, his father's concubine, and Israel heard.... The sons of Jacob were twelve." The ellipsis is actually in the text itself, represented by a paragraph break mid-sentence. We anticipate a response but there is none. Jacob ignores Reuben's attempt precisely because, unlike Abraham and Isaac, he is committed to keeping all of his sons within the inner circle of the family constellation. The sons of Jacob must be twelve.

In the Book of Genesis, families are considered complete when their children number twelve. Ishmael[11] has twelve children, Nahor has twelve children, and now Jacob has twelve children. A family with twelve children is a proto-nation. Jacob understands the significance of Benjamin's birth. He is not simply another child of the beloved wife, but the living embodiment of a turning point in Jacob's status. Benjamin is indeed Jacob's strength, as he transforms Jacob into a proto-nation.

With the birth of Benjamin, Jacob is the first Patriarch who can lay claim to being a nation-founder. Jacob is the beginning of the fulfillment of God's promise to Abraham, and that fulfillment comes, not surprisingly, immediately following Jacob's new covenant with God. Moreover, maintaining those twelve children as a unit becomes Jacob's priority. With them he becomes the fulfillment of God's covenantal promise at Beit El; without them he will fail to found a nation. All twelve children must remain inside the covenant, and Jacob's silence is both a subtle rebuke to Reuben and a way to maintain his new status. Despite the rebellious endeavors of Reuben, Simeon, and Levi (Jacob's eldest children), Jacob is in charge of his family, and all twelve sons, including the rebellious ones, are included.

---

11. Ishmael is promised twelve children by God (17:20), God's way of indicating to Abraham that Ishmael, too, will become a great nation.

This story culminates Jacob's personal odyssey. It is a journey that forces him to confront his external challenges and, ultimately, his internal ones. It is a journey that reconnects him with God in profound ways, even establishing a new covenant, and a journey that redefines him as Israel the man and Israel the father of a nation.

Jacob-Israel is also the first Patriarch to have no children fall outside of the covenant.[12] Abraham has Ishmael, Isaac has Esau, but "the sons of Jacob were twelve." As the nation-founder, Jacob has a responsibility unparalleled by his predecessors. How will he build a covenantal family? That challenge will carry him until his dying days.

THE NATION(S) OF ESAU-EDOM-SE'IR

If the nation of Israel is the product of slow and careful nurturing, Esau's emergence as a nation follows a profoundly different path. Esau is the only figure in the Bible described with two books of *toledot*, or legacies. The first is the legacy of Esau, otherwise known as Edom (36:1). Using imagery evocative of Abraham's nephew Lot, after building a family with five sons in Canaan, Esau travels eastward, crossing the Jordan, because his ancestral land of Canaan "could not support" both him and his brother, Jacob. Leaving the land to go eastward in search of better grazing follows the model of those seeking to leave the covenant for more immediate material gains.[13]

But there is a second *toledot* of Esau presented immediately afterward: Esau the father of the Edomite nation, in the mountains of Se'ir (36:9). The legacy of Esau presented here is far more complex and involves Esau marrying into and eventually merging with the people of Se'ir. The family relationships in this account are intertwined and complicated, with more than a hint of incest.[14] The merged family defies the Genesis model of twelve sons (Esau has thirteen), as well as the model of the proto-nation, and with the merger Esau flourishes into a nation

---

12. In Song of Songs Rabba 3–4 this is referred to as Jacob's bed being complete.
13. In this, Esau's essential character as a hunter living for short-term gains has not changed.
14. See Rashi, 36:2, 5, 12, 24.

almost immediately. Let us recall that when he comes to greet Jacob he already has four hundred men.

And not only does Esau become a nation right away, his nation has kings – long before there are kings in Israel (36:31). The Torah lists a long line of kings (although lacking any line of succession; each generation sports a king from a different region). Esau emerges from the womb complete, and he later emerges as a complete nation even before Jacob has his twelve sons.

Esau receives the divine blessings as promised to Abraham and Isaac. His children are numerous and they become a nation – even nations – adorned by royalty. Yet fulfillment of the promise is quite different from fulfillment of the covenant. As we've seen, being part of the covenant entails patience and endurance: four hundred years[15] of servitude, oppression, and slow development. Impetuous Esau, who sells his birthright because he cannot imagine waiting for it to become valuable, is incompatible with God's covenant. He gets his nation, complete with kings, even as Jacob struggles to establish his fledgling clan.

A single line at the close of the legacy of Esau-Se'ir captures the distinction powerfully. While Esau merges with Se'ir and builds himself a powerful nation, Jacob dwells in the land of Canaan, the land of his father's sojourn (37:1).[16] Three times Jacob narrowly escapes the kind of merger (with Laban, Shekhem, and Esau) that propels his elder brother to instant success, following instead the slow, arduous, covenantal path. It is the same kind of path Jacob chooses years earlier, prepared to wait as long as necessary to "cash in" on the birthright. Esau finds his fortunes in the immediate; Jacob returns to the land of his promise.

---

15. Esau's four hundred men are contrasted with the four hundred years Jacob must wait.

16. This is an odd verse. Based on the traditional Masoretic breaks in the Torah as well as the Christian chapter breaks, it serves as the introduction to the Joseph story. If, however, we look at the division of Genesis into eleven books of *toledot*, this verse closes the legacy of Esau-Se'ir.

Genesis 37:1–37:36

The Disintegrating Family

E
sau, with his Hittite and Ishmaelite wives, leaves the ancestral lands and merges his clan with Edom on the eastern bank of the Jordan. Within the course of a single chapter the Torah describes his legacy – his *toledot* – twice, including his thirteen sons, fourteen chieftains, and eight generations of kings. Esau achieves his destiny, and more, in this one chapter. Such is the Torah's way of describing the branches of the Abrahamic family who are distanced from the main line. Unlike Abraham, whose covenant demands enduring years of hardship, the rejected branches of the family achieve greatness quickly, after which they are relegated to the sidelines of the biblical story.

Jacob, by contrast, has worked hard – in line with the Abrahamic covenant and with the alternate interpretation of Rebecca's prophecy.[1] He settles into the land in which his forefathers were considered sojourners (37:1), and so he expects his story to conclude.[2] But unbeknownst to Jacob, his hard work is about to begin.

---

1. See Rashi's lengthy explication of 37:1.
2. Genesis Rabba reads 37:1 as "Jacob sought to live placidly."

THE PLAGUE OF FAVORITISM

Jacob's favoritism toward Joseph likely begins long before Joseph's birth. Rachel is Jacob's love, and Jacob refuses to consider leaving Laban's house until Rachel bears him a son. With Rachel's tragic death during the birth of her second son, Jacob's love for her is channeled into Joseph.

Jacob makes no secret of his affinity for Joseph – Joseph is his *ben zekunim*,[3] the awaited child born to the beloved, barren wife. Joseph is different from the other sons – he is a child neither of Leah nor of the maidservants, but he is comfortable with both and thus has the potential to be a unifying figure in the family, bridging between the bloc of Leah's children and those of the maidservants.[4]

Jacob makes a special cloak for Joseph, a *ketonet*. That word is reserved in the Bible for priestly clothing (e.g., Ex. 28:39–40) and the special garments God makes for the first couple (Gen. 3:21). Joseph's particular type of *ketonet*, a *ketonet passim*, is referenced only one other time in the Bible, and there it is a sign of royalty (II Sam. 13:18). The cloak is not just a gift from Jacob to his favored son but an unambiguous statement about that son's status. It is Jacob's elevation of Joseph and his special love which inspires his brothers' hatred toward him (37:4), much as Jacob's love for Rachel engenders Leah's jealousy and competition for his affection.

Jacob is not the first in his family to express preference for one son over the other: Abraham favors Ishmael and Isaac favors Esau (interestingly, both of those choices are rejected by God). That history of parental preferences raises an important question: Is Jacob's preference for Joseph meant to be like that of his father and grandfather – exclusive to the point of rejection of all the other children, or is it meant to be hierarchical, in which one son is elevated above the others into a leadership position, without rejection of the others?

---

3. Most read this phrase literally, as "the child of his old age." That reading is problematic, as Benjamin is born many years later and is never referred to as such. Isaac is also referred to as Abraham's *ben zekunim* (21:2, 7) even though Abraham fathers many children dozens of years afterward. It seems more accurate to read this phrase as "the child he thought he would never have."

4. Joseph tends the flocks with his brothers but also spends time with the sons of the maidservants (37:2).

A single verse in the Rachel-Leah paradigm leaves us with hope: "Jacob came unto Rachel as well and also loved Rachel even more than Leah" (29:30). While the verse is written awkwardly and yields multiple possible readings, its simplest reading indicates that Jacob did love Leah but not in the same way as he loved Rachel, suggesting that the same might be possible for her children. This is precisely where we, the omnipotent readers of the text, need to suppress our knowledge in order to understand the narrative. While we know that Jacob's preference for Joseph may not be exclusionary, Jacob's children may not be aware of that. They may understand it as a zero-sum game – him or us, with no chance of finding a middle ground.

JOSEPH DREAMS

While Jacob lights the fire of discord between his sons, Joseph does an excellent job of fanning the flames. Whether through carefully considered malice or simple immaturity, seventeen-year-old Joseph flaunts his dreams before his brothers with his grandiose self-image. To be sure, dreams in the Bible play a significant role; for many, they are an expression of divine inspiration. Just as a single generation earlier, Jacob is unsure whether God really appears to him or if his vision is a product of his deep yearnings, Joseph's brothers may secretly suspect and fear that the dreams may be a divine message. Thus, either Joseph is an arrogant, spoiled child dreaming of ruling over them, or God has determined Joseph's supremacy. Either way he does not endear himself to them.

Joseph has two dreams, and despite their apparent similarities, a close look at their subtleties as well as the differences between them is quite revealing.

Joseph's first dream is marked by avatars representing the characters. All twelve brothers, Joseph included, are in the fields gathering the wheat into sheaves, and the sheaves take the places of the brothers as they circle around and bow to Joseph's sheaf, which has risen and stands erect. While the symbolic acts are clear, both to the reader and to Joseph's brothers, it is quite telling that the dream is about wheat. After all, Jacob's clan are shepherds, not farmers. For Joseph to dream of wheat indicates that his thoughts are far from those of the rest of the family, and that he sees his superiority within the family as emerging from his ability to break from the family's traditional mold and imagine new modes.

In contrast to his first dream, Joseph's second dream is marked by the disappearance of the explicit avatars: the brothers are absent, Joseph is present and central, and the sun, moon, and eleven stars bow to him. He provides nothing to them; he is simply the object of their fealty. The brothers cease to exist; their significance is only in the subservience of their symbolic representatives to him. If Joseph's first dream could be tolerated as a product of his hope of finding a new means of supporting the family, the second is sheer arrogance.

It is this arrogance that leaps out at the reader, particularly when we notice that absent from Joseph's dream is God. Jacob, Joseph's father, also dreams twice, but both of his dreams have either God or some divine figure as central. Even at Jacob's nadir, when he dreams of sheep, there are angels directing the process. Joseph has no divine representation in his dreams; *he* is the god with the heavenly hosts bowing to him. Joseph, with his dreams of wheat and himself as a god, is dreaming like an Egyptian Pharaoh.

It is not only the hubris in his dreams which increases, but what he does with them. Joseph does not hold back. He shares the first dream with his brothers and the second with his brothers and his father. Joseph knows no bounds. He seems to lack the common sense of what should be kept to himself.

Jacob's response, however, is more complex. He publicly rebukes Joseph, not for his arrogance in telling the dreams but for the self-centered, godless dreams themselves. Jacob, more than anyone else in the family, knows the power of dreams. His public rebuke is necessary, but feeble – in his heart he holds on to those dreams of his favored son. Isn't Joseph the miracle child, the one whom he believed would never be born to the barren Rachel? Doesn't Joseph take the place of his beloved wife, the one who engineers Jacob's explosive emergence from his servitude? And why should Jacob not anticipate Joseph's pretension – does Jacob himself not elevate Joseph over his brothers and treat him like royalty?

For Joseph's brothers, his increasingly intolerable egotism breeds contempt and hatred. Even worse, their father's public rebuke of Joseph is, to them, disingenuous. Jacob is the one who created Joseph with his delusions of grandeur; his disapproval of Joseph's grandiose dreams is shallow. Their hatred for Joseph redirects their anger at their father and masks their profound jealousy: "His brothers were envious of him but his father held on to [Joseph's] word" (37:11).

RETURNING TO SHEKHEM

Given the brothers' antipathy to Joseph and their father's role in Joseph's ballooning ego, it is not surprising that the next time we find Joseph's brothers they are tending the sheep in Shekhem. Not only is Shekhem geographically distant from Jacob's home in Hebron, it is the scene of their massacre of the city and where they flex their muscles – both against the local inhabitants and against their father. It is in Shekhem that the brothers, as a group, hijack their father's talks with Ḥamor, and it is to Shekhem, where they feel powerful and reject their father's authority, that they return.[5] And while Joseph is earlier described as shepherding the flocks together with his brothers, he is now left behind. Jacob's sons, with the exception of Rachel's children, abandon him to establish their own entity in Shekhem.

In light of this, Jacob's mission sending Joseph to "see how his brothers are doing in Shekhem" is not an innocent fact-finding trip. Jacob, like Joseph, is aware that his sons are quite distant, and the trip takes on ominous overtones. Joseph's response to Jacob's summons belies his understanding: "*Hineni*, here I am." It is the same response Abraham offers to God at the *Akeda* and the same one Abraham gives to Isaac during that same fateful incident. (In fact, this mission to Shekhem bears striking resemblance to the *Akeda*: Jacob risks his son, his beloved son, echoing God's instructions to Abraham [22:2].) The *hineni* is also the response given by both Esau and Jacob in preparation for their blessings from Isaac; it expresses the import of the moment. Despite the danger involved, Jacob knows that he has no choice. If the brothers break from him he has no hope for a covenantal family, just a chosen son – like himself and his own father. Joseph must figure out how to reunite with his brothers and bring them all back home.

---

5. Rashbam, 37:13, anticipates some of this analysis as he identifies Shekhem as a dangerous place resulting from the earlier massacre there.

His success or failure in this mission may determine the future of the entire covenant.

Not only is Joseph aware of the importance of his trip, on his way to his brothers he replays a critical moment both from his great-grandfather Abraham and from his father, Jacob:

> A man found him; behold, he was lost in the field. The man asked him, "What do you seek?" He responded, "It is my brothers whom I seek. Tell me, please, where are they tending the sheep?" The man said, "They have moved on from here, for I heard them saying, 'Let us go to Dothan.'"[6] (37:15–17)

Like Abraham, who gets lost in his search for the land, Joseph gets lost in the search for his brothers; this task is far greater than it seems. Like Jacob, who has a fateful nighttime encounter with a mysterious, anonymous man who refocuses him, Joseph has an encounter with a mysterious, anonymous man who similarly redirects him.

Yet Joseph's search for his brothers is different from Abraham's aimlessness. He is not lost but he has lost his brothers. What Joseph may not yet understand is that his brothers have been lost for a long time, starting with Jacob's favoring Rachel, to Jacob's favoring Joseph and treating him like a prince, to Joseph's cavalier sharing of his dreams, and finally to Jacob's admiration for Joseph even while rebuking him in front of them. If Joseph, whom Jacob ironically sees as the unifier, successfully finds his brothers, he will save the covenantal family; if he does not, then the covenantal family will have to wait yet another generation.

So Joseph responds to Jacob with a fateful *hineni*. And if his brothers have moved to Dothan, he will find them. He must.

BACK FROM THE BRINK

When Joseph finally does find his brothers, he is not even given an opportunity to speak. As soon as they see him with his pretentious, offensive cloak, they begin to plot against him: "Let us kill him and toss him into one of the pits; we can say that he was eaten by a wild animal. We will

---

6. Dothan is located northwest of Shekhem, even farther from Jacob.

then see what will come of his dreams" (37:20). Not only do they plot Joseph's death, they conspire to deceive Jacob, giving him a taste of his own medicine.

Reuben, the eldest, comes to the rescue: "Do not spill blood! Toss him into one of the pits in the wilderness but do not send out your hand against him" (37:22). Reuben's noble effort seems to work, but he is far from the hero of the story. For sure he is planning to secretly return Joseph back home, but is that for Joseph's good or for his own? Is he hoping that Joseph will report to his father that Reuben is, indeed, deserving of the leadership because he saves Joseph? A second look reveals a deeper problem with Reuben's solution; it is based on deception – he will deceive his brothers just as they plan to deceive Jacob. Even if Jacob appoints him as leader of the clan, his leadership will be based on deceit and treachery, the antithesis of Jacob's trajectory.

Reuben's attempt to grasp the reins fails as Judah steps in: "What profit is there in killing our brother and covering up his blood? Let us sell him to the Ishmaelites and let our hand not be upon him, as he is our brother" (37:26-27). Judah recognizes the moral problematics of killing a brother, but his morality is muted by his crass practicality. There is no profit in murder; why not benefit from Joseph's disappearance? While Reuben's failure reflects his own inappropriateness at leadership, Judah's success is not exactly a resounding moral triumph. The profit motive trumps the discomfort associated with murder, and especially fratricide. Two brothers, both asserting leadership, fail at the most basic levels.

THE SALE AND COVER-UP

The next step is shrouded in mystery. Ishmaelites, Midianites, merchants, and Medanites all seem to have a hand in the kidnapping and sale of Joseph.[7] It is not clear who pulls Joseph out of the pit, who sells him to whom, and who ultimately transports him to Egypt, selling him there

---

7. It is fascinating that all those involved were descendants of the children Abraham sends away from Isaac (see 25:1-6); are they now exacting revenge on Isaac's progeny? If so, they are ironically aiding the divine plan to bring Joseph to Egypt, helping to bring about the fulfillment of God's covenant with Abraham!

into slavery. The various relevant texts themselves present what seems to be an intractable puzzle:

- *Let us sell him* to the Ishmaelites and let our hand not be upon him. (37:27)
- Some men, *Midianite* merchants, passed, they pulled and drew Joseph up from the pit and *sold Joseph* to the Ishmaelites. (37:28)
- The *Medanites sold him* to Egypt, to Potiphar. (37:36)
- Joseph was brought down to Egypt; *Potiphar bought him from the Ishmaelites,* who brought him there. (39:1)
- I am Joseph, your brother whom *you sold* to Egypt. (45:4)

Is it Joseph's brothers, the Midianites, the Medanites, or the Ishmaelites who sell him? Among the commentaries there is a range of opinions, from those suggesting that the brothers intend to sell Joseph but never actually do because others pull him out of the pit first,[8] to those who suggest that Joseph, as a kidnapped youth and Jacob's son, is a "hot potato" and sold repeatedly to cover up the tracks of the kidnapping and sale.[9] Adding to the complexity is that Reuben is apparently unaware of what had happened. When he returns to the pit to rescue Joseph, the boy is inexplicably gone, rendering Reuben so distraught that he tears his clothes in mourning.

Who actually pulls Joseph out of the pit and sells him is almost irrelevant. As Rashbam argues, the brothers intend to strip him of his clothing, toss him into a pit, and sell him, creating the conditions in which he will be transported out of their lives forever while they enjoy their picnic lunch nearby.[10] Perhaps even worse, however, is what the brothers do to Jacob.

They dip Joseph's special cloak into freshly slaughtered goat's blood and shred it[11] before presenting it to their father: "We found this – do

---

8. This is the position of Rashbam.
9. See Rashi and Nahmanides. Rashbam argues that even if they did not actually sell him, they are morally culpable for his plight.
10. Rabbi Abraham, son of Maimonides, sees their callousness in this as particularly heinous.
11. See Radak; Seforno.

you recognize it? Is this Joseph's cloak or not?" (37:32). Note that Jacob's sons deceive him using the same tools, and even the same language, that Jacob uses to deceive his father: a freshly slaughtered goat and the phrase *"haker na,"* "recognize it."

It is hard to know if Jacob recognizes the irony which the text makes available to us readers. Regardless, Jacob is inconsolable. Not only does he lose his favored son, a personally devastating loss, but his bid to build a covenantal family has failed miserably – and he has no one to blame but himself. It is he who favors Joseph and sets him up for conflict; it is he who sends Joseph off to the dangers of Shekhem to test Joseph's ability to reunite the family. More than Jacob is unable to forgive his sons, he is unable to forgive himself.

IRONIC TWISTS

While Jacob is convinced that all is lost, there are interesting developments in the story. First, even though the brothers cruelly deceive their father, the sale of Joseph and the necessary cover-up ironically brings them home. Reuben, Simeon, and Levi, who earlier try to rebel against their father, are again inseparable from the others. The brothers do not return to Shekhem; in fact, they will no longer leave home at all without their father's permission. In Joseph's absence, they grow closer to Jacob.

At the same time, while the sale of Joseph is meant to put him out of the picture, it accomplishes exactly the opposite. Because Jacob is inconsolable, he doesn't stop thinking about Joseph: "I will go down to my son, to Sheol, as a mourner" (37:35). The brothers, too, cannot put Joseph out of their minds. We later overhear their discussions among themselves; they attribute the calamity which befalls them to what they had done to Joseph: "One said to the other, 'We are guilty regarding our brother, as we heard his pleas to us and we did not listen; because of that, our current tragedy befalls us'" (42:21). Like Lady Macbeth's bloody stain, they cannot wash themselves of it. It haunts them endlessly.

And there is one further irony. Judah's decision to sell Joseph is not the result of Judah's virtue. In the context of Genesis, however, Judah's decision marks a dramatic turning point, opening a crack of hope for our grand narrative. The story of the family in Genesis begins with the killing of one brother by another and the absence of the parents. Later, while Esau plans to kill Jacob, Rebecca steps in to protect one child from the other. In our story, it is Jacob who throws Joseph into the lion's den, while the brothers, and specifically Judah – the brother – make sure that the killing doesn't happen. Had the brothers successfully killed Joseph, as Cain kills Abel, the Book of Genesis may have needed to restart. Unwittingly, Judah becomes the hero of the grand narrative of Genesis. But that heroic act will be for naught if Joseph is excised from the story. Avoiding fratricide may be important, but it does not make for a family, not to mention a covenantal family. And at this point, that family seems far away.

Genesis 39:1–41:57

Joseph, the Lost Hero

The earlier narratives in Genesis form a valuable backdrop to our story. Lot separates from Abram, moving to the area of Sodom and founding two nations, sealing his departure from the Abrahamic line. Later, Ishmael travels to Egypt, where he marries and sets up his own nation, writing himself out of the Abrahamic narrative as well. In the next generation it is Esau who marries into the nation of Se'ir and merges with them to forge his own nation, yet another example of a preferred son who is no longer the heir. The narrative does not follow them once they depart. If the narratives of Genesis are any indication, after the sale of Joseph to Egypt the story of Genesis should continue with the selection of the future bearer of the covenant. Joseph is gone and the family must continue. He is sent out of the nuclear family and ultimately marries into the Egyptian elite. His fate should be the same as Lot, Ishmael, and Esau. We are surprised, then, to discover a lengthy focus on Joseph's dramatic story in Egypt. As we will see in this chapter, Joseph's trajectory in Egypt provides us with even more reason to question.

Joseph's story is filled with twists which, were we not so familiar with the flow of events, we would find surprising. He keeps getting thrown into captivity, only to emerge in a better position. And each time he gets put down, while we think that he is getting further from his rescue, he is actually getting closer to it, because his rescue comes from a completely unexpected place.

IN POTIPHAR'S HOUSE

Joseph must have been an unusual commodity on the slave market. Upon his arrival in Egypt he is purchased by none other than Potiphar, Pharaoh's chief executioner, and it does not take long for Potiphar to notice his potential: "His master saw that God was with him and in all that he did God made him successful" (39:3). Joseph is elevated quickly by Potiphar to be in charge of the entire household, and Potiphar trusts him implicitly: "God's blessing was in everything of Potiphar's, both in the home and in the field" (39:5). Joseph's meteoric rise in Potiphar's house is even more dramatic than his fall in his own home – and, unlike at home, Joseph finds favor in everyone's eyes.

This adulation, however, comes at a price. Potiphar's wife tries repeatedly to seduce Joseph. She persists despite Joseph's resistance, perhaps even spurred by his refusal, until one day she grabs his cloak as he tries to evade her. Unlike his half sister Dinah, Joseph escapes his sexual predator without being violated, but Potiphar's wife accuses Joseph of molesting her, and there are consequences.

By all rights Potiphar should execute Joseph without hesitation. Potiphar is, after all, the chief executioner, and Joseph is nothing but a foreign slave who, according to his wife's account, tries forcing himself upon her. As with Reuben's violation of Bilhah, bedding the master's wife is not only a sexual violation but a thinly veiled power grab. In Joseph's case, his position as chief-of-staff in Potiphar's house makes the threat that much more credible.

It is surprising, then, that Potiphar does not kill Joseph immediately, instead throwing him into the royal prison. As we listen carefully to Potiphar's wife's words to the house servants we begin to get a clue as to why Joseph's life is spared: "See, *he* brought us a Hebrew man to play[1] with us" (39:14). She blames her husband;

---

1. The sexual connotation in this word echoes Avimelekh's discovery of Isaac "playing" with Rebecca. The same Hebrew word, *metzaḥek*, is used for both.

the tension between them is apparent. Later, when she reports the events to Potiphar, she repeats the same accusation against him: "The Hebrew servant whom *you* brought to us came to me to play with me" (39:17).[2] Her frustration at being unable to seduce Joseph is matched only by her disdain for her husband.[3]

It is quite possible that Potiphar does not trust his wife but is embarrassed into reacting to her accusation. Potiphar may need to punish Joseph, but he knows how valuable Joseph is. He wants to keep Joseph close, hoping to bring him back some day. Even as Joseph again sinks into the pit he finds favor in Potiphar's eyes.

Joseph finds favor in the eyes of his jailor as well: "God was with Joseph and extended him kindness; God put him in the favor of the officer in charge of the prison" (39:21). And once again Joseph finds himself having earned the complete confidence of his master, who "sees nothing in Joseph's hands, for God is with him" (39:23).

UNDERSTANDING JOSEPH'S TRAJECTORY

Joseph is successful at everything he does because God makes him successful, and everyone responsible for him recognizes his divine gift. The great irony is that the only one unaware of the source of his success is Joseph himself.

The pattern of Joseph being thrown into the pit only to emerge more popular than before marks his life until now and continues until he ends up as second-in-command to Pharaoh himself. Each down-phase of Joseph's cycle is preceded by his arrogance, believing that his success is his own. God tries to get Joseph to recognize what everyone else already knows, that it is He who is responsible for Joseph's impossible success, but Joseph has a hard time getting there. In his father's house it is those self-centered dreams, with himself as a god figure, which necessitate his being stripped of his position and his cloak. In Potiphar's house it is his

---

2. This is somewhat reminiscent of the Man's response when asked by God if he ate from the forbidden tree: "The woman whom *You* gave [to be] with me, she gave me from the tree."

3. Her attempts to seduce Joseph may be less about Joseph than about her relationship with her husband, or perhaps even her plot to have Joseph displace her husband.

hesitating recognition of God's role in his success which again requires that he lose his cloak (by Potiphar's wife) and be tossed into a pit.[4] Note Joseph's response to Potiphar's wife:

> Behold, my master knows nothing about what is with *me* in the house and all which he has placed in *my* hands, and he has held nothing back from *me* except for you, as you are his wife. How could I do such a great evil? It would be a sin to God. (39:8–9)

Joseph's primary argument is his loyalty to Potiphar and his refusal to violate the trust placed in him; he brings in God only at the very conclusion of his refusal. Even then, it is not clear whether the violation against God is bedding a married woman or violating the trust Potiphar has placed in him. Furthermore, it is unclear whether he is referring to a particular God or to the generic gods, or even if the phrase "to God" (*le'elohim*) might not refer to God at all but may be an expression meaning, "greatly."[5]

It seems as if the main obstacle preventing Joseph from succumbing to Potiphar's wife is the consequence from Potiphar himself. And, as indicated by the emphasized words in the above quote, buried in Joseph's words is his own inflated sense of self ("There is none greater in this house than I"); were it not for practical exigencies he would welcome her advances. It is no wonder she keeps trying. Joseph's words are not a principled objection but a form of flirting,[6] and it is that selfish, reckless playing with danger that brings him crashing down from his successful rise.

---

4. The prison he is in is later called a pit (40:15).
5. In Jonah 3:3, Nineveh is called a city that is "large to God" (*le'E-lohim*). Radak there writes that this means it is a very large city. Similarly, in Genesis 10:9, Nimrod is called a "mighty hunter before God" (*lifnei E-lohim*), which Rashbam explains as a "very mighty hunter."
6. *Midrash Tanḥuma* 39:8 sees Joseph's flirting even earlier: "Once Joseph saw himself [in charge], he began eating and drinking and doing his hair." The midrash carefully observes that Joseph's beauty is first expressed after his promotion in Potiphar's house. The only other person in the Bible described with the kind of beauty possessed by Joseph is his mother, Rachel (29:17). A similar, though slightly different, description is used for Esther (Esther 2:7).

Joseph experiences yet another round of this cycle. When he interprets the dreams of the royal butler and baker he sees his light of redemption – the butler is indebted to him and Joseph finally acknowledges God's assistance: "God has solutions, tell [your dreams] to me" (40:8). It appears that his time in prison has afforded him some time to think, as Joseph credits God for the interpretation. Yet his crediting of God is once again tinged with arrogance, as he assumes that God, who holds the keys to reading dreams, will share those keys with him. What gives Joseph the right to assume access to divine knowledge?

Beyond battling his own arrogance, Joseph needs to recognize his own contribution to his misfortunes. Indeed, after he interprets the butler's dream positively, Joseph asks that the butler remember him and help him to be raised from his imprisonment. Listen carefully, though, to Joseph's words: "For I was kidnapped from the land of the Hebrews and here, too, *I did nothing wrong* that they placed me in this pit" (40:15). God may know how to solve the mystery of the dreams and Joseph can take little credit for that, but he also takes no responsibility for his own downfalls. In his own eyes he remains a blameless victim. None of his fate is his fault.[7]

The need for Joseph to recognize both God's role in his success and his own responsibility for the calamities that befall him mirrors Jacob's need to accept responsibility for his own actions in dealing with Esau. Jacob does so only hesitantly, after a night of intense struggle, and even then only partially. Joseph, the wonder boy, struggles similarly. When he fails to recognize his own role in antagonizing his brothers leading up to his sale or his own arrogance in Potiphar's house, he needs more time to consider his life's path: "The butler did not remember Joseph; he forgot him" (40:23). Joseph must wait – and contemplate – for another two years.

---

7. This point is demonstrated through the careful use of a single word, *meuma*. Both Potiphar and the chief jailer know *nothing*, *meuma*, about Joseph's activities; they are beyond comprehension precisely because God is directing the course of events. Joseph, describing his own plight to the butler, describes himself as doing *nothing*, *meuma*, to deserve his fate, not realizing that both his fate and his success emanate from the same source. This story contains four of the six uses of *meuma* in Genesis, and it is used only three additional times in the entire Torah.

THE DREAM READER – ROUND 1

We first become aware of Joseph's specialness through exposure to his dreams. Later we are privy to his extraordinary talents running a household and attracting admirers. None of this automatically leads us to believe that Joseph will also be adept at interpreting dreams, yet this talent is the catalyst for the final turning points in his narrative.

Putting Joseph into prison distances him from his power in Potiphar's house yet ironically moves him closer to the ultimate source of power in Egypt, for he is in none other than the royal prison. It is there that he meets two of Pharaoh's estranged servants, the royal butler and baker, who are apparently accused of attempting to poison the king. Each of them dreams about his profession, and in both dreams the number three is significant. The butler dreams of a grape vine with three coiled branches, blossoming and bursting with ripe grapes. He takes the grapes and squeezes them to make wine, which he then serves to Pharaoh. The baker dreams of carrying on his head three woven baskets filled with baked goods, upon which the birds feast.

Regardless of whether Joseph understands the dreams as divine messages or the products of the servants' imaginations, the differences between the dreams are immediately apparent. The butler dreams of lush fruits that he is able to use to serve the king, while the baker dreams of royal baked goods that never see the king's table. The butler, confident in his innocence, imagines himself loyally continuing his work; the baker, convinced that he will be found guilty, sees himself as coming to the king empty-handed, or, literally, empty-headed. Interestingly, one particularly severe form of punishment in the biblical era is sometimes referred to as "sky burial," in which the body is never allowed to return to the ground as the flesh is eaten by the birds.[8] The baker's dream is essentially a vision of his own sky burial.

---

8. This fate was decreed for some of the worst kings of Israel. Jeroboam's family is fated for sky burial (I Kings 14:11), as are the families of Baasha (I Kings 16:4) and Ahab (I Kings 21:24). Sky burial denies the deceased from even having a grave marker, and signifies the absolute finality of the failed attempts to establish a dynasty. Interestingly, one of Saul's wives prevents the remnants of Saul's family from that fate (II Sam. 21:10).

No wonder, then, that Joseph interprets the butler's dream positively and the baker's dream negatively. Furthermore, assuming that Joseph – as well as the king's servants – is aware of the practices related to celebrations of Pharaoh's birthday and that it is but three days away, it is not surprising that they are both dreaming about their impending fates.[9]

Joseph gets the dreams right but misses his opportunity. He arrogantly presents himself as having the keys to divine secrets and takes no ownership over his own fate. He sees everything around him with great clarity but is still blind to himself.

THE DREAM READER – ROUND 2

Joseph's interpretation of this first pair of dreams serves no inherent, immediate value. The baker is beheaded and the butler is restored, but Joseph is promptly forgotten. It is only when Pharaoh experiences his own pair of dreams[10] that the butler deems it valuable to mention the talent of the imprisoned Hebrew slave.

A quick review of Pharaoh's dreams is quite revealing as well. In Pharaoh's first dream he is a bystander, standing impotently next to the Nile watching as the scrawny livestock devour the healthy ones. In the second dream Pharaoh disappears altogether; he is not present in the dream as the withered stalks of wheat make the healthy ones disappear. Pharaoh's dreams are distinctly un-Pharaohnic. Pharaoh the god is either impotent or absent. Moreover, his opening dream is of livestock, not of the Egyptian trade. If we recall Joseph's dream of wheat, it is distinctly uncharacteristic of the shepherding Hebrews. Joseph dreams like a Pharaoh, while Pharaoh dreams like a Hebrew.[11]

9. Joseph's use of drama and irony is quite striking, as he incorporates the subtle but eminently significant differences between the dreams into his interpretations. To the butler he says, "Pharaoh will raise your head and restore you" (40:13). To the baker he adds one more Hebrew word, yielding, "Pharaoh will raise your head *off of your body*" (40:19).

10. This is the fourth pair of dreams marking the second half of Genesis: Jacob has two dreams, one of a ladder and a second of sheep, separated by twenty years. Like Jacob, Joseph also has a pair of dreams. The butler and the baker have dreams on the same night, as does Pharaoh.

11. Pharaoh's disappearance in the second dream mirrors the disappearance of Joseph's brothers in his second dream.

While it seems clear that Joseph's interpretations are influenced by divine inspiration, he likely realizes the irony in the reversal of his dreams and Pharaoh's. Joseph does more than offer a divinely inspired interpretation. He offers a wise, humanly inspired suggestion. In this, Joseph departs from Pharaoh's great sorcerers and wise men. It also distinguishes him from the other great Jewish dream reader, Daniel, who understands Nebuchadnezzar's dreams as sealed, deterministic, and unalterable.[12] Joseph the dreamer's experience has taught him that dreams represent opportunity, not fate. Like his father, Jacob, who toils to make his dream a reality, Joseph recognizes that even divinely inspired dreams are meant to open doors, not close them.

Together with Joseph's new reading of dreams comes a new understanding of self. Just as dreams do not represent unalterable fate, neither do the waking events in our lives. We are not hapless victims of the stars; we can direct our destinies. Joseph can no longer present himself as the victim of other people's actions. He must own his behavior and take responsibility for how it impacts his life. Once he stands before Pharaoh, he never again refers to himself as a victim. When speaking with his brothers he repeatedly and confidently states that, despite their bad intentions, God was behind all the events, providing an opportunity for him and his family. And from the time he meets Pharaoh, Joseph does not cease to invoke God's name and presence. When Pharaoh says, "I hear about you that you can hear a dream and interpret it," Joseph responds, "Not I! Only God will answer for Pharaoh's well-being" (41:16).

THE EGYPTIAN VICEROY

Joseph stands before Pharaoh wiser than ever – not about dreams but about himself. He has learned to be humble, and in his humility he embraces the role that God plays in his life. Like his father, Joseph discovers himself and finds his own way of incorporating God into his selfhood. His rehabilitation seems complete, and with it he rises in Pharaoh's house. Just as Joseph loses his special cloak as his brothers fling him into the pit, and just as he loses his clothes to Potiphar's wife

---

12. Dan. 2:31–45; 4:16–24.

right before he is tossed into prison, with his rise in Pharaoh's palace he gets new clothes – royal garb – signifying his new status.

After his dream analysis and suggestion to Pharaoh, he is hailed for his access to special wisdom. Pharaoh exclaims in front of his entourage, "Can there be found like this a man within whom there is the spirit of God?" (41:38). Pharaoh hands Joseph his signet ring, dresses him in royal garments, and parades him through town in the viceroy's chariot. Only the throne will be held back from Joseph; everything else in his hands. By every measure of success, Joseph has made it – he achieves the highest position possible for a non-Pharaoh and accrues great wealth and power to augment his status.

Joseph is the hero of Egypt. His multiyear plan prepares Egypt for the worst of the famine, and the accumulated stores of grain turn out to be an unimaginable financial asset. People from far and wide come to purchase grain from Egypt, likely at exorbitant prices. Even the Egyptians themselves hunger for food, and Joseph's advanced planning turns them into Pharaoh's slaves (41:55–57; 47:18–26), having willingly given over even their lands to Pharaoh.[13] Joseph's success brings Pharaoh to new levels of wealth and power, both domestically and internationally.

But there is a dark side to all of this success. Joseph's brilliant economic plan turns wisdom into wealth, wealth into power, and power into oppression – like Solomon will do many years later[14] – and in doing so

---

13. In an extraordinary literary play, in this story the Torah uses the word *shever* both as a noun ("food") and as a verb ("to purchase food") a total of twenty-one times. As a noun, the word appears here seven times and only twice in the rest of the Bible; as a verb, it appears in this story fourteen times and only seven times in the rest of the Bible. Combined with the word *bar*, meaning "food," which appears five times in the story, we have a powerful combination of words highlighting Joseph's roles, both as provider and as economic czar. It also indicates that the food becomes especially significant as a hunger-breaker (the word *shever* can also mean "to break"), suggesting that the people are breaking and hence prepared to figuratively break themselves in order to break their hunger. Interestingly, the root R-A-V, meaning "hunger," also appears twenty-one times in the story, creating a powerful aural effect generated by the theme words.
14. See I Kings, chs. 3; 10; 12. Solomon asks God for wisdom, which brings him fame, extraordinary wealth, and power. His political power and wealth enable him to engage in two grand building projects, the Temple and his palace, requiring a heavy

creates the conditions for the eventual bitter enslavement and oppression of his own people. It won't be long before the Egyptians take the suffering Joseph imposes upon them and transfer it to the Israelites, forcing the latter to build warehouses to store the accumulated wealth of the Egyptian empire (Ex. 1:11).

On a personal level, Joseph is given an Egyptian name, Tzofnat Paaneaḥ, which in Aramaic means "the one who can decode the hidden," and an Egyptian wife, the daughter of the priest of On. He even has two children: Menashe, whose name means, "for God has helped me forget my suffering and my father's house," and Ephraim, meaning, "for God has made me fruitful in the land of my oppression." Joseph's new name puts him on a trajectory opposite that of his father; he is moving out of the covenant rather than into it. Similarly, his Egyptian wife is a red flag in Genesis. Marrying into the descendants of Ham – as did Ishmael and Esau and against which both Abraham and Isaac warned their own children – is a one-way ticket into the margins of the biblical story.

We expect the biblical story to continue without Joseph, and are surprised to discover that the narrative focus shifts away from Jacob's family to Joseph's adventures in Egypt. We watch the wonder boy fall from grace, only to rise and fall yet again, and are curious to see if he would ever be rescued. We are even pleasantly surprised to see that, after numerous failures, Joseph mutes his arrogance and incorporates God into his language, his selfhood, and his success. Joseph is saved, but his help comes from a completely unexpected source – Pharaoh himself, which introduces an entirely new challenge. Joseph's salvation doesn't bring him out of Egypt; it entrenches him in its heart. With every step forward in Egypt, Joseph becomes further removed from his family and its covenantal destiny. Joseph's success has turned him into a hero – an Egyptian hero. He is the hero of the wrong story.

---

labor tax on his constituents. That tax ultimately sparks the rebellion against his son, permanently tearing the kingdom asunder. See Micah Goodman, *Moses' Final Oration* (Or Yehuda: Dvir, 2014), 234–253.

The narrative leaves us with a gaping question. Will the man with the golden touch, firmly embedded in Egypt, be lost forever, or will he somehow reunite with his long-lost family, the one he so desperately wants to forget?[15]

---

15. *Midrash Tanḥuma* 39:8 suggests that with his rise in Potiphar's house, Joseph begins divorcing himself from his past.

Genesis 42:1–44:17

Joseph Needs to Know

J oseph's dream has come true: He is almost a Pharaoh, having built an empire out of wheat. People from near and far bow before him, pleading for food. Among those people, it turns out, is the family which tried to erase him from their midst but cannot escape the memory of what they did.

It seems that Joseph, too, suffers like his brothers, unable to erase the nightmares of his youth. Despite his Egyptian wife and Egyptian name and high Egyptian position, the name he gives his firstborn son expresses gratitude to God for helping him forget his family. But the very fact that he enshrines that sentiment in his son's name suggests that the more he tries, the less is he able to escape the memories and scars of his youth. The combination of Joseph's dreams and nightmares shapes his reactions when he sees his brothers among those coming to buy grain.

ESTRANGEMENT AND ENTANGLEMENT

Four times in the span of two verses the Torah plays on the word which in one form means to recognize and in another means to be a stranger: "Joseph saw his brothers and recognized (H-K-R) them, but made himself a stranger (N-K-R) to them.... Joseph recognized (H-K-R) his brothers but they did not recognize (H-K-R) him" (42:7–8). This is the same root used to describe Isaac's inability to recognize Jacob dressed in Esau's clothes, Jacob's demand that Laban identify any stolen possessions, the brothers' asking Jacob to identify Joseph's bloodied *ketonet*, and Tamar's private challenge that Judah identify the staff and cloth (38:25).[1] Jacob's deception of his father keeps coming back to haunt him and his children, and now it is Joseph's turn. He hides behind his Egyptian clothes and presents himself as a stranger to his brothers.

We can only imagine what is happening in Joseph's head at that moment. Anger? Vengeance? Possibly. Is he simply taunting them to watch them squirm? It is impossible to know. What is likely, though, is that seeing his brothers rattles him.[2] He has made it so far in building his new life and has worked so hard to put his past behind him, and he is now forced to contend with that past. Their arrival in Egypt presents him with essentially three options: one, to give them their wheat and hope that they never return; two, to exact some kind of vengeance and live with the knowledge that he is no better than they; and three, to figure out a third option.

What does seem clear is that despite his best efforts to forget his past, Joseph now knows that he cannot forget. He cannot simply give his brothers food and send them on their way. Their very presence forces him to face his buried past. Fascinatingly, the Torah does not describe that Joseph remembers they had sold him. Rather, it tells us that he remembers his dreams. The former would lead us to expect vengeance, but the latter directs our thinking differently. Nahmanides (42:9) is so taken by this description that he understands everything Joseph does as an attempt to ensure that his prophetic dreams come true, including that all eleven brothers bow before him. That is why, Nahmanides asserts, Joseph insists that the brothers bring Benjamin, using a ruse to hide his real intentions.

This interpretation is appealing, especially since Joseph's first demand is that one brother return to Canaan to bring Benjamin, but it is built on many assumptions, including Joseph's unerring righteousness

---

1. We will discuss this story in the next chapter.
2. Thomas Mann, *Joseph and His Brothers*, trans. H.T. Lowe-Porter (New York: Knopf, 1994), 1049–1072, has an exquisite development of Joseph's inner state.

and his belief that the dreams are prophetic. It also pits Joseph's righteous intentions against his cruel behavior toward his brothers and father in the attempt to fulfill that prophecy. Perhaps the greatest difficulty with this interpretation is that Joseph continues the ruse against his brothers even after that dream is eventually fulfilled with the arrival of Benjamin, drawing them back in and forcing a confrontation with Judah.

Rabbi Yoel Bin Nun suggests a dramatically different approach.[3] According to him, Joseph is under the impression that his sale is a premeditated plot to remove him from the covenantal family, just as Ishmael and Esau are removed. Moreover, Bin Nun suggests that Joseph suspects Jacob is complicit – or even the architect of this plot. Joseph's actions are his attempt to discern the truth of his own hypothesis.

Both Nahmanides and Bin Nun assume that Joseph is still deeply rooted in his past, whether in his dreams (Nahmanides) or in the covenant (Bin Nun). I'd like to suggest an alternative to both interpretations, based on the assumption that Joseph long abandoned his past identity and is now struggling with the question of how to resolve his past with his present and to figure out how to navigate this new complication. Ignoring his past is no longer possible but neither is fully embracing it, as that will endanger everything he has accomplished. Remembering his dream suddenly puts his Egyptian life into a context which Joseph hasn't considered: that his new life need not be a radical departure from the old but, in fact, a fulfillment of it. Joseph needs some time to think.

JOSEPH DEVELOPS A PLAN

The one thing which is clear is that Joseph does *not* have it all planned out initially, but is trying to figure out what to do, changing course when necessary. When he first accuses his brothers of being spies he insists that one of them go to Canaan to bring back Benjamin while the others remain imprisoned, but after placing them all in prison for three days he changes the terms – all will go back to Canaan to bring Benjamin while one remains hostage. While both plans seem to have the same ultimate goal, Joseph's tone has changed radically. Notice the dramatic differences:

---

3.   Yoel Bin Nun, *Pirkei HaAvot*, 165–180.

Joseph's initial comments	Joseph's revised comments
He spoke with them harshly (42:7)	
You are spies, you came to expose the nakedness of the land (42:9)	Do this and live
This is as I said, you are spies! (42:14)	I fear God (42:18)
You will be tested with this	If you are telling the truth
I swear by Pharaoh's life that you will not leave this place unless your younger brother comes here (42:15)	Bring your younger brother so that your words can be verified, so that you will not die
You will be imprisoned and your words tested if the truth is with you or not, and if not, by Pharaoh's life – You are spies! (42:16)	One of your brothers will be imprisoned in your guarded house
	You go, bring food to ease the hunger of your household (42:19)

Joseph's initial charge to his brothers reflects his own frustration, perhaps confusion. It is harsh, accusatory, and threatening, and assumes only the worst about them. He opens and closes with the accusation that they are spies[4] and threatens them if they do not do as he says. Joseph's initial words are not a plan; they are a defensive and desperate attempt to buy himself some time to figure things out. Three days later his tone changes dramatically. Now he is positive, encouraging, God-fearing, hopeful, and confident. Joseph assumes only the best about them; they are truthful and will vindicate themselves. It is during those three days that Joseph formulates a plan.

Joseph still wants Benjamin brought to him, but he will hold only one brother, not all ten. In doing so, Joseph is staging a new version of

---

4. This accusation of Joseph is reminiscent of Laban's verbal assault on Jacob, opening and closing with the accusation of theft.

his own kidnapping, where one brother (this time Simeon) disappears and the rest can live on happily. Will anyone come to rescue the brother left behind, or will they abandon Simeon the way they abandoned him? For Joseph, this is a very real test of his brothers' mettle and will help him decide whether he wants them back in his life at all.

THE PLAN FAILS

Joseph is taken by surprise at their reaction to this plan, as they understand precisely what is being asked of them and they immediately link their present dilemma with their sale of Joseph years earlier: "One said to the other, 'Alas, we are guilty regarding our brother, as we saw his pleading to us and we did not listen'" (42:21). Joseph, overhearing their words, is deeply moved. He needs to leave the scene to release the tears he held back for years. How do they instinctively link those distant events with their current crisis? Could it be that they, too, have been replaying that fateful day in their minds for the past twenty years?

Joseph sends them off, his hopes raised – but as he does he raises the stakes. Joseph instructs his people to secretly return the silver paid by his brothers for their food. Imagine the scene as they return home: having left as eleven brothers, they return with a load of grain and all their money, but with one son missing. If Jacob was not suspicious about what happened when Joseph disappeared, he will certainly be suspicious now, and will draw the right conclusion – that his sons sold off one of their own – but about the wrong son.[5] More than simply a gesture of familial kindness, sending the silver may be Joseph's attempt to have the truth about his own disappearance exposed.

This is significant for Joseph. After all, it is his father who initially creates the tension by favoring him, and it is his father who sends him to Shekhem, fully aware of the risks involved. Is his father complicit in what happened?[6] And if not, do the brothers ever share with Jacob, as they just

---

5. See Mann, *Joseph and His Brothers*, 1080. This approach is first referenced by Rabbi Abraham, son of Maimonides, in his commentary to 42:36.
6. This is similar to Bin Nun's approach, but without the theological overlay of exclusion from the covenant.

confessed among themselves, what they had done? Before Joseph can consider reintegrating his past into his present, he needs to know more.

The trip from Egypt to Canaan should not have taken more than a week or two, and the return trip should be the same. While Joseph continues his daily tasks as the provider for Egypt and the surrounding lands, he quietly and eagerly awaits the return of his brothers. Will they come back for Simeon? Will Benjamin, or maybe even Jacob, join them? As the weeks turn into months Joseph begins to despair. Perhaps they are still prepared to abandon one of their own; perhaps even Jacob is prepared to do the same. Hope for reconnecting with his family fades with each passing day. Little does Joseph know of the drama taking place back in Canaan.

BACK IN CANAAN

On the way back home, when one of the brothers discovers the silver in his saddlebag, they all become agitated: "They trembled one before the other and exclaimed, 'What is this which God has done to us?'" (42:28). Imagine the terror magnified ten times when they open their bags at home and discover that all their silver has been returned. Reflecting their angst, it is not surprising that as they retell their saga to Jacob they omit any mention of Simeon being left behind.

Unwittingly, they press precisely the buttons that Joseph intends, as Jacob bursts forth, saying: "You have bereaved[7] me of my children! Joseph is not here and Simeon is not here" (42:36). Their omission of Simeon's absence along with the discovery of the silver raises Jacob's suspicions as he links the disappearances of both his sons. Moreover, in their rendition of the story, the brothers add a line about Joseph assuring them that upon bringing the youngest brother they will be able to conduct their business in the land – which Joseph did not say. That addition not only conjures up for Jacob the possibility that the brothers are involved in Simeon's absence (is that also a "business" transaction?),

---

7. The Hebrew term, *shekhol*, has no English equivalent. It has the unique meaning of being bereaved of a child. Rebecca uses it to describe her fear of losing both of her children on the same day, should Esau kill Jacob. Now it is Jacob's turn to see himself as being bereaved of two sons. When Jacob finally accedes to send Benjamin he uses the term again, in a double language: *kaasher shakholti shakhalti.*

kaasher shakholti shakhalti.but also seems reminiscent of the story of Dinah in Shekhem, where Ḥamor promises they can do business in the land in return for Dinah. It is no wonder, then, that when the brothers ask to take Benjamin, Jacob refuses. He does not trust them.

Reuben, the eldest, is of no assistance. Reuben, who loses his father's trust when he violates Bilhah, who tries to deceive his brothers and secret Joseph back to Jacob, is the same Reuben who, when the brothers speak among themselves about their failure to heed Joseph's cries from the pit, can only muster up his version of "I told you so." Reuben, who repeatedly proves himself as a non-leader, offers Jacob to kill two of his children (presumably in "payment" for Jacob's lost sons) if he does not bring Benjamin back. Reuben is completely unaware of the absurdity of his offer. He is clueless about what it means to lose a child and apparently does not understand how ridiculous it is to suggest that Jacob kill his own grandchildren if Reuben does not return Benjamin. His offer convinces Jacob even further of Reuben's unworthiness. Jacob is less likely to release Benjamin than ever before.

It is not until many months later, when they finish all the food they brought from Egypt, that Judah intervenes, and only after his presentation does Jacob agree to send Benjamin.[8] The irony in the story continues as Jacob sends some delicacies to the Egyptian master – including balm, gum, and labdanum – the very items carried by the Ishmaelite traders who bring Joseph to Egypt (37:25). Joseph's gift of the silver sends a powerful message to Jacob; we can only imagine Joseph's reaction upon receiving a gift from Jacob containing the potent scents of his own kidnapping.

HIDING WITHOUT SEEKING

The return of the brothers with Benjamin confirms for Joseph that they are not abandoning Simeon, but Joseph must be curious about what took so long. From his previous experience he learns that by shaking them up he is able to overhear important information; perhaps it is worth trying again. This time, however, rather than the unwelcoming accusations, he brings them into his house as his special guests – and this stresses them greatly:

8. In the following chapter we will discuss Judah and his approach to Jacob.

413

> The men were frightened that they were brought to Joseph's house and they said, "It is over the matter of the silver which returned to our sacks from the first time that we are being brought, to find a pretext against us and to fall upon us to take us as slaves, and our donkeys." (43:18)

The ruse against the brothers does get them talking among themselves but reveals little other than their terror of the Egyptian lord. What else can Joseph do to learn more?

It turns out that Joseph has been playing a second game with his brothers. On their first sojourn to Egypt, when Joseph changes his tone toward the brothers after letting them out of prison, he opens by indicating that he fears God. That is indeed an interesting turn of phrase, and one wonders if Joseph is not trying to lay a subtle hint as to his true identity. It seems that Joseph wants to be found by his brothers, but is making it as difficult as possible. If they are truly seeking him then they will find him, and then he will want to be found – but if they are not seeking him then he wants the option of keeping his identity secret, as he does not want to reconnect with a past that does not want him. Indeed, when we look at Joseph's hospitality he drops numerous clues.

Take, for example, his instruction to the man in charge of his house to prepare a slaughtered animal for the meal. This is reminiscent of Abraham's instruction to the lad to prepare the young cow for his three guests. Or the presentation of water for them to wash their feet – again a replay of Abraham's hospitality. Likewise, giving food to the donkeys raises images of Rebecca's hospitality to Abraham's servant upon his arrival in Ḥaran.

If the subtle references to the family's legacy are not enough, Joseph asks about the welfare of their aging father. He also blesses Benjamin: "May God grant you grace, my son." What is more, the seating arrangements at Joseph's table – Joseph seats them in age order – certainly piques their curiosity: "The men were astounded" (43:33). Finally, since the Egyptians would not dine with the Hebrews, Joseph arranges for three eating zones: one for the Egyptians, another for the Hebrews, and a third for himself. Is Joseph not an Egyptian? Short of openly declaring his identity there is little more that he can do to lead them to what he considers an obvious conclusion. Yet despite the numerous clues, the brothers do not even come close to guessing his identity. Joseph wants to be found, but nobody is seeking him.

The brothers' lack of ability to sniff him out frustrates Joseph, as he needs to know if it is worth his while to expose himself, and that frustration is compounded by the mystery of the lengthy delay in their return. They offer no explanation, and even in their fear they reveal nothing in their intimate conversations. Joseph still does not know if his brothers want him back in their lives; in other words, he still lacks enough information to decide whether he wants *them* back in *his* life. And while Benjamin's presence moves Joseph to tears, just as overhearing his brothers' remorse earlier moves him, it is not enough. Once again, Joseph must raise the stakes. He must find out.

THE FINAL PLOY

Joseph decides to press his brothers one more time, this time switching Benjamin for Simeon by arranging to have his special goblet planted in Benjamin's pack. The significance of this is clear. While the brothers do not abandon Simeon, that may be because he is one of "them." Second only to Reuben, co-leader of the rebellion against Jacob in Shekhem, and son of Leah, he is closely allied with the power brokers in the group. But how will they relate to a son of Rachel, Jacob's beloved and the object of Leah's jealousy? Will they stand by him as they do for Simeon, or will they welcome his disposal as they had done so cavalierly with Joseph himself?

Joseph plays on the collective memory of the family encounter with Laban. When the brothers are accused of theft by Joseph's emissary they are as horrified as Jacob is by Laban's accusation, offering death for the thief (as Jacob does with Laban) and themselves as slaves to Joseph (which they understand would have been their fate with Laban).[9] Like

---

9. Also similar to Laban is the invocation of divination, *naḥesh*. Laban claims to use divination to explain his reason for holding on to Jacob, knowing that Jacob will bring him success. Some commentaries suggest that Rachel takes the *terafim* to prevent Laban from using those same powers of divination to track their escape route. That same word, *naḥesh*, appears four times in this scene to describe Joseph's using divination to discover the thief.

Jacob, they expose themselves to an invasive search to clear their names. How dare this Egyptian accuse the sons of Israel of theft!

While we the readers, or even Jacob himself, may have understood Rachel taking her father's *terafim* as a way to provoke Jacob into confronting Laban, the rest of the family is likely scandalized when they discover Rachel's theft – her pettiness nearly cost all of them their freedom. In our present situation Joseph has made sure that his special goblet is secreted in none other than Benjamin's pack: Benjamin, son of Rachel, the thief. Unlike in Jacob's confrontation with Laban, one of them is caught. Benjamin, Rachel's son, the child thief who must have learned well from his mother, is exposed.[10]

The die is thus cast. The test is in place. The brothers have an easy excuse to rid themselves of Jacob's other child from Rachel. But the brothers offer themselves, *in toto*, to Joseph as slaves. They will all serve Joseph; none will abandon Benjamin, son of Rachel. Yet Joseph is still not satisfied and he refuses their offer, insisting that only the guilty party remain. What is missing? What else can he want from them before being prepared to reintegrate his past life into his present one?

---

10. Genesis Rabba 92:8 presents the image of the brothers having the opportunity to abandon Benjamin, branding him as a thief, son of a thief.

Genesis 38:1–30; 44:18–47:10

Judah, the Redeemed Redeemer

A s we followed Joseph's path into Egypt we skipped an important narrative. Sandwiched between Joseph's sale and his arrival in Egypt, jarringly interrupting the flow of the Joseph narrative, is the story of Judah. This story actually takes place over an extended period of time, certainly more than a decade and probably closer to thirty years than to ten.[1] Not only is it thematically out of place in the narrative, it is chronologically out of place as well.

JUDAH STARTS, AND DOOMS, A FAMILY

Judah leaves his ancestral family to start his own. He marries the unnamed daughter of a Canaanite man named Shua, and she bears him three sons: Er, Onan, and Shela. Judah marries off his eldest, Er, to a woman named Tamar, but Er dies soon afterward, childless.[2]

---

1. Ibn Ezra, 38:1, calculates the minimum time necessary for this story to unfold, and it far exceeds the twenty-two years Joseph is away from his family.
2. Er is described as being evil (*ra*) in God's eyes, a subtle pun on his name (the name and the adjective being the same letters reversed).

The second son, Onan, is called upon to "uphold his brother's name" in some form of levirate marriage (this practice was widespread even before the Torah's explicit command), yet Onan, aware that the seed "will not be his," spills his seed on the ground. God, angry with Onan, kills him as well. Unprepared to have his last son suffer the fate of the first two, Judah tells Tamar to wait for Shela to be old enough to fulfill his levirate duties, while having no intention of ever marrying him to Tamar.

Judah's marriage to a Canaanite is itself dreadfully problematic, and emblematic of breaking his ties with his birth family. Judah's breaking of the taboo founded by Abraham signifies his purposefulness in leaving his clan; he rejects Jacob and the covenant. As opposed to his older brothers, Judah's rebellion against Jacob is not to compete for the leadership of the family but to start a new clan.

Judah's plan is substantively disrupted with the death of his two eldest sons and his refusal to allow the third to marry the widow, whom he blames for the deaths of Er and Onan. In preventing Shela from marrying Tamar, however, he must also deny Shela[3] marriage to any other woman, for when he is ready to marry he is obligated to marry Tamar. In his effort to protect the youngest son he is effectively dooming his new family to extinction.

TAMAR TAKES THE INITIATIVE

In time, Judah's anonymous wife dies, and he comforts himself by attending his sheep-shearing festival. Meanwhile, with the passage of time, Tamar realizes that she is in a bind – legally she is bound to Shela and forbidden to marry anyone else, yet she understands that she will never be given to him. Dressing up as a prostitute, she positions herself strategically at the crossroads. With her face covered, Judah has relations with her without being aware that it is Tamar sharing his bed, a bizarre replay of Jacob's wedding night with Leah. When it comes time

---

3. "Shela" actually comes from a root meaning to fool or deceive, exactly what Judah is doing to Tamar. Judah is described as being in Keziv when Shela is born. Keziv could be the name of a place, but it also means to deceive or disappoint. The first half of this story points to the great disappointment which is Judah and his deception of Tamar.

to pay her for her services it turns out that Judah has no ready means of payment, and Tamar requests collateral[4] – Judah's staff, seal, and cloak – until he can send a goat for payment.

Tamar's subterfuge works. First, she conceives as a result of her encounter with Judah, thus ensuring that she will remain within his clan despite Judah's best efforts. Second, Judah does not realize who she is throughout the encounter. When he later sends a goat with his friend to pay the prostitute, everyone in the area denies knowledge of any such woman there. Judah remains a debtor while Tamar retains his staff, cloak, and signet ring.

This tale spans many years – including Judah's initial marriage and the birth of his three children, who in time, each reach marriageable age. According to the Torah text, two of Judah's grandchildren from Tamar, conceived only after Shela reaches the age of marriage, are among those who descend with Jacob to Egypt (46:12). Given that only twenty-two years pass from the sale of Joseph until the family's final trek to Egypt, this extended account must have begun long before the sale of Joseph, and its inclusion here as a break in the Joseph narrative is clearly designed to inject necessary themes into that broader narrative.[5]

The astute reader already begins to notice how this story is being subtly woven into the larger narrative. Both Joseph and Judah marry foreign women from the house of the accursed Ham; both have seduction stories (one successful and one unsuccessful); both protagonists lose their clothes in a deception scene; both have goats as part of the deception (the brothers use goat blood to stain Joseph's tunic and fool their father, while Judah attempts to pay Tamar with a goat); and both Joseph and Judah lose their signs of authority – Joseph has his special *ketonet* torn from him, and Judah loses his staff, seal, and cloak.

---

4. The Hebrew for collateral is *eravon*, which is an alliteration built on Tamar's two dead husbands, Er and Onan (in Hebrew, *er veonan*).

5. The precise moment of intersection between the story of Judah and Tamar and that of the sale of Joseph, in which Judah also plays a prominent – though less than exemplary – role, is a matter for further exploration.

SHIRKING RESPONSIBILTY

Judah's abdication of responsibility is his signature behavior throughout the first half of this account. He denies Tamar's marriage to Shela but also refuses to be responsibly honest with her about it. He is equally irresponsible to his son; how long will he keep Shela from marrying? In his shortsighted drive to save Shela's life, he destines his younger son to permanent bachelorhood, burying the future and his dreams for establishing a new dynasty.[6] This image of Judah is consistent with his behavior in the sale of Joseph. It is Judah's idea to sell Joseph rather than kill him, with the primary motive being profit rather than morality, and like his brothers – or perhaps even leading them – he is prepared to let his father suffer in the darkness of Joseph's fate rather than own up to his deeds. Even more than Jacob, Judah has mastered the art of avoiding responsibility.

Ironically, after Judah returns to his ancestral clan, his distorted model of responsibility is emulated by his own father. When the brothers return from Egypt the first time and inform their father that their Egyptian master will not countenance their return without Benjamin, Jacob steadfastly refuses to release him – even when the food stocks are depleted. Just as Judah is prepared to sacrifice his family's future to save his youngest son, Jacob is prepared to sacrifice his entire family just to prevent Benjamin from leaving his side.

When Tamar's pregnancy becomes apparent, Judah is informed. Still unaware that it is his child she is carrying, he pronounces her infidelity and a death sentence. Without so much as a question, not to mention an investigation, Judah is all too eager to have her removed

---

6. Judah's selfish, shortsighted behavior is replicated by his son Onan, who would rather spill his seed on the ground and have no children at all than have a child who will uphold the name of the deceased Er.

   Ironically, the one area in which Judah is prepared to be responsible is his business dealings, insisting that the prostitute be paid. When his friend is unable to find the rightful payee, Judah is beside himself. In an interesting twist, he finds himself in a similar position when he and his brothers return from Egypt, their bags filled with grain but their money still intact. The fear of being accused of financial misdeed is terrifying to them all, perhaps a carryover from what they witnessed as children of their own father's drive for financial uprightness.

from his life so that he can move on. Her pregnancy could not have been more convenient.

JUDAH'S MOMENT OF TRUTH

All this, however, takes a dramatic turn when Tamar pulls out her ace. Clandestinely, she sends a message to Judah with the seal, staff, and cloak he had left with her, indicating that the owner of those items is the father of her child: "By the man to whom these items belong am I pregnant. Recognize (*haker na*), to whom belong this seal and staff?" (38:25).[7] Judah can conveniently keep those items for himself and deny the message from Tamar – consistent with his behavior until this point.

But Judah surprises, and without hesitation he announces her innocence and his own guilt: "She is more righteous than I,"[8] he declares, "for I did not give her to my son Shela" (38:26). Not only does he take responsibility for her pregnancy, he takes responsibility for improperly denying her rightful marriage to his son.[9]

Judah's acknowledgment is nothing less than life-changing. Faced with the opportunity to solve his problem at the expense of Tamar's life, he chooses instead to embrace his own wrongdoing. In recognizing his role vis-à-vis Tamar, Judah begins a process of personal transformation. He now takes responsibility, even at the cost of losing his reputation. Just as Rachel stealing the *terafim* pushes Jacob into a dramatic turnaround and into confronting Laban, Tamar's secret message to Judah forces him to confront himself.

The effects of Judah's transformation are immediate and dramatic. In the first half of the story, Judah loses two children and demonstrates irresponsible behavior. In the latter half, where he acts responsibly, Tamar bears him two children – from whom the rest of the historic

---

7. Once again, the *haker na* phrase haunts Jacob's family. It is used to describe the brothers' deception of Jacob as well as Joseph's deception of his brothers.
8. According to Rashi, his declaration can be read as, "She is righteous; [the child is] from me."
9. This is mirrored in the declaration of the brothers that the tragedy befalling them is the result of their callousness to Joseph's cries twenty years earlier.

leadership of Judah's clan will emerge.[10] Earlier, Judah sacrifices his future for his present; now, in return for the sacrifice of his present, he receives a new future.

JUDAH'S IMPACT ON JACOB

We noticed above that Judah models self-destructive behavior for Jacob. Judah's shortsighted attempt to save Shela at the expense of the future of his clan is mimicked in Jacob's refusal to let Benjamin go to Egypt at the risk of the family's starvation. Now the transformed Judah again impacts on Jacob, but in reverse: Judah convinces Jacob to release his youngest. In admitting his responsibility to Tamar, Judah sacrifices his present to ensure a greater future for the family. He expects no less of his father. Listen carefully to Judah's words:

> Send the lad with me; we will arise and go, live and not die, both us and you and our children. I will take personal responsibility for him; you may demand him from my hand. Should I not bring him to you and present him before you I will be a sinner to you for all time. (43:8–9)

The language Judah uses, "I will take personal responsibility," not only echoes his experience with Tamar but uses the same language. The collateral Judah left with Tamar is called in Hebrew an *eravon* (from the root A-R-V); the word he uses here for "responsibility" is *e'ervenu*, from the same root. The message he delivers to Jacob is one of personal commitment and responsibility.

It is hard to know whether Judah's phrasing and meter are chosen intentionally, but they are nearly identical to language Judah hears his father use years earlier. As Jacob stands before Laban defending his integrity he declares that he has taken personal responsibility for any losses to the sheep incurred over the years. Note the remarkable similarity:

---

10. The story of the birth of these twins is remarkably similar to the birth of Jacob and Esau. There is a struggle in the womb, even at the moment of birth, over which child will emerge first. For more on this, see Zakovitch, *Jacob: Unexpected Patriarch*, 23–25.

Jacob to Laban (31:39)	Judah to Jacob (43:9)
anokhi ahatena	*anokhi e'ervenu*
miyadi tevakshena	*miyadi tevakshenu*

Judah watches his father regain his integrity, internalizes that as he rises to Tamar's challenge, and now reminds his father of that very integrity.

Judah's embrace of responsibility impacts on his role in both of his clans, the one he once abandoned and the one he tries to start. His personal redemption in his new clan opens the door to the redemption of his ancestral family. In contrast to his personal *haker na* abdication regarding Joseph's tunic, the rehabilitated Judah makes himself Benjamin's personal guarantor. Those words likely take Jacob by surprise (as he knows the old Judah well) and Jacob responds immediately, planning the dreaded trip for his beloved youngest.

When we first traced Joseph's path to Egypt we noted that following his sale, the narrative should have continued with the clan in Canaan. This story of Judah is precisely the narrative we expected. Judah stands in stark contrast to Joseph: Joseph is the man whose success leads him to failure; Judah is the man who transforms his own failure into greatness. Judah's personal redemption, sparked by Tamar, opens the door for Jacob to redeem himself, and ultimately for Joseph to redeem the family.

JUDAH'S TRANSFORMATIVE SPEECH

At the end of the previous chapter we wondered what Joseph is waiting for. After all, haven't the brothers cast their fate together with Benjamin, insisting that they will all remain as Joseph's slaves? It seems that the answer is embedded in Judah's speech as he confronts Joseph, one which touches a number of core areas, including Judah's own transformation. To fully appreciate the speech we will cite it here in full, despite its length:

> Please, my master, let your servant speak to your ear and do not be angry with your servant, for you are as Pharaoh. My master asked his servants, saying: "Have you a father or a brother?" We said to my master, "We have an aged father and a small child of his *zekunim*; his brother died and only he was left from his mother,

and his father loves him." You said to your servants, "Bring him
down to me, and let me set my eyes upon him." We said to my
master, "The lad cannot leave his father, for if he were to leave
his father, [his father] would die." You said to your servants, "If
your youngest brother does not come down with you, you will
not see my face again."

It happened that when we went up to your servant, our
father, and we told him the words of my master, our father said,
"Return, buy for us a bit of food." We said to him, "We cannot go
down. If our youngest brother is with us then we can go down,
for we cannot see the face of the man if our youngest brother is
not with us." Your servant, our father, said to us, "You know that
my wife bore me two children. One went out from me and I said,
'Oh, he's been torn to shreds – I haven't seen him since.' Should
you take this one and some tragedy befalls him, you would bring
me to a bad grave."

And now, when I return to your servant, my father, and
the lad is not with us – for his soul is intertwined with the lad's,
and when he sees that the lad is not here, he will die, and your
servants would have brought our father's old age to his grave in
agony. For your servant has guaranteed the lad from my father,
saying, "If I do not bring him to you then I will be a sinner to
my father for all time." So now, let your servant sit in place of the
lad, as a servant to my master, so that the lad may go up with his
brothers. For how can I go up to my father without the lad with
me, lest I see the evil which will find my father? (44:18–34)

A number of critical elements make this speech so powerful. First, Judah
retells the events with extraordinary pathos, righteous indignation, and
artful reshaping of those events; his oration likely reminds Joseph of
Jacob's impassioned soliloquy of injustice to Laban.[11] In Judah's carefully
crafted version, Joseph never accuses the brothers of wrongdoing – neither

---

11. For example, the phrase Judah attributes to Jacob's understanding of what happened to Joseph is *tarof toraf* ("torn apart"), echoing Jacob's comments to Laban
that he never brought a *tereifa* (a torn animal) for which he did not accept personal

of being spies nor of theft. In fact, Judah subtly suggests that it is not the brothers who did anything wrong but Joseph himself, first by inquiring about their family and then by wanting to unjustly and cruelly keep behind the most special of them. Finally, with all the above, Judah remains respectful, seven times calling Joseph "my master" and thirteen times referring to himself or his family (including Joseph's father) as Joseph's servants.

Second, Judah inadvertently touches on numerous issues sensitive to Joseph. For the first time, Joseph hears one of the brothers speak about him. From their perspective he is simply "gone," but in Jacob's eyes he was torn apart by a wild beast. Joseph must have spent countless hours wondering about his father's role in his sale. Aside from knowing that his father deliberately sends him into a dangerous operation, Joseph is likely plagued by a simple question: Why does his father, a wealthy clan leader from a respected family, never try to find him?[12] Joseph now hears that his father thinks him long dead, perhaps stirring his own guilt for not reaching out to his father once he gained the ability to do so. And he now hears that his father is aged and fragile – even the removal of his youngest son could bring about his untimely death. Joseph wonders: can his insistence on bringing Benjamin have already killed Jacob?

Most powerful, however, is Judah's description of Jacob's comment: "You know that my wife bore me two children." To hear one of Leah's children describe Jacob referring to Rachel as his wife, meaning his *only* wife, yet remain committed to the father who regards their mother as someone less beloved, is profoundly moving. It means that the jealousy of the brothers for their mother has passed, that they accept their father's preference for Rachel without rejecting him. It is that preference which began Joseph's domestic troubles. Their ability to move beyond it challenges Joseph to move beyond his hesitation to bring his past life into his present one.[13]

---

responsibility. Beyond that, like Jacob, whose retort to Laban includes recounting a twenty-year history, Judah lays out the entire story. Of course, the word *arev*, guarantor, plays a central role in both narratives.

12. According to Nahmanides, he is waiting for the fulfillment of his dream. According to Yoel Bin Nun, he suspects that his father evicted him from the covenantal family.

13. This echoes the reunion between Jacob and Esau, in which (according to Rashbam) Esau has long forgotten the injustice done to him while Jacob is still stuck in his past.

Third, Judah consciously stresses one issue which is significant to his plea for Benjamin, but significant to Joseph in a profoundly different way – his own personal responsibility. The lack of responsibility is Judah's greatest weakness before Tamar presents him with his fateful choice, and his preparedness to accept responsibility is what convinces Jacob to send Benjamin with him. Joseph never heard any of his brothers take personal responsibility. Even recently, he has heard Reuben absolve himself from the communal responsibility which the others accepted. Judah's cavalier, "Let us sell him," has rung in his ears for decades, and is now replaced by Judah declaring himself Benjamin's personal guarantor. Even beyond this, the flip side of Joseph's suspicions regarding his father's role in his disappearance is the possibility that his father is not involved, and if so, then how could his brothers have so cruelly tortured his father, their father? Judah's personal commitment is not only to Benjamin but to Jacob.

Joseph has been unsure whether he can embrace his family and integrate them into his life. He has also been hoping that they will discover him, their unconscious seeking of Joseph allowing Joseph to consciously embrace them. Even though his brothers do not discover him, Joseph slowly and painfully discovers that they are not the same regarding their relations to each other, their acceptance of Jacob's preference for Rachel and her children, their responsibility to Jacob, and now, even their own sense of personal accountability. Their transformations do not heal Joseph's wounds, but they do help put them behind him and live with them, and embrace his estranged family.

REUNITING THE FRACTURED FAMILY

Joseph can hold back no longer. Listen to the first words out of his mouth: "I am Joseph, your brother! Is my father still alive?" (45:3). Two things stand out in this release of pent-up emotion. First is Joseph's declaration of brotherhood. Listening to Judah's tale convinces Joseph of their preparedness for brotherhood. He indicates that he, too, seeks their kinship – just as he earlier seeks out his brothers in Shekhem. Second, Judah's description of Jacob's frailty and yearning for his "true" sons, the children of Rachel, has melted Joseph's resolve: "Is my father still alive?"

Readers of the story exult in joy as years of tension are brought to resolution. The mask is dropped, the family reunited. The language of Joseph revealing himself to his brothers is quite powerful as it echoes Jacob's deception of his father, but in reverse. When Joseph first announces himself, his brothers recoil in terror. Seeing that, he implores them, "Approach me." The verb he uses, N-G-SH, is the same used by Isaac asking Jacob to come closer so that Isaac can smell (and thereby identify) him, and the twist is fascinating: Isaac's request is an unsuccessful attempt to uncover Jacob's identity, while Joseph's is a successful attempt to unmask himself.[14]

Joseph's speech to his brothers is filled with pathos and forgiveness, and the brothers never have an opportunity to respond.[15] He has it all figured out: There will be a reunion of the entire family. He bears no grudge; after all, it is God's plan that brought him to Egypt to save his family from the famine. He has fulfilled his potential as the family unifier, albeit in ways that even in his dreams he could not imagine. He is successful beyond belief; they should all join him in Egypt. He sends his royal chariots to pack up the family and bring them to him, and it is these royal chariots which convince the skeptical Jacob that indeed, "Joseph is still alive and it is he who rules over all Egypt" (45:26).

JUDAH IS SENT AHEAD

For Jacob, the impossibly good news about Joseph probably raises many questions. How, exactly, did Joseph escape the wild animal which shredded and bloodied his special tunic, and end up as an Egyptian viceroy? If Joseph is, indeed, the ruler of Egypt, why does he put this family through so much agony? These questions, however, deal with

14. Interestingly, the same verb is used to describe Judah's approach to Joseph just prior to his speech. Could that be the Torah's way of describing Judah's hidden motive – the unmasking of this Egyptian tormenter – or is it meant to explain Joseph's N-G-SH as the result of Judah's?
15. After Joseph weeps on Benjamin's neck, his brothers are able to speak with him (45:14). This finally reverses the historic enmity expressed even before Joseph's dreams, where his brothers could not speak with him civilly as a result of his being favored by Jacob (37:4).

the mystery of the past. More important ones face Jacob, and the reader, about the future. Who, or what, has Joseph become? Will Jacob find in Joseph the same lad who left him twenty-two years earlier, or will he find an Egyptian prince showing kindness to the aging father from the old country?

Jacob has every reason to fear, especially when he recalls his own sojourn from home. After twenty years in Laban's house he is nearly completely absorbed into Laban's culture, and he is saved only by an act of God (with an assist from Rachel). Without divine protection and assistance Joseph stands no chance of maintaining who he is, and the evidence from the past few months of famine does not bode well.

Not only does Jacob have good reason to fear, the biblical reader should be concerned as well. When Pharaoh hears that Joseph's brothers have arrived, there is noticeable relief. Pharaoh had apparently been apprehensive all along about Joseph's mysterious origins and whether he would one day return to them. Pharaoh's reaction to the brothers' arrival is unequivocal:

> Load up your beasts and go, return to the land of Canaan. Then take your father and your households and come back to me, that I may give you the best of the land of Egypt and you will live off the fat of the land. (45:17–18)

Pharaoh suggests that they leave their (Canaanite) belongings behind, as he will provide them with the finest that Egypt has to offer (45:20). Pharaoh's plan is clear; Joseph's family will merge into Egypt. Joseph apparently has a similar idea, as he gives each of them a change of clothes, likely Egyptian clothes, to ease their transition into Egyptian society. Interestingly, he gives Benjamin five changes of clothes and three hundred pieces of silver, probably preparing Benjamin for a place next to him in the Egyptian aristocracy.

Joseph is aware that the transition into Egyptian culture will not be smooth. When the brothers do arrive, he instructs them to tell Pharaoh that they are shepherds, to justify his decision to settle them in Goshen, apart from the Egyptian wheat-growers (46:34). While Pharaoh is planning for a fast acculturation to Egypt and Jacob plans to resist that acculturation, Joseph tries to engineer a generation-long process, perhaps with Benjamin playing a significant role in the transition.

The Torah provides additional evidence for the reader to be concerned: "Joseph accumulated food, a lot of food, as numerous as the sands of the sea, until it could no longer be counted because there was no number [large enough]" (41:49). The phrases here remind us of God's promise to Abraham that his children will be uncountable (15:5), as numerous as the sands of the sea (22:17). For Joseph, the Egyptian grain has replaced the covenantal promise of prodigious progeny. Egypt is the new future.

Jacob has resisted attempts to be absorbed by Laban, Esau, and Shekhem, but those attempts, by people Jacob sees as antagonists, pale in comparison to this new challenge – resisting the embrace of his beloved, long-lost son. So troubled is Jacob by this turn of events that God comes to reassure him: "Do not fear the descent to Egypt, for I will make you a great nation there. I will go down with you to Egypt and I will also bring you up from there" (46:3–4).[16] These words should comfort Jacob, but God's next statement undoes that comfort: "Joseph will lay his hand on your eyes." This last statement could be a reference to the practice of closing the eyes of the deceased at the moment of death,[17] or it could mean that Joseph will take care of everything.[18] If Joseph is the Egyptian grain-master who can torture his family and hide his identity so thoroughly from both the Egyptians and his own brothers, can Jacob

---

16. Up until this point, Jacob may have believed that his twenty-plus years in Laban's house fulfilled the conditions of the Covenant between the Pieces: he was a stranger in a foreign land who was overworked and oppressed. With God's message to him, however, that illusion is shattered. Far from being behind him, his exile is about to begin.

We have already noted that the eleven books of *toledot* in Genesis follow a pattern in which each new book opens by repeating a critical element from the prior one (see Introduction, note 8). The detailed list of Jacob's seventy descendants in 46:8–27 is repeated briefly in the opening of Exodus (1:1–5), thus highlighting Jacob's essential role as the father of the Israelite nation. It is the experience of that nation, not of Jacob the individual, which serves as fulfillment of the Covenant between the Pieces.

17. Ibn Ezra.
18. Rashbam.

truly trust him? Can he depend on Joseph to ensure the future of the covenant? Moreover, God's language to Jacob evokes Abraham's *lekh lekha* journey: "They took their cattle and their belongings which they acquired in the land of Canaan, and they arrived in Egypt" (46:6). This is remarkably parallel to the language in 12:5, but in reverse! Abraham's *lekh lekha* brings him into the land, while Jacob's journey takes him out, permanently.[19]

In fear, Jacob turns to Judah, the only son he has learned to trust. Judah earns Jacob's respect because he turns a crisis into an opportunity for self-redemption and he turns his self-redemption into redemption for Jacob, and his masterful oratory ultimately serves as the impetus for Joseph to take on the role of the family redeemer. Jacob sends Judah ahead to Goshen to "instruct" (46:28), likely meaning to ensure that Jacob is received properly, including establishing that Jacob's arrival is not to be read as a surrender of identity. The Midrash, picking up on the enigmatic statement, suggests that Jacob sends Judah ahead to set up a yeshiva for Torah study.[20] While anachronistic, the rabbis of the midrash were trying to convey a powerful idea: Jacob wants to ensure that the family's identity will not get devoured by the dominant Egyptian culture.

On at least a symbolic level, Judah is successful. Rather than wait for Jacob to come to the palace, Joseph travels to Goshen to greet Jacob and personally escort him to the meeting with Pharaoh. That largely symbolic act orchestrated by Judah notwithstanding, Jacob is still concerned. What will the future bring if it is placed in the hands of a son who is married to the daughter of an Egyptian priest, whose children are being raised as Egyptian princes, and who looks, speaks, and acts like Egyptian aristocracy?

For the reader, this question has a slightly different formulation. Joseph, the hero of the Egyptian story, is now the hero of Jacob's story as well – he saves the clan from famine. Joseph, who as a lad

---

19. Although Pharaoh tells them not to bother with their earthly belongings, as he will provide for them, Jacob insists on retaining the objects which connect him to his home and help preserve his identity as a non-Egyptian.

20. Genesis Rabba 95:3.

shepherded with Leah's sons but played with the sons of the maid-servants (37:2), successfully bridges the divide in the family and reunites it after a lengthy period of painful division. But what are the implications of that reunification? Will Joseph become part of Jacob's narrative, including the covenant with God, or will he co-opt the narrative and absorb Jacob and the entire family into his own story as the successful immigrant to Egypt?

Genesis 47:28–50:26

The Struggle for Legacy

T he great Abrahamic narrative, spanning more than ten chapters in Genesis, essentially ends with the marriage of Isaac. We hear almost nothing about Abraham afterward other than his death. The same is true for the much shorter narrative of Isaac's life. Once Jacob leaves home, the focus shifts; Isaac disappears, returning to the narrative only to be buried. Jacob is the only one of the Patriarchs to return to the central stage of the narrative even after his children get married.

From the time Jacob leaves Laban, he maintains control of the family despite five rebellions: Reuben's incident with Bilhah, Simeon and Levi's massacre of Shekhem, the sale of Joseph, Judah's attempt to break away, and Joseph cutting off all contact with his family even after rising to power in Egypt. Ultimately, his sons remain in his household and he decides who leaves the house and when; the brothers will not make a move without him.

With the invitation from Joseph, Jacob faces his greatest challenge yet. Jacob escapes from Laban's attempt to swallow him through a combination of deceit (a midnight flight) and ultimately a divorce – Jacob and Laban part ways at the *matzeva* stone, and the pile of rocks Jacob builds becomes a boundary to eternally separate Jacob from his father-in-law. Esau's attempt to merge Jacob into his nation ends similarly. Even though Jacob has almost admitted his wrongdoing to his elder brother, offering him the blessing in return and choosing to be Israel, their meeting ends with a parting of ways and a less-than-honest promise by Jacob to eventually join his brother. Esau returns to Mount Se'ir while Jacob continues his plodding return to Canaan and his ancestral home. And after the rape of Dinah, when Ḥamor offers a merger of the clans, Jacob avoids it via the sons who learn well from their father. They, too, engage in deception, and follow it with a massacre to prevent the merger and hasten Jacob's departure from that place.

The challenge with Joseph, however, is far more complicated. Jacob is committed to keeping the family intact, despite the many obstacles. He is now intent on the final reunification of the family, but faces a battle for the family's future – will it be Jacob's vision into which Joseph will be drawn, or will Joseph absorb the family into Egypt? How can Jacob win this battle without divorcing himself from Joseph? How can Jacob ensure that his vision wins without alienating the son who has the acumen and capacity to steer a different course?

Three key encounters in Jacob's final days highlight the tension between father and son.

JACOB SUMMONS JOSEPH

With Joseph's assistance, Jacob settles with his clan in the land of Goshen, away from the political and cultural center of Egypt where Joseph continues to dwell. Seventeen years later, Jacob senses that his end is near and summons Joseph to his bedside:

> If, please, I find favor in your eyes, place your hand under my thigh and do for me a kindness and truth – do not bury me in Egypt. When I rest with my fathers, carry me from Egypt and bury me in their burial place." (47:29–30)

After an extended stay in Egypt, Jacob is familiar with its culture, and particularly its culture of death. In Egypt, death is merely a passageway into a new form of embodied life. The body is preserved and entombed in an elaborate structure with the many provisions it needs in the next world. The more important the deceased, the grander the structure. Jacob wants no part of that.

Moreover, like Abraham, who understands that a final resting place designates permanence, Jacob understands that Egypt cannot be his final resting place. Egypt is but a stop on his long and complex journey, and that journey must end back in the land promised to his ancestors and enshrined in the covenant. No foreign land can provide the anchor for the future of Jacob's clan. He must be buried in the only place he can call home.

The parallel to Abraham is strengthened by a bizarre symbolic act, placing the hand under the thigh. While it may be difficult to decipher the specific symbolism of that act,[1] it appears only twice in the Bible, once as Abraham asks his servant to find a wife for Isaac from his homeland and another as Jacob asks Joseph to bury him in Canaan. Like Abraham, Jacob is worried about his future, and believes that the request is essential for ensuring that future. And, like Abraham, Jacob insists on an oath.

Yet this is where the two differ. Abraham demands an oath as an integral part of the request that his servant place his hand under his thigh, while Jacob demands the oath even *after* Joseph agrees to fulfill his father's request (47:31). Why would an oath be necessary over and above the symbolic act, especially when the son responds, "I will do as you said"?[2]

It seems that Jacob does not fully trust that Joseph will follow through, even after the symbolic commitment. In hindsight, Jacob's initial request of Joseph indicates that he is not expressing merely a preference for burial in Canaan, he is rejecting Egypt as a possibility. Look at what he could have said and what he actually does say:

---

1. In Jacob's case the act may have an additional meaning, as the hip is where Jacob is wounded in his mysterious nocturnal encounter.
2. It is possible that while Joseph verbally agrees to his father's request, he never performs the symbolic act of the hand under the thigh, as there is no mention of it in the text. If so, Jacob's request for an oath is even more significant because Joseph seems to initially deny his father's request.

What Jacob could have said	What Jacob said
If, please, I find favor in your eyes,	If, please, I find favor in your eyes,
	place your hand under my thigh and do for me a kindness and truth – do not bury me in Egypt.
when I rest with my fathers,	When I rest with my fathers, *carry me from Egypt and*
bury me in their burial place.	bury me in their burial place.

The phrases "do not bury me in Egypt" and "carry me from Egypt," which Jacob could have omitted, point to his rejection of Egypt and compound his mistrust of Joseph ("place your hand under my thigh"). Even the request that Joseph do for him "a kindness and truth" suggest that from Jacob's perspective the burial in Canaan is a truth; its necessity is clear. But Jacob understands that Joseph fundamentally disagrees with Jacob's assumptions about Egypt and Canaan, and therefore frames it as a request for kindness from Joseph.

Joseph and Jacob understand each other, and recognize that each sees the future of the clan differently. Joseph sees it in Egypt, with Canaan being the primitive old country left behind. Jacob believes that Joseph's infatuation with Egypt is misguided and that the future is in the land of his fathers, the land of the covenant. Were Jacob's concern merely about his burial place he would likely have summoned Judah, the son he trusts more than any other. It is clear that he is more interested in confronting Joseph than on ensuring his appropriate burial.

Jacob asks for an oath and Joseph obliges. That seems to be enough to allay Jacob's concerns, and so he bows to Joseph.[3]

JACOB FALLS ILL

Sometime later a messenger informs Joseph that Jacob has fallen ill. Joseph takes his two sons, Menashe and Ephraim, and brings them

---

3. Jacob's bowing to Joseph only *after* Joseph swears his oath may be further indication of the tension. Jacob cedes authority to Joseph only once he is sufficiently secure that Joseph will fulfill his request. As such, Jacob becomes Israel as he resumes the reins of his family's destiny.

to Jacob's bedside. Jacob sits up on his bed and tells Joseph the following:

> El Shaddai appeared to me in Luz, in the land of Canaan, and blessed me. He said to me: I will make you fruitful and numerous – you will be a community of nations – and I will give this land to your seed after you as a permanent holding. And now, the two sons who were born to you in Egypt prior to my arrival, they are mine; Ephraim and Menashe will be mine, like Reuben and Simeon. Those whom you father afterward will be yours; they will be called after their brothers with regard to their inheritance. And I, on my return from Padan Aram, Rachel died upon me in the land of Canaan, some distance from Efrat, and I buried her there on the road to Efrat, which is Beit Leḥem. (48:3–6)

This speech appears to be a jumbled collection of disconnected thoughts without a coherent message. What is the connection between God's promise and Jacob's taking Ephraim and Menashe as his own? What does it even mean for Jacob to take the two boys as his own, and how does that connect with Rachel's untimely death?

When we look further we realize that Jacob has conveniently conflated two separate divine messages connected only by the location of their delivery. God's promise to make Jacob numerous, particularly as he formulates it here,[4] is given only upon Jacob's return *from* Laban's house (35:11), while the promise of the land is first given on his way *to* Laban's house (28:13). It is precisely in this blending of messages that we have a clue regarding the structure of Jacob's speech. He opens recalling the divine message on his way to Ḥaran, that he will be numerous, and closes with how that message is challenged by the death of Rachel upon his return. Since, in Jacob's eyes, Rachel is his primary wife and the only one whose children can be considered a fulfillment of the divine promise, according to Jacob, then, God's promise has yet to be fulfilled. As such, in order to fulfill the divine promise, Rachel's

---

4. This includes the use of the name El Shaddai and the terms "to be fruitful" and "to be made numerous."

grandchildren – Joseph's sons – need to be surrogates for the additional children Jacob never has from Rachel.[5]

Further examination of the passage, however, reveals an additional layer Jacob has carefully interwoven. In his opening line, he references Canaan as the land of revelation, in the following verse he notes that God promises *that* land to him, and in his closing line he goes to great lengths to describe the geographical location of Rachel's death and burial – *not* in Padan Aram but in the land of Canaan, just shy of Efrat, on the road to Efrat which is Beit Leḥem. Jacob's message is clear: the land of the family's past and future, the land of divine revelation and promise, is Canaan. If that were not enough, his identification of Menashe and Ephraim is also geographically linked. They are the two sons born to Joseph *in Egypt.*

When we put the entire speech together it becomes clear that Jacob wants to transform Menashe and Ephraim from Egyptian children born to an Egyptian lord into Hebrew children tied to their ancestral land of Canaan. Making these children his own means leapfrogging Joseph in the chain of inheritance: they get their inheritance, their portion in the Promised Land, directly from Jacob.

The conversation which follows now actually makes sense and is quite meaningful. After speaking about Menashe and Ephraim, who have been standing at Jacob's bedside, and co-opting them as his own, Jacob asks, "Who are these?" The question is not like Isaac's question trying to identify the son awaiting his blessing,[6] but an existential one. Now that Jacob has claimed the boys for himself, he challenges Joseph to acknowledge his decision: "Who are they, your Egyptian children or my Hebrew ones?" Observe carefully Joseph's response: "They are *my* children, which God gave *me, here*" (48:9). Joseph refuses Jacob's

---

5. The theme of the two children runs throughout the narrative. Jacob loses two children (Joseph and Simeon), as does Judah. Judah's two children are "replaced" via Tamar's twins, and now Jacob is claiming Joseph's two children as replacements for the children denied him from Rachel. Furthermore, Reuben offers two of his children to Jacob should he fail to return Benjamin.

6. Note that even though the Torah does indicate that Jacob's eyes were heavy from age, that description only appears *following* the conversation, as Jacob prepares to bless them.

request, insisting that the boys are his – Egyptians, not Hebrews. They belong to the future of the clan, in Egypt, not to its humble beginnings in the backwater of Canaan.[7]

Jacob does not give up easily in the tug-of-war between himself and Joseph regarding the custody of the boys. Joseph presents them to Jacob for his blessing, but they remain "between his knees" (48:12). Ultimately, Joseph bows before his father, reversing the earlier scene, ceding the children to Jacob's blessing.

Jacob places his hands, intentionally crossing them, upon their heads. He opens his blessing invoking their ancestry and the God with whom their predecessors had a profound relationship, continues by referencing the "angel" who redeemed him from his encounters with foreign cultures which nearly devoured him (Laban and Esau), and concludes with the intonation: "Let my name and the name of my fathers, Abraham and Isaac, be called upon them, and may they flourish like fish in the midst of the land" (48:16).

Jacob insists on pronouncing upon Ephraim and Menashe the names of their ancestors and inducting them into the God of their ancestors. Moreover, he blesses them to flourish like fish in their land, the land of Egypt. Fish do not flourish on land;[8] Jacob packs a punch in his message that any success the family experiences in Egypt is unnatural and ultimately will not last. "God will return you to the land of your ancestors" (48:21), he proclaims to his grandchildren. Jacob's clan in Egypt is like a fish out of water. He reinforces this by allotting Ephraim and Menashe portions in the Promised Land; their future, he asserts, is in the ancestral land, not in the new land of their birth.

All this is highlighted further when Jacob, responding to Joseph's protestations about the crossed hands, explains his preference for

---

7. We earlier noted Jacob's justified anxiety about the descent to Egypt and Joseph's intentions to make Egypt the future home of the clan. Those intentions become even clearer when Joseph's family prospers in Goshen and as he turns the Egyptians into Pharaoh's slaves (47:11–27), effectively transforming his family into an economic aristocracy. Ironically, in doing so, Joseph also creates the precedent for the enslavement of an entire population as well as the pretext for the eventual enslavement of his own clan.
8. I first heard this idea from Rabbi Shlomo Riskin.

Ephraim. Menashe's name celebrates Joseph's attempt to forget his past: "For God has helped me forget my suffering and my father's house" (41:51). Ephraim, the younger, reflects Joseph's subtler understanding of his position: "For God has made me fruitful in the land of my oppression" (41:52). Ephraim's name includes recognition by Joseph that the land of his success is also the land of his oppression, and it may be that very element that Jacob wishes to emphasize.[9]

Jacob stakes his claim, Joseph rejects it, and Jacob refuses to accept Joseph's rejection. The debate goes far beyond the two boys. They are but the flash point in a fundamental disagreement. Where will the future of the clan be? For Jacob the future is rooted in his past, while for Joseph the future is completely disconnected from the past. And neither is prepared to concede to the other.[10]

ON THE DEATHBED

Jacob takes one final opportunity to convey his message. On his deathbed, he blesses his children. When he gets to Joseph, after identifying the munificent blessings which have already been bestowed upon him as well as his troubles with those who despised him, Jacob adds:

> His arms were made strong by the Mighty One of Jacob, from Israel's Shepherd, the God of your father, who helps you; Shaddai, who blesses you with the blessings of heaven above, blessings of the deep which crouches below, and blessings of the breast and womb. The blessings of your father even surpass the blessings of my ancestors … may they rest upon Joseph's head and be his crown among his brothers. (49:24–26)

---

9. Jacob is the first leading male figure in the Torah to *intentionally* prefer the younger to the elder. Both Sarah and Rebecca do so, each for their own reason. In preferring the younger, Jacob has assumed the roles of both Patriarch and Matriarch. What further distinguishes Jacob is that his choice is not exclusive. Menashe will *also* be a full-fledged covenantal member. We will soon see that Jacob extends this to the rest of his children.

10. Interestingly, throughout this scene Jacob is referred to consistently as Israel. He has clearly taken charge in his attempt to guide the destiny of Joseph's children, Joseph himself, and – ultimately – the entire clan.

Jacob invokes his own God and Protector in addition to the God of his ancestors, suggesting that the blessing God gives to Abraham increases with each successive generation and that Joseph is the crowning climax of the progression. Jacob consciously tries to drive home the point that Joseph's success is not personal, it is part of a greater divine plan in which Joseph is a continuation of his past rather than a dramatic departure from it. He concludes his comments with the invocation of Joseph's ancestors as the crown upon Joseph's head. Jacob does not give up; he takes one final shot at Joseph in an attempt to convince him that the future lies in embracing his covenantal history rather than in abandoning it.

JACOB INSTRUCTS HIS SONS

Yet even after his final message to Joseph, Jacob remains unconvinced that Joseph will change his position. Joseph's oath to Jacob does not pacify Jacob's concerns, and the later encounter with Menashe and Ephraim confirms Jacob's fears. Jacob will not rest until he knows that he has exhausted every possibility. After blessing his sons individually, Jacob instructs them all as a group:

> I am being gathered unto my people; bury me with my fathers, in the cave in the field of Ephron the Hittite, in the cave which is in the Makhpela field which faces Mamre in the land of Canaan, the field which Abraham bought from Ephron the Hittite as a burial-holding. There they buried Abraham and his wife Sarah, there they buried Isaac and his wife Rebecca, and there I buried Leah; the purchase of the field and the cave which is in it are from the Hittites. (49:29–32)

Jacob has already sworn Joseph to this request. Why does he need to make the request of the rest of his sons? To be sure, one could argue that he wants them to feel included in the process, but it is just as likely that he still does not know if he can rely on Joseph to carry it through, and so he instructs them all – Joseph included – together.

A closer reading of Jacob's request reveals a sharper focus on the issues he raised earlier with Joseph as well as some significant omissions. He refers twice to Abraham's purchase, twice to the fact that his ancestors were buried there, three times to the burial cave, and four times to the field. Missing from this speech is the explicit rejection of Egypt, which Jacob mentions twice in his earlier request of Joseph.

Jacob's reference to the place as a family burial plot with a three-generation history is designed to strengthen the bond with the past, building upon and sharpening the idea he raised briefly with Joseph. Similarly, the references to Abraham's purchase of the land are intended to deepen the bonds with that ancestral plot.[11] He does not need to reject Egypt in front of his other sons, as they are foreigners in Egypt, but the rejection of Egypt is apparently replaced by a subtler, hidden polemic against Egyptian burial rites. At Makhpela there are no monuments and nothing above ground to catch the eye. Instead there is a field with a cave, an underground burial. Jacob's message remains consistent even as his formulation has changed – the Egyptian way is not the way of his clan.

This is Jacob's final attempt to secure the future of the covenant, and it concludes a lengthy narrative. We first hear of Jacob's impending death in 47:28: "Jacob lived in Egypt for seventeen years; the total years of Jacob's life were 147 years." When we read the parallel verse at the end of Abraham's life (25:7), it is followed immediately by Abraham's death. But Jacob is not yet prepared to die. He summons Joseph, takes Joseph's sons as his own, blesses them with not-so-subtle messages about Canaan, blesses Joseph similarly, and finally instructs the remainder of his children regarding his burial. All of that is part of Jacob's desperate effort. It is only when he has exhausted all avenues that he "draws his feet onto the bed" and dies (49:33), something we expected two chapters earlier.

Tragically, Jacob dies without knowing if he is successful. And we, the readers, are held in suspense as well.

JACOB'S BURIAL

Joseph obeys his father's wish and buries him in Canaan, precisely where he requests. But the funeral and the arrangements have all the trappings of an Egyptian funeral:

---

11. Referring to the purchase emphasizes that this is the only place that the clan can truly call its own. The legitimacy of Shekhem, purchased by Jacob, was compromised as a result of the massacre carried out by Simeon and Levi.

Joseph commanded his servants, the physicians, to embalm his father, and the physicians embalmed his father. The forty-day period of embalming was finished, for that is the length of the embalming period, and Egypt cried for him for seventy days. (50:2–3)

Jacob receives a royal Egyptian burial treatment as Joseph organizes the funeral procession, asking permission from Pharaoh to bury his father in Canaan. Listen to Joseph's words and how different they sound from his father's: "My father made me swear, saying, 'Behold I am about to die; bury me in the grave which I dug for myself in the land of Canaan'" (50:5). No rejection of Egypt, no critique of Egyptian burial practices, not even a reference to the ancestral lands – simply that Jacob had already dug his own grave (which Jacob never actually said).

Pharaoh accedes to the request and Joseph leads a prominent Egyptian delegation, replete with "Pharaoh's servants, the elders of his house, and the elders of Egypt," Egyptian horses and chariots (symbols of Egyptian power and culture), with the brothers "tagging along" as an afterthought (50:7–9). If there is any doubt that Joseph arranges for an Egyptian funeral, listen to the comments of bystanders observing the funeral procession: "This is a heavy mourning for Egypt" (50:11). Just as Joseph's brothers see him as an Egyptian, the Canaanites witness in Jacob's funeral an Egyptian procession.

Joseph follows the letter of his father's instructions but not its spirit. Even after his father's death, he rejects Jacob's message. It appears that Jacob has failed. Joseph will not be Jacob's successor; there is no successor. The covenant is buried with Jacob.

JOSEPH'S BROTHERS – EGYPTIAN OR CANAANITE?

After Joseph conducts the royal Egyptian funeral for his father, his brothers carry out Jacob's final wish, providing for him the burial in the Makhpela cave back in their native Canaan:[12]

---

12. It is unclear if Joseph is present with them at the burial. If he is, then he is there as just one of the twelve rather than as their leader. In Canaan, Joseph has no status in the family.

His sons did for him as he instructed. His sons carried him to the land of Canaan, and buried him in the cave of the Makhpela field, the field that Abraham had bought as a burial-holding from Ephron the Hittite, in front of Mamre. (50:12–13)

It is hard to know where the brothers stood earlier in the debate between Joseph and his father. Were they loyal to Jacob throughout or were they getting comfortable in Egypt and adapting to its ways? (After all, hadn't Joseph provided them with Egyptian clothes to ease their transition?) It is possible that Jacob's final instruction to them is his last, desperate act to kindle within them, if not within Joseph, a bond to their ancestral home. The language describing their burial procession matches that of Jacob's wish. They apparently understand their father; they try to preserve Jacob's legacy. In insisting on fulfilling his final wish, however, they may be creating a new source of friction with Joseph.

It is not surprising, then, that after Jacob's death and burial, Joseph's brothers approach him, fearful of retribution now that their father-protector is gone. Just as Esau is prepared to wait for Isaac's death to exact retribution from Jacob (27:41), the brothers fear that Joseph will do the same, particularly in light of their betrayal of their absorption into Egypt by granting Jacob his final wish.

Joseph weeps at the thought that he is suspected of such pettiness, and reassures them: "Fear not. Am I in God's stead? You intended it for me with malice, but God intended it for the good, so that I could do as I do today, supporting many people" (50:19–20). Joseph's rhetorical question of being in place of God echoes his father's insensitive retort to Rachel's demand that he provide her with a child (30:2).[13] By invoking that same language, Joseph seems to be suggesting that the God who initially denies Rachel a child is the same God who ultimately provides

---

13. Zakovitch, *Jacob: Unexpected Patriarch*, 72, notes the dramatic difference between Jacob and Joseph regarding this statement, suggesting that whereas Jacob's comment is a callous rebuff to his pained wife, Joseph's use of the same phrase is intended to allay his brothers' fears. In that sense, Joseph redeems his father's insensitivity with a display of profuse sensitivity. See also Rafi Vaknin, "Jacob and Rachel," [Hebrew] http://www1.biu.ac.il/Parasha/Vayetze/Vaknin.

her with a child, and that the purpose of that birth is to bring the family to Egypt and ultimately ease the transition of the clan to their new home.

As if to drive the point even further, Joseph "comforts [his brothers] and speaks to their hearts" (50:21). That language is familiar, as it is used earlier to describe Shekhem's attempts to convince Dinah – whom he rapes and captures – that she is better off in his home (34:3). Whether this is Joseph's intention or the text's commentary, Joseph has become the benevolent despot who holds his family captive, regardless of their renewed bond with the ancestral land. The links to that land, the ancestors, and the covenant are part of the past; Joseph is a man of the present and the future.

JOSEPH'S LEGACY

Jacob dies when Joseph is fifty-six years old. Joseph lives for another fifty-four years, confident in his belief that he is fulfilling his divine role in securing the family's financial future and well-being in Egypt – until just before his death.

The aging Joseph has a chance to view the landscape of his life and that of his family. Joseph, the man of the future, sees that it does not hold the promise he imagined, and he begins to reflect on his past and on a different kind of future. The conversations he has with his father prior to Jacob's death haunt him. Joseph asks himself, "Could it be that my father was right, and that I, blinded by my own success, missed what was so clear to him?" While Joseph never says these words, before his death he summons his brothers and makes a declaration:

> "I am dying, but God will remember your destiny[14] and bring you to the land which He promised to Abraham, Isaac, and Jacob." Joseph made his brothers take an oath, saying: "God will remember your destiny and will bring you up out of this land; bring up my bones from here." (50:24–25)

---

14. The Hebrew root P-K-D has a particular nuance, meaning "remembering the individual's destiny." This same language of destiny (P-K-D) is invoked in the Exodus story (Ex. 13:19) as Moses gathers Joseph's bones for transport to Canaan. The destiny of the people is saved by Joseph's turnaround; Joseph brings them into the Egyptian exile and he needs to bring them out of it.

Joseph finally understands, and demands of his brothers – as his father demanded of him decades earlier – that they reassess where their future lies: not in Egypt, but back in the promised, covenantal land. When Joseph refuses his father's initial request for Menashe and Ephraim, he emphasizes that they are the children that God had given him "*in* this place" (*bazeh*). Now that Joseph understands that the future is not in Egypt, he asks his brothers to remove his bones "*from* this place" (*mizeh*). Just as Abraham, in his old age, accepts Isaac and not Ishmael as the covenantal son, and just as Isaac, in his old age, acknowledges his error about his choice of covenantal successor, Joseph, in his old age, accepts his error of rejecting the past for the illusory glitter of the Egyptian future.

"The children of Makhir, son of Menashe, were raised on Joseph's lap" (50:23). Joseph takes responsibility for his great-grandchildren just as Jacob takes Menashe and Ephraim under his wings. Later in the Torah, we are witness to the impact of Joseph's tutelage when the daughters of Tzelofhad, who is himself a descendant of the same Makhir of Menashe, petition Moses for a portion in the Promised Land: "Why should our father's name be diminished?" they argue, because he died before having the chance to enter the land.[15] Their desire to have their father's name enshrined in the Promised Land is a testament to Joseph's adopting Jacob's mission. Joseph raises four generations in this spirit, just as God promises Abraham in the Covenant between the Pieces that the fourth generation will return to the land. Joseph becomes not only a believer in the land but makes himself the guarantor of the covenant.[16] As the guardian of that covenant, Joseph needs to do more than simply teach his own children and grandchildren. Like Jacob does to him, he insists that his brothers take an oath: "God will remember your destiny and will bring you up out of this land – bring up my bones from here" (50:25).[17]

---

15. Num. 27:1–11.

16. It is therefore fitting that Joshua, an Ephraimite, who leads the Israelite conquest of the land, is also a descendant of Joseph.

17. Joseph, like his father and all Egyptian royalty, is mummified. He is aware of what will happen to him, yet asks that "his bones" be reinterred in the ancestral land. This suggests that just as Jacob rejects an Egyptian burial, Joseph belatedly attempts to do the same.

In the end, long after Jacob's death, Joseph finally internalizes his father's message. The future is not in Egypt; it is in the unique, ancestral, promised land. That land represents not only the past, but the future as well. That land is more than just a place. It is the symbol of the destiny of a family chosen by God for a mission – a mission waiting to be fulfilled since the beginning of Creation.

Genesis 49:1–33

Jacob's Legacy

J acob's tortured life could easily have led him down the same path as his fathers before him. He himself nearly lost his way twice – once by getting involved in the deception of his father and brother and the second time by getting crushed by his uncle Laban and nearly becoming absorbed in the inhospitable culture of Ḥaran. Jacob struggles to find his voice (vis-à-vis Laban) and his self (vis-à-vis Esau), and eventually emerges as Israel.

Finding himself, however, is not Jacob's ultimate goal. Rather, it is a means to a much greater end – creating the family which will not be rent asunder and which will become a standard-bearer for a set of values. Creating this family is a formidable challenge. Two rival sisters and their maidservants bear him twelve sons, who themselves carry on the rivalry between their mothers. Jacob contributes to this by preferring the son born to him by his primary love. Somehow, despite those challenges and five filial rebellions against his authority, Jacob remarkably maintains control of the family, which is almost intact. Judah's heroic efforts to transform himself are the catalyst for Jacob to take a leap of faith and bring Joseph back into the family.

Ultimately, Jacob struggles with Joseph as he tries to help his son realize that a meaningful reunification of the family demands that he must return to his roots rather than sever his family from them. Genesis cannot close without Joseph's final move, as God will still be lacking His partner. Joseph's final transformation brings Jacob's work to fruition and provides what God has been waiting for: a family, united within its diversity, committed to the covenant defining both its past and its future.[1] To understand what made Jacob successful where Abraham and Isaac were not, we will examine three important endeavors he takes on, all in the final chapter of his life.

PARENTAL BLESSINGS

Genesis is filled with blessings. Initially it is God who bestows them; later, parental blessings are given by Noah, Isaac, and Jacob.[2] Noah's and Isaac's blessings (and, in Noah's case, a curse as well) invoke the divine and are intended to confer something upon and determine the future of their children.

Jacob's blessings to his sons, however, are of a completely different nature. He avoids invoking divine assistance, electing instead to identify characteristics within his children, including their strengths and weaknesses, with the intention of providing guidance for their future. In doing so, Jacob redefines the nature of blessing in the Torah and redeems his own past. Jacob, who usurps his brother's generic blessing, now issues only personalized blessings, which can be neither transferred nor stolen and for which there can be no jealousy or competition.

Here are Jacob's blessings to his first four sons:

Reuben

> Reuben, you are my firstborn, my strength and the first fruit of my manhood; you had extra rank and extra power. But because you were impetuous and unstable as water, you will have nothing extra, for you mounted your father's bed; you profaned where I lay as you climbed on it. (49:3–4)

---

1. Jacob descends to Egypt with a clan of seventy, a microcosm of Noah's seventy nation-descendants which emerged from his three sons. God's plan for all humanity, which was derailed by human behavior, can finally find expression through Jacob's family, proto-Israel.
2. There are other blessings offered by Melchizedek and Laban, but they are not our focus here.

Reuben could have been the leader,[3] but he squanders his position as a result of his impulsivity – anything "extra" he had is no longer. Identifying his mistakes of the past serves as a warning for the future. Reuben needs to be aware of his nature. Only then does he generate the possibility of controlling it. It appears that Jacob's words fall on deaf ears, as Dathan and Abiram, Moses' antagonists, are Reubenites. Their rebellion against Moses is an expression of frustration that the leadership passed over them, descendants of the eldest (Num. 16). By the time we reach the end of the Book of Numbers the tribe of Reuben is already requesting to secede from the union and settle in Transjordan.[4]

Simeon and Levi

> Simeon and Levi, the brothers, tools of violence are their trade. In their secrets I did/will[5] not partake, in their gathering was/will my presence not to be found. For in their fury they slaughtered men and willingly maimed the ox.[6] Cursed be their fury, as it is fierce; and their rage, so intense. I will divide them in Jacob and disperse them in Israel. (49:5–7).

If Reuben's weakness is rashness, for Simeon and Levi it is their zealotry which needs to be curbed. Simeon and Levi provide an extraordinary example of the Jacob model. Jacob's words sound like a curse rather than

---

3. We will soon see that Jacob tries undoing the institution of the firstborn. Despite this effort, on a psychological level the firstborn stands out in both the eyes of the parents and the child's own eyes. From the perspective of the parents, the firstborn gives them a new identity and turns them into parents. From the perspective of the child, the firstborn is the only one to have the experience of being an only child, garnering all of the parental attention.
4. See Grumet, *Moses and the Path to Leadership*, 156–165.
5. As we noted earlier, Jacob's comments in his blessings are intended to be both retrospective and prospective.
6. The reference to the ox (*shor*) puzzles the commentaries. Rashi suggests that it refers to Joseph, Ibn Ezra posits that it refers to the wall of the city of Shekhem, and Radak proposes that it refers to the chieftan Shekhem himself. I submit that it is a play on the name Israel (*shin, resh*, the central letters of *Yisrael*), indicating Jacob's displeasure that they undermined him in the incident of Shekhem.

a blessing, and indeed, that is certainly the way Simeon understands them. It is the tribal leader from Simeon who parades his Midianite consort in front of Moses in a direct challenge to Moses' leadership. Angered by Jacob's stinging rebuff over the defense of Dinah following her rape by an outsider, Simeon's descendant reverses the scene and it is *he* who is having relations with a foreign woman, challenging anyone to rebuke him in light of the ancient story (Num. 25:6, 14). Not surprisingly, when Moses blesses the tribes at the end of his life he omits Simeon altogether, and soon after the entry into the land the tribe of Simeon is subsumed into Judah and ultimately disappears from the Bible.[7] Jacob's "curse" becomes a self-fulfilling prophecy; the name Israel will soon no longer be associated with Simeon.

By contrast, those same words are directed at Levi but he transforms them into a blessing. Levi learns to control and direct his zealotry, unleashing it twice in the Torah. First, as Moses calls, "Whoever is for God come to me!" (Ex. 32:26) following the incident of the Golden Calf, it is the tribe of Levi who answers the call, but not until being invited and authorized to act. Second, in a twist of poetic justice, when the scion of Simeon parades his Midianite woman before Moses, it is a descendant of Levi, Pinḥas, who takes up the spear and impales him (Num. 25:7–8). The former partners in the massacre of Shekhem are now on opposite sides of the conflict. Simeon becomes the cynic while Levi takes Jacob's words to heart, understanding that his zealotry can be both his weakness and his strength.[8]

For Levi, too, the name of Israel is no longer called upon him. In the beginning of Numbers (1:1–16), God instructs Moses to count the entire Israelite nation, and names twelve tribal leaders to assist him, yet the tribe of Levi is not represented. Moses executes the census with Levi excluded, yet the Torah insists that this total is the number of "all of Israel" (Num. 1:45). If the implication weren't enough, the concluding verse is explicit: "But the Levites, by the tribe of their fathers, were not counted

---

7. Unsurprisingly, not a single one of the leaders in the Book of Judges is from the tribe of Simeon.

8. For more on Levi's zealotry, see Grumet, *Moses and the Path to Leadership*, 27–57.

among them" (Num. 1:47). The Levites become a nation within a nation. They are not counted among the Israelites, nor do they camp together with the rest of the Israelites (Num. 2:1–3:10). Ultimately, when the nation enters the Promised Land, the Levites are not assigned a portion in the land as are all the other tribes (Num. 26:62). Instead, they live in cities scattered among the people, to serve as God's emissaries embedded within (Num. 35:1–8; Josh. 21:1–40), fulfilling the final line of Jacob's blessing to them.

Judah
Judah is originally named by his mother, who derives his name from the Hebrew word for "thanks." His father now changes it to mean the alternative definition, "to acknowledge" or "to admit":

> Judah, now your brothers will acknowledge you; your hand on the nape of your enemy's neck, your father's sons will bow to you. Judah is a young lion; you rose up from the tearing apart of my son. He crouched, lay down like a lion – like the fierce cat – who can pick him up? The scepter shall not pass from Judah and the lawgiver from between his feet, until he comes to Shiloh and peoples submit to him. (49:8–10)

Judah's admission of responsibility with regard to Tamar earns him the respect of his brothers, and he becomes their leader. It is that very ability to readily acknowledge wrongdoing which catapults Judah into leadership, hence the scepter shall be his. The young lion had fallen from grace into the laps of a Canaanite woman and Tamar; no one can pick him up other than himself, until he is ready to bring his third son, Shela (a play on the word Shiloh). Ultimately, Judah redeems himself from his involvement in Joseph's sale and the deception of Jacob, in which Jacob is led to believe that Joseph has been torn apart. In picking himself up from there, he brings redemption to the rest of the family.

Indeed, later in the Bible, when David is confronted by the prophet Nathan regarding the incident with Bathsheba (II Sam., chs. 11–12), David's reaction parallels Judah's as he immediately declares, "I have sinned."[9] He offers no excuses or justifications, just an acknowledgment of wrongdoing. Jacob identifies Judah's strengths so that Judah's descendants may learn from them.[10]

Jacob's blessings to his children reflect a deep understanding of who they are and an acknowledgment of their strengths and weaknesses, which are often the same. His blessings are not suffused with magic and assume no special divine authority, but they acknowledge and encourage the recipient of the blessing to be the best possible iteration of his own unique self. As such, they become a model for Jacob's descendants.

THE FIRSTBORN

More than anyone in the Bible, Jacob knows about the importance of the birthright, having purchased it from Esau. Reflecting on Genesis, however, reveals that this book is not enamored of the firstborn. While Cain is the preferred son of his parents, God gives attention to Abel, and ultimately humanity survives only through Seth, the youngest brother. Among Noah's children Shem is not the eldest, but the Abrahamic line comes through him. Abraham's oldest is passed over in favor of Isaac, and Esau is eventually shunted aside in favor of Jacob. Even among Judah's children, Zeraḥ is born first, but it is Peretz's descendants who sit on the throne.[11]

The rejection of the inherent specialness of the firstborn pervades Genesis. Leadership is not automatic; it must be earned – as Judah demonstrates. Jacob emphasizes this as he blesses Menashe and Ephraim,

---

9. For more on the parallels between Judah and David see Zvi Grumet, "Patriarch and King: Two Models of Repentance," in *The Tent of Avraham*, ed. Nathan Lopes Cardozo (Jerusalem: Urim, 2012), 127–144.
10. The end of Judah's blessing suggests that Jacob has offered Judah a double portion in the Promised Land. Whereas the farmer and the shepherd cannot coexist, Jacob blesses Judah with both the bounty of the vine and an abundance of milk, the implication being that there will be ample space, perhaps even different geographical regions, within Judah, to support two dramatically different areas. Ultimately, the portion Judah is allocated in the land includes the agriculturally fertile land west of the central mountain region (appropriate for viniculture) and the wilderness east of those mountains (appropriate for grazing sheep).
11. See Ruth 4:18–22.

mentioning Ephraim first and crossing his hands so that his right hand falls on Ephraim's head. Joseph objects, insisting that Menashe is the firstborn, but Jacob is adamant. Given the deliberateness of his action we expect to find some special blessing for Ephraim, but none is forthcoming. It seems that Jacob is trying to make the boys equal; there is no firstborn.

In a reversal of the scene from his earlier life, in which his father's blindness allows for confusion between the two sons, Jacob's switching of the sons is intentional: "I know, my son, I know." Indeed, Jacob's blindness (47:10) is not the cause of the reversal, as Joseph believes.[12] That is precisely Jacob's intent: despite Joseph's insistence on the significance of the firstborn, Jacob prevails in his assertion that birth order is irrelevant. Jacob understands the folly of his past along with the underlying message of Genesis that actions, not birth order, determine supremacy. Thus, in the final days of his life, Jacob tries to create two revolutions, one undoing conventional notions of blessing and the other undoing prevailing ideas about firstborns.[13]

THE COVENANTAL FAMILY

We opened the previous chapter with a question: How does one ensure the continuation of his or her own legacy without alienating the children or fracturing the family? Both Abraham and Isaac struggle with this question and are unsuccessful in resolving it. Jacob struggles with the same question and succeeds. How does he do it?

Jacob's blessings to his children convey an important element of his approach. In those blessings he does not hold back his critique of their actions, yet he does not allow that critique to turn into rejection of the child. Furthermore, his blessings are not generic like Isaac's blessings to Jacob and Esau; they are personalized. Jacob understands each

---

12. Throughout the Torah, Ephraim is usually listed first. One notable exception is Numbers 26:28. Joshua 16:4–17:13 initially presents Menashe first, but explicates Ephraim first in an A-B-B-A structure.

13. Jacob's and God's attempts to eradicate the cult of the firstborn are only partially successful. The laws regarding inheritance for the firstborn are the Torah's last vestige of primogeniture, a concession it allows for a people unable to completely disabuse themselves of the notion of the specialness of the firstborn.

of his children, recognizes their strengths and weaknesses, and uses his fatherly status as an opportunity to share his perspective.

Regarding the Abrahamic blessing, Jacob does not attempt to bestow it on only one of his children. Rather, he nurtures a covenantal family in which the Abrahamic blessing is their joint heritage. Jacob's instruction to his sons, even after Joseph's solemn oath, to bury him in Canaan with his fathers, is his way of directing them to remember that they are all heirs of the Abrahamic covenant. Jacob ends the era of exclusivity within the covenantal family.

In Genesis, competition within the family is over a particular commodity: God's recognition, parental love, spousal love, parental blessing, or preferential treatment. When there is but a single commodity the competition is increased. When, however, the focus is shifted to helping each individual achieve his or her own potential, the number of desired commodities in the family increases with the number of children. The strength of the collective emerges not from its numbers but from the ability of that collective to acknowledge and harness the unique contributions of each of its members.

One of the many functions within any corporate unit is leadership. Leadership does not imply superiority, but a different quality which knows how to bring out the best of all of the parts and make the bold decisions necessary to move forward while maintaining a vision of what is best for the members of the group and its ultimate goals. Leadership belongs to leaders, not to those who arrive first by accident of birth. Jacob learns this on a deeply personal level, initially chasing Esau for the birthright and ultimately surrendering it.

When he initially prefers Joseph he repeats his father's error, favoring one child over the others. Jacob and his family pay heavily for that error, and in his ultimate blessings to his children he tries to undo it as he accords what is appropriate to each. Joseph demonstrates one form of leadership, Judah quite another – and Jacob acknowledges the need for both.

The profoundly different leadership roles of Joseph and Judah play themselves out through all of Jewish history. Joshua is from Joseph and Saul descends from Joseph's younger brother, Benjamin, as does Mordekhai. Paralleling those, we have the entire line of the Davidic dynasty descending from Judah. For too long those two lines forget Jacob's blessing, believing that leadership belongs to themselves exclusively. Tension, even open warfare, marks the relationship between the kingdoms of Israel (identified often as Ephraim) and Judah, each believing that it alone owns the sole legitimate right to leadership. Ezekiel's vision (Ezek. 37:19), in which the branch of Judah unites with the branch of Joseph without one devouring the other, is a vision of the mutual recognition of the value of both.

Jacob's ability to correct his earlier errors both inspires his own children and is inspired by them. His oration to Laban profoundly moves his young children who witness it, and they cite it in different ways at critical moments in their own lives. The dynamic between Jacob and Judah, in which each learns from the other to self-correct their earlier errors, provides for the redemption of his family and is perhaps one of Jacob's most important contributions to its unity.

We earlier suggested that Jacob's mission to send Joseph to Shekhem parallels the *Akeda*, in which the first of the Patriarchs is asked to sacrifice his beloved son. In retrospect, there are two profound differences between Abraham's *Akeda* of Isaac and Jacob's of Joseph. First, while Abraham accedes to God's request only because it is God's request, Jacob understands the necessity of his for the future of his family, and enters into it of his own volition. That, of course, adds to his pain, as he knows that he is solely responsible for the ensuing tragedy. Second, Abraham is asked to sacrifice his beloved son, but Jacob ultimately sacrifices the entire notion of a beloved son. In doing so he saves his family and the future of its covenantal destiny.[14]

Additionally, we have Jacob's interactions with Joseph in his waning moments. Jacob is firm and unwavering, even in the face of Joseph's resistance to his initiatives, but he does not force Joseph to accept his position. Jacob dies without knowing if Joseph will accept and adopt his reorientation of the family. He has done everything in his power to teach, coach, and guide his children, yet he has no guarantee of success. Nobody does. He leaves this world with faith in God and in his

---

14. Ironically, Abraham's preparedness to go through with the sacrifice ultimately costs him his son; Jacob's actual sacrifice of Joseph ultimately brings Joseph back to him.

children, and that his message and values will endure. Ultimately, they do. He successfully forges a covenantal family, and the nation of Israel bears his name until today.

Finally, Jacob is the first biblical figure to explicitly play the role of grandfather. To be sure, Abraham was alive when Jacob was born and Isaac would have met Jacob's children upon their arrival from Ḥaran. Yet there is no record of their interaction. By contrast, Jacob adopts Menashe and Ephraim as his own children. The significance of this is not merely sentimental, it is a profound statement of the continuity of a legacy. We recall that the foundation of Abraham's revolution was in his understanding that the family was the primary vehicle for transmitting values and legacy and hence he teaches his children his values of *tzedaka* and *mishpat*, righteousness and justice. Jacob takes this one step further, working actively to ensure that the legacy is continued beyond his immediate children. This lesson is learned well, as Jacob's act is repeated by none other than Joseph, who raises his great-grandchildren on his knees. To ensure the future of the covenantal family, Jacob tends to the family, to the covenant, and to creating a self-perpetuating mechanism for ensuring their continuity.

CHILDREN OF ISRAEL

The Hebrew term *Benei Yisrael* can alternately be translated as "the children of (the man named) Israel" or the Israelites, the first referring to a family unit and the second referring to a national identity. In Genesis the reference is always to the former; in most of the rest of the Torah and the Bible it is to the latter. The shift takes place at the beginning of the Book of Exodus (1:7): "The children of Israel were fruitful, swarmed, became numerous, and became very powerful; the land was filled by them" – a fulfillment of the promise God makes to Abraham. Note that the language here also parallels the language of Creation (1:28; 9:7), indicating that in their emergence they are beginning to fulfill God's initial hope for humanity.[15]

---

15. The beginning of Exodus is filled with language describing Egypt in terms reminiscent of the stories of the *Mabul* and the Tower of Babel, while the Israelites are described in the language of God's blessings to humanity in the Creation. Israel

Immediately afterward, however, there is a profound shift. Pharaoh sees "the nation of the Israelites" as becoming too numerous. For the first time, ironically from the mouth of an outsider, we hear them being referred to as a nation rather than a family. It is this shift, fulfilling another of God's promises that Abraham's descendants will become a great nation (12:2; 17:4–6), that creates the conditions for God's fulfillment of His covenant with the forefathers. The redemption of the Israelite nation is followed by the Revelation at Sinai, where they elect to become God's "nation of priests" – His vehicle for communicating with the rest of humanity, fulfilling God's desire that through Abraham shall come blessing to all the families of the earth (12:3).

All this is made possible by Abraham's boldness, Isaac's preparedness to be a faithful transmitter, and Jacob's Herculean task of creating the covenantal family. It is now that God's story can begin.

---

emerges from the chaos of an Egyptian world gone out of control, much as Noah and Abraham emerge from the *Mabul* and Babel. For a different take on these parallels see Judy Klitsner, *Subversive Sequels in the Bible: How Biblical Stories Mine and Undermine Each Other* (Jerusalem: Maggid Books, 2011), 35–72.

Conclusion

The search for covenantal family begins with the first family. That initial family introduces one of the great challenges of all families: sibling relationships. Cain's killing of Abel hovers in the background of the three central families of the narrative. The need for Isaac's exclusive succession of Abraham necessitates the expulsion of Ishmael (whose descendants play a key role as Joseph's brothers seek an expedient way to expel Joseph from their lives). Jacob's rivalry with Esau drives both out of their home, and only Rebecca's desperate move saves her sons from following in the path of Cain and Abel.

Joseph's brothers almost follow Cain's path as well; only the combined efforts of Reuben and Judah save them from that ignominious ending. Ultimately, the brothers redeem that rivalry as they learn to accept Jacob's preference for Rachel over their own mothers. As for Jacob, giving his sons personalized blessings renders moot the struggle for blessing (and the accompanying jealousy) which haunts us from the beginning of Genesis. In fact, the blessing Jacob gives to Judah (which includes both wine, the produce of the farmer, and milk, the produce of the shepherd) demonstrates that he sees within Judah the capacity to end the rivalry between farmers and shepherds, bringing us full circle back to Cain and Abel.

The heroes and heroines of Genesis aren't born heroes. They emerge as they transform themselves and those around them. Our humanistic reading of these individuals transforms them into archetypes. Their stories are our stories, their struggles ours, and their stumbles and ultimate successes provide us with models of personal transformation.

GOD SEEKING PEOPLE SEEKING GOD

Genesis describes God's multiple, frustrating attempts to connect with humanity. We hear about those attempts both from God's perspective (primarily in the narrative prior to Abraham) and from the perspective of the people and the family through whom He elects to reach the rest of humanity. Along the way we, the readers, learn many profound ideas from the heroes and heroines of the saga.

The first Man and Woman highlight what it means to be human, while the sad story of Cain and Abel, along with their genealogies, teaches us about what it means to be a human living with other people and struggling with mortality. The stories of the Great Confusion (*Mabul*) and the building of Babel provide for us the limits, on both the minimum and maximum ends, of God's tolerance for human empowerment.

Abraham introduces a new era in which Man must seek God and learn His ways. In the process, we learn from him that obedience to God is not always the highest value, and that the nuclear family is the prime vehicle for transmission of the Godly values he embodies. Isaac, together with Rebecca, tries to refine that model, but he and Rebecca demonstrate the danger of what happens when family communication breaks down.

Jacob demonstrates powerfully the need for honesty, both with regard to others and vis-à-vis oneself, and the long-term dangers resulting from dishonesty. Jacob also presents the model of being able to learn from one's mistakes, a critical element for personal growth. Indeed, Jacob learns from his own errors, from Rachel, and even from his sons, and his future is ensured only when he embraces his family as his redeemers. His openness to learning from others only strengthens his conviction to pass on the covenant to all his children, without exclusion.

God chooses Abraham because he will teach his children, and they will teach their children, creating a reliable means of perpetuating

God's message. God also chooses a particular land so that the bearers of His message come into contact with the maximum number of people. After all, the creation of Man was focused on Man's potential to connect with God. The land, destination of Abraham's first search, is to function as God's embassy to humanity. Listen to Solomon's prayer upon the dedication of the Temple:

> And [listen] also to the gentile – not Your people, Israel – who comes from a faraway land for Your name. When he hears of Your great name, Your mighty hand and outstretched arm, and comes to this house to pray, [please] listen [in] heaven, Your established place, and do all that the gentile calls to you, so that all the nations of the earth will know Your name and will be in awe of You as are Your people, Israel. (I Kings 8:41–43)

When the People of Israel in the Land of Israel cease to function as beacons of the divine message, God will need to once again activate the RESTART button. Exile from the land, the silencing of the Jewish voice emanating from its native land, is God's way of helping the nation reorient itself properly and rededicate itself to His mission. The return from exile is not just to restore the Jewish people to its glory, it is God's attempt to restart the process of the Jewish people – descendants of the Patriarchs and Matriarchs – being able to impact positively on the rest of humanity and bring it closer to "establishing the world with God's sovereignty."[1]

BIBLICAL COVENANT

The idea of covenant, so prominent in Genesis, is central in the Bible, and Genesis presents a remarkable progression of its development. The first covenant is not even explicit. We know about it only by inference from God's promise to Noah: "I will uphold My covenant with you" (6:18). Implied in these words is that there is some preexisting covenant with humanity, about which we are never told, which God will keep with Noah. Later in that same story, God establishes a new covenant with

---

1. From the second paragraph of the *Aleinu* prayer.

Noah and his descendants, complete with a sign. That covenant, however, is rather different from what we might expect, as it is one-sided. God makes a promise to humanity, but no expectations are made of Man.

Although the above are called covenants in the Torah, since they lack mutuality they are more like promises. The same can be said about the next one, the Covenant between the Pieces (ch. 15). Although called a covenant – and it is a significant one in that it is the first time God selects a single member of the human race with whom He establishes it – it is still essentially a one-sided promise: after a long period of exile and suffering, Abraham's children will return to the land with great wealth. It is, however, significant in that it takes the first step toward mutuality. Abraham need not do anything actively as part of this covenant, but his descendants must endure before God will fulfill His part.

The Covenant between the Pieces serves as a significant transition in the history of covenant-making, for the following one, the covenant of circumcision, demands action from Abraham and his descendants. We have finally achieved a pact of mutuality; the Abrahamic family must circumcise its children and God will fulfill His promise. What this pact is missing, however, is voluntary agreement. God commands Abraham to circumcise himself; he is not given a choice. This changes when we turn to the covenant at Sinai, where God instructs Moses to "place His words before the people" so that they may decide whether to accept them or not. At Sinai, humanity finally achieves a mutual, voluntary covenant with God. This is an essential component of what makes the Sinaitic agreement so theologically significant.[2]

This progression in covenant is designed to be instructive. A covenant is essentially a set of mutual, unconditional commitments between two parties. Each side is committed regardless of whether the other party is fulfilling its side. In this way a covenant is profoundly different from a contract, in which a breach by one party typically absolves the other of responsibility. Before God can expect Man to enter into a covenant with Him, He must model what that means, hence the initial covenants in

---

2. According to one opinion in the Talmud (Shabbat 88a), the Sinaitic covenant was also coerced, making the later reaffirmations of the covenant that much more significant. For a fascinating discussion of this see Goodman, *Moses' Final Oration*, 221–224.

Genesis are one-sided, as God demonstrates what that commitment looks like. As the book unfolds, covenants demand increasing levels of commitment from Man – until we reach the great covenant at Sinai in Exodus 20.

Genesis' concern with family and covenant lays the foundations for the subsequent books of the Torah. In Exodus the family is expanded into the nation and the covenant plays a central role, both in the Revelation at Sinai and with regard to the endeavor to build a resting place within that nation for the Ark and Tablets of the covenant. Leviticus concludes with a moving statement on the dangers of violating the covenant, as well as with a discussion of the relative value of family members. The end of Numbers prepares the people for God's fulfillment of the covenant as well as enumerates laws designed to prevent friction within families. Finally, the entire final section of Deuteronomy is about Moses renewing the covenant between the nation and God, closing with an updated replay of the blessings Jacob bestowed upon his children prior to his own death.

LAND AND COVENANT

The emphasis on family as a vehicle for transmission of covenant should not mask the centrality of land. Abraham falls into that trap and rediscovers the need to bond with the covenantal land only after Sarah's death. In the Bible, family and land are inseparable. Throughout Genesis, abandonment of the land results in exclusion from the covenant,[3] and the attempt by Reuben and Gad to remain outside of the Promised Land is understood by Moses as a rejection of the covenant.[4] Exodus 23–24, which describes the covenantal ceremony following the Sinaitic revelation, includes an extended section on the uniqueness of the Promised Land. Similarly, when the covenant is renewed following the schism caused by the Golden Calf, it is introduced by God's commitment to bring His people into His land (Ex. 34:11). The integration of land and covenant could not be any more seamless than the presentation in Leviticus, where the consequences of Israel's violation of the covenant result from their nonobservance of the sabbatical year:

---

3. This is evidenced in Lot and Esau. For Ishmael, it is his lack of rootedness in the land which marks him as a covenantal outsider.
4. See Grumet, *Moses and the Path to Leadership*, 156–165.

> I will remember My covenant with Jacob and also My covenant with Isaac and also My covenant with Abraham, and I will remember the land. And the land shall be forsaken of them, and it shall expiate its Sabbath years when it is desolate of them. (Lev. 26:42–43)

Throughout the rest of the Bible, Israel's ability to remain in the land is repeatedly linked with its adherence to the covenant.[5] But beyond the element of punishment for nonadherence, the linkage of covenant to land is essential for the covenant's purpose – for the people to establish a society that could shine a light unto the nations:

> I the Lord, in My grace, have summoned you, and I have grasped you by the hand. I created you, and appointed you covenant people, a light of nations. (Is. 42:6)

> For He has said: "It is too little that you should be My servant, in that I raise up the tribes of Jacob and restore the survivors of Israel. I will also make you a light of nations, that My salvation may reach the ends of the earth." (Is. 49:6)

It is for this purpose that God initially sends Abram to Canaan, the crossroads of the ancient world – to share his light with all humanity. The land is the vehicle for the flourishing nation to accomplish God's task by becoming a paragon of justice, righteousness, and Godliness. Hence the consequence of the failure to live up to that task is exile from that land.

COVENANT OF THE FUTURE

In the first four books of the Torah, the covenant between God and people is initiated by God. Deuteronomy (27–30) marks a significant shift, when Moses initiates a renewal of the covenant just prior to Israel's entry into the land:

---

5. Josh. 24; Judges 1–2; 10; II Kings 17; 21. This idea is ubiquitous in the prophetic literature.

You stand here today, all of you, before the Lord your God – your heads, your tribes, your elders, and your overseers, every man of Israel. Your little ones, your wives, and your sojourner who is in the midst of your camps, from the hewer of your wood to the drawer of your water, for you to pass into the covenant of the Lord your God. (Deut. 29:9–11)

Moses is the first to bring the people to "renew their vows" with God, but certainly not the last. Joshua conducts a similar ceremony (Josh. 8:30–35; 24:1–28) after Israel enters the land. Asa, one of the early kings of Judah, initiates a recommitment to covenant (II Chr. 15:8–19), as later does Yehoyada the High Priest (II Chr. 23:16–20). Many years later, after Israel sins in violation of the covenant, King Josiah conducts a covenantal ceremony in which the people recommit themselves to God (II Kings 23; II Chr. 34). Jeremiah tries unsuccessfully to get the people to recommit to covenant (Jer. 11), presaging the exile from the land, but after that exile Ezra conducts a ceremony of recommitment with the returnees from Babylonia (Ezra 10).

The renewal of the covenant attests to both its significance and its fragility. It is the Jewish people's *raison d'être*, but is easily threatened by complacency, apathy, and ignorance. It is perhaps for this reason that the Torah, in the context of Moses' covenantal ceremony, commands the *Hak'hel* ceremony every seven years – it requires gathering the entire people for a public reading of the Torah, reminiscent of Sinai:

At the end of seven years, in the set season of the sabbatical year at the Festival of Sukkot, when all Israel comes to appear before the presence of the Lord your God in the place that He chooses, you shall read this Torah before all Israel, in their hearing. Assemble the people, the men and the women and the little ones and the sojourner who is within your gates, so that they may hear and so that they may learn, and they will fear the Lord your God and keep all the words of this Torah. And your children who know not will hear and learn to fear the Lord your God all the days that you live on the land, which you are about to cross the Jordan to take hold of. (Deut. 31:10–13)

While it is clear that the Sinaitic covenant needs renewal, the prophets envisioned yet one further step in the covenant-making process – covenants initiated by people in their search for God. Such a covenant is envisioned by Isaiah (Is. 2:1–4; 11:1–9), Micah (Micah 4:1–5), and Jeremiah (Jer. 31:31–34), and it represents the Bible's vision of the ultimate covenant with God. It returns us to the beginning of Genesis, where God hopes that humanity as a whole will use its Godly *tzelem* to guide and refine its internal interactions and its relationship with God. It is the universal vision expressed in the second paragraph of the *Aleinu* prayer, which closes every Jewish prayer service and which stands at the center of the Rosh HaShana and Yom Kippur services:

> Therefore, we place our hope in You, Lord our God…when the world will be perfected under the sovereignty of the Almighty, when all humanity will call upon Your name…all the world's inhabitants will realize and know that to You every knee must bow and every tongue swear loyalty.

Isaiah describes this in terms reminiscent of the Garden of Eden, where there is neither competition nor enmity between animals, or even between animals and people, and where that state is achieved through a heightened awareness of God and Godliness:

> The wolf shall dwell with the lamb, the leopard will lie down with the kid; the calf, the beast of prey, and the fatling together, with a little boy to herd them. The cow and the bear shall graze, their young shall lie down together; and the lion, like the ox, shall eat straw. A baby shall play over a viper's hole, and an infant pass his hand over an adder's den. In all of My sacred mount nothing evil or vile shall be done; for the land shall be filled with knowledge of the Lord as water covers the sea. (Is. 11:6–9)

GOD'S CORRECTIVE

Genesis is where this vision is initially presented. The book describes the initial challenges in achieving it, and how God repeatedly adjusts His plan to enable it to come to fruition. The unfolding of that plan is expressed in the *toledot* structure of the book, with each stage of *toledot* indicating yet one further refinement of who Man is and how God interacts with him. Man must discover himself before he can engage with his partner. Brothers must figure out how to get along in order to ensure the health of the family. Parents need to learn to reign in their children while at the same time empowering them.

One useful paradigm we referred to in this book is that of God as parent. God wants to empower His children as well, but not to the extent that they sever their relationship with Him. In the process, God both rewards and punishes, much as a parent does. Punishments for misdeeds take on a striking pattern, which was first introduced as the Man and the Woman were being expelled from the Garden: they are designed to be corrective rather than punitive.[6] Cain must learn what Abel's existence was like; the builders of the city and the tower, who wanted to crush human independence and creativity, are corrected by an explosion of language and thought; Abraham's false accusation that Avimelekh is not God-fearing haunts him as he needs to prove his own awe of God in the *Akeda*.

One particular expression of this approach is through God's blessing and curse, blessing referring to an endowment of increased potential and curse being the diminution of that potential. Thus the animals are endowed with increased potential for procreation and the seventh day is endowed with potential that remains unfulfilled until Israel receives the Torah. Most significantly, humans are repeatedly blessed with potential. When they violate the understanding implied in a blessing, God's response is to diminish the potential, i.e., to bestow a curse.[7]

---

6. Rabbinic literature refers to this as "measure for measure." See, for example, *Kalla Rabbati* 1:13; Shabbat 105b; Sanhedrin 90a; Genesis Rabba 9:11. This extends even to the legal system. For example, a thief has to pay back double what he steals, so that he experiences the loss that he inflicted on his fellow.

7. This is most strikingly demonstrated in the extended passage of blessings and curses in Deuteronomy 28, in which the detailed blessings in verses 1–14 are contrasted one by one with the ensuing curses.

Diminishing of potential is specific to the word *arur*, from the root A-R-R. The Torah uses two other roots to describe curse, K-L-L and K-B-H. The root K-L-L is likely a strong form of the root meaning "lightweight," and in the context of curse means

Genesis lays the foundations for this mode of interaction between God and Man, and it is continued throughout the Bible. For example, the Israelites demonstrate their unpreparedness to enter the land, and God responds by decreeing that they are not ready to go in and that only their children will enter to conquer it. God's interest is not that we pay the price for misdeeds but that we learn from them as we continually strive to become better, both as individuals and as a people. Likewise with regard to God's blessings and curses – one is the inverse of the other, with blessing indicating an increase of goodness and a curse being the decrease of that very goodness.

GENESIS AS VISION

Genesis tells a profound story of God's relationship with Man in terms that are both very Godly and simultaneously very human. It is accessible and meaningful to the naïve and the learned, young and old, novice and expert. Genesis tells the story of every man, woman, and child, of parents and children, of siblings and families, of mistakes and recovery, of growth and development, of tragedy and triumph, and of personal crisis and redemption. It tells the story of individual people and national identity, of promise and sacrifice, and of ideas both grounded and sublime. It is both particular and universal.

A deep understanding of Genesis transforms the way we read the rest of the Bible and the way we read the rest of human history. It challenges, confounds, and inspires as we follow its heroes and heroines. It provides a vision of what was, what could have been, and what the future can possibly be. Finally, Genesis is a story of God's profound faith that humanity, endowed with His spark, will ultimately succeed in its mission.

---

for something to be regarded as non-serious or unsubstantial – essentially, the inverse of K-B-D, which means both "heavy" and "respected." The root K-B-H is probably related to making holes, N-K-B, which suggests finding the weakness in the other.

Selected Bibliography

Aharoni, Yohanan. *Eretz Yisrael BiTekufat HaMikra*. Jerusalem: Yad Ben Zvi, 1987.

Alter, Robert, trans., *The Five Books of Moses*. New York: Norton, 2004.

Aviezer, Nathan. *In the Beginning*. Hoboken, NJ: Ktav Publishing House, 1990.

Baden, Joel S. "The Tower of Babel: A Case Study in the Competing Methods of Historical and Modern Literary Criticism." *Journal of Biblical Literature* 128:2 (2009): 209–224.

Bazak, Amnon. *Ad HaYom HaZeh*. Tel Aviv: Miskal – Yedioth Ahronoth and Chemed Books, 1983.

Berman, Joshua. *The Temple*. Northvale, NJ: Jason Aronson, 1995.

Bin Nun, Yoel. *Pirkei HaAvot*. Alon Shevut, Israel: Tevunot, 2003.

Blumenthal, Fred. "Who Wrestled with Jacob?" *Jewish Bible Quarterly* 38:2 (2010): 119–123.

Breuer, Mordechai. *Pirkei Bereshit*. Alon Shevut, Israel: Tevunot, 1999.

Buber, Martin. *Darko Shel Mikra*. Jerusalem: Mossad Bialik, 1978.

Cassuto, Umberto. *Commentary on the Book of Genesis*. Jerusalem: Magnes Press, 1969.

Dershowitz, Alan. *The Genesis of Justice*. New York: Warner Books, 2000.

Ellickson, Robert C., and Charles DiA. Thorland. "Ancient Land Law: Mesopotamia, Egypt, Israel." Yale Law School Legal Scholarship Repository. Faculty Scholarship Series. Paper 410 (1995). http://digitalcommons.law.yale.edu/fss_papers/410.

Feliks, Judah. *Nature and Man in the Bible*. London: The Soncino Press, 1981.

Fokkelman, Jan P. *Narrative Art in Genesis: Specimens of Stylistic and Structural Analysis*. Second edition. Sheffield, UK: JSOT Press, 1991.

Fox, Everett, trans. *The Five Books of Moses*. New York: Schocken Books, 1983.

Fromm, Erich. *Escape from Freedom*. New York: Farrar & Rinehart, 1941.

Goodman, Micah. *Moses' Final Oration*. Or Yehuda: Dvir, 2014.

Grant, Deena. *Divine Anger in the Hebrew Bible*. Washington, DC: Catholic Bible Association of America, 2014.

Grumet, Zvi. "Ideal and Real." *Tradition* 34 (2000): 3.

———. *Moses and the Path to Leadership*. Jerusalem: Urim, 2014.

———. "Patriarch and King: Two Models of Repentance." In *The Tent of Avraham*, edited by Nathan Lopes Cardozo, 127–144. Jerusalem: Urim, 2012.

———. "Within and Without the Encampment: The Ambivalent Acceptance of a Biblical Convert." *Tradition* 27:3 (1994).

Hawking, Stephen. *A Brief History of Time*. New York: Bantam Books, 1996.

Helfgot, Nathaniel. *Mikra and Meaning*. Jerusalem: Maggid Books, 2012.

Kass, Leon. *Genesis: The Beginning of Wisdom*. New York: The Free Press, 2003.

———. "Why the Dietary Laws." *Commentary* 97 (1994).

Kaufmann, Yehezkel. *The Religion of Israel*. Translated by Moshe Greenberg. New York: Schocken Books, 1972.

Kellner, Menachem. *Must a Jew Believe Anything?* Oxford: Littman, 2006.

Kierkegaard, Søren. *Fear and Trembling*. Edited by Stephen Evans and Sylvia Walsh. Cambridge, UK: Cambridge University Press, 2006.

Klitsner, Judy. *Subversive Sequels in the Bible: How Biblical Stories Mine and Undermine Each Other*. Jerusalem: Maggid Books, 2011.

Klitsner, Shmuel. *Wrestling Jacob*. Jerusalem: Urim, 2006.

Leibowitz, Nehama. *Iyunim BeSefer Bereshit*. Jerusalem: World Zionist Organization, 1975.

Mann, Thomas. *Joseph and His Brothers*. Translated by H. T. Lowe-Porter. New York: Knopf, 1994.

Matt, Daniel C. *God and the Big Bang*. Woodstock, VT: Jewish Lights, 1996.

Medan, Yaakov. *Daniel: Exile and Revelation*. Alon Shevut, Israel: Tevunot, 2006.

Moore, A. W. "Williams, Nietzsche, and the Meaninglessness of Immortality." *Mind* 115 (2006).

Muffs, Yochanan. *The Personhood of God*. Woodstock, VT: Jewish Lights, 2005.

Pollack, Robert. *The Faith of Biology & The Biology of Faith*. New York: Columbia University Press, 2000.

Pritchard, James B., trans. and ed. *Ancient Near Eastern Texts Relating to the Old Testament*. Princeton: Princeton University Press, 1969.

Sacks, Jonathan, trans. *The Koren Siddur*. Jerusalem: Koren Publishers, 2009.

Sacks, Robert. *A Commentary on the Book of Genesis*. Lewiston, NY: The Edwin Mellen Press, 1990.

Samet, Elhanan. *Iyunim BeFarashat HaShavua*. Second series, vol. 1. Maaleh Adumim: Maaliot, 2004.

Sarna, Nahum. *The JPS Torah Commentary: Exodus*. Philadelphia: JPS, 1991.

————. *Understanding Genesis*. New York: Schocken Books, 1970.

Scholem, Gershom. *Major Trends in Jewish Mysticism*. New York: Schocken Books, 1954.

Schroeder, Gerald. *Genesis and the Big Bang*. New York: Bantam Books, 1990.

Shapiro, Marc. *The Limits of Orthodox Theology*. Oxford: Littman, 2004.

Simon, Uriel. *Reading Prophetic Narratives*. Jerusalem: Mossad Bialik, 1997.

Soloveitchik, Joseph B. *The Lonely Man of Faith*. Jerusalem: Maggid Books, 2012.

————. *Reflections of the Rav*. Jerusalem: World Zionist Organization, 1979.

Steinmetz, Devora. *From Father to Son: Kinship, Conflict, and Continuity in Genesis*. Louisville: Westminster, 1991.

Sternberg, Meir. *The Poetics of Biblical Narrative: Ideological Literature and the Drama of Reading*. Bloomington: Indiana University Press, 1985.

Tanakh: The Holy Scriptures. JPS translation. Philadelphia: Jewish Publication Society, 1988.

Tirosh-Samuelson, Hava. "Gender in Jewish Mysticism." In *Jewish Mysticism and Kabbalah: Insights and Scholarship,* edited by Frederick E. Greenspahn, 191–230. New York: New York University Press, 2011.

Tonnies, Ferdinand. *Community and Society.* Translated and edited by C. P. Loomis. New York: Harper & Row, 1957.

Vaknin, Rafi. "Jacob and Rachel" [Hebrew]. http://www1.biu.ac.il/Parasha/Vayetze/Vaknin.

Viorst, Judith. *Necessary Losses.* New York: The Free Press, 2002.

Wahrman, Miryam Z. *Brave New Judaism.* Lebanon, NH: Brandeis University Press, 2002.

Williams, Bernard. "The Makropulos Case: Reflections on the Tedium of Immortality." In *Problems of the Self,* edited by Bernard Williams. Cambridge: Cambridge University Press, 1973.

Zakovitch, Yair. *Jacob: Unexpected Patriarch.* Or Yehuda: Dvir, 2012.

Index

A

Abel, 58–65, 67–69, 71, 73–75, 78, 89, 92, 99, 117, 180–181, 235, 273, 303, 311, 454, 461, 469

Abraham. *See also* Abram
  Akeda. See Akeda
  and Isaac, 190, 234, 237–238, 243, 253, 265, 268
  and Sarah, 192–193, 198, 200, 202, 208, 214–215, 219–220, 222, 226, 238, 243, 246, 253, 265
  and Yishmael, 182, 190, 192, 225–226, 246
  burying Sarah, 247–248, 250–251
  faith, 198
  God's partner, xvi, 186–187, 190, 200, 202
  hospitality, 204, 208
  impact, 205, 210
  laughter, 190, 198, 246
  Lot, 202
  negotiating with God, 201
  the land, 248–251, 266
  universal and distinct, 189–190, 214

Abram. *See also* Abraham
  and Nimrod, 111

and Sarai, 119, 176–179, 246
  becoming Abraham, xvi, 190, 240
  childless, 138, 158, 269
  faith, 158–159, 161, 163–164, 172, 175
  family, 118–119, 121, 124, 140, 145, 170, 174, 238, 240
  impact, 153
  in Egypt, 177–178, 216
  journey, 120, 126, 128, 130, 132–133, 135
  Lot, 138, 140, 142, 144, 147, 152–153, 159–160, 162, 170
  promise of land, 143, 145, 156, 160, 168–169, 174, 233
  reading God's sign, 132–134, 136, 162
  uniqueness, 116, 121–122, 124, 158
  warrior, 153

Akeda, 232, 238, 240–241, 243, 254, 263, 268–269, 271–272, 294–295, 299, 313, 389, 457

Akedat Yitzhak. See Akeda

altar, 58, 130, 132–133, 219, 234–235, 237, 242, 277, 349, 363, 375

ambiguity, 26, 30, 49, 67, 133–134, 155, 196, 227, 234–236, 272, 284–285, 318

anokhi, 318, 320, 340, 358, 360, 423

and Joseph, 386, 388, 393, 412, 425,
427–429, 433–436, 438, 440,
456–457
and Laban, 331–337, 339, 343–344,
346–350, 384, 415, 424, 428,
433, 449
and Leah, 333–334
and Rachel, 327–328, 334, 340, 347,
360, 379, 428
becoming Israel, xvi
birthright, 290–291
burial, 434, 441–443
conferring blessing, 440, 454–456
dream, 318, 324, 338, 341, 375
Isaac's blessing, 300–301, 303, 306,
354, 358–359
Israel, 362, 369, 373, 376–379, 382–383
Joseph's sons, 437–438
rebuking children, 373
schemer, 289, 292–293, 307, 408
tam, 270, 293, 302, 307, 328,
334–335
vow, 323
wrestling, 357–358
Joseph
and God, 397, 399, 402, 427, 444
and his brothers, 387–390, 392,
408–411, 414–416, 426–427, 444
and Jacob, 386, 409, 411, 425, 428,
436, 438, 440, 442
arrogance and humility, 388, 397,
399, 401, 404
burial, 446
dream, 387, 400–401, 408
dream interpreter, 400, 402
hero, 403, 430
in the pit, 391, 397, 399
sale, 265, 391–392, 395, 408–409
successful, 397, 404
unifier, 386, 426, 430

Judah
and Jacob, 413, 422, 430, 449
and Joseph, 393, 420, 423, 425
and Tamar, 408, 418–421, 423, 453

K
ketonet, 55, 386, 408
ki tov, 5–6, 40–41

L
Laban
with Abraham's servant, 258, 262
Leah, 245, 284, 291, 333–335, 364, 368, 381,
386–387, 415, 418, 425, 431, 441
lekh lekha, 116, 123, 135, 187, 232–234, 238,
243, 255, 260, 263, 272, 282, 285, 300,
325, 363, 377, 430
Lemekh
descendant of Cain, 66–68, 70,
72–74, 76
descendant of Seth, 72, 74
Levi, 368–369, 371, 373, 380–382, 393, 433,
442, 451–452
life span, xxi, 44, 68, 76
Lot, viii, 118, 120–121, 130, 137–140,
142–144, 147–148, 152–153, 159–160,
162, 170, 196, 201–210, 213–215, 217,
220, 231, 238, 243–244, 247, 253, 277,
284, 313, 331, 337, 353, 383, 395, 465

M
mabul, 81, 85, 87, 92–94, 96–99, 107–108,
110, 209
Makhpela, 249–250, 266, 441, 443–444
makom, 321–322
matzeva, 322–323, 325, 349–351, 379, 433
meaningful mortality, 43–44, 51, 53–54
meaningless immortality, 43–44
Melchizedek, 142, 154–155, 159–160, 163,
247
Menashe, 404, 436–441, 446, 454–455

The fonts used in this book are from the Arno family

Other books in the
Maggid Studies in Tanakh series:

Joshua: The Challenge of the Promised Land
Michael Hattin

I Kings: Torn in Two
Alex Israel

II Kings: In a Whirlwind (forthcoming)
Alex Israel

Isaiah (forthcoming)
Yoel Bin-Nun and Binyamin Lau

Jeremiah: The Fate of a Prophet
Binyamin Lau

Ezekiel (forthcoming)
Tova Ganzel

Jonah: The Reluctant Prophet (forthcoming)
Erica Brown

Nahum, Habakkuk, and Zephaniah (forthcoming)
Yaakov Beasley

*Haggai, Zechariah, and Malachi:
Prophecy in an Age of Uncertainty*
Hayyim Angel

Ruth: From Alienation to Monarchy
Yael Ziegler

Nehemiah: Statesman and Sage
Dov S. Zakheim

Maggid Books
The best of contemporary Jewish thought from
Koren Publishers Jerusalem Ltd.